D1572536

THE CHOICE of the JEWS UNDER VICHY

THE CHOICE
of the JEWS
UNDER VICHY

Between Submission and Resistance

ADAM RAYSKI

Foreword by François Bédarida

Translated by Will Sayers

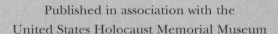

Published in association with the
United States Holocaust Memorial Museum

University of Notre Dame Press • Notre Dame, Indiana

Manufactured in the United States of America

Translated by Will Sayers from Adam Rayski, *Le choix des Juifs sous Vichy:
Entre soumission et résistance,* published by Éditions La Découverte, Paris.
© Éditions La Découverte, 1992

Published in association with the United States Holocaust Memorial Museum.
The assertions, arguments, and conclusions contained herein are those of
the author or other contributors. They do not necessarily reflect the opinions
of the United States Holocaust Memorial Museum.

Library of Congress Cataloging-in-Publication Data
Rayski, Adam.
    [Choix des juifs sous Vichy. English]
    The choice of the Jews under Vichy : between submission and resistance /
Adam Rayski ; forward by François Bédarida ; translated by Will Sayers.
        p.   cm.
    Includes index.
    ISBN 0-268-04021-4 (alk. paper)
    1. Jews—Persecutions—France.   2. Jews—France—Politics and government.
3. Holocaust, Jewish (1939–1945)—France.   4. World War, 1939–1945—Jewish
resistance—France.   5. France—Ethnic relations.   I. Title.
DS135.F83R3913   2005
940.53'18'0944—dc22

                                                            2005043066

∞ *This book is printed on acid-free paper.*

CONTENTS

FOREWORD

It would be an overstatement to assert that the history of the Jews of France has been obscured or repressed for years, but it is true that it was long relegated to the second rank of historical inquiry and that there is a striking contrast with the eminent place it occupies today. Testifying to this ubiquity—which reflects the fluctuations and ongoing questioning of the French conscience—is the abundance of books and studies devoted to persecution and genocide, and the constant media attention focused on the tragic past.

In fact, the present situation is above all the result of two phenomena. The first—and by far the more interesting—is the revival of Jewish memory that has been in progress for the past quarter century. The affirmation of Jewish identity that accompanies this revival has led to a process of reconquering history and of reinterpreting the destiny of a people dispersed and scattered over the centuries. Yet, how can we not accord a privileged position to an exceptional era, that of the Shoah, marked by a brutal rupture in the continuity of Jewish life under the effects of an implacable policy of extermination, in order to follow the unfolding of Jewish history and understand its significance—all the more so in that this recent past marked a decisive turning point in a bimillennial history?

The second phenomenon, more conjectural, relates to dates. Between 1990 and 1995 we had a round of fiftieth anniversaries, and one commemoration succeeded another: that of the anti-Jewish legislation, the roundup at the Vélodrome d'Hiver and the deportations, even the liberation of the camps. The memory of Vichy and of the Occupation assails the French, besieges them, lashes them, the process further driven by notorious "affairs" (Bousquet, Papon, Touvier). From all this comes a will to know even more, to comprehend the components and mechanics of such a controversial past, to explain the great transformation of Jewry in France that occurred in the space of a few years. It is to this task that Adam Rayski has passionately set himself, at the heart of a historiography in full development, and with the aid of a vast body of documentation, quite often unpublished.

Rayski himself belongs to the rare and invaluable category of witness-turned-historian. After having been a privileged actor in this past, as the head of the Jewish section of the Main-d'oeuvre immigrée (MOI—Immigrant Labor Association), whose extraordinary adventure he has retraced as co-author of the fine book *Sang de l'étranger* (Blood of the Foreigner), he has elected to present a more probing and reasoned synthesis of the destiny of the Jews in France from 1940 to 1944, while conforming scrupulously to the rules and canons of historical method. This allows us a double vision and double reading: a view from the interior but, as well, a distanced view, a critical but also engaged reading.

From this comes the breath of life that permeates the book, challenging the reader, recalling to life the Jewish tragedy in all its intensity, translating the author's will to understand the indelible trauma at whatever cost. But in following the unfolding of events—the French defeat in World War II, the occupation of France, the policies of the Vichy regime, the "Final Solution"; in following the accounts of the trials overcome, the suffering, the fear, the raids; in following the drama of the hunts, the arrests, and the deportations, the camps, the hideouts, the false papers—in all this the author maintains a remarkable concern for weighing the evidence, forcing himself to balanced and equitable judgment. It is thus that after illuminating the paradox and the specific nature of the "Jewish Question" in France, which unlike other European states was characterized by a double persecution—by both the Nazis and Vichy—supported by a solid tradition of native anti-semitism, Adam Rayski devotes his analysis to the rescue of the Jews, whether of French or foreign nationality, arguing that those who escaped death owed their salvation above all to the solidarity, mutual aid, and sympathy of the French. Admittedly, it happens that here and there his indignation comes to the fore (and why, for that matter, should we be surprised?), but most often it is contained, while the work as a whole is informed by ethical rigor and is vibrant in its appeal to honor, respect for life, the dignity of every human being, through which we sense the very soul of the Jewish struggle.

The focal point of this work is the relationship between French Jews and foreign Jews. Even if this relationship long took the form of radical divergence in mentality and conduct, entailing endless stereotyping, multiple conflicts, and constant mutual recrimination from 1940 to 1943, a major evolution was also generated by the pressure of events. In the face of a common persecution, not only the awareness of a common fate but a rapprochement evolved among groups that had hitherto been competitors or antagonists, with a view to bringing together the whole of "Jewry in France."

Yet, initially, this divide between Jews "of French stock" and those considered foreign appeared immense, even unbridgeable, as Rayski illustrates in numerous examples, with great candor and without sparing anyone's feelings. Two cultures confronted each other, each founded in a different conception of Jewish identity. On the one hand, French citizens of Jewish faith, assimilated citizens, tended to define themselves half by religion and half by culture, however vague the definition may have been in the minds of some. On the other hand, Jews who had come from Central or Eastern Europe identified rather, and often very strongly, as a community at once ethnic, national, and religious. Between the two, incomprehension was profound. Thus, we find the chief rabbi of Nancy speaking out against the use of Yiddish, which he characterized as a "jargon."

Among members of the first group, with a strong tradition of obedience to the laws and regulations of the country, there was a great tendency to give in to illusion and to place trust in the authorities, in a respect for legality, while trying to manage misfortune as well as they could. Suffer and endure: so might we characterize their line of conduct. Rayski offers a merciless analysis of the strategy of the religious leadership of the Consistoire central des Israélites de France (CC—Central Consistory of the Jews of France) in this respect, and of the path taken by the Union générale des israélites de France (UGIF—General Union of the Jews of France) from the last months of 1941 onward. With document after document from trustworthy sources, the author exposes the mechanism of Vichy allegiance that hid the trap set by occupation authorities: exploiting the legal and superficially legitimate power of the French state and its instruments, both the police and the administrative apparatus, in order to mount and implacably execute the German policy of annihilation.

The behavior of foreign Jews was quite different, and understandably so in the light of their historical experience—at least among the best organized of them, starting with the communists and Zionists of the left. Refusing to be isolated and turn inward, the equivalent of entering a "ghetto without walls" in Rayski's telling phrase, they found means of resistance to the Vichy state and to their fierce enemy, the Occupation. For them the very condition of survival was clandestinity, an underground existence. Instead of accepting misfortune to the point of martyrdom, the order was simple:

stand up, fight rather than submit. "Everywhere Present, Face the Enemy!" exhorts the slogan of the Jewish Scouts, which became the Organisation juive de combat (the Jewish Fighting Organization).

Throughout their common trial, the two constituents of Jewry in France, instead of continuing to follow separate paths, effected a movement of convergence. While official Judaism, from whose eyes the scales finally dropped, moved toward an underground mode of operation, the Jewish resistance organizations, composed for the most part of foreigners, came to adopt a strategy of unification, with the communists taking the lead. The result of this transformation of cultures and mentalities was the creation, in the spring of 1944, of the Conseil représentatif des Juifs de France (CRIF— Representative Council of the Jews of France) recognized by both camps as the interpreter and representative of French Jewry in its totality.

Here, then, under the threat of extinction, we see a community reconstituted, reestablishing its links—moving beyond a recent generation marred by contradictions and misunderstandings—to a more distant past. Here too we see how the drama of genocide led many native French "Israelites" to shed their skin and become "Jews." In the striking words of Robert Badinter, the anti-Jewish legislation of 1940 had "a conceptual victim: it killed the French Israelite; the Jew took his place." Among foreign Jews, combat and the struggle to rescue community members generated a sense of belonging, of integration into the national French community. In short, at the end of a dramatic itinerary of persecution and death, Jewish consciousness and national consciousness—the one and the other revitalized—found themselves reunited and reconciled.

Another original feature of this book is the light thrown on the Jewish resistance, taken in its broadest sense, by closely associating armed action and rescue. For the struggle to survive was one and indivisible. René Mayer summarized this in a lapidary phrase: "To safeguard French Jewry, it is necessary first of all to save the Jews." Far from limiting himself to a specious distinction between active and passive resistance, Adam Rayski shows with pertinent facts the interdependence of the different forms of the battle that was waged—the armed struggle, urban guerrilla activity, escape networks, participation in other resistance movements, and in intelligence networks such as that of "Free France," the forgery of identity papers, the hiding of children, and various social services. Differentiating their times, rhythms, and spaces, the author takes as his point of departure the separation of the two zones of France, which accentuated even more the rift between French Jew and foreign Jew, the consequences of which would not be totally effaced until the last months of the Occupation and the very eve of the Liberation. Here we find an opposition between two basic behaviors: the position of compromise and resignation—"that great school of cowardice" for an intransigent activist such as David Knout—and the resolute will to wage the battle for survival by any and all means outside the law.

Those who made the latter choice had a precious trump card in their hand: the prewar community organizations that served as structures ready-made for undercover activity (while the Jews who joined resistance movements, instead of benefiting from this same framework, engaged themselves individually). This is certainly the case for the MOI in the communist camp but also for the Éclaireurs israélites (Jewish Scouts), the Oeuvre de secours à l'enfance (Children's Relief Agency), the Organisation reconstruction travail (ORT—Organization for Reconstruction and Labor), and the Armée juive, linked with the Zionist movement.

In the final analysis, what Adam Rayski seeks in his book, what constitutes its informing purpose and its strength, is to liberate historiography of the cliché of the Jew as victim. Instead of permitting learned memory as represented by historians to stay fixated on an image of Jewish passivity, his mission is to illustrate the emergence of a collective consciousness of self-affirmation, growing over the course of events and through the history of terrible suffering: the consciousness of an absolute, congenital adaptability in the face of mortal danger, but one that opens onto a consciousness of identity and of fidelity through a common historical destiny; a consciousness that finds expression in individuals as well as in families, and that voluntarily assumes the option of defending its identity, along with all the consequences that such a choice entails; the consciousness of a founding experience that, once the time of grief was over, would renew the sense of bond with the French nation and forge new modes for the integration of identities. For this horrible experience caused the proscribed Jews to encounter the sympathy and support, active or passive, of a major portion of the French population, indignant over the inhumanity of their persecution. From this stemmed the success of the politics of rescue, which permitted three-quarters of the Jews of France to escape the "Final Solution."

The fact remains that the Jewish tragedy wears at one and the same time two faces. On the one hand, the bold combat against the beast for survival, a combat in darkness that long remained obscured but is today restored and projected in full light, a combat moreover bearing within it a new future. On the other hand, suffering, sorrow, the death of dozens and dozens of thousands of innocents. But did the latter allow themselves to be passively exterminated, as there has been too great a tendency to claim, under the weight of a debilitating secular tradition? Or did this happen only under the blows of a mortal enemy vastly better organized and armed? Without any doubt, the heroes of the resistance saved Jewish honor, even if one may still ask what dishonor might reside in being the victims of a massive and systematic operation of extermination. Can one think of reproaching the hostages killed in reprisal for armed resistance to the Germans for having been shot? Or the victims of Oradour-sur-Glane, or of the Ardeatine Caves, for letting themselves be massacred?

On such a controversial subject it is naturally permissible not to share totally the argumentation and judgments of Rayski. One might debate, for example, the severity of his accusations against the Jewish notables of the Consistory: after all, they were deeply influenced by their own memories of World War I, and its effect on the nation as a whole, and they acted accordingly (on this subject, think of a man like Marc Bloch, who, however, was hardly a notable!). Contrast those whose Jewish self-identity was disappearing due to assimilation, on the one hand, with the lucidity of leaders of the various organizations of foreign Jews in France, on the other. And indeed, outside narrow and closed circles, was so much known about the "Final Solution" and its unfolding? As Pierre Vidal-Naquet states in his timely reminder, "in order to understand historical reality it is sometimes necessary not to know its outcome."

From this we see how interesting this book is, devoted to the "choice of the Jews" and from beginning to end resting upon the dialectic of submission/ refusal; legality/clandestine illegality; turning inward and opening to exterior alliances. Rich in insight and reflection, the book not only contributes to the understanding of a tragic period but illuminates today's debate on Jewish identity and its integration in the French community.

François Bédarida

ACKNOWLEDGMENTS

I would like to express my gratitude to all those whose counsel has assisted me in better penetrating the complex reality of an era that is so intensely studied but nonetheless poorly known. My particular thanks are due to Alexandre Adler and Henry Bulawko (who were kind enough to read the manuscript), Jacques Adler, Lucie and Raymond Aubrac, Jean-Pierre Azéma, Gaby Cohen, Jean Laloum, Denis Peschanski, Claude Urman, and Pierre Vidal-Naquet.

I spent almost a year and a half in various archives in France and abroad, where I met curators and archivists who do honor to their calling and whose cooperation gave me access to collections that have been little or not at all explored. My thanks go to Jean Favier, director general, Chantal de Tourtier-Bonazzi, head curator, and archivist Jean Pouessel at the French National Archives; Sarah Alperine, Sarah Mimoun, and Vidar Jacobsen at the Centre de documentation juive contemporaine (CDJC); Yvonne Lévyne and Jean-Claude Kupferminc of the Alliance israélite universelle (AIU) Library; Bernard Garnier, executive director, and Isabelle Sauvé-Astruc of the Historical Archives of the Prefecture of Police; Jean Astruc and Anne-Marie Pathé of the Library of the Institut de l'Histoire du temps présent (IHTP); Monique Cohen of the Municipal Library of Toulouse; Bronia Klibanski and Shimshon Eden at the Yad Vashem; archivists at the YIVO and the Jewish Theological Seminary in New York; Norman N. Eden at the Hebrew Union College, Cincinnati; and lastly the student of political science Nicolas Offenstadt.

François Bédarida was kind enough to write a foreword to this book, and I have benefited from his most valuable comments on the manuscript. I hope that I may be permitted to see in his acceptance of that task not only a mark of sympathy but perhaps equally a mark of recognition that my nearly ten-year long participation in the seminars of the IHTP has not been in vain. I must also pay homage to François Géze, executive director of La Découverte publishers, who has kept company with this undertaking from one end to the other. In him I discovered an editor overwhelmed by the history of the Holocaust, one who has proved himself an attentive, collegial, and passionate reader.

I owe particular thanks to Benoit, my son, who, although he has no memory of that time, bears deep imprints in his subconscious of the hunt for children, for reading and correcting the manuscript as it progressed; to my grandchildren Jean-Marc and Yaël, who sacrificed much of their free time to provide technical assistance; and to Annie, my wife, whose presence at every stage of my work, intelligent collaboration, remarkable sense of organization, and encouragement at critical moments, permitted me to complete a book whose scope, as time passed, became ever broader.

Finally for their help with the English-language edition, let me thank Michael Gelb and Benton Arnovitz of the United States Holocaust Memorial Museum, and Brewster Chamberlin, previously of the same institution. My appreciation goes, too, to the staff of the University of Notre Dame Press.

INTRODUCTION

Jewish history has increasingly become a rare combination of
national history and world history.

— Salo W. Baron[1]

The history of the war years in France presents a situation unique on more
than one count. After defeat by Nazi Germany, much of France was occupied, but the rest, supervised by the compliant regime at Vichy, remained unoccupied, enjoying some elements of autonomy. This satellite state, Vichy
France, nevertheless lent its political, administrative, and police cooperation to the fulfilment of the anti-Jewish policy of Nazi Germany. Its participation, and even its voluntary initiative, were so substantial that a close associate
of its leader, Marshal Pétain, would tell him "France, along with Germany, is
the country that persecutes the Jews the most."[2] And yet—a paradoxical
distinction—that country shows one of the highest percentages of Jews
who survived. Ultimately, during the course of the confrontation of two opposing wills, death against survival, both occupiers and Jews would call on
the assistance of France, each seeking its allies in opposing camps of French
citizens.

   The occupation forces did not have a police apparatus capable of carrying out the tasks of internment and deportation. Conscious as they were
of the monstrous nature that anti-Jewish measures were to assume, they also
saw the importance of precluding, or at least of limiting, Jewish resistance
or hostile reactions among the French public.[3] The collaboration of as many
French citizens as possible appeared indispensable. The Germans would find
the kind of Frenchmen they were seeking in the senior administration of

1

the Vichy state and in those social groupings already inclined to antisemitism and xenophobia.

From the very first German and French antisemitic measures it was possible to make out the Nazi strategy of isolation and concentration, the same strategy already being implemented in Poland, where walls were going up around those neighborhoods in which Jews were being forced to live. But geographic ghettos could not easily be imposed in France, so the occupiers conceived instead a social and moral ghetto. Two instruments would assist them: the Commissariat général aux questions juives (CGQJ—General Commissariat for Jewish Questions) and the Union générale des israélites de France (UGIF—the General Union of Jews of France). We will see that ultimately it was Frenchmen and Jews who were in charge. The anti-Jewish legislation of October 1940, completely French in provenance, would inaugurate the processes of exclusion and isolation, actually predating German initiatives.

For the Jews, simple common sense dictated the attitude they should adopt: refuse to be isolated. From this followed imperative choices, since each new phase of anti-Jewish persecution called for new decisions, not only on the part of organizations but also individuals. In short, the dilemma posed by the enemy's strategy could be stated as follows: to turn inward, toward isolation, or to seek an alliance with well-disposed forces that were not Jewish. Depending upon the strategic option that groups and individuals selected, they would be locking themselves into a near suicidal legality or entering a salvationist but highly risky clandestine and illegal existence. Called to submit by the occupying authorities in Paris in January of 1941, and in the "Free Zone" by the Vichy government in December of the same year, the majority of Jewish leaders obeyed, some in a spirit of cooperation, others with exceedingly heavy hearts. They chose legality, with all the disastrous consequences events would soon demonstrate.

For the Jewish population, in particular those of foreign origin living in Paris, the decisive moment of choice arrived in the course of the great roundup of 16 and 17 July 1942. A change in collective behavior then occurred. Its most notable component was to avoid constraints of anti-Jewish legislation in order to try to hide among the non-Jewish population. To do this, Jews had to find French men and women who despised the Vichy government. But in the face of widespread indifference, these Jews had to be truly convinced that the "real France," the France of 1789, had not disappeared. From this assumption, an alternative and a prospect of salvation could be glimpsed.

With time, the sum of individual decisions generated a collective, a majority phenomenon, a situation with few parallels in the history of humanity: the immersion of a civil population of tens of thousands of persons of all ages, of entire families, into a clandestine existence more natural to cells of militants organized for such a mode of life. The life of the Jews of France during these terrible years has, to this date, not been fully described, in large part because the historiography of the genocide favors the image of the Jew as victim. But if the Jews were victims they were by no means passive ones. For those who perished, like those who survived, engaged in a solitary struggle every moment of their lives, without resonance and without glamor, but a struggle that does not lack for grandeur in the eyes of history. In this regard, one should not suspect the author, himself a former resistance activist, of wishing to depreciate organized Jewish resistance. That organized resistance, it should be emphasized, in fact worked actively to foster all sorts of clandestine efforts and to furnish means for their success.

Oral and written testimony, and unedited archival documentation, reveal the importance that the Gestapo and the French police accorded to the hunt for fugitive Jews, against whom they found themselves obliged to adopt ever more innovative methods. In this light, the victims appear in their capacity as subjects, as actors. They are no longer the "object of rescue actions," but performed these actions themselves, admittedly with the assistance of non-Jews. What is even more striking is that children, too, went underground, even some as young as five or six: they knew how to keep silent, to no longer mention their parents' names—not even the word "mama"—because they were supposed to be orphans. Thus, the shadowy zone of the "passivity" of the Jews of France needs to be illuminated to reveal the realities under the surface.

On the level of methodology, it has seemed necessary to enlarge the investigative space by leaving the conventional boundaries of metropolitan France, the "hexagon." The destiny of the Jews of France reached its tragic dénouement beyond these national borders and also because, despite the oppressive secrecy that surrounded the camps in occupied Poland, Auschwitz cast its shadow across France. This approach also reflects the practice of the Jewish resistance of the Main d'oeuvre immigrée (MOI, Immigrant Labor Association), which continuously sought information on the fate of those deported from France and, in general, on what was taking place in the camps.

Another line of inquiry concerns the impact of Jewish behavior on the evolution of French public opinion in the face of the horrors it so often witnessed: would the French have translated their feelings of disapproval into action if the victims had remained passive? The answer reveals the interaction among the worsening of persecution, the defensive reactions of Jews, and the response of public opinion. The study of this dynamic leads to the conclusion that the turning point in public opinion that occurred in summer 1942 was to a considerable extent preceded by a reversal of position among the Jews of Paris. The personal archives of Pétain reveal that the reaction of Catholics and Protestants to the inhuman persecution of the Jews was of paramount concern to his government.[4]

The initial limits of this research broadened during the exploration of archival holdings in various institutions abroad (United States, Israel) and in France, where—and this must be emphasized—historians regularly receive dispensation for the opening of archives they wish to consult. In the course of the work, which proceeded from one discovery to another, and often from one surprise to another, it became ever more necessary for the author to revise his previous stock of understanding, bolstered as it might have been by personal memory. A tension arose between the witness-actor sure of his own recollections, and the historian, confronted with numerous and varying unpublished versions of events and responses. The reader will judge whether this tension has been overcome.

PROLOGUE

The summer of 1939 was oppressive, but the sun did not shine on everyone in the same way. Three years later, the fires of the summer of 1936 were only ashes: the Popular Front had ceased to exist, no more than a past electoral episode. Republican Spain was no more, having crumbled under the blows of General Franco and his foreign supporters. The Nazi flag flew over Prague after Hitler's Germany had swallowed Bohemia and Moravia in the predictable aftermath of the Munich Agreement. Austria, incorporated into the Third Reich, had seen Hitler parade down the streets of its capital.

And the far right in France, reinvigorated by the triumphant advance of fascist dictators, launched its campaign against the "warmongers" (in the first instance, the Jews), and clearly announced its intention not to go to war against Hitler's Germany, which it promoted to a "rampart against Bolshevism." At the same time, the far right declared that Poland, the traditional ally of France, must make concessions. Nurtured by an ideological antisemitism, a kind of popular xenophobia was born: Unemployment? It was the fault of the far too numerous foreigners in France. The war? If there were a war, it would be the fault of the Jews seeking vengeance on Hitler. It was in this noxious environment, where the defeat of the founding ideas of the French Republic seemed assured, that the one hundred and fiftieth anniversary of the French Revolution was celebrated.

Numbers of Jews of eastern European origin—some of them communists, and others Zionists with socialist leanings—celebrated the event with two large rallies. The former, at a grand banquet in the sumptuous salons of the Palais d'Orsay, where almost six hundred persons had responded to the invitation of the Union des sociétés juives (USJ—Union of Jewish Associations), which was under communist influence; the latter, in more modest fashion, under the aegis of the Fédération des sociétés juives de France (FSJF—Federation of Jewish Associations of France),[1] at their premises on the Avenue de la République in Paris. They expounded similar views at this time, strongly stamped by the events of the day. The two organizations also had another characteristic in common: a desire to celebrate the event not in Jewish isolation but in common with other representatives of French democracy. Despite the ideological divide, which at the time seemed unbridgeable, their strategy in the face of the National Socialist danger was based on Jewish unity, open to an alliance with the French left.

They each appealed to political figures and intellectuals who were sympathetically disposed toward the Jews. Alexandre Zevaës, a celebrated historian of the First Republic, spoke at the USJ's banquet of 23 June. Zevaës "linked the memory of the Revolution," Jacques Bielinky reported in *L'Univers israélite* the same day, "with both the era of the Dreyfus Affair and the sad events of today": "Forty years ago . . . I expressed my solidarity with those who fought on behalf of a Jewish officer who had been unjustly condemned. And today, when a storm of barbarity howls across the world, I am proud to lend my support to the whole nation of Israel, so unjustly hunted and persecuted. The French Revolution was universalist in character. It sought the liberation of all men, not just of the French [repeated cries of *Vive la France!*]. But today we are witnessing the destruction of the ideas of the Revolution by a terrifying human regression." Other speakers at the USJ banquet included its president, M. M. Levin; Julien Racamond, secretary of the Confédération génénalé du travail (CGT—General Confederation of Labor); and Édouard Tcharny.[2] The FSJF's rally invited as its guest of honor Victor Basch, president of the League for the Rights of Man, who evoked the situation in an eloquent address: "Today we are in utter dejection and ignominy, and the whole world must now rise against the killers from Berlin." Marc Jarblum, president of the federation, took the podium after André Spire, the author and member of the Conseil d'Etat (Council of State, the highest administrative court in France); Paul Grunebaum-Ballin, also a member of the Conseil d'Etat; and Professor Albert Bayet of the Radical Socialist Party. According to Bielinky, Jarblum made a very pessimistic observation: "At the time of the Revolution, the act of emancipation affected 50,000 Jews, while one hundred and fifty years later, seven million Jews are being persecuted in central Europe [as] ghostly [refugee] ships sail the oceans in search of a haven."[3]

The one-hundred-and-fiftieth anniversary was not ignored by the religiously centered Consistory. The commemorative activities of the *Consistoire*, few in number in any case, were situated in the spiritual domain, outside the current political context, and in a purely Jewish framework. The June issue of its organ *L'Univers israélite* reported on an address given by Rabbi

Maurice Liber to an assembly of young people. The meeting took on the air of a history lesson, punctuated by the *Marseillaise* and the *Hymne à la liberté* sung by a student chorus. Liber's theme was "The Liberating Work of the Revolution, the Revolution and Judaism," and gave pride of place to the "Motion on Behalf of the Jews" of the Abbé Gregoire a century-and-a-half earlier, to the speech given at the Assemblée Nationale by Berr Isaac Berr, and to other important statements symbolizing the Enlightenment-era march toward emancipation. Liber drew a parallel between the ideals of the Revolution and those of Judaism, but he insisted above all on the spiritual concerns of the two systems of thought as reflected in the religious accent of the declarations of French Jews during these last days of peace.[4]

These commemorations of 1789 were the last public manifestations in which the two Jewish communities, the foreign and the French, would outline the orientations they would assume when confronted with the outright abolition of the same "Rights of Man and Citizen."

At the same time, other Jews, veterans of the International Brigades during the Spanish Civil War, who had been interned by the French government in the South of France, marked the anniversary in a far different atmosphere. Their mimeographed Yiddish-language news-sheet recorded their rally: "We, too, celebrated the 14th of July, the sesquicentennial anniversary of the French Revolution. Over some of the huts, the French tricolor snapped in the wind. . . . We made candles of suet and wrapped them in colored paper and lit up the insides of the barracks. . . . But this made the contradiction of the situation hit us with even greater force. . . . We, the new fighters for liberty, . . . were behind the barbed wire fence."[5] The author of these lines, Jonas Geduldig, who soon escaped the internment camp and joined the Jewish resistance, became a member of the military branch of the immigrant Resistance (FTP-MOI), along with Missak Manouchian, Marcel Rayman, and other heroes of various nationalities. Geduldig was eventually captured. He was shot on 21 February 1944, just a few short months before the Liberation.

PART ONE

1940–1942: The Logic of Persecution

CHAPTER ONE

The First Anti-Jewish Measures

Dark Forebodings

"A single injustice, a single crime, a single inequality, if it is
universally, legally, conveniently accepted, suffices to dishonor
an entire people."

—Charles Péguy

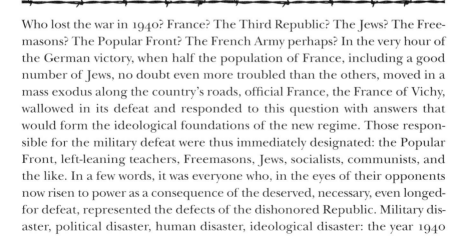

Who lost the war in 1940? France? The Third Republic? The Jews? The Freemasons? The Popular Front? The French Army perhaps? In the very hour of
the German victory, when half the population of France, including a good
number of Jews, no doubt even more troubled than the others, moved in a
mass exodus along the country's roads, official France, the France of Vichy,
wallowed in its defeat and responded to this question with answers that
would form the ideological foundations of the new regime. Those responsible for the military defeat were thus immediately designated: the Popular
Front, left-leaning teachers, Freemasons, Jews, socialists, communists, and
the like. In a few words, it was everyone who, in the eyes of their opponents
now risen to power as a consequence of the deserved, necessary, even longed-
for defeat, represented the defects of the dishonored Republic. Military disaster, political disaster, human disaster, ideological disaster: the year 1940

left France at the mercy of the occupiers and at the disposition of a reactionary "national revolution" regime that fully intended to take its revenge at last for the Revolution of 1789 and the humiliation of the Right in the Dreyfus Affair.

"Who Is a Jew?"

The Jews found themselves the target of two convergent and destructive passions. None of them could ignore it, even if they, too, experienced the general collapse that obscured thought and anesthetized the fighting instinct. These passions were the Nazi "racially" motivated antisemitism, which promised the Jews' prompt elimination for having "corrupted" the world, and the traditional French antisemitism that sought to exclude them from a society they allegedly had perverted and made gangrenous. The severity of the catastrophe for the Jews was without precedent in the long history of France. Would they prove capable of meeting the challenge? Would the analysis they made of the defeat determine their reaction to the occupation? They were in every sense of the word disoriented: tens of thousands of French and immigrant Jews found themselves buffeted from one city and to another, stunned by the collapse of a France that, especially for those coming from the East, had recently been a land of asylum; now they were desperate because they did not know what awaited them.

Very quickly—it was clearly a priority for both the government of Marshal Pétain and the German Occupation—the regime proclaimed the first anti-Jewish measures: on 22 July 1940, Vichy established a commission charged with reviewing prewar naturalization decisions; on 27 August 1940, the Marchandeau Decree from 1938, which prohibited antisemitic propaganda, was abrogated; on 27 September, the German military commander in France gave the Jews of the Occupied Zone until 20 October to submit to registration; on 3 October, Vichy promulgated the "Law Concerning the Status of Jews," signed by Pétain and the principal members of his government, defining who would be considered Jewish and barring them from employment in a broad array of jobs; on 7 October came the abrogation of the Crémieux Law of 1870 granting French citizenship to Algerian Jews. The rapidity with which laws for the exclusion of Jews followed one another prompts the assumption that this legislation had already matured in the minds of some politicians well before the military defeat. A real "legislative" fever seized the "justice" apparatus of the Vichy government. From the beginning of October 1940 to

16 September 1941, the *Journal officiel* ("Legislative Gazette") published the texts of twenty-six laws, twenty-four decrees, six orders, and one regulation concerning the Jews. "They were not idle in France: fifty-seven bills in less than a year, quite an antisemitic accomplishment!" wrote Pierre Chaillet, the Catholic cleric who protested the persecutions.[1]

Modeled on the Nuremberg laws, the anti-Jewish legislation established the definition of "a Jew" and enumerated the types of social activity that would henceforth be forbidden to Jews.[2] "Every person descended from three grandparents of the Jewish race, or from two grandparents of the same race, if the spouse was also Jewish" would be considered a Jew. The public positions that would be closed to Jews included those of head of state and cabinet minister: the memory of former prime minister Léon Blum, or of former cabinet members Georges Mandel and Jean Zay (who openly declared his Jewish background), must have troubled the nights of Vichy officials. But the list of forbidden activities restricted access to many fields, including the civil service, the armed forces, the news media, and the cinema. Other posts remained open only to veterans of the war of 1914−18 or to those who had been decorated in the 1939−40 campaign. Beyond all these details, what really counted was the objective and the sense of the legislation: the exclusion of Jews from the national community.

For its part, Nazi headquarters in France had a specific vision of its anti-Jewish policy, even if the exact meaning of the term *Endziel* (final objective)—frequently employed during the initial period—was never stated. In the minds of the Germans, the policy was to close off the least maneuvering space for any existing or future Jewish organization. The only accommodations foreseen related to the possible international repercussions of this or that measure, as well as to the statist sensitivities of the Vichy administration, which they took pains not to ruffle. Several memoranda, drawn up by the German general staff in consultation with Otto Abetz, the German ambassador in Paris, bear witness to this determination, accompanied by formidable tactical intelligence. In a memo from 22 August 1940, based on directives received from Berlin and in accord with instructions from the embassy, military headquarters set the broad policy lines that would guide its participation in the anti-Jewish program. "For all administrative measures that it may be called on to take," the memorandum states, "the military administration should in principle employ the channel of the French authorities."[3] Thus, there was created something like a "purely French space" where the Vichy regime could and ought to legislate "freely." The Germans believed that the goal of definitively removing "Jewish influence from all domains of public life" could be reached only if "the French people itself determines to free it-self of Jewry." The Germans counted on Vichy, but they also kept score.

German headquarters insisted on these points, deeming it important to avoid "any suspicion of annexation" (the assumption seems to be that the appropriate German apparatus would eventually replace the French authority in matters concerning the Jews, but this could not be hinted at for the time being).[4] Most likely this concern stemmed from dependence on the collaboration of French administrative and police personnel. The Germans were, in fact, quite conscious of the insufficiency of their own numbers. Moreover, the German military saw other advantages in maintaining a certain camouflage. They considered that a series of partial or individual measures "would sow more fear among Jews if they were less systematic, in other terms, appeared more arbitrary." Why, in fact, would it be necessary at the beginning (August 1940) brutally to weed out the Jews when for the moment it seemed more effective "to poison their existence even there where they are not yet troubled."[5]

Following the same train of thought, the Germans declined, not only out of prudence but also with a concern for efficiency, to pressure Vichy to intensify anti-Jewish measures in the non-occupied Southern Zone, "where only the French government is authorized to act." Indeed, German policy consisted in reinforcing "the parties and movements within the French people with antisemitic tendencies," which would encourage the Pétain government to move in the desired direction.[6]

This tactic paid off, since it took into account the antisemitism of the new French authorities and their desire to cling to the tatters of sovereignty that were left to them. As the 3 October legislation making Jews second-class citizens would show, the Germans had not been mistaken. They wrote the rules for a game in which they would hold the upper hand, and they found it useful to show their dominance: before Vichy could act, they published their own anti-Jewish ordinance on 27 September: "We have judged it necessary to make [our law] public before the French" the occupiers stated, in order to show that "the settlement of the Jewish question originates with the German authorities."[7]

Who Went Back to Paris?

As the Jewish communities came to know and comprehend the situation, a number of Jews who had left Paris in the exodus to the South preferred to remain in the Free Zone, although some would eventually return to Paris. As far as we can judge, their choice in 1940 was often determined—and this is only normal—by economic and social considerations.

Which Jews did return to the Nazi-occupied capital? An unpublished, anonymously authored text entitled "Étude sur la situation des Juifs en zone occupée" (Study of the Situation of Jews in the Occupied Zone), contains an excellent sociological and demographic analysis of an extremely confused situation, furnishing in addition precise information on the daily life of Parisian Jews in 1940 and early 1941.[8] To the question "who went back to Paris?" the author states, "The French Jews, on the whole more fortunate than the immigrant Jews, returned in lesser numbers. The percentage of returns decreases as the social category . . . rises (certainly more Jewish lawyers than tradesmen stayed away)."[9] The census carried out in the Occupied Zone in October would show a figure for foreign Jews that is very close to prewar estimates.

For the Jews, as well as for Parisians generally, the capital had changed. The German presence was evident in signposts that had been put up overnight. The city turned into an alien landscape filled with innumerable acronyms that the French had difficulty in deciphering. And then there were the German soldiers whom one encountered out walking: like tourists they exclaimed before every monument or every young Parisienne, "*Ach! Paris!*"

Other images reinforced the strange atmosphere. Huge billboards with the caricature of a Jew—a bogeyman to terrify children but also to bolster the propaganda of the antisemites—announced the screening of the film *The Jew Süss* in the cinemas of the Champs-Elysées and Grands Boulevards. This was the new shock film of Nazi propaganda, a monstrous travesty of the novel by the great German-Jewish author Lion Feuchtwanger, a refugee huddling at that very moment in Les Milles, an internment camp in the South of France.

To reinforce the effect, the Germans also showed what purported to be a documentary on the noxiousness of the "Jewish race," the film *Der ewige Jude,* seen through the history of the Rothschild "dynasty." At regular intervals, rats spill onto screen as if to invade the theater. But as yet, few imagined that the identification of the Jews with vermin implied the concept of their planned extermination.[10]

By the autumn of 1940 Parisian Jews rarely attended public performances, even if their presence was not yet expressly forbidden. After the 27 September ordinance for the census of Jews, the most varied rumors spread, awakening a heavy sense of foreboding and anxiety. The collective unconscious still bore the traces of past persecutions: each time an emperor, prince, or some lord ordered Jews to be counted, it ended badly for them.[11] How far would it go this time? The worst that most expected was economic despoliation. Some spoke of the revival of the ghetto. But where? "At the flea market in Saint-Ouen," said someone who did not lack a sense of irony, but the prospect was enough to reawaken old anxieties. Still, fear is malleable: it can be repressed, denied.

All this, we've seen it before. The sense of déjà vu was passed along like a directive. "Jewish optimism," writes the author of the "Étude," "has its roots in the evocation of persecutions already endured and overcome. We survived Haman, why not Hitler?"[12] Here the author of the study pinpoints the belief in a victorious outcome to the war as the principal source of hope.

Because the times were dark, numerous anecdotes soon circulated, generally of "Jewish origin." The joke that best caught the spirit of the times concerned Hitler's frustration at the German failure to invade England. He turned to an old rabbi and promised to save his life if he would divulge the secret Moses employed to open a path through the Red Sea. The rabbi told Hitler that Moses' strength lay in the magic power of his commander's baton. "I must have that baton," cried Hitler, "Where is it?" The rabbi replied with dry mockery, "It's in the British Museum."[13]

The Jews' forebodings, however, proved insufficient to prompt nonsubmission to the census ordinance. And how could it have been otherwise, in light of the fact that refusal was tantamount to outlawry, to serious (if unknown) consequences for individuals and their families? With heavy hearts, Jews reported at the offices set up for this purpose in the police stations.

"A number of Jews were certainly not registered," as the author of the "Étude" notes, "often on the advice of the local chiefs of police, who pointed out to them that neither their name nor that of their parents betrayed them. The overall impression is that these were not very numerous, since many . . . who could have escaped the census on the contrary made a point of honor of acquiescing to it." In this connection a rumor circulated in Parisian society about the appearance shortly before his death of the philosopher Henri Bergson before the chief of police. Bergson had been told informally that he did not need to appear; he died two months later, on 4 January 1941, at the age of 81. Paul Valéry, the great poet and member of the Académie Française, delivered a funeral eulogy on 9 January before a group of friends who had gathered around the coffin in the philosopher's apartment. Fernand de Brinon, the official delegate of Vichy to the occupation authorities, represented the French government on the occasion. "I have no doubt," said

Valéry, who at no point made any allusion to the Jewish origins of the great thinker, "that he was cruelly afflicted by the disaster whose effects we have all borne." As a matter of fact, after the entry of the Germans into Paris, Valéry had not called on Bergson. After pressing the widow's hand, everyone accompanied the casket to the door of the building.[14] From one solitude to another. . . .

In October and November 1940, 113,462 men and women over age fifteen were registered in Paris and its surrounding suburbs. Of these, 57,110 had French citizenship; 55,849 were foreigners, and 503 came from French protectorates. Among the foreign Jews, those from Poland were in the majority (26,158); followed by those from Russia (7,228) and Romania (4,382).

A closer analysis of this data reveals that among Jews with French nationality, the number of naturalized Jewish citizens was almost equal to the number of French origin, 28,502 and 25,989, respectively. The census allowed a special category for children under fifteen years of age, who numbered 34,557, 30.5 percent of the registered population. A substantial proportion of children had French nationality as a consequence of the registration of their birth, totalling almost three-quarters of all the children of immigrant families. While children in families of French origin numbered 13,212, those with French nationality in foreign families were no fewer than 21,345. Most would later share the fate of their parents.[15]

A Shattered Community

Is it possible, at this stage, to speak of the Jewish population in terms of a collectivity? The exodus, the military defeat, the first antisemitic legislative measures shattered the previous cohesive structures, the framework that gave shape to the social, cultural, and political life that had been so intense before the war. This collapse was further aggravated by a geographic dispersion that had not previously been experienced in France. The Franco-American historian Zosa Szajkowski has identified almost eight hundred towns and localities where Jews went into temporary exile after 1940.[16]

The demarcation line that split France into two parts became almost impassable, especially for Jews of foreign nationality. A further division, this in the very center of the Jewish population, came from the decision by most of the mutual aid organizations and political groups to move their offices to the Free Zone. The distance thus created between decision-making centers in the south and the Jews of Paris created very differing situations, perceptions, and experiences, differences lasting at least until the entry of German troops into the Southern Zone. This was so much the case that with only a few exceptions the national offices were in the South politically and psychologically incapable of advising their Parisian staff.[17]

On the communist side, the administration of the Jewish section of the Main d'Oeuvre Immigrée (MOI—Immigrant Labor Association) had regrouped in mid-July 1940. Adam Rayski had escaped from a POW camp in Nantes and returned to Paris on July 14. The head of the MOI, Louis Gronowski (né Bruno), accompanied by Jacques Kaminski (né Hervè) returned to the capital at the end of August.[18] The members of the organization, operating illegally since September 1939, when the French Communist Party (PCF) and groups under its influence had been banned, favored the rapid reconstitution of base groups in several parts of the city. Propaganda and social assistance activities were put into the hands of a new front group, Solidarité, which devoted itself to activities judged to have immediate priority, such as fundraising and the distribution of relief to households struck by unemployment or whose head was a prisoner of war in Germany. Particular attention was devoted to propaganda at meetings organized by apartment building, and to the distribution of the Yiddish-language newspaper *Unzer Wort* ("Our Word"), which resumed publication in late September.

An exceptional observer, the author of the "Étude sur la Situation des Juifs en Zone occupée," paints this picture of Jewish political life in Paris: "It is only the 'Jewish Communist Party'[19] that has remained fairly active after going underground, by holding small meetings of cells. It frequently publishes tracts in Yiddish, most often simple translations of Communist Party texts. If, during an initial period, they took noncommunist Jewish leaders to task for their absence from Paris, their emphasis shifted to criticism of the Vichy government's racism and to resistance against Hitler, while inviting the 'Jewish proletariat to put its trust in communism and in Soviet Russia for its liberation.'" No similar signs of activity can be noted in the other Jewish parties, Zionist or socialist. "There is no publication of pamphlets; the activists are content to put their trust and hope in a British victory," the author writes. "They meet in canteens, along party lines."[20] *Unzer Wort*, like numerous other publications that started to appear, would come to play the symbolic and practical role of a center around which the movement took form.

Neither the French police nor the occupiers underestimated the threat posed by the circulation of clandestine publications in Jewish circles otherwise condemned to ignorance of what was being planned for them. Police collaboration between the French and Germans did not, in fact, have to wait for the political agreements of Montoire on 24 October 1940. Collaboration was formally justified by Article 3 of the Armistice Convention, which granted "all rights to the occupying powers" and obliged the French administration "to ensure the implementation of German regulations."[21] Sent to Berlin scarcely two months after the fall of Paris, a report from the German commander illustrates how the occupiers sought to legitimize in advance measures to come: "The hostile attitude of the Jews in the Occupied Zone toward the Third Reich cannot be in doubt." As a consequence, the Jewish population of the Occupied Zone "constitutes an ever-present threat to German troops. Effective and radical measures against this danger are [therefore] perfectly compatible with the armistice convention."[22] What must be borne in mind is that the Jews were automatically qualified as "enemies," their repression and persecution encompassed by the armistice terms. This would furnish Vichy with the necessary alibi—if one were even needed. From the outset, then, the efforts of the French police against Jewish organizations were considered by the occupying authorities as one of the preconditions for their own success.

The first acts of police repression in the autumn of 1940 had as their objective the moral and political "disarmament of the enemy," and took the form of attacks against the framework and social fabric of Jewish community life. The unit charged with the task was the "Direction générale des renseignements et des jeux" (General Administration for Intelligence and Gaming) at the Prefecture of Police, which on the orders of the occupying forces established a special section for the "surveillance of Jewish circles" to make monthly reports to the commandant of *Gross Paris* (the Greater Paris region).[23]

Between October 1940 and April 1941, the agents of this bureau claimed to have carried out two hundred raids and five hundred investigations concerning private individuals or the headquarters of former "Zionist or political organizations." In particular, those of the Ligue internationale contre l'antisémitisme (LICA—International League against Antisemitism), the Alliance israélite universelle (AIU—Universal Israelite Alliance), and the Alliance juive pour la Palestine (Jewish Agency for Palestine) were the targets of searches or close surveillance. At this time, the Paris Prefecture of Police assumed on its own authority the repression of Jewish organizations begun by the Gestapo in August 1940. Numerous apartments were the object of searches carried out on the personal orders of Herbert Hagen, the head of the Gestapo in Paris.[24] The prominent figures investigated included numerous members of the Rothschild family, George Mandel (Jeroboam Rothschild), Bernard Lecache (president of the LICA), Marc Jarblum (leader of the Zionist-Socialists and president of the Federation of Jewish Societies), the lawyers Moro-Giafferi and Henri Torrès, and Chief Rabbi Isaïe Schwartz.[25] The French and German police gave evidence of special interest in "the new activities of the Consistory and its affiliated organizations," which meant the Comité de coordination des oeuvres de bienfaisance israélites du Grand Paris (Committee for the Coordination of Jewish Welfare Agencies of Greater Paris). The *Renseignements Généraux* note:

> It has been determined that aside from the recently reorganized Consistory . . . there are no other active Jewish organizations. However, a certain number of former members of the above-mentioned Jewish section of the Communist Party have continued to circulate the marching orders of the Third International among French Jews and the foreign Jewish colony of the capital. They have sought to attack the moral standing of Marshal Pétain. To this end, clandestine tracts, entitled *Unzer Wort* and written in Yiddish, have been disseminated or slipped under the doors of lodgings occupied by Jews, in particular in the 4th, 5th, 10th, 11th, 19th and 20th city districts.[26]

The First Internments

For its part, the Jewish population of Paris alternated between anguish and hope. On the one hand, the first anti-Jewish legislation, accompanied by a rabid campaign to arouse antisemitic feeling, reminded Jews of the tsarist pogroms or of Poland between the wars. But weeks passed and—with the exception of some clashes in Jewish neighborhoods provoked by rowdies of Jacques Doriot (the former communist turned fascist and founder of the radical right-wing Parti populaire francais [PPF]) or similar groups—a near calm returned. This led to ephemeral feelings of relative physical safety.

Paradoxically, news from the Free Zone caused the greatest anxiety. The Vichy government did not wait for the anti-Jewish laws before establishing camps and other "reassembly centers." Foreign Jews were arrested "in great numbers," and sent to join political refugees from other countries (Germans, Austrians, Czechs, and others) in the camps in Gurs and Argelès. The only echo of what was happening there, except for censored private correspondence, was the news reported in *Unzer Wort,* which in its 21–29 September issue denounced the outrageous internment of foreign Jewish volunteers in the French armed forces: "The Jewish soldiers at the Septfonds camp report that they have been rounded up by the French government like murderers and criminals. . . . It is not enough that thousands of them have fallen for France; those who survived must now be locked up in concentration camps or work camps after having been sent to the front with neither guns nor bullets."[27]

In its 20 October issue, the paper provided additional information about these internments. "Thousands of Jews, men, women, and children have already been interned in concentration camps where there is a total lack of hygiene, without food and without care." This is the first occasion when the presence of children in the camps is mentioned. The newspaper does not spend too much space on the matter, however, probably considering it an episodic occurrence, but writers continued to denounce Vichy's treatment of the volunteers: "Hundreds of foreign volunteers who were in Algeria have been sent to forced labor in Africa. They were told that after three months they would be sent back to France, but seven months later they are still there, under the torrid sun. . . . Anyone who wants to return to France must produce a work permit for the non-occupied zone or show proof that he has the sum of 5,000 francs, both impossibilities."[28] With the internment of Jewish volunteers on the pretext of their irregular status, Vichy touched an extremely sensitive nerve among immigrant Jews who could never have foreseen such ingratitude on the part of France. They were as proud as the French-born Jews of having served the country, but they would not experience the same difficulty as the latter in choosing between the France of the Rights of Man and the France of Vichy.

This same ignobility found expression beyond the camps. It enjoyed a privileged place in the Fédération des anciens engagés volontaires étrangers (Federation of Former Foreign Enlistees) headed by General Goudouneix. He displayed not the slightest concern for the Jewish volunteers, curtly excluding them from the association. "The Jewish enlistees," he opined, "are only defectives, untrustworthy." In an undated circular letter numbered "15," the general justified this exclusion in terms reminiscent of antisemitic tracts. "It is then indispensable," he wrote, "to strengthen supervision over our membership. . . . It is clearly a case of Israélites who only now come to us [Goudouneix is insinuating that the Jewish volunteers had not seen combat] and who are largely animated by the desire to find refuge and do not offer, in the sense of our bylaws, resources of interest." But he is very specific in his praise of "non-Israélite" Poles and Italians. Xenophobia on request, and unlimited antisemitism.[29]

Internment actions were also initiated in Paris. They were limited in scope and aimed at a certain number of militant Zionists, in addition to Jews carrying passports from Palestine. Little noticed because they were isolated cases, these arrests did not seem to worry Jewish opinion excessively.

Considerably more troubling were the consequences of the 18 October 1940 edict that imposed "Aryan" administrative commissioners over companies and businesses belonging to Jews. Unemployment, due to the general crisis, became even more widespread. According to the author of the "Étude sur la situation Juifs," already cited, "A certain number of Jews, merchants, or salaried workers who have remained without work through the loss of their activities, find new ones by reverting to ancestral forms. . . . These people were now peddling from house to house, hawking in the markets without license, etc. Thus, in a singular evolution of things, the forms of Jewish commerce that had disappeared with the emancipation of the Jews by the French Revolution returned in force and are imposed on the great-great-grand-children of those emancipated in the past."[30] The handwriting was on the wall for those perceptive enough, but most had no premonition that things would soon become much worse.

The Question of Final Objective (*Endziel*)

All of these measures, however, were only the first steps in the persecution of the Jews. During the summer of 1940 little gave the impression of a coordinated plan: only sporadic, if sharp, harassment and intimidation, the most optimistic (or naïve) might tell themselves. But by early September the *Judenreferat*, the Gestapo office for Jewish matters, was already established in Paris to deal with the "question." At its head was twenty-seven-year-old Obersturmführer Theodor Dannecker. A determined man in a hurry, Dannecker reported to Adolf Eichmann and had been his collaborator for the previous three years, when Eichmann was the head of Section IVb at the Berlin headquarters of the *Sicherheitsdienst* (SD — Security Service). Dannecker arrived in Paris with almost unlimited power, held in check only by the necessity of coordinating activities with the embassy and army. He was also equipped with the notorious telegram that the head of the SD, Reinhard Heydrich, had circulated to all the commandants of *Einsatzgruppen* after the fall of Warsaw on the 21st day of the Polish campaign (21 September 1939).[31]

In this directive, Heydrich set out the general lines of the Nazi policy with regard to Jews in the occupied territories of Eastern Europe and spelled out the means for its implementation. The top-secret document deals with "the set of measures," including the final objective. Just what lies behind this phrasing? There is nothing precise, but "it is important to distinguish between 1) the final objective (*Endziel*), which is of the long term, and 2) the stages (*Abschnitten*) toward this objective, which may be achieved in the short term." The first stage, "the concentration of Jews in the large cities," should be completed rapidly. The territories of Danzig, western Prussia, Poznan, and Upper Silesia were to be "freed" of Jews. In the other occupied territories of Central Europe it would be necessary to create a certain number of concentration points in order to facilitate "subsequent measures." For this reason, cities with railway junctions or at least near a railway line were to be considered. All Jewish communities numbering fewer than five hundred persons were to be dissolved and their residents brought to the nearest concentration centers.

In the second part of the directive Heydrich requires each Jewish community to create a "council of elders" (*Ältestenrat*) composed of twenty-four influential persons and rabbis. This council, also known as the *Judenrat,* would be "fully responsible" for the faultless and timely implementation of evacuation and concentration. Acts of sabotage would expose the councils to the most severe "counter-measures." Point 5 of the directive explicitly mentions the establishment of ghettos, which would at one and the same time constitute the keystone of the concentration efforts and would define the territorial framework within which the "power" of the Jewish councils was to be exercised. The Germans legitimized the anti-Jewish measure by noting, "the decisive role the Jews played in attacks by irregular troops and in pillaging."

Adapting Heydrich's instructions to the French situation—where, for reasons as much political as practical, Vichy's participation had to be relied on—naturally fell to Dannecker. In a memorandum sent to the concerned German offices on 21 January 1941, he gave a broad-brush account of the goals to be reached and the means to achieve them. In his opinion, this meant undertaking a task that was "gigantic, and whose success can be assured only by the most meticulous preparations." The preparations in question were "for the carefully implemented complete deportation of the Jews prior to a colonization action in a yet to be determined territory." Does Dannecker's un-nuanced use of terms like "deportation" and "colonization action" reveal an absence in Berlin at this time of a precise definition of the final objective, or rather a deliberate intention to keep this objective vague in order better to conceal it? Whichever the case, Dannecker reveals a firm will not to be overwhelmed by the enormity of the task. "It may happen that with the deportation of the Jews, which will eventually take place, we shall have before us a task that is beyond our resources."[32]

From the perspective of eventual deportation, Dannecker went on, it was desirable, first of all, to proceed with "locating and eliminating Jews from all professional and social networks." Subsequently there would be created a "centralized administration for Jews and their property until the time of their deportation." Considering the attitude of the French authorities, who "showed no political understanding of the necessity of a general purge," Dannecker insisted on the urgent creation of a "central Jewish office." With a view to increasing pressure on the Vichy government, he did not hesitate to criticize it for its "decentralized tinkering." Among other features of the deportation preparations, it would be important to control a "compulsory association of the Jews which is already organized in broad terms and under our surveillance as the communal body responsible for all Jews." Dannecker is here alluding to the Comité de coordination des oeuvres juives (Committee for the Coordination of Jewish Organizations) of Paris, which he was then setting up. From the Nazi perspective, the Vichy government's Central Jewish Office (which in March 1941 would become the Commissariat général aux questions juives, or General Commission for Jewish Affairs)[33] and the compulsory association of the Jews established by the Germans complemented each other. These two organizations would then play leading roles in the resolution of "the Jewish Question" in France.

CHAPTER TWO

The Consistory between Religion and Politics

Our religion directs us to consider the law of the prince as the
supreme law in civil and political matters.
> —Declaration of the assembly of
> prominent Jews brought together at the
> instigation of Napoleon on 4 August 1806

In its August 1940 decision not to return to the French capital and to establish itself at Vichy, the Central Consistory—in particular Chief Rabbi
Isaïe Schwartz and his vice-president Jacques Helbronner—failed to recognize that this choice of location would not only bring it geographically
closer to the new regime but would also risk hitching it to Marshal Pétain's
cart. It is certainly normal for such a representative body to have its headquarters in a capital city, even if the latter is only temporary. But, this said,
should they have lost sight of another criterion: the presence in Paris of
the great majority of France's Jews, alone in the face of the occupying forces,
first in line and most threatened?[1] In any case the German edict prohibiting
Jews from returning to the Occupied Zone eased the Consistory's choice.

First Message of Allegiance

A "closed session" held by the Central Consistory in Vichy in August 1940 invested Chief Rabbi Schwartz with "full authority" to speak on its behalf. Shortly thereafter, on 3 September 1940, the first meeting of the Association du rabbinate (Association of the Rabbinate) was held in Lyon under Schwartz's leadership. The rabbinical corps sent a telegram to Marshal Pétain, "in whom France in its distress has placed its hope," assuring the head of state "that, ever inspired by the commandments of Judaism, it exhorts the faithful to serve the fatherland, promote the family, and honor labor."[2] At almost the same moment, Cardinal Pierre-Marie Gerlier of Lyon informed Pétain of his and the Catholic Church's support in the same terms: "Work, Family, Fatherland, these three words are our own."[3] Two years later, however, Schwartz would be one of the first leaders of the Consistory to advocate disobedience to the anti-Jewish legislation.

It is true that great confusion reigned in the country as to the role that the Marshal intended to play. Yet some of the prominent figures close to the Consistory expressed their skepticism by deciding in late August 1940 to establish in Marseille "a collective body for defense" that would, in their view, be "seen as representative of the Jewish community."[4] Even though they might recognize the authority of the chief rabbi, these figures were nonetheless of the opinion that the latter was not up to the task before him. Was this a conflict of personalities? Did it reflect political differences? In any case their initiative reflected a reaction to the unconditional act of allegiance the rabbinate had just made. The name "Defense Committee" suggests that the new body was intended to act in the political sphere, where the Consistory had no mandate to intervene. At its head was General André Boris, who would be struck from the ranks of the army by virtue of the anti-Jewish legislation and, at his side, Léon Meiss, a magistrate from Strasbourg with socialist leanings who later would play a prominent role in the Consistory. Others included Professor David Olmer, a physician and researcher with an international reputation; René Mayer, a politician who had been active under the Third Republic; and Jacques Meyer, president of the association of Jewish WWI veterans.

Their project foresaw formation of individual "defense committees" in the various cities, in order to create the impression of a "movement whose objective was to protest against the antisemitic propaganda orchestrated by the Vichy people, as well as against new legislative measures that had already been enacted or were in the course of preparation." Here we can see the first hints of resistance, and at a moment when it was scarcely conceivable. The political character of the initiative did not fail to arouse worry within the Consistory, particularly in the person of its vice-president Jacques Helbronner, who "on the pretext of avoiding a schism in French Jewry invited the Marseille Committee to incorporate itself into the Consistory." Some members of the committee were swayed by his argument. But in so preempting the nascent protest of the Defense Committee, had not Helbronner (who had in the meantime been named president) delayed the Consistory's acknowledgment of the full seriousness of the situation? Would the Jews of Vichy France now have to depend on men such as Schwartz and Helbronner as their representatives?

Shortly after publication of the anti-Jewish legislation, the chief rabbi approached the Marshal to voice a protest, but its strength was attenuated by passages resonating with the slogans of the Pétainists: "We recognize, as we have always recognized, the superiority of the common good, the necessity of a hierarchy, and the primacy of merit. But we note with sorrow that in the name of a civilized society we are refused equality before the law. The new order that has been proposed to the country by the head of state is founded in work, family, and fatherland. No concept could be dearer to us." The legislation appeared not to have affected the Consistory's loyalty to the government.[5]

While this behavior seems in hindsight naïve, it should be recognized that a clear awareness of the actual intentions and the long-term implications of the new laws would have been difficult in their immediate wake. The members of the Consistory were Frenchmen of the Jewish faith, absolutely sure of the definitive character of their integration into the nation: nothing had prepared them to confront antisemitism on the part of the state; the Dreyfus Affair, despite its far-reaching echoes, was still accounted as an episode rather than a bellwether. Thus, in accordance with the Talmudic principle that "the law of the kingdom is the law," the Consistory would find itself before agonizing moral choices since the "kingdom" was here incarnated in Pétain.[6]

Helbronner's Counter-Proposal

In November 1940 Jacques Helbronner submitted, very probably in his own name, to Pétain and the Conseil d'État (from which he had just been excluded) a draft of a bill intended to offer an alternative to the anti-Jewish legislation.[7] This "counter-bill" would have redirected toward immigrant Jews the thrust of the recent antisemitic laws, which had been armed primarily at the French "Israélites."[8] According to Helbronner, the objective of the government should not be "to strike at freedom of conscience nor to initiate religious persecution but to eliminate from political and public life those foreign elements that are unassimilated to the national spirit."[9] Helbronner develops his claim with the aid of a historical review of integration from the sixteenth century to his day, citing King Louis XVI's extension of the citizenship to France's Jews in 1791, disingenuously ignoring the fact that Louis was by then a prisoner of the Revolution. (Mention of the 1789 Declaration of the Rights of Man and Citizen would not have helped Helbronner's cause in 1940.)

More shocking, Helbronner averred that "the Israelites are not all descended from the Jewish people, a Semitic race that inhabited Palestine at the moment of its dispersal." Scattered across Europe, Asia, and Africa, he wrote, the Jews showed their aptitude for proselytizing and "converted to their faith various peoples, some of which today still possess the ethnic character of their original race, very different from that of the Semitic race: yellow tribes of Mongolia, negroes from Abyssinia, Jews from Poland, Khazars from Russia." What then do the Israelites of France have in common with these tribes that were "converted" to Judaism? Nothing, thinks Helbronner. But, Helbronner argued by extension, "we can today affirm, after numerous scientific studies, that the modern Jewish communities of western Europe are, for the most part, the descendants of Latins, Gallo-Romans, Iberians, and Germans": more noble origin could scarcely be imagined.

Things were fine in France, Helbronner continues, until the close of the nineteenth century, at which time a "danger" appeared before the eyes of French Israelites: successive governments opened the frontiers of France to "foreigners" who had been persecuted in their native lands, and even facilitated access to French citizenship. Helbronner thus made the same case against the Third Republic as the far right. The "invasion"[10] assumed ever more troubling proportions, but, "despite the warnings of French Jewry the governments did nothing (in fact, did the very contrary) to meet the danger." To believe Helbronner, the government of Marshal Pétain had initially taken the right course, neutralizing the danger by undertaking to "review all the naturalizations that had been made since 1919," and to modify the law on French nationality by limiting the rights of naturalized citizens.

Helbronner's conclusion heralds the purpose of his bill: "If it were desirable to deny the important functions of the state or the exercise of professions that influence public opinion, it would have been simple to require . . . national ancestry for the holders of these positions, without having recourse to the erroneous German ideology of race." Helbronner cited the practice of the monarchy under which candidates, for certain appointments, had to adduce proof of "several generations of French nationality." Helbronner's draft nonetheless employs the terminology then in use for classifying people according to their ethnic, racial, or national "characteristics." The bill reiterates the whole list of positions—political, military, and public—in the areas of journalism, cinema, and entertainment that would be permitted only to "French citizens having at least three grandparents of French nationality."

The clear goal of the bill is to spare French "Israelites" at the expense of "unassimilable" Jews who came from Romania, Russia, Poland, and elsewhere. It was a deplorable betrayal, but the latter were destined for the French internment camps anyway. In any case, we have no reason to believe that either the rabbinate or the Consistory knew of, or were party to, Helbronner's questionable initiative.[11]

How to Manage Misfortune?

The Consistory was—or believed itself to be—the symbol of Jewry persecuted but still standing, in the person of those who represented it to Vichy. It was—or thought itself—the necessary representative in the management of misfortune. It was—or in any case saw itself as—the incarnation of a Judaism suffering injustice with dignity, but bound to respect the articles of the armistice and to submit to the law of the victors. It still held to the notion that the head of the Vichy state could be dissuaded from the strictest application of the new antisemitic laws.

The Consistory claimed that, along with the rabbinate, it represented the only Jewish "space" still tolerated in France. Deprived of civic rights, subject to multiple restrictions on employment, economically threatened, the Jews of France did not experience any restrictions in the practice of their religion. There was a great temptation, therefore, to concentrate on what could be preserved, even if it were at the price of accommodating to the new regime's antisemitic legislation. But the space that would be protected this way shrank as more exclusionary legislation was passed. The Consistory obstinately refused to face up to the political content of the "National Revolution," touted from the very beginning as revenge for the one that had proclaimed the Rights of Man and the emancipation of the Jews—"in the mind of Marshal Pétain, the battle of France had been lost in 1789,"[12] wrote Arthur Koestler, who was then interned in the Vernet Camp in Ariège. In 1941, all juridical, moral, and political foundations for the integration of Jews in the nation collapsed. All the more striking to note in Consistory documents is the absence of any reference to the French Revolution of 1789 or the Declaration of the Rights of Man. Its leaders seem to have forgotten that the integration could survive only in a republican climate.[13]

However earnestly the Consistory may have protested, it is patent that it saw no other choice than to appeal to Pétain. But could the Consistory have been pursuing a two-pronged policy, something that would have been almost an elementary resistance tactic for a legal organization; might it have been speaking the language of necessity to Vichy and the language of reality to the persecuted Jews? No, not even that. With the one, it evinced wounded good faith; to the others it counseled obedience while, of course, invoking only one courageous principle: the retention of dignity in misfortune.

Confronting the Second Anti-Jewish Law

In June 1941, as a consequence of the promulgation of a new law establishing more severe measures to exclude Jews from the economy and public administration, the Consistory adopted an official analysis of almost a year of persecution against French Jews in the two zones. The statement did not mention the massive internment of foreign Jews in the Free Zone nor the similar action a month earlier in Paris. It did, however, note that this new law came on top of "numerous measures of an administrative or corporative nature" that had already intensified the effect of the first anti-Semitic law." The aim of the new legislation was to complement, adapt, and codify what had already been done "with a view to removing Jews from executive positions in banking, business, journalism, cinema, theater, and publishing." The Consistory rightly observed that the new statute brought a moderation in the definition of who was a Jew: "It is worth noting that this text, which concludes with an exemption for Jews who converted before 25 June 1940, proves explicitly that it is not the idea of race, however debatable this may be, that is envisaged, but religious observance that is targeted."

Still, it was the foundations of Jewish identity that were under attack. The new exclusion struck at the very mandate of the Consistory. This is why it argued—with a goodly amount of inner conviction—that the new misfortune derived solely from the Nazi occupier. Was it not trying to save what it could of its legitimacy in the eyes of French authorities by doing so? The following text boils down to an argument that "we didn't deserve that" and to appeals for recognition of the dignity and loyalty of the French Jewish community. Desperate to believe in the basic decency of Pétain or other members of the Vichy government, the members of the Consistory felt the second law as a cruel insult. In their distress, they still hoped: "The community of French Israelites, through the voice of their Central Consistory, requests of the head of state that the measures to be undertaken not be presented to the general public as a governmental decision, dictated solely by reasons of national interest, but as a ransom exacted by external coercion. . . . And this will be [the French Israelites'] only consolation while awaiting the hour of . . . justice."[14]

Viewed from another vantage point, the Consistory seemed to be saying that for French Jews to submit, it was enough to present the anti-Jewish measures as a concession to Germany! Even if the Consistory still thought itself the recognized representative of French Jewry, did it have the moral right to speak "in the name of the collectivity of French Israelites"? Did it really know the latters' feelings? Was this stance valid for the foreign Jews? For those in the Occupied Zone?

This declaration constitutes an implicit justification of the policy of collaboration, and the hope that Pétain—with at least Helbronner's support—might spare France even more suffering by sacrificing the foreign Jews. To add weight to his intervention Helbronner appended the full list of all the members of the Consistory council, including their occupation, military rank, and military and civil decorations. Given the communications conditions of the period, it is unlikely that all of them had been consulted. Addressed to the Marshal, the letter was received by the General Commissariat for Jewish Questions on 30 June 1941. The leaders of the Consistory must have hoped that France (but which France, one wonders) would appreciate their willingness to sacrifice on its behalf. Still and always this spirit of sacrifice for the nation, as if there were something in common between this abnegation and bloodshed on the battlefield in relation to the honor of French Jewry. And what did they demand in exchange? The impossible! That Vichy save the dignity of French Jews by naming the occupier responsible for the antisemitic persecutions that were an integral part of the regime established by Marshal Pétain.

This is how the Consistory envisaged the survival of Jewry in these circumstances. From the deliberations, protests, supplications, and oaths of fidelity that it sent to Pétain, we see what, in fact, lay at the core of the Consistory's reasoning: an attachment to the values of Judaism, to Jewish identity, and to the reputed traditional values of France, which against all evidence they hoped to find in Pétain. This hope against hope appears in Jacques Helbronner's written account of his visit to the Marshal in March 1941. Pétain is reported to have asked Helbronner to stay to dinner. In the course of their conversation, the Marshal declared that he, unfortunately, was not the master; that the legislation had been extracted from him under duress by a few rabid members of his government (now out of office — Minister of Justice Alibert, and Minister of the Interior Peyrouton); that its consequences horrified him; that all of it would all be abrogated the day he became the true master. Appended to this document one may still find a draft of Helbronner's proposed adoption of a motion of confidence in and fidelity to the Marshal, fealty conceived in the following terms: "The members of the Council of the Central Consistory of the Israelites of France and Algeria, meeting in Lyon, in the harsh circumstances of the trials now afflicting the French of Israelite faith, address to Marshal Pétain the assurance of their absolute fidelity and their unwavering devotion, as well as their confidence that his justice and goodness will re-establish them in their honor and full dignity as citizens."[15]

The text did not fail to provoke a stir among council members. General Boris stated that he was resolutely against it, but Helbronner and his supporters convinced the general of the necessity of the appeal in order to forestall further anti-Jewish depredations. Then, overcome by his doubts, he rushed to the railway station where Helbronner, with the motion in his briefcase, was about to take the train to Vichy. Boris begged him not to submit the text, for it would be "dangerous to leave such a document in the hands of the Marshal." In the end, Helbronner agreed to limit himself to a "verbal communication."[16]

The Census and the Honor of Being Jewish

The new law was followed by an edict mandating the compulsory census of "all persons belonging to the Jewish race." The Consistory needed to take a position in response, and made Chief Rabbi Isaïe Schwartz its spokesman; he then made his statement from both religious and political perspectives.

Should one or should one not submit to the census? Rabbi Schwartz averred that "Jewish honor obliged [Jews] to conform to the provisions of the law. Not to state one's Jewish identity in the present circumstances is to be considered an effort to conceal one's religion and one's origin, tacitly to disavow one's ancestors and brothers."[17]

Could not this same Jewish honor have legitimated a stance of refusal? This was not the view of the chief rabbi, who continued: "Others have asked me whether, by way of protest, we ought not to obey a law ordering the census of French Jews who have fully honored their duty toward their country. To these persons, I can only reply: However cruel this law may appear to us, we must obey it. By what right could I encourage you to expose yourselves uselessly to severe sanctions?"[18] The anxiety to which Schwartz was trying to respond had, in fact, spread to the entire community, prey in a thousand ways to the antisemitism of the state. Thus the Légion française des combattants (French Veterans' Legion),[19] in which Vichy hoped to make a principal base of popular support, wanted no Jewish members. It stated so publicly, with the blessing of its leader, the Marshal himself. A poster on the theme "The Legion honors its fallen," which specifies that only Catholics and Protestants might be enrolled, was widely distributed. On the radio program "La Légion vous parle" ("The Legion Speaks to You"), the exclusion of Jews was reaffirmed in a series of talks on the topic, "The Jews Against France."[20]

The theme of Jewish responsibility for the recent defeat was constantly reiterated in publications and manifestos of the legion: "The disaster of 1940 was not only military. . . . International Marxism, international capitalism, and stateless Judaism have joined in a monstrous alliance to gnaw at the state and at France."[21] The marching song of the Service d'ordre légionnaire (SOL), the legion's service for public order, transformed later into the notorious Milice, was apparently inspired by this theme:

> For the men of our defeat
> there is no punishment too harsh
> We want their heads.
> SOL, make France pure once more!
> Bolsheviks, enemies, freemasons,
> Israel, vile corruption,
> Heart-sick, France vomits!

Professor Lévy-Bruhl, charged by the Consistory with drawing up a response to the legion, argued for calling on Jews to quit the organization without waiting to be expelled. His proposal was not approved:[22] the title of veteran (*ancien combattant*) was among the most glorious Jews could cite in support of their claim to membership in the French nation and should not be given up willingly. This stance was perfectly logical, except that it bound the Consistory even more tightly to the regime that less and less incarnated the real France. The Consistory did, however, ask Xavier Vallat—first director of the General Commissariat for Jewish Questions—to instruct local sections of the legion to admit Jewish veterans on an equal footing, and to cease all antisemitic campaigns. But in his reply, dated 29 April 1941, Vallat claimed that it was not in his jurisdiction "to give instructions to the Legion that Jewish veterans be treated on footing equal with non-Jews," and even added quite cynically, that "no antisemitic instructions had been given" to the legion.[23]

The purge continued. It deprived Jews of their rights and "freed" them from their duties as citizens. Young Jewish men were no longer obliged to perform youth labor service. "We, the Marshal of France," states the text of the new law, "decree that every male French citizen who is not a Jew shall complete in the course of his twentieth year a service period at a youth labor site." The Consistory, continuing to defend the principle of equality, protested by communicating to Pétain "the deep emotion sparked in French Israelites by a text that seems destined to exclude their sons."[24]

Could one be a Jew and a friend of the Marshal? No. The following statement was written on the application form of the association "Friends of the Marshal" (Les Amis du Maréchal, under the patronage of the head of state): "I declare on my honor that I am a Frenchman, born of a French father and mother, and am neither a Jew nor a Freemason." The objective of the association was "to rebuild the house of France on the unshakable rock of French unity." Admittedly, this was not the worst misfortune—not being counted among the friends of the Marshal. But it did indicate clearly enough that for the Marshal and his admirers there was no place for the Jews in the house of France.[25]

What remained of the Consistory's representative function? Serious attacks had been made against its freedom of expression. The Consistory's weekly radio broadcast, "Voix d'Israël," had ceased in May 1940 during the exodus from Paris, briefly resumed in Vichy, but was suppressed shortly thereafter. Xavier Vallet personally rejected the Consistory's appeal of 21 April 1941 to be invited as in the past to official functions: "It does not seem opportune to me to invite the representatives of the Israelite faith to . . . official ceremonies."[26]

Aware of a radicalization among French Jews as a consequence of the government's discriminatory measures and the climate of hostility created by antisemitic propaganda, the Consistory increased its announcements in support of the service that religion—and as a consequence the Consistory—could render as a rampart against this danger. Chief Rabbi Schwartz charged

Jewish community leaders to "make efforts to calm minds by pointing out to
our coreligionists that the necessary approaches had been made to the Marshal."[27] At the same time Consistory secretary Robert Kiefe told Catholic organizations that Jewish victims could not be counted on to indefinitely "listen to counsels of moderation and patience." As an example he cited the
situation in Algeria, where "the indigenous leaders of the anti-French movement have already made numerous efforts to incite the 125,000 Algerian
Jews, who had been reduced to the status of the indigenous population, to
join forces with them." Though "the religious feelings of a population over
which the rabbinate holds great influence have rendered these efforts vain
until the present time," he urged these organizations to consider how long
they would continue to remain without effect.[28]

Was the Consistory heard? The Vichy police, for their part, noted "in Israelite circles of the Free Zone a great deal of ill will with regard to the forthcoming census of the Jews." This was a state of mind that Vichy spies, on the
basis of intercepted telephone calls and correspondence, qualified as a veritable conspiracy. According to the police report, it would appear that this
"conspiracy" had yielded results and that "a certain number of Jews are refusing voluntarily to state their religion." The same document noted with
anxiety "many conversions to Catholicism."[29] A report by the Vichy intelligence service, worried that "Jewish circles in the Free Zone observe with scorn
that the French government is resolutely engaged on the course of collaboration." More bizarre still is the observation that in "Marseille, Lyon, and Saint-
Étienne, many [Jews] believe that the synagogue will not offer them . . . sure
refuge and . . . are looking for locations more suited to resistance."

The Experience of the Belgian Consistory

Inside the Consistory, some began asking questions about the leaders' strategy,
and neglected nothing in the effort to base their criticism on facts. A document of exceptional interest found in the archives of the Consistory reveals a
conversation that took place on 19 April 1941, between a member of the Consistory or its staff (who remains anonymous) and Rabbi Brodt of Antwerp,
who fled Belgium for Palestine and was in transit in Lyon.[30]

At the heart of this discussion we find the stance of the Belgian Consis-
tory in the face of German demands for cooperation. In the summer of 1940,
Brodt said, "the German authorities asked Jewish leaders to reconstitute the
Consistory, "which had broken up as a consequence of events." The Belgian

Jews understood the Germans' concern to appear to be acting "legally." The authorities, Brodt reported, sent the Belgian Consistory "an action plan" consisting of three points:

- All Jews (according to the National Socialist definition) were to be gathered into the organization, be they Belgian-born, naturalized, or foreign, even those who had converted;
- The Consistory was to extend its funding activity to the social [welfare] sphere, and Jews were to renounce any kind of funding from non-Jewish sources;
- [The Consistory would] create Jewish schools; parents were to withdraw their children from municipal and state elementary and secondary schools.

In sum, according to Rabbi Brodt, the Consistory was required to create an intellectual ghetto that would complement the social ghetto.

The Belgian Consistory replied with a flat refusal. This it justified on the one hand by juridical considerations that invoked the Belgian constitution, which limited the mandate of the Consistory to religious matters, and on the other by its lack of authority, as a purely religious institution, to "renounce voluntarily, in the collective name of the Jewish population, the rights that it possessed."[31] The Belgian Jews mounted another clever argument: since the country was wholly occupied and had no legal government, no one was qualified to approve, in the name of the Belgian nation, the anti-Jewish measures being enacted by the occupiers.

The representative of the French Consistory drew a first lesson from the Belgian experience in the form of a question: "We can then ask ourselves whether French Jews are not . . . at a disadvantage in the defense of their interests in the unoccupied zone in comparison with the integrally occupied territories." In other words, this is a denunciation of the policy of "maintaining a presence in Vichy." The second observation might have been meant as the basis for a new policy of resistance on the part of the Central Consistory: "It would then be an error to follow a policy that sought simply to limit damage. On all the fronts on which we are attacked, it is vital that we resist with maximum energy. Whether the occupiers take *aim at foreigners or at Frenchmen, at naturalized citizens or citizens of old stock, the greatest possible resistance* [is necessary]. We would fall into the trap that is set for us if we accepted making the sacrifice ourselves."[32] Regrettably, this warning would remain without effect, at least in the short term.

Pétain and the "Huge Jewish Fortune"

The forced "Aryanization" of businesses and property belonging to Jews became a major part of the overall program of "dealing with" the Jews in France. The increasing action aimed at removing Jewish owners alarmed Helbronner, and he intervened personally with the Marshal, who received him on 17 June 1941. The former was struck by Pétain's "profound ignorance" concerning French Jewry: "The Marshal," he wrote, "took up as his very own the grievance [voiced] against the majority of Jews of having made colossal fortunes in parasitic vocations."[33]

On the other hand Pétain expressed a wish to be better informed "about the creative activity of Jews." Hypocrisy on Pétain's part? Naïveté on Helbronner's? We don't know, but in order to respond, Consistory General Secretary Albert Emmanuel and his assistants worked for two weeks with regional delegates to compile a thirty-page report, which they submitted to Pétain's office at the end of June. Since, in Helbronner's mind, the assignment was to illustrate "creative activity in industry and in the business world," the file contained a list of French Jews who headed important businesses, starting with the steel producers Forges de l'Est, passing through the paper industry, and ending with "silks and trimmings": large fortunes, but "acquired through tireless labor." These business leaders, although driven from their positions, "have confidence in you," Helbronner wrote, "and ask that you have confidence in them, without supporting the exclusionary laws that affect them, which are an offense to their honor and their patriotism."[34]

Aside from the unreal nature of this intervention, one notes Helbronner's choice to survey exclusively the "Israelite" bourgeoisie and to name only men who were major employers. Admittedly, these were the circles where he was most at home and with whom, in addition, he had close family ties.[35] But is this sufficient to explain his skipping over middle- and working-class people who were also both Jews and patriots and who also had been ruined by the legislation? We shall return to this question below.[36] Invoking the name of an André Schwob d'Héricourt of the Forges de l'Est would, however, impress the Marshal more than those of a Bloch or Lévy (or so Helbronner may have thought). In any case, in the climate of the times, such a list could only throw oil on the fire of anti-Jewish propaganda.

Considerable time had had to pass before the president of the Consistory gave up all hope that the "victor of Verdun" might one day justify his confidence. "Will the persecutions never end? Can we not have a word of hope from you?" This is none other than Helbronner speaking, now seemingly at the end of his patience and quit of his illusions, writing to Pétain as late as 8 December 1942. The same day, in a letter to his friend Mounier, attorney for the Conseil d'Etat, he speaks of the Consistory as a "kind of ministry of misfortune that [he himself was] directing."[37]

De Gaulle to Cassin: "You've come at just the right time"

Other Jews not linked to the various official institutions of the community made a choice to support Charles de Gaulle, then in British exile. "You've come at just the right time," said de Gaulle to René Cassin, who sought an audience at the general's office in Stephen's House on 29 June 1940, the day after his arrival in London. De Gaulle seemed to be greeting him as the eminent jurist that he was. Yet Cassin remarked in his notebook: "I did not hesitate to tell the General that I was Jewish. . . . He told me that he knew that."[38] Once de Gaulle had set up the Council for the Defense of the Empire (Conseil de défence de l'empire) on 27 October, Professor Cassin was appointed to it, along with General Georges Catroux, Colonel Philippe Leclerc (de Hautecloque), Governor Félix Éboué, and other leaders of Free France.

What is to be said of the occasionally ambiguous quips about Jews that have been attributed to de Gaulle? Did he really care about the origins of those who were rallying to his side? He never denied the fact that he exclaimed about Pierre Mendès-France "Another Jew!" From Gaston Defferre, Mendès-France learned of the general's remark, but did not take offense, judging that "antisemitism was foreign to him [de Gaulle]. But he was sensitive to the need for balance and to public opinion that, especially in North Africa, was from this point of view less innocent than he."[39]

The question of balance did in any case preoccupy de Gaulle. Sure of his historical choice, he was less sure of the response the country would make to his appeal. Whom did he see coming to his side? Much later, he confessed his doubts to Pierre-Louis Blanc: "To my surprise I [had] found myself alone in London. Without any political figures of any standing. What did I have in the way of Frenchmen around me? Clear-sighted Jews, a handful of aristocrats, all the good fishermen from the Île de Sein."[40] These "clear-sighted Jews" were Raymond Aron, Jacques Bingen (who would parachute into France as de Gaulle's delegate), Pierre Dac, Maurice Schumann, Jean-Pierre Bloch, and a good many others.

Yet all these men plus the "handful of aristocrats," even if they were without doubt an integral part of France, were not by any means France itself. Thus de Gaulle faced major political questions: the degree to which he could rightly be said personally to represent the French nation, and of the legitimacy of the government that he was trying to put into place. This concern was also observed by another witness, Daniel Cordier: "He [de Gaulle] had hoped that a fairly large number of unattached figures, and representatives of different trends in French public opinion and of the interests of various categories of the French people, would become part of it so that his committee would give full expression to public opinion."[41]

On the tactical level, de Gaulle, like Churchill, Roosevelt, or Eden, seems to have taken into account the possible public opinion effect of Nazi foreign propaganda calling the war against Germany the "Jewish war"—but to a lesser extent than they did. In his immediate circle, however, were found individuals—politicians or military officers—who were sensitive to the possible effects of this propaganda and were convinced that by appearing to be associated with Jewish organizations, they could lend credibility to the Nazi's identification of "Free France" with the Jews. Captain Jean Escarra, René Pleven's associate in de Gaulle's London offices, sent the latter a memorandum which repeated all the classic themes of French antisemitism, from Édouard Drumont to Charles Maurras to Pétain.[42]

But de Gaulle would not have been de Gaulle if he feared Vichy propaganda. On 9 August 1940 he received Albert Cohen, the well-known writer charged by the World Jewish Congress with a mission to the Free French. After this interview, de Gaulle wrote him to reaffirm his confidence that "liberated France will [see] that justice is done for the wrongs against groups who were the victims of Hitler's domination, among these the Jewish communities which, in the countries currently subject to Germany, are unfortunately the targets of intolerance and persecution."[43]

In the spirit of this profession, there was established a durable relationship between de Gaulle and the World Jewish Congress. On 11 November 1940, from Libreville in Gabon, which had rallied to the side of Free France, General de Gaulle addressed a long and quite basic message to the New York offices of the WJC. He had been appalled by "the cruel decrees that are being directed against French Jews, which will not and can not have any validity in a free France. These measures are no less a blow struck at the honor of France than an injustice done to its Jewish citizens." He stigmatizes the violation by Vichy of the principles "on which the French Republic was based," confidently aspiring to return France to its traditional place "as the defender of liberty and justice for all men, without distinction of race and religion, in a new Europe."[44]

This message would be followed by others. De Gaulle was evidently court-ing public opinion in the United States, where the doors of the White House remained closed to him as long as Washington was playing (without too many scruples) the "Pétain card." A good strategist, the general reinforced his contacts with American Jewish leaders, who had been shocked by the an-tisemitic legislation and the first internments of foreign Jews in Vichy. On 4 August 1941, through the intermediary of Jacques de Sieyès, head of the Free French delegation to the United States, the general addressed Rabbi Stephen S. Wise, president of the American Jewish Congress. His message was intended to dissipate any ambiguity with regard to the doctrine of the Free French on the Jewish Question by underlining forcefully that a liberated France would enforce only legislation dating from before 18 June 1940, or edicts of the Free French themselves. The racist laws of Vichy would be con-sidered "null and void."[45]

On 4 October 1941, de Gaulle used the occasion of the one hundred and fiftieth anniversary of the emancipation of the Jews of France (27 Sep-tember 1791) to define again "the policies of France with regard to all the French." The choice of date was more than symbolic, going to the heart of Pétain's Jewish policy, which "by striking Jewish citizens from the national register, by opposing their emancipation and their integration, serves to re-alize the objectives the National Revolution [i.e., the establishment of the puppet government], which is the rejection of the values of the Revolution of 1789." General de Gaulle reaffirmed his fidelity to the founding prin-ciples of the republican France: the Proclamation of the Rights of Man and Citizen along with the decree on the emancipation of the Jews. These could not be abrogated by the officials of Vichy: "We consider null and void the changes brought to the Constitution and to French laws by the self-proclaimed government of Vichy, whose origins and actions are anticonstitu-tional and illegal."[46]

For their part, the Parisian collaborationists seized the opportunity that the general had offered them. A poster pasted up on the walls of Paris shows him before a microphone, surrounded by caricatured Jews. The poster paro-dies the general's recent statement: "I accept the charge to reinstate the Is-raelites after the war in all their rights and functions in France." At the bottom of the poster appears the caption, "General 'Mike [microphone],' quarter-master of the Jews!"[47]

CHAPTER THREE

Preliminaries to a Massacre

Men and women of France! We must find among you an Émile
Zola who will raise against this crime his powerful "J'accuse!"
— Appeal from the Union of Jewish Women

Persuaded that the French "front" was the most important in the persecution of the Jews, the zealous Theodor Dannecker explained in a voluminous
report to Berlin on 1 July 1941 the actions that had been taken already and
what he thought the objectives for the future should be.[1] A preamble heads
the document. Laboriously antisemitic and without much originality, it is
nonetheless interesting: every one of its thoughts has been copied from the
prewar anti-Jewish press as well as the new "collaborationist" press then flour-
ishing in Paris to present a dubious history of the Jews of France. In order to
establish their influence the Jews had "tried to corrupt the kings of France
by offering them enormous sums"; Jewish domination (incarnated in the
Rothschilds) had begun under Louis-Philippe and lasted until 1940. Most
significantly, Dannecker charged that "through the intermediary of the
banks," Jewish influence was "still being perpetuated in the Free Zone."
(The Parisian collaborationists—who suspected that Vichy's antisemitism
was too moderate—harped continuously on this theme.)

But beyond the jumble of Dannecker's clichés (which no doubt reflected the vanity of a man seeking to parade his "culture" before his superiors), his plan owes nothing to borrowings. The man, in fact, was experienced. He had taken part in anti-Jewish activities in Austria after the *Anschluss* (annexation) in 1938, and then again in 1939 in Prague, which after the dismantlement of Czechoslovakia had become the capital of the German Protectorate of Bohemia-Moravia. His French experience would subsequently stand him in good stead during the deportations of Jews from Greece, Italy, and, near the end of the war, Hungary.

Dannecker defines Germany's strategy clearly: set up a "compulsory association of Jews"—a French version of the *Judenrat*, whose function would initially be exercised by Comité de coordination des oeuvres juives (CCOJ—Coordinating Committee for Jewish Agencies) in the Occupied Zone; a second stage would transfer this function to the Union générale des israélites de France (UGIF—General Union of the Jews of France), with a mandate for the whole of France. Dannecker even details the place that the "Jewish organization" should have in the deportation program—the idea is already explicit even if the ultimate form is not yet specified.

All in all, the situation is quite well analyzed from a Nazi perspective: France was not Poland, where the cornerstone of policy was concentration of the Jews in ghettos, which would have been difficult, if not entirely unfeasible, in France. Moreover, however strong the occupiers' desire to shake up the Pétain administration, whose anti-Jewish activities seemed to them only "tinkering," it was necessary, politically and diplomatically, to take the Vichy government into account. To overrun the "last [Jewish] entrenchment on the European continent," therefore, Dannecker would adapt the rhythm and method of the "Final Solution" to French conditions. He did not omit to complain of the "lack of understanding on the part of the Jews themselves"; of inept "French legislation"; and of the attitude at Wehrmacht headquarters that saw France's "Jewish Question" as the responsibility of the French authorities. All this entailed, he understood, "unforseeable delays." On Berlin's orders, though, Dannecker would do his best to expedite matters.

A Ghetto without Walls

Since the creation in Paris of a ghetto on the model of Warsaw was at that time excluded (for both practical and political reasons),[2] recourse to other methods of isolating the Jewish population would be necessary. To gather the

Jews into a "tight organization"—a kind of ghetto without walls—Dannecker had to proceed in stages, and above all with cunning. As it happened, he was not ignorant of the importance Jews had traditionally accorded to social solidarity and mutual aid. He understood that "German legislation will not fail to bring about a continuous worsening of Jewish social problems," which would accelerate the "creation of a terrain favorable to a general organization of the Jews."[3] The relationship between the German project of despoliation on the one hand, and the establishment of a single body for Jewish relief on the other, was the means Dannecker employed to reach his goal.

Nonetheless, his efforts to bring the Paris Consistory to assume responsibility for drawing Jewish aid agencies into a "central Jewish organization" initially met with refusal. Persisting, he gave Marcel Sachs, president of the Paris Consistory, an order to convoke a meeting of delegates from the most important agencies. This meeting would finally take place in December 1940, with Dannecker attending.[4] The Paris Consistory upheld its refusal, citing French legislation concerning associations (the law of 1901). This, apparently, decided Dannecker upon an incremental policy. And thus he launched—this was the trap—a charitable collection, donations to which might be used to offset taxes soon to be imposed on the Jews. In early January 1941 Dannecker announced that he was no longer disposed to tolerate separate activities outside a "coordinating committee" and he demanded that the Jews create one. By the end of the month, such a committee was in place, and included, in addition to the Paris Consistory, the Comité de bienfaisance israélite (Committee for Jewish Welfare), the Organisation reconstruction travail (ORT—Organization for Reconstruction through Labor), the Oeuvre de secours aux enfants (OSE—Children's Relief Agency), and the Amelot Committee.[5]

First Refusal of the Directive

The Arbeiter Orden (Order of Workers) and associations controlled by "Solidarité," which ran a canteen and a dispensary, refused to join the committee and closed down their operations following a decision to this effect by the Jewish Section of the Main d'oeuvre immigrée (MOI). The representatives of the Amelot Committee, David Rappoport and Yehuda Jakubowicz, and Dr. Eugène Minkowski of the OSE set conditions for their participation. The common concern was to preserve the autonomy of the agencies—which, naturally, ran counter to Dannecker's objectives.

The issue of the coordinating committee would absorb all the attention of agency officials for months, in the absence of their political leaders, who were in the Southern Zone. It faced them with an extreme dilemma: to give in to Dannecker's pressure, or to say "no" without having any basis on which to predict the possible reactions of the German authorities. They appreciated the danger for the Jewish population, so they decided to resist as long as possible by dragging out negotiations. At this juncture, Dannecker, anxious to get the committee totally into his grip, brought two "experts" from Austria in mid-February. These were Leo Israelowicz and Israel Biberstein, who had been useful in the *Judenvereinigung*, the Austrian *Judenrat* totally controlled by the Germans. He made Israelowicz's presence at committee meetings obligatory. "When the SS, their patience exhausted, brought in from Austria the two traitors Israelowicz and Biberstein, who took control over the Coordinating Committee," runs an internal note of the Amelot Committee, "our delegates fought back furiously at the risk of their lives to have the Committee resign publicly. Then, when such an act came to be seen as impossible . . . the Amelot Committee withdrew. This attitude won Rappoport a summons from Dannecker, who ordered him to renounce all social activity if he didn't want to end his days in a prison."[6]

The imposition of these two "experts" sounded the hour of truth for officials of the agencies. Dr. Minkowski judged that the Coordinating Committee "was changing its nature"; he resigned, invoking "numerous engagements."[7] In fact, next to Israelowicz and Biberstein, to whom Dannecker had given arbitrary power, the representatives of the various agencies saw themselves reduced to the role of yesmen for the policies of the occupying forces and, in particular, for the weekly *Informations juives* (Jewish News), launched by Dannecker under the editorship of Israelowicz.

The first issue appeared on 19 April 1941. It contained a message from Chief Rabbi Julien Weil on the occasion of Passover, and included an appeal for philanthropic financial support for the relief agencies under the committee umbrella, an appeal that paradoxically concluded with a scarcely veiled threat: "It will be possible," Israelowicz wrote, "to give advice or provide aid only to those who openly belong to the Jewish community of Greater Paris." For "Coordinating Committee" we here find "community," which better translates German intentions, the objective of which was control over the entire Jewish population.[8] The real functions of the future UGIF, which would be imposed throughout the Occupied Zone, were outlined in the 25 April number of *Informations juives:* "Everyone who registers [for assistance] will receive a certificate. This will bear witness . . . that the registrant has freely adopted the idea of a Jewish community." Reflecting the actual place of free choice in the arrangements, the authors of the editorial conclude on a more menacing tone: "It is understood that we can take up the cause only of our own people. And the few whose hearts and minds remain closed to our words? They will have to bear the consequences."[9]

Nazi Propaganda Exploits Address Lists

The first three issues of the newspaper were sent to 60,000 addresses, nearly all of the Jewish families that had been registered during the month of October 1940, the address information having been made available by the Prefecture of Police on Dannecker's orders.[10] It is very likely that the same file was employed somewhat later to send out an illegal "counter-appeal," whose author or authors are not known; this large-scale counter-mailing required someone on the inside of the "intelligence fortress."

"Jews beware!" begins the tract, "the Coordinating Committee whose call you have received has its offices on the fourth floor of 17 rue Saint-Georges. If you go there, you will be received by two Galician Jews whom the occupiers have brought from Vienna in order to build the Jewish Community of Greater Paris. Everyone who has received the newspaper and who has understood the situation has sent nothing [i.e., contributions] and has determined to refuse delivery of the next issue. Follow their course of action and tell everyone else to do the same."[11]

The newspaper was poorly received, and not only for the ideas it expounded. People distrusted the use of the registration index: "Everyone who got it . . . knows that his address is not in good hands," wrote Jacques Bielinky in his diary. "Those who did not receive it think themselves in greater safety."[12] The whole experience suggested the idea of "leaving without a forwarding address." The *Informations juives* announced the inauguration of a "special section to maintain contact with readers." Noting that "in the last few days the number of inattentive people who did not sign their letters [i.e., anonymous letters, usually insulting] has shown a tendency to increase," the paper made a new threat: "Such behavior deserves to be sanctioned!" Nonetheless the letter writers persisted. The reader liaison section disappeared.[13] The most vehement opposition came from Eastern European Jews. This prompted Israelowicz to try to reach an understanding with them in late May and early June at the synagogue on rue Pavée, in the Marais district, and at the one on rue Julien-Lacroix in Belleville.

As the account published in the *Informations juives* has it, in each of the synagogues Israelowicz found "a great number of friends, a great number of the undecided, and also a great number of adversaries." In fact, what this meant was that the "friends" could be counted on the fingers of one hand. Concerned above all to put an end to "all the unreasonable rumors in circulation," Israelowicz explained the reasons for his arrival in Paris, which he said had no objective other than "to provide some direction to Jews who were without a leader in the grave times that we are going through." It was because the Viennese community "has by now accomplished the most useful and symbolic work" that two of its employees "have been sent" to Paris. Of course, at the moment when he spoke these words, he could hardly have been ignorant of the deportation of the Viennese Jews to Poland, which was already in progress.[14]

Israelowicz thought he had been understood by "those persons [who] have become our friends." But he had words of warning for those "who choose not to understand us." These he urged to "understand this, understand it in time, for the good of us all!" The threat implied in such words appeared too in the "technician's" editorial of 1 May 1941: "Reflect on it a bit. To admit what fate has reserved for us, is this not more honorable than always seeking to escape one's destiny?" The dictatorial manner of their boss Dannecker was not long in rubbing off on his collaborators, as in the following instructions: "Solicitations for money [i.e., any direct solidarity among Jews], without the previous approval of the authorities are forbidden. They may be undertaken only by the Coordinating Committee. Not only the solicitors but also the donors are to be condemned."[15]

Either on his own initiative or on the advice of Israelowicz, Dannecker required, beginning on 6 June, the publication of a supplement in Yiddish to the *Informations juives*. Since the deportation and internment measures would initially affect the Jews of Eastern Europe, the majority of whom spoke Yiddish, logic dictated that the paper's propaganda should be oriented toward them. The use of Yiddish seems to have distressed the chief rabbi of Nancy, Paul Haguenauer, who wrote to André Baur of the Coordinating Committee to complain of the problems the Yiddish-speaking Jews from Eastern Europe had caused French Jewry: "I have received the bulletin and have distributed it among our coreligionists. Since you have asked me for suggestions, I must tell you that the Judeo-German family is extremely displeasing to us. . . . I cannot help thinking that all our misfortunes come from books, newspapers, and journals in this jargon that foreign members of our faith introduced into

France after the armistice. [Publishing in Yiddish] is a grave error that must not be perpetuated."[16] But where was Vichy in this reasoning? Or for that matter the Germans? It seems as if the rabbi was deliberately obscuring the true responsibility, whether due to a misplaced patriotism, fear of the occupiers, or perhaps a bit of genuine xenophobia. The final words of the letter, point out that "we have not particularly suffered here. We have had no incidents thus far." Foreign Jews were already being hunted down in Nancy and its surroundings, as everywhere in France; so far the French Jews were physically safe, but could one really say that they were not suffering from the anti-Jewish legislation, which not only attacked them in their dignity as citizens and human beings, but was also destroying the very bases of their existence?

Concentrate and Isolate

Naturally, the directors of the Parisian agencies—engaged in supposed negotiations with a pitiless conqueror who imposed his law on nations much stronger than the Jews—could not know all that was being hatched in the greatest secrecy in Berlin, Paris, and Vichy. But, in order to take a stronger stand in the face of the demands of the Occupation authorities, would one really have had to know the ultimate goal of their policies? The extent of persecution in France ought to have inspired greater mistrust. As of January 1941 the juridical framework for the concentration and isolation of "foreigners of the Jewish race" on the basis of the law of 4 October 1940 was already in place, and it was actually being implemented in the Southern Zone.

In Paris the authorities seemed to be taking their time, not for reasons of principle, but rather with a view to leaving the initiative to the Vichy government. In a letter of 28 February 1941 to administrative headquarters, the chief of the SD and the security police in France, Helmut Knochen, noted the German intention to push the Vichy government to action. Unlike Dannecker, however, he insisted on the urgency of a lightning strike: the creation of concentration camps for the Jews. Knochen's views on the possibility of inoculating the French with racist ideology are of interest for the study of the evolution in public opinion. As head of the SD, Knochen was certainly well informed. He worried that "the development of anti-Jewish sentiment among the French is scarcely possible on the ideological level." On the other hand, he hoped that, by involving the French population in their despoliation, "approval of the struggle against the Jews could more easily be obtained." More specifically, he urged on his superiors the idea that "the internment in concentration camps of about 100,000 foreign Jews resident in Paris would give numerous Frenchmen the possibility of moving from low social status to the middle class." This was a strange, precocious anticipation of the failure to win over the French.[17]

According to the German principle of making the victims themselves administer their own misfortune, the plan for the "lightning strike" required, in addition to the collaboration of the French authorities, two principal instruments: the compulsory Jewish association (*Judenrat*) and a central Jewish office within the French government. The German ambassador to Vichy, Otto Abetz, along with Dannecker and Knochen, were already fully engaged in the task of creating such instruments.

Creation of the "Judenrat" seemed to be under way by January 1941, but that of the Jewish office, dependent on Vichy, remained in an embryonic state. In this, Abetz was taking care not to ruffle the French, although this prudence was probably quite superfluous in relation to the Jews. For his part, Dannecker seemed eager for the establishment by Vichy of a central office— the future Commissariat général aux questions juives (CGQ J—General Commissariat for Jewish Questions)—because it would mark the moment when the Pétain government could fully enter into collaboration in the anti-Jewish policies of the occupying forces.[18]

The CGQ J was ultimately created on 23 March 1941 with Xavier Vallat at its head.[19] By appointing this minister Vichy seemed to be reassuring the occupation authorities that it was confronting the Jewish "problem." If legislative tasks such as economic aryanization and supervision of the application of "the statute" appeared as the priorities, soon a new law gave the CGQ J an operational capacity in the domain of persecution, and in particular the task of "stimulating" against the Jews "all police measures dictated by the national interest."

In the course of a first meeting at the beginning of April 1941 at the German embassy, Abetz explained to Vallat the way the Germans conceived the task of the commission. Along with supervision over the anti-Jewish laws, "the reconciliation of French laws and German edicts" and the elaboration of "new French anti-Jewish laws" were seen as the priorities. Although obliged to admit for the time being the difference between "foreign Jews" and "Jews of long standing," Abetz specified that at a "later stage" it would be necessary to apply to the latter the same measures as to the former. "It is necessary . . . to enact a law that authorizes the Commissariat to consider as aliens those French Jews who have attacked the social and national interests of the French state." This phrasing would permit all imaginable arbitrary accusations.[20]

Abetz's ideas were explained just as clearly two days later during the visit Vallat made to military headquarters, where he was told that "the Germans are interested in progressively ridding Europe of Jewry." In France this was to be begun, as they suggested, by interning 3,000 to 5,000 Jews of all nationalities, as well as "Jews with French nationality who are particularly dangerous or undesirable."[21] Some weeks later the occupiers and Vichy initiated the long series of internments of Jews within the framework of a deportation plan called "Clearance" (*Débarras*). First, on Wednesday, 14 May, came the arrest of nearly 4,000 Jews, mostly Poles, who were taken by the French police to the camps in Pithiviers and Beaune-la-Rolande (Loiret), which had earlier served as German prisoner-of-war camps and had since been transferred to French administration. Then followed the operation of 20–22 August, directed against immigrant Jews and also against French Jews living in the Eleventh Arrondissement of Paris. All these people first saw the Drancy camp without suspecting the role they would be called on to play in the tragedy in which they would be actors and victims. And then came the raid of 12 December against "prominent French Jews" on the pretext of reprisals for attacks against the occupation forces. The plan was carried out in clearly logical fashion and reached its culminating point in mid-December with the execution of fifty-three Jewish "hostages," along with the same number of gentile French resisters.

Social Assistance and Resistance

The Amelot Committee, from the very first days, mounted a substantial program of material relief to families who were left without support and to those interned. Solidarité (MOI), which was not a beneficiary of subsidies from the American Jewish Joint Distribution Committee, collected perforce limited sums of money, distributing it to needy families. Even if the principal concern remained material solidarity, it was not long before political objectives were drafted by the leaders of the "Jewish Section" of the MOI. Their analysis of the situation, after the 14 May 1941 internments, led them to initiate a new strategy of trying to sensitize public opinion to the consequences of the anti-Jewish policy.

This step took concrete form in an "Appeal to the French" signed by "a group of Jewish women and children" and published at the beginning of June after the internments in the Loiret camps. This was the first underground text to come from the "Jewish Section." As the Paris newspapers had presented the internees as "black market traffickers," the tract stressed that for the greater part they were tailors, cabinetmakers, shoemakers, and the like, "who live from their hard work and not off investments." Moreover, 60–70 percent of those interned had been volunteers in the French army. The authors called upon the French to protest: "French men and women! We must find among you an Émile Zola who will raise against this crime his powerful "I Accuse" [*J'accuse*]. We appeal to you in the name of your glorious past, in the name of the Declaration of the Rights of Man and Citizen, in the name of your great men such as Voltaire, Jean-Jacques Rousseau, Victor Hugo, Émile Zola, and [Jean] Jaurès, so that you will join our protest."[22] For the East European Jews in particular these figures incarnated justice, the permanence of France, and the principles of 1789.

After having too easily been lured into the trap, France's Jews now seemed to grasp the scope of events: the establishment of a concentration camp scarcely sixty miles from Paris may have been a turning point. The families of internees traveled to Pithiviers in the hope of communicating with their loved ones. They wanted to see with their own eyes the "camp" where the men were to live. Jacques Adler remembers the day in June 1941: "I saw my father standing behind rows of barbed wire that seemed to me enormously high and deep. I had gone to the camp where he was interned in the hope of seeing him, and there we tried to catch each other's words above the voices of hundreds of others who had come with the same intention. The French gendarmes were running around trying to move us away from the camp perimeter. It was the last time I saw him; I was fourteen years old."[23] Two years later Adler joined the Resistance.

The reaction of the general Jewish population was not long in coming. The Coordinating Committee received an amount of mail extraordinary for the times. The authors, naturally, remained anonymous, but they belonged to the disadvantaged immigrants rejecting the "compulsory community" being imposed by the occupiers. From the very outset, the gap between these common people and the Coordinating Committee was great. Among other things, the letters indicate the deep abyss between the bulk of the Jews from Eastern Europe and the Coordinating Committee: "If you have too much money, make better use of it than by spending it on stamps!" "Why do you address yourselves to women whose husbands are in concentration camps and not to the rich Jews who are paying not to be kept in the camps?" "My husband . . . is in the camp at Beaune-la-Rolande [and] I am left with three children and no help." "For your charitable work, appeal to Monsieur Ch. who is locked up in the Pithiviers camp where no one comes to his aid." "Hello, you gang of charlatans, thieves, and bandits. The hour of your end is near."[24]

Protests by the Wives of the Interned

Very quickly the despair of the 14 May internees' mothers and wives found public expression. The latter poured their anger onto the Coordinating Committee, justly or unjustly holding it accountable for the internments. They demonstrated angrily before the offices of the Committee at 29 rue de la Bienfaisance, calling for assistance in liberating their sons and husbands. From Pithiviers and Beaune-la-Rolande. An internal report of the Committee gives one account of events.[25] On Thursday, 24 July, it reads, Israelowicz tried to calm the demonstrators by explaining that "the internees are martyrs who are expiating the faults of others, [but] without their sacrifice pogroms would have taken place." The next day the women returned. A delegation made its way to the offices, shouting and calling for the return of their husbands. The report continues: "They no longer wanted assistance, they said that the Committee is to blame for the arrests, that 'the rich Jews pay to run the camps because they hope to escape the measures that would be taken against [the others].'"

The *Informations juives* was also taken to task. Israelowicz, its editor, defended himself vigorously. The atmosphere grew more heated until he laid a hand on one of the women. At this moment a true scuffle broke out: the women cuffed the editor, and when he took refuge in his office, they followed him in and continued to shout and make threats. At this point, the report notes, "Monsieur Israelowicz telephoned Dannecker and, citing the authority of the latter, asked that the police be called. Marcel Stora [secretary general of the Committee] was against the idea and prevented him, on his own authority, from doing so." Stora then went to the police station with a delegation of women. There, Robert de François, director of the Aliens Bureau, told them that the arrests of their men had taken place on Dannecker's orders and that neither the Coordinating Committee nor the Prefecture of Police was responsible. But from this moment on, the Committee would be under the direct surveillance of the police, which did not prevent the women, little convinced by François's explanations, from coming back to rue de la Bienfaisance in great numbers on Monday, 28 July.

Further details of these events appear in the same document:

> Toward two in the afternoon, the women began to gather around the building and a quarter of an hour later invaded the premises. They could not be prevented from coming up, and it was impossible to calm them down. They immediately invaded the offices on the second floor, breaking everything and throwing the objects and furniture that they found there at Monsieur Stora and Monsieur Israelowicz. They went after Monsieur Biberstein, who tried to get up to the third floor but was caught on the landing, and they beat him. After these incidents, Monsieur Israelowicz called the police who cleared the building and drove the women back out of rue de la Bienfaisance. Monsieur Longue, of the Institut d'étude des questions juives [Institute for the Study of Jewish Questions] appeared in the company of SS officer Heinrichson, Dannecker's adjutant. They looked over the building and then left, having expressed their disapproval and their opinion that the Jewish question ought to be resolved "not by protests but in a constructive manner."

Radio Paris officially, if dishonestly, reported that "the wives of the internees held a rally to protest the [meagerness] of the sums allocated to them." Bielinky's information was more accurate when he noted in his diary for 2 August 1941 that "the wives of the internees . . . protested against the internment of their husbands and not as a way to call for assistance."

Immediately after the Drancy camp was opened on 21 August 1941, occupation authorities asked the Coordinating Committee to recruit volunteers for agricultural work in the Ardennes. Neither the internees in Pithiviers nor those in Drancy were to be considered since they were already concentrated and controlled. While aiming to secure cheap labor, the Germans also intended to create yet another reserve population for deportation through this recruitment scheme. The *Informations juives* of 29 August 1941 published the following announcement and appeal, printed in large type: "Through the exceptional good will of the responsible authorities we have the possibility of engaging 6,000 Jewish men and 1,000 Jewish women in agricultural labor in the Ardennes. . . . Join the agricultural sector!" This "recruitment" continued even after it became known that the "volunteers" were being treated like prisoners, that their wives and children who remained in

Paris were being interned, and that groups of workers themselves were first being taken to Drancy.[26]

By means of this recruitment the Militärbefehlshaber in Frankreich (MBF—military commander in France) furnished an exploitable labor force to the German enterprise "Ostland," which had been charged with the colonization and development of land in the so-called "forbidden zone" in northeastern France. The Germans drove off the French farmers in a series of expropriations and expulsions under scandalous conditions (the farmers were given just a few hours to abandon everything), most frequently invoking the justification only that "the farm was being poorly run. By the end of May 150 expropriations, of which certain of them more than 150 hectares in size, have been carried out and the project should be completed by the end of June."[27]

The Appeal from Moscow

The Wehrmacht's attack on the Soviet Union on 22 June 1941 marks not only one of the pivotal dates of World War II, but also the beginning of a new stage in the anti-Jewish policy of the Third Reich, that of large-scale massacres. After extremely rapid progress in pursuit of the rapidly collapsing Red Army, the vanguard of the German forces reached the outskirts of Kiev in the south and of Leningrad in the north. They were soon within striking distance of even Moscow. Hitler's prophecy that by the close of 1941 the Soviet Union would no longer exist now seemed considerably more credible than a few months earlier.

Four groups of SS troops, called Einsatzgruppen, began to implement the specific directives that were appended to the Barbarossa Plan regarding the "political administration of the Soviet territories."[28] The plan ordered the summary execution of "citizens suspected of activities hostile to the Reich," especially communists and in particular military or political commissars, categories identified in the Nazi mind with the Jews. The Einsatzgruppen interpreted broadly the official conception of the "destruction of the ideological enemy," and initiated the first stage of the "Final Solution" even before all the details had yet been worked out. In practice this meant the deliberate, planned, and systematic slaughter or concentration for forced labor of the Jews in the occupied territories. Berlin accorded the greatest importance to the work of the Einsatzgruppen, and in August Gestapo chief Heinrich Müller (acting as deputy of Reinhard Heydrich, chief of the Reich Security Main

Office) ordered the four commanders to keep the Führer informed of the results of their operations.[29]

Until Sunday, 24 August, two months after the attack, the world remained largely ignorant of the Einsatzgruppen. On that day, however, Radio Moscow revealed (in Yiddish) that the *extermination of the Jewish people* was in progress in the occupied territories of Eastern Europe. The Soviet government had just created a "Jewish Antifascist Committee" to activate Jewish support for the war against Nazi Germany and its allies and fill the void left by the dissolution of many cultural organizations as a result of Stalin's purges during the 1930s. The new committee held its first meeting on 20 August. A radio program four days later broadcast for two hours the statements of prominent figures such as Ilya Ehrenburg, David Bergelson, Peretz Markish, Sergei Eisenstein, and a number of highly decorated Red Army officers. The broadcast ended with an appeal "to brother Jews throughout the world."

The victims of the Nazis' "ideological" war numbered in the tens of thousands; they included men and women who belonged to the party apparatus or who worked for the state, but their families and children were generally spared. Jews, however, were killed without distinction: men, women, and children. This was fully evident in the statement of the Jewish Antifascist Committee in Moscow: "For all oppressed peoples, Hitlerism is synonymous with slavery, persecution, and war, but for us Jews it means complete extermination. The very question of the existence of the Jewish people is today raised to its fullest extent. At the moment in which you hear these words, women and children are being buried alive by these brown thugs. . . . On the millennial path of the diaspora, which passed through Roman times, the Middle Ages, and the rule of the tsars, the Jewish people has never known a similar catastrophe." The Moscow appeal is undeniably the first document that revealed to the world the coldly organized massacres of the Jewish populations of Poland, Romania, the Baltic countries, and the USSR. It called on Jews to enlist in the Allied armies, or in partisan detachments in those areas conquered by Hitler. "*Our people will not perish,*" it proclaimed. "This is the people that thousands of years earlier said to its oppressors: '*I shall not die, but live.*'"[30]

In Paris and Lyon monitoring units of the "Jewish Section" of MOI simultaneously picked up the Moscow broadcast. "The appeal" was perceived by the Jewish left as a primary source on the condition of the Jews in the East, news received with all the emotion one might imagine. It is true that everything that came from Moscow enjoyed near absolute credibility in these circles. Nor did events fail to confirm the tragic truth of the news from Moscow. The Jewish resistance fighters in the MOI and the readers of their underground newspapers were thus the first in France to learn that in Eastern Europe the Nazis had embarked on the complete extermination of the Jewish people. The entry of the USSR into the war the lifted spirits among those whose morale had suffered after the Hitler-Stalin Pact of August 1939. Knowledge of the nature of the Nazi plan, however, even though at first confused and accompanied by doubts about its possible application in Western Europe, lent a new gravity to the political and practical aspects of Jewish response in France.

A special edition of *Unzer Wort* of 1 September 1941 reprinted the appeal in its entirety, following it with a commentary entitled "What Do We Do?" which set out the essential elements on which the strategy of the Jewish resistance of the MOI would be founded, taking into account the extermination plan from which the Jews had to be saved and the Allies' chief objective, the defeat of Hitler: "The choice is clear, we shall choose the path of resistance, of defence by every means against the *war of extermination* that the barbarians have declared on the Jewish people."[31] This was the first time the notion of a "war against the Jewish people" appeared in the underground press. Today the debate between the "intentionalists" and the "functionalists" turns in part on the question of whether the Einsatzgruppen massacres were the first stage in a plan of genocide that had been prepared long in advance. Whatever that case may be, we know that at the time there was only one perception: that of a vast massacre.[32]

In Palestine the appeal from Moscow had great resonance. The transmission was rebroadcast in Tel Aviv and other locations over loudspeakers in the streets, and in theaters and movie houses, where performances were interrupted for the event.[33] The BBC in London soon relayed back to Moscow messages in Hebrew, Russian, and Yiddish, affirming the reborn hope of renewed ties between the Jews of the rest of the world and those of the USSR, gradually choked off during the 1930s. Isaac Ben-Zvi, president of the Jewish National Council, forerunner of the future government of Israel, went to great lengths to let Soviet Jews know that their message had been heard: "You have proclaimed that the Jewish people will not die but will live, to which we reply that we shall not die, but live. The enemy of humanity shall not have us."[34]

CHAPTER FOUR

The Creation of the UGIF, the "Compulsory Community"

"If I didn't do it, there's another worse than me who would."
One MUST refuse, and one always can, in every circumstance.
—Primo Levi[1]

It is not philanthropic bureaucracies that will save our people.
You cannot combat catastrophe with donations.
—David Knout[2]

As we have seen, from January 1941 onward the Gestapo's *Judenreferat* attached great importance to the establishment in Paris of a "compulsory Jewish organization" in the form of the Coordinating Committee. The German Military Command in France (MBF), however, judged this body insufficient "because it does not possess the necessary authority [and] since it encompasses only the organizations that voluntarily affiliated themselves."[3] In other words, too many organizations were likely to escape its control. In addition, the Coordinating Committee was not the product of any French law that would have engaged the Vichy government in the Reich's anti-Jewish program.

To urge the necessity of a "compulsory community," the MBF evoked the danger for society of a "human mass deprived of its means of existence," declaring that "security and public order require appropriate measures to organize social assistance for all the Jews of the Occupied Zone."[4] The key word was *assistance,* as if the misery of the Jews resulting from their expropriation was a genuine concern for the occupation authorities. What was important for the occupiers was that the creation of a "compulsory Jewish organization" be backed by Vichy. Xavier Vallat, head of the General Commissariat for Jewish Questions (CGQ J) since the end of March 1941, wanted to wait for an opportune moment when he could make the initiative look like that of an antisemitic but independent French government. But on 29 November 1941 he gave in to Dannecker's long-standing threat to impose the creation of the Union générale des Israélites de France (UGIF—General Union of French Jews) by decree, and began negotiations with the directors of the Consistory's various agencies.

Vallat's "Worst Case Scenario": Blackmail

In November 1941 "discussions" began in a climate of strong opposition from both the Consistory and the FSJF. The former felt the proposal for a coordinating committee would irrevocably legitimate the exclusion of French Jewry from the national community. For the FSJF as the representative of Eastern-European Jews, the UGIF symbolized the total takeover of Jewish communal life by hostile forces.

Helbronner reacted to the draft legislation creating the UGIF like a jurist—scarcely surprising for a former member of the Conseil d'État (highest administrative court in France). He thought that a legislative text of such importance could not bypass that institution. On 24 November 1941, André Lavagne, legal counsel of this body and deputy director of the Marshal's civil cabinet,[5] confirmed Helbronner's interpretation: the bill would be submitted to the scrutiny of the Conseil d'État. On 7 November 1941, however, Vallat notified Raymond-Raoul Lambert, secretary general of the Committee for Assistance to Refugees (CAR),[6] that the decree would not be submitted to the Conseil d'État.[7] Yet, according to off-the-record remarks made by "an important political figure in the Vichy government," the Conseil d'État did indeed debate the draft, finding it to be "in disagreement with the essential principles of the French state"; they approved it anyway, apparently hoping to appease both the Germans and the antisemitic faction in French politics.[8]

In contrast to what had happened in Paris a year earlier, when the Coordinating Committee had been imposed by a *Diktat* of the occupying forces, Jewish agencies in the Free Zone continued to enjoy some maneuvering room, and could express their disapproval of the draft UGIF legislation. Thus the Commission for the Coordination of Jewish Relief, which met in late October 1941 in Marseilles, freely debated the draft without fear of personal sanctions. (Opinion was divided over whether their disappearance or the state's takeover of the welfare agencies would be worse.)[9] Certainly it was better to live in the Free Zone than under the Nazi boot. It is equally true that while thousands of foreign Jews were rotting in the Free Zone camps, representatives from the Jewish relief agencies were considered negotiators with authority.

But for how long? Léo Glaeser, a member of the Amelot Committee in Paris, had fled *in extremis* to the Free Zone when he learned that his arrest had been ordered by Dannecker. During the meeting of the Commission for the Coordination of Jewish Relief, he cautioned against too positive an appreciation of the situation of the Jews under Vichy; things could get worse, as he suggested in his report about his experience of the "sixteen-month struggle between the Coordinating Committee in Paris and the occupation authorities," which had caused some of its members to be thrown in prison. He insisted that those at the meeting not adopt an attitude that would risk "annulling the efforts of our co-religionists in Paris."

This danger added to the drama of the debate that started with the presentation of Marc Jarblum, president of the Federation of Jewish Societies of France, who called for a protest in the form of unequivocal boycott of the UGIF, and urged delegates to draw inspiration from "the great principles in the history of Judaism." Israël Jefroykin, honorary president of the FSJF, did not share Jarblum's view, and declared that "in the opinion of a Jewish nationalist . . . the draft bill offered a basis for possible discussion." By using the term "nationalist," of course, Jefroykin signaled acceptance of the identification of the Jews as a "national minority," a conception that was common to nearly all the Eastern European Jews. As opposed to Jarblum, for Jefroykin the UGIF seemed to correspond to the idea of *kehillah*, the autonomous self-administration of Jewish communities in Poland. Indeed he had been advocating the creation of a similar institution in France since the 1930s. But as Joseph Fischer, the representative of the Zionist groups, responded, "It is not a national minority that [the government is] seeking to create, but a minority outside the [protection of the] law": an *outlawed* minority.

André Kessler of the *Éclaireurs israélites de France* (EIF—the Jewish Scouts) also agreed with Jarblum. "Discussion with the general commissioner is unworthy and unavailing. This meeting has a historical significance, and we should not respond with subtleties where we must be firm." Did the national board of the EI agree? Apparently not, for some weeks later their head, Robert Gamzon, agreed to sit on the Administrative Council of the UGIF.

Julien Samuel, the representative of the Oeuvre de secours aux enfants (OSE—Children's Welfare Agency), urged a compromise position by insisting that "everything be done in order to prevent the disappearance of the welfare agencies." Lambert was of the opinion that more was to be gained by lobbying administrative officials on the level of the prefectures, who, should the Jewish agencies disappear, would find themselves "faced with social problems that were difficult to resolve." This technical approach to a problem that was essentially political would prove fatal for the outcome of negotiations.

From this debate there finally emerged a common position that both denounced "the attack made . . . on the citizen's rights of French men and women of the Jewish religion" and called the attention of the government to "the danger of an attack on agencies which are currently providing relief to thousands of families." Overall, the attitude was so hostile that during the course of a joint meeting of the Consistory and delegates of the CCOJA a decision was taken "to forbid members of the agency boards . . . to sit on the administrative council of the UGIF."[10]

It took Xavier Vallat one hundred days—from 24 September to the end of December 1941—to set up the UGIF. From the beginning he granted Raymond-Raoul Lambert, secretary general of the CAR, the status of privileged negotiator: indeed, by the conclusion of talks Lambert was his sole negotiating partner. Lambert was received at the Hotel Algeria in Vichy, the seat of the CGQ J. Lambert would soon report, though, that Vallat "speaks to me of the Jews in the Occupied Zone and gives me to understand that the Occupation authorities are considering even more brutal measures."[11] Vallat's blackmailing technique—pointing to the Occupied Zone and telling Lambert that things would only get worse if the Jews of Vichy were not compliant—seemed already to have been well refined.

On 21 November Lambert called again on Vallat, who seemed ready to make some concessions because of pressure from the Consistory, desirous of staying outside the UGIF. There would be no reference to education in the law. The large agencies incorporated in the UGIF, Vallat promised, would retain a technical independence. If prominent figures agreed to be named to the UGIF council, there would be no Aryan commissioner. While there would be "obligatory membership fees," these would not be taxes. With the exception of independence for the Consistory in religious matters, however, a respect that would also prove quite temporary, all the concessions were purely formal.

At this same time, Vallat informed Lambert of his intention to cease receiving delegations, which "end up making ineffectual protests." He no longer wanted to get advice, either from the Coordinating Committee of Jewish Relief Agencies or from the Federation of Jewish Associations of France. Their officials were to understand that "the regime has changed, there is no longer a place for parliamentary dickering." But Vallat's closing promise got Lambert to bite: "priority to the experts and down with phrase-makers." In other words, policy is not your business, we will take care of that. Then Lambert committed the fatal error that allowed the creation of the UGIF with the alleged agreement of the Jews themselves. "After all those words, it was difficult for me not to agree to return alone to Vichy," he noted later. The Central Consistory observed that, "in full agreement with the president of CAR [Albert Lévy, Committee d'Aide aux Refugies]," Lambert "believed himself able, without mandate and alone, to pursue negotiations with the Commissioner General."[12] Discussions entered a decisive phase marked by a one-on-one conversation between this solitary "expert" and the commissioner in whom resided the power of the Vichy state and the German occupiers. With not a single representative of the Jewish organizations present at the birth of the UGIF, its only organizational matrix was the offices of the Gestapo in Paris and of the Commissariat Général in Vichy.

On 30 November Vallat informed Lambert by phone that the UGIF was a *fait accompli*. In fact, the law instituting it had been signed the day before (!), though it would appear only on 2 December in the *Legislative Gazette* (*Le Journal officiel*). In addition to the signature of Pétain himself, it bore those of Vice-President of the Conseil d'État Darlan, Minister of Justice Joseph Barthélemy, Secretary of State for the Police Pierre Pécheu, and Secretary of State for Economy and Finance Yves Bouthillier. According to the law, the union was to "assure the representation of Jews before the public authorities, in particular as concerns matters of aid, contingencies, and social restructuring." Article 2 specified that "all Jews resident or lodging in France are compulsorily affiliated with the Union. . . . All existing Jewish organisations are dissolved with the exception of legally constituted Jewish religious bodies." Assets of the dissolved associations were to devolve to the union. The financial resources of the union would come from the CGQJ, from "Jewish solidarity funds,"[13] and from compulsory dues paid by the Jews themselves. The union would be divided into two sections, one for each zone, with separate councils "as long as current communications difficulties persist."

As of early December Helbronner still hoped to block implementation of the law by presenting a new line of argument to the Marshal. In effect the UGIF had just obtained an exceptional judicial status of a public institution, thus integrating it into the machinery of the Vichy regime. But, Helbronner argued, "the status of public institutions is reserved for entities that exercise a degree of public authority,"[14] which could not be the case with the UGIF. Nevertheless, as a cog in the Vichy machine, the UGIF would soon enjoy the de facto right to levy taxes and exercise other privileges. Helbronner suggested review by the Conseil d'État of this "departure from the principles of our jurisprudence."[15] His demarche produced no result.

The new legislation had no guarantee of success, and would have remained a dead letter if representative Jewish figures had not joined the board of the UGIF. Here was the most delicate part of the affair. With Lambert's willing (and not uninterested) complicity, Vallat set out to find persons capable of legitimizing the UGIF both in the eyes of the French and German authorities, and in the eyes of the Jews themselves. The Consistory expressed its disapproval of Lambert, censuring Albert Lévy in the minutes for subverting its injunction against acceptance of the UGIF board. As of early December, almost all the prominent persons who had been approached by Vallat to join the UGIF board had declined (invoking the most diverse pretexts). After taking cognizance of the refusal of René Mayer of the Consistory[16] and of Gaston Kahn, who would subsequently accept, Vallat was prepared to name the members of the board himself. At the "insistence" of Lambert, Vallat agreed to receive on 12 December for the last time William Oualid and André Weil (representatives of the ORT and Consistory, respectively), Joseph Milner (in charge of the OSE), and Lambert himself. André Weil made a tumultuous declaration which won him exclusion from the board: he later told Lambert that he had done it on purpose.[17] William Oualid was not satisfied with Vallat's verbal assurances as to the positive role that the government was planning for the UGIF. On 5 January 1942 Vallat shared his discontent with the results in a telephone call to Lambert. The responses of Jarblum, Oualid, and Professor Olmer, another possible candidate, had been negative, and they would have to be replaced by others whom Vallat would select. Vallat then brought out his ultimate weapon—blackmail—threatening to put "eight crooks" at the head of the UGIF.

Lévy now caved in, joining Lambert in citing this threat as alibi and falling for the rationale Primo Levi condemned as both immoral and ineffectual:

"If I didn't do it, there's another worse than me who would." Albert Lévy who, it seems, had a less clear conscience than Lambert, later justified his decision to accept the presidency of the UGIF by his concern not to displease the CGQ J: "Aware that my resignation, even for reasons of health, would probably provoke an angry reaction from Monsieur Vallat, I decided to retain this appointment." Still, after having exercised his function for some months, Lévy left for Switzerland without alerting anyone, not even Lambert, who characterized his departure as "lacking elegance." (Had Lévy been concerned for his personal safety? He would not be the only one to abandon ship under such circumstances. Certainly he must have realized that he had fallen into a trap.) Concerned about "saving the agencies" as Lambert claimed to be, did he know what was at stake, did he understand his political responsibility when he agreed to Vallat's proposal? The Consistory was well aware that acceptance of the UGIF was tantamount to accepting the legislation excluding the Jews from the French nation, a victory for Vichy.

At its very first session on 20 January 1942 in Paris the UGIF board for the Occupied Zone, with André Baur at its head, addressed a declaration to Pétain which, excepting a few formal reservations, greatly resembled a gesture of allegiance: "We agree—with emotion—to fulfill among the members of our faith the mission of aid that you have delegated to us." But they conceived of a much grander role for the union, in particular as the "intermediary" between the Marshal and the Jews. By bringing to the foreground this role, the members of the UGIF-Paris perhaps wished to signify that their mandate did not originate with the occupation authorities, but with the French government. Yet they knew well that in Paris the occupiers made the law. Had not Vallat said as much to the Jewish representatives?

The Parisian Jewish representatives promised to carry our their mission "to the full extent, [short of] abandoning our double dignity as Frenchmen and adherents of the Jewish religion."[18] Did this conditional mode not reveal the skepticism of these men about the unlikelihood of preserving that dignity? On the agenda for the same 20 January session of the board was the matter of a billion-franc "fine" the Germans had imposed on 17 December, ostensibly in reprisal for the assassination of some German soldiers by "Jews and communists" in November. (Dannecker rounded up and held hostage 700 Jews at Drancy.) The UGIF was required to collect the fine (in three installments) in both occupied and unoccupied France. Here was a moment of truth when they should have grasped the intentions of the occupiers, who expected of them much more than the distribution of relief. Their declaration illustrates how out of touch they were with attitudes even in circles close to the Marshal, where signs of disenchantment with him were by this time fairly frequent.

Marc Bloch and the Letter of the Twenty-Nine

In the Free Zone the creation of the UGIF had been such a painful experience for French Jewish intellectuals that it provoked a protest that resonated both in France and London. Prominent academics, in particular Marc Bloch and Professor Georges Friedmann, joined forces to make known their total opposition to the new institution. Their correspondence was intercepted by "postal control" and handed over to the regional offices of the CGQ J in Montpellier (for reasons of an administrative nature), which, after drawing up a file entitled "Jewish Protestations of Fidelity to France," sent it on to the administration in Toulouse.[19]

The initiative had come from Friedmann, an early member of the resistance movement "Combat" in Toulouse.[20] He proposed an original version to Marc Bloch, who sent back a text much more temperate in tone. The final "letter" was signed by twenty-nine prominent figures, most of them respected academics or senior-level civil servants.[21] Bloch wanted the initiative limited to intellectual circles. "We must take care," he wrote to Friedmann, "that no one be able to accuse us [of being] the agents [of] financial circles," alluding here to the bankers and industrialists on the board of the Central Consistory.

The underground declaration was surreptitiously circulated at the end of February 1942. It was also sent to the Information Bureau of "France Combattante" in London by "Combat" in Toulouse.[22] The signatories denounced the law establishing the UGIF, which in their view would legitimate the exclusion of the Jews from the French nation: "As Frenchmen of Jewish descent," they stated, "we cannot recognize the members of the administrative board of the Union as our representatives. We would warn them . . . concerning the answerability which they are incurring in the eyes of French public opinion . . . and before posterity." The signatories rejected the welfare functions assigned to the UGIF and the bait invoked as much by the Germans and Vichy as by Lambert: "We know the necessity of relief agencies. . . . But we believe that they, too, must above all avoid becoming the instruments, be it involuntary, of a separation that would run counter to the most deeply felt sentiments of Frenchmen of Jewish faith, for this is the real purpose of the UGIF." What must come first was "the preservation of moral values which bind [the French Israelites] to the whole of the French nation." There should be no "withdrawal into mutual assistance," they said, since the Jews could count on the "generosity of spirit of so many of our fellow-countrymen, . . . well known to us since we have received from them so many moving testimonials of solidarity."

Bloch, Friedmann, the writer Benjamin Crémieux, and the other signatories thus rejected a policy being undertaken in their name. They saw their stance as an act of resistance, and distinguished themselves from institutionalized circles of French Jewry that sought to act from within the official Vichy order. They felt no need for a "Jewish policy" implemented either in the name of, or by, the collectivity. They fought Vichy as individual Frenchmen; they were French citizens first, then Jews. They acted for an element of society which was far from negligible—Jewish intellectuals—and had no intention of letting themselves be represented even by the Consistory, let alone the UGIF.[23]

Was it in reaction to Marc Bloch's initiative or because he was ignorant of it that Lambert went to Montpellier in May to meet him? In either case, the director of the UGIF sought to recruit him to the administrative board, where prominent figures were notable primarily for their absence—the only official who could be called representative was Robert Gamzon, the national head of the Jewish Scouts. Lambert gave Bloch a text providing "explanations of the conditions under which the UGIF functioned in the Free Zone." Lambert's misunderstanding of the situation was total. By that time Bloch already had the nom de guerre of "Narbonne" in the Francs-Tireurs (the "Irregulars"). At the 10 July 1942 session of the administrative board, Lambert gave an account of their discussion: "Because he is not involved in the work of the welfare agencies, he could only adopt a position of principle."[24]

Meanwhile the Alliance israélite universelle, the second organization in order of size and importance after the Consistory, did everything possible to avoid submitting to the UGIF. The alliance had drawn the particular attention of the occupying power, above all because its name resonated in the fantasies of Nazi leaders, but also because of the role it played in French cultural expansion in North Africa and the Middle East. Its funds, which were considerable, also drew the envy of the Germans, Vichy—and the UGIF. The AIU was on the list of Jewish organizations (the Jewish Agency, the LICA, and others) whose Paris premises the Gestapo would search, where its offices were pillaged and its archive plundered.[25] Having removed to Vichy, the few members of the alliance's board still in France tried as best they could to assure its autonomy in relation to the CGQJ and the UGIF. The still heterogeneous character of the Vichy regime may have afforded them some room to maneuver. The alliance doubtless hoped to draw some advantage from the fact that the interests of the secretary of state for foreign affairs did not entirely coincide with those of the CGQ J. In a letter of 20 September 1941, Admiral Darlan, in his capacity as minister for foreign affairs, called the attention of the CGQ J to the possible repercussions of blocking the bank accounts of the alliance for the "services it renders for the expansion of the French language in the Near East." Without too many illusions about the independence of the commissariat in relation to the occupation authorities, Darlan advised it to make the Germans understand that the alliance was an important instrument of influence and that the British government (and, implicitly, de Gaulle?) would inherit that influence "if we are not careful."[26]

Vallat, who made no secret of his interest in the assets of the alliance, informed Lambert that he wanted to transfer the 13 to 18 million francs that the alliance had in Paris to the Southern Zone "so that they don't fall into the hands of the Germans." In the end, it was the UGIF-Paris that would be authorized to sell the alliance's assets, to meet the financial requirements both of the occupying forces and of the CGQ J, and the union's operating and relief budgets.

To the degree possible the alliance resisted turning over its assets to the UGIF. The delegate from Morocco was ordered not to correspond with Lambert. When the latter offered the alliance the possibility of setting up offices in the "sumptuous premises" of the UGIF in Marseille, he met with refusal. Initially housed in a hotel room in Vichy, from which it would be ejected (like the Consistory and all the other Jewish institutions) on 14 June 1942 (thence retiring to Creuse, some 100 kilometers east of Vichy), the alliance ceased all activities in occupied France in November 1943.[27]

Some of the officials of the alliance—according to André Chouraqui—established relations with the Resistance fairly early on, and gave their financial support to Paul Petit, a diplomat who had been dismissed by Vichy and who then helped edit and distribute the clandestine publication *La France continue* ("France Goes On"). For the period during which it appeared—May 1941 to February 1942, when Petit was arrested by the German police—*La France continue* was without a doubt the underground paper that devoted the most space to the persecution of the Jews by Vichy. Paul Petit was condemned to death and was shot in Germany on 24 August 1944.[28]

Darlan had not been mistaken when he anticipated that Britain would soon take an interest in the Alliance israélite universelle. The idea of reconstituting the alliance under the auspices of the "France combattante" movement came from René Cassin, who had been in London since the end of June 1940. A year later Cassin was appointed to Free France's "Commission for Justice and Public Education." At the beginning of May 1943, General de Gaulle gave his agreement for the formation of a "Provisional" Committee of the Alliance "in consideration of the fact that the Central Committee of the Alliance universelle israélite [in France] was unable to function."[29] This event was a great moment in Cassin's historical achievement of reconstituting the "republican legality" that had been swept aside by Vichy.

Must We Break with Pétain?

If the Consistory made its refusal to join the UGIF fully evident, nothing suggests that it foresaw any modification in its loyalist stance toward Vichy. This immobility, however, became intolerable for some. In May 1942 Louis Kahn presented the Consistory board with a "draft letter to Marshal Pétain."[30] The responsibility for antisemitic persecution, Kahn argued here, was to be laid squarely at the feet of the French government. He did not accept the alibi of "the Armistice," and asserted that it was erroneous to see developments in France as exclusively the effects of German desires, as did many of the French, among them a majority of Jews. He quotes a member of the armistice commission whom he knew: "Never, either during the negotiation of the armistice or in discussions on . . . its application, did the Germans demand anything of the kind. All that can be said is that if we wanted to return to the way things were before, they would impose their veto." Kahn continues: "The fact that these laws are an internal initiative results from [the input] of the Action Française, whose director was appointed by you [Pétain] as a member of the National Council." Kahn specifically targeted the responsibility of Pétain: "The radio and editorial propaganda, the uninterrupted antisemitic activity of the French Legion of Veterans and Volunteers of the National Revolution, of which you are the honorary president—nothing is done there, nothing is said there, that does not come from you and your closest circle."[31] But Kahn did not stop with this new attack on Pétain.

Turning to a general issue theretofore taboo for the Consistory, Kahn addressed the causes of the military defeat: *Mein Kampf* "spelled out the action to be pursued against the adversary before the conflict. . . . Antisemitism was to play a capital, multiple, and prolonged role. From this source, the parties that opposed [the Third Republic] received sure reinforcement in their effort to undermine the loyalty of the national civil service. . . . From this [source], defeatism drew its fundamental argument, [for use in] the combat units themselves: it was not for its own existence that France had taken up arms but to save the Jews. Was such a cause worth dying for?" Kahn identified those who profited by the defeat: "After the armistice, antisemitism weakened the French resistance; [the antisemites'] France had everything to gain from its defeat. Only the Jews would pay."

In Louis Kahn's eyes the deportations from Compiègne in March 1942, primarily of French Jews, constituted the explicit avowal of those in power that they would no longer make any distinction among the Jews. "The Germans deported the Jews only because your government turned them over," Kahn wanted the Consistory to charge Pétain. "But what other government before yours . . . handed over to the enemy, on the soil of the France, several hundred of its citizens guilty only . . . of having four grandparents of the same religion as their own?"[32] In conclusion Kahn charged that the Consistory's mode of protest to Pétain was questionable: "What is the use of protesting in the name of principles of justice and principles of law, when justice has been disarmed and the law negated?"

Kahn's reflections were intended more for the Consistory than Pétain; the virulence of his tone; and the analysis of Vichy's responsibility in the exclusion that was striking the Jews of France, were likely all aimed at provoking a rupture with the Marshal and the end of the policy of allegiance. But the majority of Members of the Consistory were not yet ready for such a step. For his part, Louis Kahn joined de Gaulle in London shortly thereafter. A British submarine had waited for him off Sète in southern France. Chief engineer of the navy, Kahn could not have dreamed of a better means of transport for the adventure that would lead him one day to the position of director of naval construction.[33]

"They are ruining the Jews"

The debate on cooperation with the UGIF at the plenary session of the Federation of Jewish Associations in France (FSJF) at the end of 1941 revealed profound divisions. The difference of opinion between Israël Jefroykin (honorary president of the FSJF) and Marc Jarblum, already evident at the CCOJA meeting in October 1941, now grew more passionate. Against Jarblum, who argued for a categorical refusal to sit on the UGIF board, voices were raised in favor of options that were more nuanced but at times radically opposed. Jefroykin argued that if the CCOJA adopted a hostile attitude it would lose its ability to function: "There is no means of reconciling a welfare agency with illegal activity; the terms are mutually exclusive." Jules Jefroykin, his son, favored cooperation with the UGIF under certain conditions, asking, "Isn't the UGIF the realization of what has been so long desired: a community [*kehillah*] representing the totality of Jews living in France? There are examples," he affirmed in contradiction to what was already known, "of acceptance in Germany and in Poland where the results have been positive." The illusion that the *Judenrat* could play the role of a *kehillah,* that is, a community organization that ran its own affairs, had been fairly widespread in Poland, at least until they were forced to provide assistance in deportations.[34]

Beyond the question of participation in the UGIF, the ideas advanced by the Jefroykins, père and fils, betray the existence within the federation of strong opposition to Jarblum's firm stance. Because he was a socialist, Jarblum's vision of the Zionist ideal did not exclude—quite the contrary— alliances on the national as well as the international level with forces favorable to the creation of a separate Jewish state. On the other hand, the idea of Jewish autonomy espoused by Jefroykin favored a latent penchant for Jewish isolationism that always came to the fore when the enmity of the exterior world reinforced Jewish skepticism about humanity.

A compromise solution, brought forward by Zvi Lewin, an important leader of the FSJF and a Zionist-socialist like Jarblum, was accepted with twenty-one votes for and one abstention, probably Jarblum's. The motion condemned the UGIF while still admitting of some collaboration on the purely technical level. Lewin was appointed "Steward of Funds," would accept a job in the administration of the UGIF, and there was to serve as a kind of liaison. Jarblum was not supported by his friends, but others congratulated him for his "proud and worthy attitude." And the resolution does make it quite clear that the federation "could never recognize the spirit that informed the creation of the UGIF and which, in contradiction to the principles of the Declaration of the Rights of Man, puts Jews outside the common law."[35] This was a principled position, but unfortunately their honor did not save them from paying in human lives for their "technical cooperation" with the UGIF.

Marc Jarblum, isolated from his friends in France but not from world Zionist bodies, held firm, categorically refusing the very idea of "cooperation." In a report to the Palestine Office in Geneva and to the Vaad Hatsala (Rescue Council, created by the Jewish Agency), he speaks of his general anxiety: "In a few days our agencies will be dissolved; . . . I have refused to go and see the 'Brith' family [the Hebrew term for union] . . . , the people who are . . . creating misery for us all. . . . The Brith family is taking over everything, supported by Vaks [from the initials of Xavier Vallat written backwards]." But Jarblum also wrote that "With a lot of *kessef* [money] you can do a great deal despite Vaks and Brith"; in other words Jarblum was asking for funding that would not come through official channels, i.e., affirming the necessity of illegal social action. In the same report Jarblum warns of the de facto right of the UGIF to raise taxes on the Jewish community: "Of the billion [franc fine] the Brith has already turned over one half; it has contracted a loan in order to pay interest and depreciation costs. They are ruining the Jews."[36]

Leftist Jewish organizations in the Occupied Zone were not long in reacting to the creation of the UGIF, even as the bargaining continued. The Jewish Section of the MOI reacted without delay in *Unzer Wort* of 6 December 1941, by declaring that the body "was being called on to play an economic role during an initial period by facilitating the pillaging of the funds of Jewish welfare agencies and draining off what remained of Jewish assets through taxes and special contributions." This denunciation of the union's political function identified the true end of the UGIF: "to prepare the groundwork for the isolation of all the Jews among the French people, to create the ghetto demanded by *Le Pilori*."[37]

The assessment of the Bundists (Jewish socialists) was no less categorical: "Our reply," we read in their underground newspaper *Unzer Kamf* (Our Struggle), is "No! A thousand times No! We have nothing in common with a government that discriminates against us, robs us, imprisons thousands of people in concentration camps. They say that we have to join the UGIF in order to reduce the misery and suffering of the masses of the Jewish population. To that we reply that they have allowed thousands of people to die of hunger in the camps; let the executioners do their work themselves. There are many other ways to relieve the suffering of the Jews."[38] A letter sent from Paris to the central offices of the Bund in New York notes that "very few people have gone to the UGIF offices for help." The letter also deplores the recent decision of the American Jewish Joint Distribution Committee to turn the funds intended for the Jews of France over to the UGIF. The proposal ought "to be considered an unheard-of scandal from both the material and political points of view."[39]

Apparently, the trap laid by the Vichy government and the German occupation forces did not work when the "prey" were politically sensitized. The idea that the Jews of France had to evade the constraints of the UGIF was early expressed in positions adopted by the federation, the Bund, and the

MOI, despite their ideological differences. The Consistory reached similar conclusions by a different route, dictated by its fear of seeing the Jewish community likened to a "national minority." In essence, the Jewish organizations of France had to confront the problem of the *Judenrat* just as did those of Poland, with the only difference being that in France isolating the Jews could be effected only by means of a social and moral ghetto and, in this case, by assembling all the cultural and social structures into the arms of the UGIF. For this project to succeed, the precondition was that Jewish leaders succumb to the ancient tendency to turn inward and to cut ties with the non-Jewish population.

How to Save Honor?

The prison-like ghettos of Poland allowed no alternative, largely because the concrete wall was backed by the hostility or indifference of the majority of Christians. The policy of withdrawal was imposed by the reality of the situation. Any survival strategy had to take into account the geographical and political limitations of the ghetto. The principal advantage in the French situation, by virtue of the deeply rooted humanitarian tradition and the favorable evolution in public opinion at the time, was the existence of a real alternative, and thus the possibility of choice. Choice offered itself on the level of the family and the individual, as well as of the community. Naturally, decisions taken by the latter were not without consequences for the former. The elaboration of a global defense strategy against antisemitic legislation and deportation, of a strategy of survival, would ultimately depend on an accurate perception of, and some degree of consensus on, the particular nature of the French situation.

The choice between submission to the legislation, on the one hand, and seeking alliances with non-Jewish forces that would ultimately lead to civil disobedience and the clandestine life, on the other, became the principal (if not the only) conundrum on which the history of the Jews of France under Vichy and the Occupation would be written in tears and blood. In the final analysis, the attitude of the responsible community leaders who faced the choice constitute the basis on which one can judge and appreciate the orientation of one or the other.

In an extremely complex situation, sacrificing their charitable organizations or submitting to the will of the enemy, the Jews, especially those who had no ideological reference points, had only one compass to help them determine what attitude to adopt: honor. Honor is not only an abstraction conveniently maintained to allow one to post facto judge this or that act, this or that human behavior. It is also a principle of reality, an infallible criterion of judgment, although instinctive, the application of which allows the achievement of the ends and the means without the former having to justify the latter.

During the debate prompted by the creation of the UGIF, in the Occupied Zone no less than in the South, the question of honor was not a matter of political rhetoric. It was certainly the case that in the context of an exclusionary action fraught with unprecedented menace, the honor of the Jewish people could not be measured only in terms of noble gestures or panache either: honor consisted of saving by all and every means each Jewish life that could be saved. Were these means better concentrated within the framework of global resistance to the Nazi enemy, or rather in a forced, but external, submission?

On 18 September 1942, Marc Jarblum wrote to the president of the Consistory asking him to initiate a regrouping of Jewish organizations in France "with a view to saving the existence and honor of the Jewish population before it is too late." For him, existence and honor went in tandem, one conditioning the other. It is similarly with reference to honor that William Oualid, a member of the Consistory and one of those who negotiated with Vallat, asked the Council in the course of a dramatic session in early December 1941 to refuse to participate in the UGIF: "How will posterity judge us?" To Albert Lévy, who protested having been censured, Helbronner replied in nearly the same terms as Oualid: "The future will judge to what extent your personal initiatives could have alleviated the sufferings of our coreligionists without compromising the political and moral traditions of French Judaism, which cannot and will not be distinguished from the national community."[40]

As events turned out, submission to the dictates of the German enemy, and to the antisemitic regime in Vichy, would lead neither to the saving of human lives nor to the preservation of honor.

CHAPTER FIVE

The Yellow Star

Stigmatize, Humiliate, and Isolate the Jews

I am not the only one in my school. Several of us wear it
and they call us "the kids with the star."
— Daniel Darès[1]

O God! Was it truly necessary that in the end it should be
that star?
— Vercors (Jean Bruller)

The ordinance promulgated in the Occupied Zone in June 1942 requiring Jews to wear a yellow Star of David, along with the acceleration of internments that soon followed in both the Free and Occupied Zones, were, we now know, the first large-scale operations of the "Final Solution" in France definitively settled at the Wannsee Conference in Berlin on 20 January 1942.[2] The victims were ignorant of the decision, as was the rest of the world, including Allied intelligence. It was not until the opening of the Reich archives in 1945 that that meeting in suburban Berlin became known, a conference so important in the history of genocide and for the fate of the Jews.

Even if it is true that until then public opinion had given little significant sign of hostility toward Vichy's anti-Jewish policies, it is no less true that inside the government there was already concern over the unfavorable public attitudes. The government sought to reassure the country by asserting that only foreign Jews would be affected. But the unilateral promulgation by the occupation authorities of the yellow star did not take Vichy's considerations into account. On 30 May 1942, Paris Jews learned of the German ordinance, which was to take effect on Sunday, 7 June. "Each Jew will receive three badges in exchange for points on his textile ration card," the ordinance stipulated. The insignia was to be in black on a background of yellow cloth, and was to be worn on the left side of the chest, sewed to the garment and not hidden, either partially or wholly, by a lapel or any other item, purse, fur, etc. There was ostensibly no charge for the badges, but later it was learned that the invoice had been sent to the UGIF, which, naturally, paid it.

"Support the wearers of the yellow badge!"

In Paris, the first reaction from the Jewish side was not long in coming. At the announcement of the ordinance, the "Jewish Section" of MOI responded in the newspaper *J'accuse* with an appeal to the population of Paris to "support the wearers of the yellow badge." Pointing to the example of Holland, where "Jews are greeted respectfully by passers-by" after the former had been obliged to bear the "shameful yellow stain," the paper encouraged the French as well to show their solidarity with the victims of Nazi barbarity. By marking the Jews with a distinctive sign, the occupiers "hope to humiliate them, distance them from non-Jews, invite incidents."

But the paper did not encourage its readers to disobey the ordinance. Was this a failure to perceive the danger that the yellow star represented, or was it rather skepticism as to the efficacy of such a protest? In either case, for the Jews generally there was no alternative to "wearing without shame the insignia that was imposed on them." Recalling that in the camps in Germany, the French, as "Aryans of the Second Zone," were marked with the letter F, like the Poles with the letter P; and that "human beings see themselves branded like cattle under the scornful eye of the 'race of lords'"; the newspaper asked the French "to find a hundred ways of demonstrating sympathy for the bullied and persecuted Jews."[3]

How many were the Parisian men and women who on Sunday, 7 June 1942, "found ways" to show their condemnation of the infamous measure? We do not know. Early *Renseignements généraux* from the police note that "the public remains indifferent to the recent measures imposed on the Jews; only those with a personal stake have made a fuss." Many may have feared being singled out for harassment by antisemitic elements. Minor incidents did mark the first day. One account runs as follows: "In the course of the afternoon, about 4:15 p.m., a dozen members of the Rassemblement National Populaire [National Popular Rally] on the Boulevard de la Madeleine and Rue Royale incited the staff of cafés not to serve Jews, and forced those [Jews] who were eating and drinking on the terrace outside to go inside. About 5:30 there were similar demonstrations on the Champs Elysées, Avenue de Wagram, and Avenue des Ternes by young people led by two uniformed members of the Légion Voluntaire Français."[4]

The police made some arrests for infractions of the ordinance. The count for day one went: without insignia, fourteen arrested; in compliance but protesting against wearing the star, two; Aryan wearers of the star, three; spurious insignia, twelve; altercations between Jews and their "opponents," nine. The wearing of "spurious" insignia was attributed by the police to "student circles."[5] Dr. Helmut Knochen, head of German security, did not share the optimism of the French police, and was struck by the "slight—or totally lacking—comprehension" for the yellow star of which "large portions of the population" gave proof: the French felt sorry for the "poor Jews, in particular the children." According to Knochen, the German police knew of forty cases in which Gentiles, "out of sympathy for the Jews," put on yellow stars with inscriptions such as: "Swing, Sousou [sic., *Zouzou,* 'hepcat' in contemporary slang], Victory, Catholic, etc." Knochen thought this was also a way of expressing "Anglophile" opinions.[6]

As the days passed, a change in public opinion could be noted, evidence of increasing disapproval, to the point that the police corrected their first observations: "The implementation of the ordinance, while appearing to have left the public indifferent, nonetheless runs counter to the feelings of a good number of Parisians, who do not see this measure as necessary in terms of the national interest."[7] Daniel Darès (né Zaydman) remembers the kindness with which his teacher received him: "When I came in, I was ashamed. The pupils looked at me curiously and they moved off, turning their heads. Our teacher came up to me, put his hands on my shoulders, and said, 'You are a good boy and the best of my pupils, so don't worry. It's as if the whole class wears stars. Let's get back to our lesson.'"[8]

The reactions of such Parisians encouraged many Jews. In a letter from the Amelot Committee addressed to the FSJF in the Southern Zone one Jew stresses that "the conduct of the Christian population provoked great anger in the little clan of antisemitic officials. . . . The [ultra-nationalist, antisemitic rightwing] press strives from one day to the next to attack us even more savagely." The city was swamped with posters mocking the "French idiots" who out of sympathy for the Jews do not even notice that the Jews are lifting their wallets.[9]

Any sentiment of pride at being able to proclaim one's Jewishness in public, experienced as defiance of the Germans, was inevitably succeeded by anxiety. The sympathy expressed by Parisians for bearers of the star allowed Jews "to get through these first tragic days. . . . But their hearts are heavy; we encourage each other, but we feel very depressed and morally weakened." For their part, the Germans proceeded "in fits and starts," which had an extremely demoralizing effect. "The vice is slowly tightening" wrote one witness, "with each turn, your chest is more constricted and your back even more bowed. The weakened morale even got to Brodati who more the less remains in better humor, firmer and younger in character than I am."[10]

Protestants and Catholics Begin to Question

There was no immediate reaction published in the French underground press. Nor did the hierarchy of the Catholic Church make any comment. Yet, without waiting for his superiors to take an official stand, Father Dillard, parish priest of the Saint Louis Church in Vichy (who counted among his flock the Marshal himself), attacked the yellow star at Mass on Sunday, 14 June 1942. He invited the faithful to pray "not only for the prisoners of the Stalags [POW camps] and Offlags [Officers' POW camps] . . . but also for all the Jews who are held up to ridicule by being made to wear a yellow star." Pierre Limagne, an excellent chronicler of the era, expressed admiration for his act, but also concern: "It is so rare that a free word can make itself heard in public. It will not take long for the Reverend Father Dillard to pay for that act of boldness and for several others."[11] And indeed, Dillard was eventually deported to Dachau, whence he never returned.

The Protestant Federation reacted as early as 5 June through the voice of its vice-president, the Rev. Bertrand. The protest, which was delivered to the Marshal, conveyed the "emotion" felt by the churches in the face of a measure that imposed "an undeserved humiliation" on an entire population of veterans, six-year old children, and also "baptized persons who are forced before others to bear the title of Jew, while before God they have the honor of bearing that of Christian." Bertrand's statement is all the more remarkable if we take into account the frame of mind of the conformist elites of all denominations who were still "worshipping the Marshal." Indeed Bertrand himself made the statement ambiguous by observing that wearing the star in no way "advanced the solution to the Jewish Question." And, furthermore, Bertrand warned the faithful against any erroneous interpretation of his statement as a call to political protest: it was vital to "take care to avoid all allusion to political events and to secular ideologies." If one could not remain silent before the attack on the dignity of man, one ought, on the other hand, to "stay in the domain of ideas and Christian action."[12]

The leaders of the Protestant Federation were clearly concerned, like their Roman Catholic counterparts, with developments in their rank and file; the symptoms of indignation over the anti-Jewish measures seemed to threaten a rupture with the Vichy government. In a letter to congregations, the Rev. Boegner expressed his anxiety over an "imposed separation" from the ruling powers. But although the statement bore witness to nascent rifts, it was important, he makes clear, that this not undermine "the communion of faith and obedience."[13] As we shall see, it would prove difficult to maintain this fragile equilibrium.

The sense of helpless embarrassment many French people felt at the practices of the occupiers and their sympathizers found expression in a novel by the writer and resistance activist Vercors (pseudonym for Jean Bruller), *La Marche à l'étoile* ("The Way to the Star"), published clandestinely in 1943 and read widely at the time. At one point in the novel, Vercors's protagonist recalls the approach of a half-Jewish friend forced to wear the star. "As always, I blushed. (I have never been able to meet one . . . without blushing.) And already I was turning my face away, with that miserable cowardice that always prevents me from conveying in a glance the message of fraternity which alone could attenuate my humiliation." The friend was the hero of the novel, Thomas Moritz, a "half-Jewish" Protestant who had fled Moravia, a man for whom the France of 1789 was a lodestar. Seeing him approach with the yellow star on his chest, knowing that he was inexorably going to his death, the protagonist cries silently to himself, "O God! Was it truly necessary that in the end it should be that star?"[14]

Reactions and Exemptions

Among the Marshal's men, satisfaction at the Jews' humiliation was clearly evident, even if the measure was limited to the Occupied Zone. Simon Arbellot, head of the Press Bureau in the Ministry of Information, announced at a press conference, "his eyes sparkling with glee," that in Paris "before eight in the evening [i.e., curfew for Jews] can you see a considerable number of yellow stars in the streets." One journalist, supported by others, shot back: "I don't find that funny at all!" To which another, faithful to the "National Revolution" cried, "I wouldn't feel harassed if they made me wear a sign saying 'Christian' or 'French.'"[15]

What sordid hopes the "yellow star" produced among the Vichy journalists who cheerfully approved the marking of the Jews! The newspaper *Le Progrès de Saône-et-Loire* saw in the star "the chance to get rid of the Jewish leeches. France can now take the national fortune back into its own hands and have it managed by its own sons, decent people of the French race."[16]

Expecting the new persecution to be unpopular in Christian public opinion, the mainly Catholic *L'Union française* sought doctrinal justification: "The Papacy," it wrote, "has always cut the Jews off from the Christian community. Catholics could contemplate the yellow star in tranquillity: its justification came from Saint Peter's throne."[17] This affirmation was hardly gratuitous. "In every Christian kingdom at all times," wrote the Church father Saint Thomas Aquinas in the thirteenth century, "the Jews of both sexes should be distinguished from the others by an exterior sign."[18] Louis Darquier de Pellepoix (who replaced Xavier Vallat at the head of the CGQJ on 6 May 1942) called for the extension of the yellow star to the entire country, which would, he argued, contribute to separating the Jews from the nation.[19]

Exemptions from the obligation to wear the yellow star were granted sparingly by the IV J office of the Gestapo, the *Judenreferat*. Several prominent persons nevertheless benefited from exemptions, among them the wife of Fernand de Brinon, the Vichy representative to the Occupation in Paris. On the other hand, certain Jews thought that because of their loyalty to the Marshal they should also benefit from the exemptions. Less well known are dispensations "earned" by special services. The CGQJ sought dispensations for four Jews who served as *Nachrichtengeber,* that is, informers.[20] Companies that had been nationalized or requisitioned for the war effort also intervened on behalf of Jews whom they considered "irreplaceable." For example the *Reichskommissar* of the Unilever Trust in France requested that the head of the German security service relieve "Simon R." and his wife from the obligation to wear the star.[21] Jean S. of Grenoble wrote to the wife of the Marshal to seek exemption from the yellow star if the measure were to be extended to the Southern Zone. His sister in Paris had already benefited from such a waiver. His status as a Jew "did not make [him] blush." But "on every occasion having shown [his] loyalty and devotion to the Marshal," wearing the star would give him the appearance of one who "entertained feelings contrary" to the Marshal's.[22]

Deport 1,000 to 5,000 Jews per Month

In Berlin and Paris in February 1942 the Germans began to prepare for the large-scale deportation of France's Jews. In order not to ruffle the sensitivities of the French unnecessarily, the German Embassy in Paris judged it necessary to take the temperature of Vichy. "The French government would be disposed," Foreign Affairs Counselor Carl Theodor Zeitschel reported to Berlin, "to make the most extensive concessions on the Jewish Question." And yet, according to the German consul in Vichy, Krug von Nidda, it would be possible to count on an agreement with the French "to transport [only] 1,000 to 5,000 Jews [i.e., from both zones] each month." Still, Zeitschel contended that "the French government would be happy to be rid of the Jews whatever the method, without making too much noise about it."[23]

Counselor Zeitschel had well judged French readiness to cooperate in the deportations, even if during the course of discussions Vichy representatives René Bousquet (secretary general for police) and Jean Leguay (Bousquet's deputy in the Occupied Zone), conveyed Pétain's nervousness about the public reaction. Between 27 March 1942, the departure date of the first convoy of deportees from Compiègne, and 5 June, the date of the second convoy from France, no departures to the east took place. The next deportations did not get underway until 22 June.

This period of relative calm may also be explained in part by the total mobilization of railway stock during preparations for the spring offensive on the Russian Front.[24] In fact, Dannecker, who returned from Berlin on 22 March 1942 (having visited his boss, Eichmann) with only a single train to show for his efforts, explained that even his boss's boss could find no more than that: "SS Obergruppenführer Heydrich succeeded in having [only one] train put at our disposal." In any case, concerned to assure themselves of the political support and practical cooperation of the French government, the Germans seemed to control their impatience to see the deportations assume the desired volume and frequency. In Berlin it was expected that deportations from France would eliminate 100,000 Jews, to be rounded up in both the Occupied and the Free Zones, over a period of eight months.[25]

Back in Paris, Dannecker reduced the scope of the program for the first operational phase to 38,000 men and women, presenting this figure to Leguay as the fulfilment by the French of the agreement Cavalt and Bousquet had made with him earlier. Finally, on 2 July, Knochen and Bousquet agreed on the arrest of 30,000 Jews: 20,000 in Paris and 10,000 in the Free Zone.[26] For the Germans, the two zones could not be dissociated. This is why the July raids in Paris and those in August in the "Free Zone" were decided at the same time: they were to lead Vichy into full collaboration in the hunt. The Germans made no secret of their intention to deport all the Jews of France; the "evacuation" of foreign Jews was to be only a first step. For Ambassador Otto Abetz "there [had been] reason, in the interests of the psychological effect on the great mass of the French people, to proceed so that the evacuation measures begin by affecting Jews of foreign origin";[27] but Berlin clearly hoped to draw the French into the persecutions a step at a time.

Louis Darquier de Pellepoix, the new commissioner for Jewish Questions in Vichy, towed the German line during the preparations for the large-scale roundups to take place across France in July and August. He spoke only of Jews in general, not distinguishing between French and foreign Jews, between the Occupied and Free Zones. Nor was Vichy ignorant that in the convoys that left Compiègne on 27 March and 5 June 1942, a large number of Jews of French birth were among the 2,112 deportees.[28] The Germans invoked the pretext that this was a "reprisal" action, but they were actually testing Vichy "resistance" to the deportation of native-born French Jews.

On 3 July 1942 Laval reported to the Council of Ministers on the deportations, and though no formal vote was taken, the Council signaled by its silence its de facto approval. The Marshal reiterated the need to distinguish between foreign and French Jews, a principle that "would be understood by public opinion."[29] The Marshal and Laval were concerned that French public opinion not extend to the Jews any of the sympathy it felt for the workers being sent to Germany. But in their faith that the French public would have no sympathy for the stateless Jewish "trash," Laval and the Marshal were badly mistaken, as events would prove.[30]

Once agreement had been reached on the number of Jews to be arrested in the two zones, it remained only to finalize the plan for Paris at two meetings of the coordinating committee Vichy and Germany had set up in 1941, the first at Gestapo headquarters (Avenue Foch), and the second at the Prefecture of Police. Moved by so-called "humanitarian feelings," Laval spoke against separating children from their parents. Berlin had favored their separation because it lent credence to the rumor that the "unknown" destination of the parents was in reality work camps. Laval's recommendation that children be taken as well was accepted by Berlin, welcome proof that Vichy was prepared to go even further than originally requested.

On 13 July the Prefecture of Police circulated a secret memorandum detailing the execution of the raids planned for 16 and 17 July. More than a simple instruction, however, the eight-page document laid out a veritable plan of attack against a civil population, a plan of eight typed pages whose precision would command admiration if its intent wasn't criminal. "The occupation authorities decided on the arrest and internment of a certain number of foreign Jews," declared Émile Hennequin, the director of the municipal police in charge of the operation in his directive. The targets of the action would be Jews of the following nationalities: Germans, Austrians, Poles, Czechoslovakians, Russians (refugees or Soviet citizens), and the stateless, without regard to sex, ages sixteen to fifty-five years. And, in a tone of shameful precision: "Children under the age of sixteen would be taken at the same time as the parents."

Neither Dannecker nor his replacement, Heinz Röthke, mention anything in their directives on the deportations about children under the age of sixteen. Laval's initiative regarding the departure of children with their parents apparently astonished the occupation authorities. "It was the French who first proposed that Jewish children should be included on the deportation trains."[31] What motivated Laval to take this sort of action? Two hypotheses are possible. One, in an attempt to put off the moment when French Jews would be deported, Laval decided to use foreign Jewish children to meet the quotas. Two, he wanted to calm down public opinion which, ignorant of their fates, would have been scandalized at the separation of the children from their mothers.

Paris police stations obtained from the UGIF 25,432 cards with city addresses and 1,427 for the suburbs (information based on the 1940 census). For the capital alone 4,412 uniformed and plainclothes officers were assembled in teams of three. Students at the Police Training Academy (École pratique de police) were mobilized as reinforcements: leave was suspended until the morning of 18 July. Police officers guarding "German buildings" were also taken off duty for forty-eight hours and reassigned to the raids. The teams were distributed by arrondissement according to the relative density of the target population, eight teams for the First Arrondissement, two hundred fifty-five for the Twentieth. The latter and the Eleventh were also assigned inspectors from the judicial police (250 and 220, respectively), probably as a precaution against difficulties that might arise in heavily left-leaning areas. On average one officer was assigned for every five persons. For the transportation of arrestees, twenty-seven buses were requisitioned from the City of Paris, along with ten police wagons, all to be guarded by supplementary teams. Once collected at the "primary centers" in the districts, families without children and unmarried persons were to be taken to Drancy, all the rest to the Vélodrome d'Hiver (Winter Cycling Stadium), which under normal circumstances could hold just over 10,000 people. An important point: "The windows of the buses will remain closed and the platforms will be reserved for baggage." Police headquarters attached great importance to being informed at each stage of the operation. A certain number of motorcycle officers would assure liaison between the police stations and headquarters. The operation would begin at 4:00 o'clock in the morning on 16 July and be completed by 4:00 o'clock in the afternoon of the following day. The teams were urged to proceed with the greatest speed possible, without unnecessary words and without commentary.[32]

Dispensation for certain categories was foreseen, including (among others) women who were pregnant or nursing, the wives of prisoners of war, and men or women with a non-Jewish spouse; members of the Union générale des israélites de France were also included, a "favor" that focused even more hostility toward the puppet organization.[33]

The Eve of the Great Roundup

So July arrived, the month when the "Spring Wind" (the code name of the operation) beat down upon the foreign Jews of the capital with a force that turned the blood in their veins to ice: the great raid of 16 and 17 July showed a barbaric antisemitism in action, but also marked the first large-scale Jewish countermeasures against the internments and deportations with the active complicity of numerous Parisians. Many Jews were still under the impression of the sympathetic words Parisians had shared with them when they had been forced to wear the yellow star. The general climate, however, quickly deteriorated. Jacques Bielinky noted in his diary the succession of measures intended to heighten the isolation of the Jews and make their deportation easier. (He had judged the situation sufficiently serious to take refuge with his wife at the home of a Protestant friend.)

1 July: Jews are no longer allowed into the city-operated canteen in the various neighborhoods; they are referred to the Jewish canteens that operate only in the 4th and 13th Arrondissements.

2 July: At the Préfecture, continual disruptions by the panic-stricken Jewish women protesting the arrest of their husbands and that they had no idea where the men had been sent.

3 July: A rumor circulates that Harry Baur, the famous cinema actor, has been shot. He is related to the family of André Baur, a banker and vice president of the UGIF.

4 July: In today's issue of *Comoedia,* there is a eulogy for Victor Behar, actor and director, Sephardic Jew. Probably negligence of the censor. But the publication has never insulted Jews.

7 July: In the Metro a big working-class fellow suddenly bends over toward me and says: "Why are you wearing that? In your place, I would have refused."

8 July: For the first time *Les nouveaux temps* printed an announcement that confirmed the existence of an order forbidding Jews to ride in any cars of the Metro except the last one. This is published as a decision taken by the transit company.

9 July: In the Jewish community clinics in the Rue Ancelot, the Rue des Francs-Bourgeois, etc. the numbers of the sick increases rapidly, ruined Jews offer less resistance to illness.

10 July: The newspapers announce new measures against the Jews. Prohibition against walking on the Grands Boulevards, the Avenue des

Champs-Elysées. . . . Entry prohibited into cafés, restaurants, shops, etc. Crowds gather in the Metro in front of yellow posters that have just been pasted up with a notice in French and German that in the event of an assassination attempt, all the male relatives of the aggressor will be shot, the women sent to forced labor, and the children put in juvenile delinquent centers. Emotions ran very high, but an hour later the posters were gone.

12 July: We are installed at Plessis-Robinson thanks to the hospitality of a French Protestant friend. Bedroom, kitchen and lovely garden.

13 July: The poster from 10 July was published [again] in the newspapers this morning. It was not rescinded, then. They are even pasted up or re-pasted in large numbers. Even in Plessis-Robinson.

14 July: The national holiday began at 1:00 o'clock in the morning with an alert that lasted one hour. But no bombardment occurred. A sad day even so. . . .

15 July: A new announcement affecting Jews. They are forbidden to go to restaurants, cafés, cinemas, theaters, concert and music halls, swimming pools, museums, libraries, exhibitions, castles, historical monuments, sporting events, races, camp grounds, and even telephone booths, fairs, etc. It appears that Jews and Jewesses between the ages of eighteen and forty-five will be arrested and sent to forced labor in Germany.[34]

CHAPTER SIX

July 1942

The Great Roundup and the First Acts of Resistance

> Don't wait at home. . . . Make every effort to hide yourselves,
> and first of all your children, with the help of sympathetic
> members of the French population.
> —Appeal from Solidarité on the eve of the raids

By the beginning of July signs of nervousness in the Jewish neighborhoods of
Paris were multiplying. The internees in the Pithiviers and Beaune-la-Rolande
Camps informed their families of preparations for impending departure to
an "unknown destination." Internment was now viewed as tantamount to deportation. The rumors grew more alarming: new measures, new raids. Against
which categories this time? Jewish organizations found themselves confronted
not only with rumors but with very precise information, including information about "Spring Wind," *Vent printanier,* the anticipated July deportation.

At this time there were, in addition to the UGIF, three other centers in
Paris: the Consistory; the semi-legal Amelot Committee (connected with the
Fédération des sociétés juives de France and also including representatives
of the Bund and the left Zionists); and the Jewish section of the MOI, which
encompassed within its influence groups such as Solidarité, the Jeunesses

communistes juives (Jewish Communist Youth), the Union des femmes juives (Union of Jewish Women), the Commission intersyndicale juive of the CGT (embracing members of several trade unions), and the Second Detachment of the FTP-MOI (the military branch of the immigrant Resistance).

The board of the UGIF learned in early July of the imminence of a "vast new deportation measure" when the Commissariat General for Jewish Questions made the blunder of sending a confidential letter dated 1 July asking the Paris UGIF to collect and furnish a large quantity of equipment indispensable to the deportees, such as camping supplies, work-boots, mess-kits, canteens, and similar items.[1]

A Difficult Secret

In a letter of 6 July 1942, André Baur, vice-president of the UGIF, explained to the commissariat the impossibility of procuring such objects. He advanced another justification that betrays both his distress and the complexity of his position: "It seems particularly dangerous to us," he wrote, "to let the Jewish population know that it may expect a vast new deportation initiative. It is not our role to sow panic by giving it even partial foreknowledge of your letter."[2] What would the UGIF do with this terrible information? Nothing indicates that its leaders thought of disseminating it. However, the staff was also aware of what was in the offing, having been called on to make sequentially numbered cardboard badges, apparently for the children. Did these employees, knowing that their own and their families' security depended on their obedience to the new order, have the courage to leak the news? Certainly—inevitably—information leaked from this source.

The Paris Consistory, associated with the UGIF, had no mandate of its own save in matters of religion. It also took no official initiative to sound the alarm. On the other hand, the Amelot Committee, in the absence of any legal means of printed communication, actively circulated the information by word of mouth. Thus, after learning that the UGIF was counting on the presence of its physicians at the Vélodrome d'Hiver, the members of the Amelot Committee refused, unwilling to become involuntary accomplices.

The only printed information that circulated among the Jewish population was a tract produced by Solidarité, which would have been read primarily by the immigrant Jews. For the Resistance, fully aware of all rumors but also precisely informed by a source within the Prefecture of Police, the dissemination of this information assumed top priority (as a sort of mobile

Judenrat, the UGIF leadership were afraid to participate). In fact, since the early internments in the camps of Loiret, Compiègne, and Drancy, this was the first time that the Resistance found itself in a position to attempt to derail the roundup. During the last days of June the leaders of Solidarité printed an appeal in Yiddish entitled "The Enemy is Preparing an Unheard-of Crime against the Jewish Population," but it would not leave the print shop until 10 or 11 July. Thus, many immigrant Jews learned only at the last minute that raids were imminent and that neither women nor children would be spared. "According to the information that we have from a sure source," the tract states, "the Germans will shortly organize an immense roundup and deportation of Jews. . . . The danger is very great. . . . *To close your eyes to this tragic reality is the equivalent of suicide. To open your eyes, to become conscious of the danger, leads to safety, to resistance, to life.*" In the impossibility of collective counteraction, the text emphasizes individual action: "each Jewish man, each Jewish woman, each Jewish teen should act: do not wait at home. . . . Make every effort to hide yourselves, *and first of all your children, with the help of sympathetic members of the French population.*" The tract also advises "barricading doors and alerting your neighbors." All these were acts of defense to be accomplished in near total isolation, but without losing sight of their ultimate collective character, because the fight for personal safety was also the fight for the survival of Jewish identity: "Not a single Jew ought to fall victim to the Nazi beast. *Each free, live Jew is a victory over our enemy, who must not and will not succeed in our extermination!*"[3]

Despite all repressive measures the foreign Jews maintained a certain social cohesion thanks to family ties, networks of friends, neighborhood and professional relations, but also through contact with Resistance groups. More than three hundred Solidarité activists and trade union activists experienced in undercover activity contributed to the widespread circulation of news from one neighborhood to another.

Resonance of the Appeal against the Raids

In every instance, without exception, the testimony of those who got away evokes the resonance the call had: "Resistance people are distributing the tract at the risk of their lives, slipping it under doors, stuffing it quickly into surprised hands: Pass it on!!" was the motto hurriedly whispered throughout the Jewish neighborhoods.[4] At the head of a group of young left Zionists, Henry Bulawko was in contact with members of the various Jewish communist youth groups, in particular Roger Trugman, the deputy of Henri Kra-sucki, who headed one of the groups. "A few days before 16 July," he recalls, "I was advised by my contact [Trugman] that a large-scale anti-Jewish action was being prepared. A tract was being disseminated by Solidarité (in Yiddish). He gave me a number of copies. Our comrades were invited to distribute them and to warn the maximum number."[5]

Another witness, Israël Belchatowski, evokes in his memoirs the mental climate in the Jewish community on the eve of events:

On the 12th of July we already knew . . . that the police were mobiliz-ing. . . . Our interpretation was that it was all connected to the patriotic celebrations on July 14 [Bastille Day]. But we learned at the same time that at police headquarters they were drawing up lists of Polish Jews to be arrested and that they would also be taking women and children. No one could believe it. Was this due to naïveté? No, it was our profoundly human conscience that prevented us from admitting that such horrors were possible. . . . On the 15th of July people in the Jewish Resistance said that they knew from a sure source that an extraordinary raid was being prepared and that Jews should not stay in their homes. This news spread like lightning. Terrified, the Jews didn't know how to escape this new misfortune. Those who could, left their lodgings, but most of them had nowhere to hide.[6]

A decision accompanied by insurmountable difficulties, raising endless ques-tions: Daniel Darès heard his parents endlessly turning over the question all night long: "Hide ourselves? Not hide? And if we hide, then where?"[7]

The information was taken seriously, although many were skeptical that the police would go so far. Belchatowksi remembered that, "I had difficulty convincing my wife of the necessity of leaving the house. She just wouldn't believe that they would take women and children."[8] Madame Lichtenstein re-ceived one of the tracts. One of her neighbors recalled, "She never doubted for a minute the truthfulness of the information. Terrified, she decided not to sleep that night. She packed her bags. When they knocked, she would take her daughter and leave by a window. They lived on the ground floor and planned to get away through a back courtyard."[9]

Some young people gave a copy of *Unzer Wort* to the Tselnick family, who had difficulty believing that they were in danger because there was a rumor that people would not be arrested twice. "Monsieur Tselnick, picked up by the police the preceding August, had already spent eighty-seven days at Drancy.

He had been released without knowing how or why, sixty pounds the lighter for the experience. Did they really have to run away now? The Tselnicks took the middle way: they stayed home at 181 Rue Faubourg Saint-Antoine, but that night they did not sleep in their apartment and instead crowded, all five of them, into a small maid's room on the fifth floor."[10]

"It was on Thursday, 16 July that the French police inspectors and officers, accompanied by young followers of Doriot, began to knock on the doors of the Jews whose names were on their lists," reports the first underground document about the raids, a pamphlet entitled *Témoignage* ("Testimony").

> They took away women and children over the age of two, women in the seventh, eighth, and even ninth month of pregnancy; sick people were pulled out of their beds and carried on chairs or stretchers. One paralysed woman was taken away in a wheelchair. Old men aged sixty or seventy were not spared. . . . But it was especially the roundup of children that must be emphasized. From the age of two and up they were considered candidates for the concentration camps! In a number of cases, mothers were forcibly torn away from their little ones. Screaming and weeping filled the streets. Neighbors and passers-by could not keep from crying.[11]

"I looked up in the dictionary," Daniel Darès noted in his "Carnets intimes," "a word that I didn't know, *rafle*. From the German *raifen* 'carry off forcibly'; a police operation carried out without warning in a suspect location; to catch little birds.' Yes, that's what a *rafle* is, a raid. Why are they talking so much about a raid tomorrow?" Early on the morning of 16 July, taken away with his parents—his gravely ill father on a stretcher—Daniel had the feeling that everyone considered them suspect: "The dogs, the cats, the people watched us leave. At the windows, in front, in back, they could see, they watched us, they wondered. We, who were being arrested, being led off. . . . Why, what did [we] do? The good people. . ."[12]

Communications from Headquarters

The roundup was executed with a logistical expertise worthy of a military offensive. Throughout 16 and 17 July communiqués to the relevant authorities, both French and German, were systematically distributed by the office of the superintendent of police, the central agency to which information was flowing: on 16 July, eight; on 17 July, two. In addition, instructions intended to result in more accurate figures were issued in rapid succession.

At 8 a.m. on 16 July police headquarters reported up the chain of command: "The operation against the Jews began this morning at 4 a.m. Many men left their residences yesterday. Some women remain at home with a young child or with several. Others refuse to open their doors. Locksmiths have to be called. At 7:30 a.m. the municipal district police report that ten buses arrived at the Vélodrome d'Hiver." In the margin is written, "9 a.m., 4,004 arrests." Updates continued to be sent at regular intervals, and results were recalculated hourly: by 10:30 a.m. on the sixteenth, 6,587 arrests; 11 a.m., 7,730; 11:40 a.m., 8,673; 3 p.m., 10,832. At 5 p.m., the last communiqué of the day reported 11,363 persons arrested. At the end of the next day, the prefecture gave the totals for the operation: 3,031 men, 5,802 women, 4,051 children—for a total of 12,884 persons.[13] Even if the *Propagandastaffel* (the German censor) had imposed a total gag on the press, which "until further notice [had to] abstain from any article dealing with the action," no one could prevent Parisians from seeing what was happening.[14]

The publication of the underground *Témoignage* under these circumstances became an act of defiance against the Gestapo and the French police. In order to learn what was going on at the Vélodrome d'Hiver, it was necessary to get an observer on the inside. The idea was born on the very morning of 16 July.[15] During the course of a meeting with Alfred Grant, one of the leaders of Solidarité, in the Passy Metro Station at 9 in the morning, Adam Rayski (who had gone underground, and was no longer living with his family) could see buses filled with men, women, and children going along the quays toward the Grenelle Bridge. The suitcases on the bus platforms, the presence of one policeman next to the conductor and another at the rear, and especially the distraught faces of the people behind the windows, allowed him to understand what was going on. The two formulated a plan, and that same day Grant sought out "Alex" (Léon Chertok), one of the leaders of the Mouvement national contre le racisme, who took charge of the operation by enlisting two comrades, the Cathala sisters, who were not Jewish. The next day the latter showed up at the cycling stadium as volunteer social workers to help relieve the police in maintaining order and to distribute whatever food was delivered. They worked there several days, as a result of which the historical record includes a unique report on that hell in the heart of Paris:

The first day the Vélodrome d'Hiver must have held about 12,000 persons. Nothing had been done in advance for them. There wasn't even straw. The internees were "installed" on the bleachers or sitting on the ground. At night the children lay on the ground and the adults stayed seated on the bleachers. There was no food the first two days. Those who had not brought provisions with them remained with empty stomachs. There was no water to drink or to wash with. The toilets, twelve in number, soon became blocked. This situation was not long in producing a number of fainting spells, nervous collapses, attacks of illness, and suicide attempts. There were only three doctors and an insufficient number of nurses. One girl had fainting fits all day after she was freed . . . because she was French. Once she was feeling better she declared: "It was a real slaughterhouse, the sick people were spitting blood, people were fainting all over the place. The screams of the children were deafening. It drove you crazy."[16]

The Secours national (National Assistance), the official relief agency under the direct patronage of the Marshal, sent him a report on 20 July concerning relief activities undertaken on behalf of the "foreign Jews arrested on 16 July." Its teams were initially denied access to Drancy and the stadium. The next day the horrible conditions forced the police to relent: "The National Assistance," states one of their reports, "brought in eighteen mobile kitchens and was able to distribute a basic meal: a little coffee and once a day some noodles and beans that *detainees took in their hands for lack of dishware* [emphasis mine]." The National Assistance representatives knew the internees were going to be deported, and worried about the fate of the children and their own inability to do anything for them: "When the Jews are sent to Drancy, they will be sorted in order to send the parents away in groups of fifty in sealed railway cars after they have been separated from their children. The question of the children, who number 4,000, will soon come up. They cannot, in the short term, be taken into custody by Public Assistance."[17] Mothers urged their children to escape, however possible, out of this hell, saying: "Run away, child, ask some good people to take you in; your mother is lost for ever." Some of the survivors later recorded their observations, including Sarah Lichtsztein, who recalled, "I saw them bring in sick people, the crippled, amputees on stretchers. But they had told us that we were being sent to work in Germany. How did they plan to employ all those poor souls? The brutality of the policemen was disgusting. We had not been accustomed to such treatment in France."[18] The inclusion of children, the elderly, the sick, and the disabled was proof enough that the Germans' French stooges were not fitting out contingents for forced labor; those who could therefore sought to "escape at all cost." Outfoxing the policemen on duty, some of them were able to slip out of the stadium.

The Hidden Face of the Raids

Elsewhere in Paris men and women, often accompanied by their children or elderly parents, tried by whatever means they could devise to escape the clutches of the police. The accounts of those who escaped constitute a pageant of individual acts, but also a collective phenomenon of noncompliance.

Ida Zaïontz:

> In a gabled room under the eaves, pressed one against the other, my parents, my two younger sisters, and I, we held our breath and every step we heard made us jump. The concièrge knew about our hiding place. . . . She told the police that we had left. But she was afraid of our staying there and urged us to go. But where? There were five of us. Who would take us in? We would have to break up. My parents and my younger sister, aged five, [went] to a cousin of my parents in Lilas. My other sister and I, we remembered a French girl in my class, Marie, who had seemed friendly to me, but I didn't know her parents. It took a lot of courage for me to knock on their door at 35 Rue des Écoles in Lilas. We were received in a very kindly way by a rather young woman, Marie's mother. I explained to her that we were asking her to shelter us for two or three days. She asked us to come in. Those three days became three months! We became part of the family. We made two attempts to pass over into the Free Zone, but each time we had to turn back. Finally, the eldest daughter . . . , Jeannine, went with us and crossed the demarcation line with us.[19]

Lucie Aubrac remembers going to the Place des Vosges,

> where I knew I could find a bed and meals with a childhood friend, an elementary school teacher. Madame Collin opened up for me and brought me into the kitchen. A little girl, about eight years old, her elbows on the table and her head in her hands, was chanting the multiplication table for seven. "This is Germaine," my friend told me. "She's the daughter of a cousin out in the country whose husband is a prisoner. She has been living with us since July and has been in my daughter's class since school

began in the fall." Later, when we were alone, my friend told me how the child came to her: "Last July, on the Rue du pas de la Mule, I was present when three buses [prepared to drive off], filled with Jewish families the police had dragged from their rooms. Incredible! . . . I knew almost everyone by sight. . . . A woman gestured for me to come over. 'Take my little girl away, Madame. With you she won't be afraid of leaving me. I don't want her to know what I sense is coming; it's going to end in our deaths.' The girl took my hand and followed me home. I did it because it was the only thing to do."[20]

When Jeanne R. came home with three-year-old son Benoit at 8 o'clock in the evening — curfew for Jews — she found all the tenants gathered in the courtyard of the building (342, rue des Pyrenées) in discussion with the concièrge, whose husband was a police officer. The latter had warned all the residents. Without losing time, Jeanne went up to her apartment and stuffed a few things in a bag. Just as she was leaving, passing in front of a mirror, she saw the yellow star on her jacket. She tore it off but the cloth still showed the mark. She carried the child in her left arm, hoping to cover it up. Jeanne and Benoit spent the night in a small hotel in the Rue de l'Aqueduct in the Tenth Arrondissement. Very early in the morning the hotel-keeper woke them up: "Madame, you have to leave, it's too dangerous for me to keep you." Downstairs in the hotel's café she could see what was happening in the streets: groups of men, women, some with children in their arms, all surrounded by policemen. She started to cry. "You're not going to put her outside with the kid, are you?" a customer said to the hotelkeeper. Other customers chimed in. "Go back upstairs," he said finally, "I'll come and tell you when everything has calmed down." Jeanne left the hotel around noon, and the hotelkeeper wouldn't accept any payment: "Keep your money. It's disgraceful to see [what's going on]. And keep your wits about you!" he told her.[21]

An anonymous witness recorded this memory:

The owner of a small apartment building at 19, Passage d'Eupatoria, had agreed to rent rooms or small apartments to Jews with false papers, or even to let former tenants stay on under cover. At certain times, there were as many as twenty. The concièrge, Monsieur Désiré, knew what was going on. He checked the papers, but it was to see whether they were well done. If he discovered an error, he never failed to give advice. Since the tenants were obliged to leave their hiding places to find . . . work, he would agree to meet them in a nearby street on their way back in order to warn them in case of danger.[22]

Hélène Edelmann-Kupermann and others survived in part thanks to an anti-German, anti-Vichy conspiracy of an entire village:

All the inhabitants of Pont-Saint-Maxence (Oise) knew that we had escaped from the July raids [in Paris]. There were twelve of us: two families with children, two wives of prisoners of war, and an elderly woman. As the first to arrive in the home of a family whose address had been given to me in Paris, I took their advice and went to see the mayor. His first gesture was to give me a counterfeit food ration card. He did the same thing for the other Jewish families as soon as they arrived in the village. He found me day-work as a seamstress for the residents. Most of us were without any resources. I have to recall the memory of the Marquise de Luppé, whose manor house was in the vicinity and who looked after us with touching devotion. In numerous cases, knowing the situation of the family, it was she who asked the storekeepers to sell us things on credit and, in the case of some families, she even paid the bills. Even though the village was full of Germans, we all felt ourselves protected by the local police; from the chief down to the last policeman, every one seemed to be looking out for us.[23]

How different was the mood of those close to the UGIF. Though informed, many were as if anaesthetized, deprived of the power to react, and they waited for the raids, as it were, seated on their suitcases. "I am staying home," one of them wrote to a friend in the Southern Zone,

Between now and tomorrow we expect the arrest of all the foreign Jews, men and women, in order to deport them to labor camps. Our bags are in any case ready and we are staying home expecting that they will come and get us. What will they do with the children? No one knows exactly. People are talking about a special center for several thousand children in the Occupied Zone. But it can't be excluded that they will be sent to the Free Zone or that they will go along with their parents. The Union [UGIF] has provided its members with a special identity card, which should result in their being left in peace. Volunteers like me have not been able to get such a card. We got a certificate that we are volunteers, but this is no guarantee. But you can't exclude the possibility that we will be freed later on. In any case it's uncertain.[24]

We find the same fear combined with passive waiting among others who felt protected because they were French citizens. Mathilde Jaffé, who had been left along with her two-year-old sister Esther by their widower father at the Rothschild Orphanage in 1938, did not forget what she called her "first memory of persecution": "It was in the month of July 1942, when I was sixteen years old, that a policeman accompanied by a German soldier came to take the children of refugees from Germany and Austria, the "little Germans, the little Viennese" as we referred to them after they had gone. . . . They screamed and cried, some of them put up a struggle. Turned to stone, the rest of us watched the scene." In fact, on the day of the roundup the French police picked up a total of twenty-three children there, the majority belonging to families that had fled Germany, in one case four from the same family, the youngest five, the oldest fourteen. All were transferred to Drancy. At the bottom of a list drawn up by the orphanage we find this note: "We do not know the dates or destinations of those who left for Germany, nor the presumed addresses. There is no one to inform." The director and his wife, Jaffé remembers, were taken as well, but they were able to return. "They explained to us that [the authorities] were after the children only because they had left Germany. . . . That didn't mean that we stopped being upset, but we were less worried about our own lot as French citizens."[25]

Seeing which way the wind was blowing, however, resistance organizations went into action. "After the tragic days of 16 and 17 July, hundreds of Jewish families were in hiding from the police," relates Sophie Schwartz, one of the Solidarité leaders. "Along with their children, they stayed closed up in cellars or attics with eight to ten people in the same place."

Our organization immediately got involved with the fate of these unfortunate people by sending a number of children to live with farm families in the countryside. Between 16 July and 1 October, almost one hundred children, in groups of three, four, or five, were placed in villages in the departments of Seine, Seine-et-Oise, Marne, Aisne, Sarthe, and Loiret. In a parallel action, we created groups of "godmothers" and about twenty of these agreed to subsidize the upkeep of these children. Fifty-five per cent were children one of whose parents had been deported; ten per cent had [seen] both parents deported; twenty-five per cent had parents in hiding; ten per cent belonged to families that had not been affected by the raids (e.g., French Jews and/or when the father was a prisoner of war). We paid between 600 and 700 francs per month for each child [one 1942 franc was about one fifth of a 2002 U.S. dollar]. Our monthly expenses amounted to 50,000 francs. The boys and girls between fourteen and fifteen [why only these ages remains unknown] we tried to place in private schools. With this objective in mind we conducted ongoing discussions with teachers and other influential people who were ready to help us.[26]

In the course of the raids and during the days that followed, the Amelot Committee mounted a remarkable rescue and camouflage action. "We decided," Henry Bulawko recounts,

> to increase the placement of children and the distribution of false identity papers to assist in passing into the Southern Zone. Our "Aryan" assistants, often accompanied by their non-Jewish husbands, crossed and re-crossed the various regions in order to find hideouts. Parents who had escaped the raids or who had not been implicated that day and who had until then hesitated to confide their children to our charge, now changed their minds. This obliged us to increase our efforts. . . . Fortunately the papers of our emissaries were authentic.[27]

Röthke's Deficient Numbers

SS-Obersturmführer Heinz Röthke did his sums. In his report of 18 July, for example, he raised the question of why the raids netted only 12,884 (4,500 of them children) out of 23,000 anticipated. He notes in particular the loss of the surprise factor: "a considerable number of stateless Jews had caught wind of the raids and were able to go into hiding. Members of the French police force appear in several cases to have informed the persons they were to arrest in the planned raids. . . . While about 9,800 persons were arrested during the first day of raids, on 17 July the French police succeeded in detaining only about 3,000."[28] Just as disappointing was "the attitude of the French population," which all too often demonstrated sympathy for the arrested Jews and "its deep regret particularly with regard to the children."

The "disappointing" totals moved police headquarters to furious activity. Check-ups on residences and in the streets, however, produced meager results. Flight had been aided by an omission in the operational instructions, for all efforts had been directed against residential buildings, while no surveillance had been planned for the streets, so that those who escaped could move about the city without too much risk. On 18 July the police began checking identity papers in the streets and on the metro. The prefecture also sought to improve its numbers by posting plainclothesmen at the municipal offices on 22 July, the day for renewing food ration cards ("the Jews who are being sought will be forced to come forward.").[29]

The determination of the police found expression in a raid carried out at the UGIF children's center on Rue Lamarck near the end of July 1942. The building was suddenly surrounded by policemen who checked the identity papers of every person who left. Quite a number of parents who had been living underground since the raids had put their children in the care of the UGIF, hoping they would be safe there. But they came to visit. The raid caught some of them unawares, and they were forced to look for places to hide. The police now began a real hunt inside the building, including the cellars. The center staff gathered the children in the recreation room "in order to spare them the . . . spectacle of the pursuit and arrest of which their parents were the object."[30] Larissa Wouzek, a seven-year-old refugee from the Netherlands placed in the Lamarck Center after the deportation of her mother, still remembered the event forty years later: "One day, a Sunday, there was a raid during the parents' visit. It was terrible, because the adults were trying to hide everywhere."[31]

The hunt continued in the streets and the metro. According to police statistics, fifty-eight people were apprehended during the second half of July. In August the police nabbed seventy-seven, thirty-six of them for "not wearing the star" and fourteen for having "false papers and complicity [in their abuse]." Henceforth, the charge "for false papers" reappears regularly. In September, the reports give "forty-three Jews turned over to the Germans," of whom thirteen for false papers and thirty for not wearing a star. October saw fifteen arrests without stated reason, nineteen for not wearing a star, five for "false papers," and eight for infractions against the Statut des Juifs. The fact that the number of arrests for refusal to wear the star is greater than that for false papers suggests that by this time not everyone had yet acquired counterfeit identities, but that in order to leave their hiding places a considerable number were removing their stars.[32]

The arrests of foreign Jews, noted the superintendent of police, provoked numerous comments from the public, a majority of whom believed that the operation was also directed against French Jews. "In general, these

measures would have been fairly well received if they had involved only foreign adults, but numerous persons were distressed by the lot of the children,
since rumors were soon in circulation that they were being separated from
their parents. . . . Although they felt but little sympathy for the foreign Jews,
inhabitants as a whole judged that these measures should not be imposed on
French Jews, especially former servicemen." In conclusion, the superintendent called attention to a feeling that would increasingly mark the evolution
of public opinion: the fear of one day seeing the raids on Jews extended to
all the French.[33] The same tone is apparent in the *Renseignements Généraux:*
"The measures . . . have quite deeply distressed public opinion. . . . Even
though the French population as a whole . . . is quite antisemitic, none the
less it severely condemns these measures, which it characterizes as inhumane."[34] The informants who contributed to the *RG* attributed the reaction
of the population to brutalities committed against women and against children who were torn away from their parents. "It is this separation that most
touches the general population and gives rise to . . . severe criticism of the
government and Occupation authorities."[35] Since the execution of the raids
was entirely the work of the French police, the Parisians who witnessed them
condemned from the very outset both the occupiers and Vichy.

Until that time the war had been a matter for men. It was they who fell
at the front, it was they who died as hostages or Resistance fighters. Except
for the mental and material suffering that affected the families of the soldiers, the war itself had never directly struck women and children. Now, one
witnessed for the first time an attack against the most sacred of values: the
family, in the person of its children. It mattered little that the stricken families belonged to a category for which Parisians did not overflow with sympathy: disgust prevailed over prejudice. The shock the population experienced
was profound and would not soon be forgotten.

A Double Turning Point

With good reason historians are at pains to pay homage to the attitude of the
Paris population toward the Jews during the terrifying days of July. But for
there to have been *solidarity,* it was necessary that Jews cease to behave as *victims* and to become *subjects,* actors in the drama into which they had been
thrown. Documentation and testimony both attest that the reaction of the
Jews appeared as a sudden burst of energy: at least 8,000 to 9,000 evaded
the police and owed their salvation above all to their own courage in breaking

with the generally passive response to previous raids. This time the element of surprise did not work to the advantage of Franco-German headquarters. The demonstrated malice directed at the family as a whole proved that respecting the law or refraining from flight had lost all justification and thus changed the thinking of Parisian Jews. But what were they to do? Even when the will to escape existed, most of them could not imagine how. Where would they go? How would they get there? The complex of questions was sufficient to cloud their thinking and paralyze their ability to act.

Little or not at all integrated into French society, locked in a kind of social and vocational self-sufficiency, the majority of immigrant Jews had not formed widespread relations with non-Jews. Paradoxically, even those who belonged to trade unions or to the Communist and Socialist Parties failed to integrate with their French comrades. Symptomatic was the rarity of mixed marriages, rare not so much for religious reasons as cultural. Only the children were close enough to school friends, or at times their school "mistress," to know their home addresses. For fugitive Jews in general the sole way out was simply knocking at an *unknown* door and asking *strangers* to hide them — persons whose reactions no one could predict. "You can count on the solidarity of the French people!" proclaimed Resistance activists, without proof or evidence beyond their faith in an idealized France of humanitarian traditions: a certainty perhaps for militants, but an abstraction for ordinary people. In reality, it was a leap in the dark. And yet, fairly rapidly Jews began to receive signs of encouragement from non-Jews.

In the final analysis, the event is to be seen as the first confrontation, admittedly indirect, between the Jews of France and the Franco-German police apparatus. Two new facts, essential and inseparable, emerged after the roundup: the self-defensive reaction of Parisian Jews, on the one hand, and the spontaneous and courageous support of non-Jews, on the other. A common moral and political front demonstrated the means to resist deportation, even though undertaken by an overwhelmingly superior police power. It also marked a diminution in the fear of the crushing power of the enemy. In August 1942 the Jewish Section of the MOI analyzed the new situation in the following terms: "The risk of deportation is indeed recognized as the primary and immediate danger. . . . [But] the number of those who remain unconvinced of the possibility of successful resistance to deportation is small."[36] Isolation could be broken — even if at a high cost in energy and courage — if people put themselves in determined contravention of the law.

It should be stressed that Catholics and Protestants alike adopted the same attitude, and that they did so spontaneously, before the church leadership had taken official positions. As Lucie Aubrac said, "The concièrge on Rue des Rosiers who picked up a Jewish child so that it wouldn't be deported had a sense of performing an everyday act, as did the farmer's wife who hid guns."[37] The summer of 1942 was marked by a turning point in public opinion, but one assuming as precondition a change in the conduct of the Jews themselves. Pierre Laborie has observed that the interaction of these two currents resembles double mirrors that reflect each other's images, so that the failure of the racist and antisemitic propaganda could become more and more evident. Foreseen by Vichy as a factor for the unification of the French, and by the occupying forces as the basis for collaboration, the persecution and the antisemitic propaganda that accompanied it had a boomerang effect. According to the historian Henri Michel, "The recognition of the total noxiousness of Nazism and the generalized movement of rebellion that it stimulated, were born of the spectacle of the fate inflicted on the Jews."[38] This humane rejection of persecution, Laborie observes, marked the "beginning of the . . . rupture between the populace and the government."[39] In the end, this dynamic movement became a major factor in the rise of resistance throughout the entire country.

A Letter to the Marshal from a Jewish Child

The people of Paris may have reacted to events in the streets, but that does not mean they necessarily fully appreciated the disaster striking the broken homes where children were left without their parents. Here is the story of a girl of thirteen whose parents were interned; she herself recounted it in a letter to the Marshal, the man who once boasted on posters, "I have replied to two million children!" Little Sarah Boruchowicz was not one of them![40]

At 52, rue d'Angoulême in Paris, Towia and Yohewet Boruchowicz lived with their five children, of whom the eldest, Madeleine, was eighteen in 1942 and the youngest, the twins Daniel and Nicole, eighteen months old. Between them were Sarah and her brother Armand, aged eight and a half. The parents' lives could not have been more typical: arriving in France in 1927, Towia and Yohewet set up as tailors working from home. When war was declared Towia enlisted in the Foreign Legion, but was discharged fifteen days later: he only weighed one hundred twelve pounds! He worked the treadle long into the night for he had five mouths to feed! Then came the raid of 20 August 1941, targeting foreign Jews in the 11th Arrondissement. Still awaiting his naturalization papers as the father of five children—all of whom were French nationals—Towia was taken to Drancy and deported with one of the first convoys in the spring of 1942.

One day in July 1942, Yohewet Boruchowicz, as a foreigner anxious "to have her papers in order," went to police headquarters to renew her identification card. She returned home only late that evening, and in the accompaniment of two police officers who gave her time only to pull together a few belongings and hastily kiss the children she would never see again. Madeleine, employed as a stock-girl in a pharmacy, quit her job to concentrate on saving her brothers and sisters. She spent much of her time knocking on the doors of various offices such as the UGIF and National Assistance in order to get some financial help (they were receiving child welfare assistance of 690 francs a month). It was Sarah, thirteen years old, who stayed at home to watch the others and listened to the little ones cry all day long and call for their mama. Where did she get the idea of writing to the Marshal with the request to free her mother? Perhaps in school, where with the other children she wrote to the Marshal words dictated by the teacher? Perhaps from the counsellor at the Secours national who forwarded letters to the director's office?

From the first words of her letter, dated 10 October 1942 and written in the style of an appeal to the king (as was taught in the schools), Sarah evoked the misfortune that had struck their home: "Monsieur le maréchal de France! My hand trembles, my voice is faint. By the doorway which gives no other echo than from the wind four little hands are stretched out in a double cry of distress 'Mama, Mama!' But the gentle voice that consoles all things does not answer." Was this a literary talent making a precocious appearance, or simply the measureless grief of a child dictating phrases as grave as the drama experienced by this family? In very neat handwriting, Sarah recounts the history of her parents, their love for France. "Papa worked hard; work was getting scarce but he never complained." In less than a year both their father and mother had been taken from the children. "Fairy tale time is over, the time of God and of man is with us." And the man was the Marshal, for it was only he "who can bring Mama back." Sarah impresses us with her acuity or her intuition, writing that there is time to save only Mama, who was still at Drancy, while for Papa there was no longer hope, *because when you leave for an unknown destination, it's all over, truly over.*" This is a child of thirteen writing to the head of state who would ignore this truth until the end of his days.

Some days later, in the absence of a response, Sarah reiterated her appeal in a letter to the National Assistance. The director, after inquiring into the situation of the Boruchowicz family, turned the "file" over to Fernand de Brinon, the Vichy representative in the Occupied Zone, accompanying it with a letter in his own bureaucratese, but which nonetheless hints at his sympathy. But the Marshal never replied, he did not write to children who had ceased to exist for him even before they were physically done to death.

CHAPTER SEVEN

The Inhuman Hunt in the Southern Zone

> The peoples who turn over their Jews surrender with them their
> way of life determined by the false, Jewified ideal of liberty. . . . It
> is only then that they can be enlisted in the fight for a new world.
> —Dr. Werner Best, chief civilian administrator of
> the German Military Command in occupied France

> France, take care lest you lose your soul!
> —*Témoignage chrétien*

In early June 1942 the representatives of Vichy—in particular police chief
René Bousquet; the Vichy police representative in the Occupied Zone, Jean
Leguay; and the commissioner general for Jewish Questions, Louis Darquier
de Pellepoix—committed themselves to turn over to the Germans roughly
15,000 Jews from the "Free Zone." They knew that they could count on the
reserve constituted by the internment camps in the South, which alone could
supply slightly more than two-thirds of the requisite total.

At one time or another between the fall of the Third Republic and the
dawn of the Fourth, more than two hundred camps blemished the French
countryside: "internment" camps, "billeting" camps, "transit" camps, "classification" camps, and even "concentration" camps.[1] But the first internment

center for "foreigners judged dangerous" (primarily left-wing, refugees from Germany and Austria or defeated Spanish Republicans and the like), was created on 21 January 1939, in a place called Rieucros in the municipality of Mende (Lozère). One month later, the frontier at the Perthuis pass in the Pyrenees was opened to let in the flood of defeated Republican forces from the Spanish Civil War: over the next several weeks 240,000 regular soldiers, 7,500 volunteers from the International Brigades, and 25,000 civilians were interned in Argelès, Saint Cyprien, and Barcarès, concentration camps that were of necessity improvised from one day to the next.

The number of aliens interned for reasons of "national security" expanded sharply in the days after the declaration of war against Germany, when male nationals of the Reich were rounded up. This measure was extended to women in May 1940, just when German troops were breaking through in Belgium and the Ardennes. During the earlier "phoney war" against National Socialist Germany, the French government had been suspicious of antifascist refugees, fearing the infiltration of Hitlerite "fifth columnists" among them. The latter certainly existed, but the German Embassy in Paris provided them with better cover than that afforded by refugee ID cards, which would have left them open to the ongoing surveillance of the Prefecture of Police. The Daladier Government that had replaced the left-liberal Popular Front seemed to be acting as if it had adopted the position of the extreme right, in particular the *Action Française,* which, blinded by antisemitism, had long characterized the refugees as potential enemies of France. "It is very clear that the Semitic immigrants among us, in their desire to regain the good graces of the German authorities, would put themselves under the orders of the latter in the event of war."[2]

In the history of the camps in the South of France the period from 1939 to 1941 is the best known, thanks to the numerous writers and intellectuals who lived there then.[3] Arthur Koestler, interned at Le Vernet, would express the sense of outrage of the interned refugees in a single bitter sentence: "Our only contribution to the war, which was our war much more than theirs, was to remain behind the barbed wire."[4]

With the armistice, the internment of the German refugees would be extended by Vichy because they were purportedly "enemies of the Reich." Among the clauses of the Armistice Convention was Article 19. In comparison with all the other constraints the agreement entailed, this one seemed rather anodyne, since it stipulated "the return without delay to the occupation authorities" of German nationals held in French camps.[5] At a moment when all France was still on the roads, the internees from Argelès and

Saint-Cyprien (Pyrenées-Orientales), Gurs (Pyrenées-Atlantiques), or Le Vernet (Ariège) were guarded more closely than ever behind the barbed wire fences, since the French administration had to comply with the occupiers' injunction to return them. As in the case of so many other repressive measures dictated by Germany, senior officials of Vichy discovered their own "French" reasons for implementing the stipulation. The national director of police, for instance, insisted on the beneficial aspects of sending back all the "extremist agitators," of whom it seemed "undeniably advantageous to rid French soil."[6]

Sometime shortly before 18 July a commission appointed by Berlin and led by a certain Dr. Kundt of the Ministry of Foreign Affairs arrived in the South of France to inspect the camps. The Kundt Commission appears to have visited thirty-one camps, whose combined population has been estimated at 32,000; among these it counted 7,500 German and Austrian nationals, 5,000 of whom were Jews.

Interned in a country that had granted them the right of asylum, many refugees and exiles retained their confidence in France. "They had not counted," noted Arthur Koestler, "on the loyalty with which the National Revolution was observing the treaties," i.e., Article 19. Politicians as experienced as Rudolf Breitscheid and Rudolf Hilferding, both important figures in the Social Democratic Party of Germany, could not believe that "there would be an extradition request." Vichy, however, remanded them to the Germans, who killed them. Some committed suicide, although "the French authorities took special precautions to deliver them alive."[7]

As scandalous as may seem the arbitrary internment of anti-Nazi refugees and Spanish Republicans in 1939, the Vichy camps were no simple continuation of those of the Third Republic (a proposition justifiably criticized by Anne Grynberg in her already cited book on the camps). Admittedly some sites were the same, but for Vichy the criterion was racial since the ordinance of 4 October 1940 authorizing the internment of the "excessive numbers" of all foreign Jews. This was the new spirit of the "National Revolution."

Numbers at the Gurs and Saint-Cyprien Camps increased sharply in late October 1940 with the arrival of 7,663 Jews—men, women, and children—expelled from the German territories of Baden, the Palatinate, and the Saar. On 22 October the Gauleiters of these provinces had forced their entire Jewish population onto four trains for the Free Zone of France. Why France? This question has given rise to numerous hypotheses none of which contain a definitive explanation.[8] For all that, the Vichy government judged itself obliged to accept the convoys and to proceed with the internment of the Jews.

At the close of 1941, the number of Jews interned in the Free Zone was between 15,000 and 16,000 (not counting a small group from Algeria and Morocco). The greatest number were concentrated in Rivesaltes: approximately 8,000. Gurs held about 5,500; the Noé Camp, reserved for the ill and elderly, 1,350; the Le Vernet Camp, considered the most repressive, 1,500. At the Les Milles Camp, designated for persons waiting for exit visas, there were 1,100. We do not know how many Jews had been assigned to labor under the Groupement de travailleurs étrangers (GTE—Foreign Worker Groups); the number is estimated at two hundred.[9]

On the initiative of Chief Rabbi Hirschler, the Jewish agencies created a Camp Commission in early 1941 to provide moral and nutritional aid to internees. It mounted a substantial relief program by dispatching whole railway cars of fruit and vegetables to complement the insufficient official rations. Nor did this replace individualized aid in the form of packages. The commission employed two hundred people, internees for the most part, many of whom were freed along with their families in order to look after administrative or other work. Yet Dr. Joseph Weill, director of the OSE, seems not to have been satisfied with the functioning of the commission of which he was a part. As early as May of that year he was sharing his misgivings, and by a year later he had come to acknowledge the futility of charitable undertakings in the absence of political action.[10]

Collecting the Trash

"You will not hesitate to crush all resistance that you may meet [in the populace] and call attention to officials whose indiscretions, passivity, or unwillingness may have made your task more complicated." These are the orders—very forceful, but given by men who trembled before the occupiers—in an official telegram of the Ministry of the Interior to police chiefs after the occupation authorities ordered the delivery of more than 15,000 foreign Jews following the great raids of July 1942 in Paris. Henri Cado, Bousquet's deputy, who signed the communiqué, specified that there was reason to "mobilize the foreign workers at the various shelters and UGIF centers."[11] The objective was the same as in Paris, to rid France of its "trash" in the words of Laval. Darquier de Pellepoix was of the same mind: he spoke of deportation as a "question of public hygiene."

The chiefs of police were held responsible for checking on the progress of operations. Vichy appears to have anticipated a strong reaction among the Jews, but what was judged more troubling were the "indiscretions" of officials suspected of reticence. In the same harsh tone—as if they anticipated a reluctant police response that might allow evasion—the ministry ordered the police to "proceed . . . to extremely strict checks on the validity of identification papers . . . with a view to entirely freeing [your] region of the Jews whose assembly is in progress." Bousquet and the General Secretariat for Police drew a lesson from the great roundup in Paris, during the course of which almost half the targeted persons evaded the police.[12]

Fearful that it would not be able to fulfill the objectives agreed upon with the Germans, Vichy suspended all foreign emigration as of 18 July, even by those who held exit visas.[13] This measure affected nearly 1,000 teenagers and adults waiting in semi-liberty at the transit centers to leave for the United States. Most of these were directed to the camp at Les Milles (just outside Aix-en-Provence).

In order to avoid the anticipated hostile reaction in public opinion, the Vichy government stepped up its antisemitic propaganda, the principal theme of which became denunciation of the Jews as solely responsible for the black market. Vichy wanted a visceral reaction from the French. Before and during the raids the most prominent figures in the government fed this propaganda.

"Crisscrossing the countryside," Bousquet wrote the police chiefs, "the Israelites [illegally] attempt to replenish their food supplies from farmers . . . creating an intolerable black market [that jeopardizes] the nation's food supplies." He ordered the internment of all "guilty parties." Laval also justified his part in the pursuit of the Jews to the Papal Nuncio using the same argument. The Nuncio reported that Laval had said that he "was in a hurry to be rid of the Jews, since they were responsible for the state in which France found itself."[14]

Laval, like Bousquet, knew very well that it was all lies. Reports that these men received from their secret services painted a dark picture of the state of food supplies, but it is apparent that illegal economic activity was widespread in rural areas and among shopkeepers in the towns and cities. Police reports complained of counterfeit food-ration stamps and of illegal bartering activity among shopkeepers and peasants. "It is the populace as a whole," states one, "which each and every day looks for ways to get around the regulations. . . . There is also good reason to point out the intense trafficking that railway employees are engaged in." Other police reports mention "non-authorized shipments" of cereals and wine, illicit price hikes, underground markets, the discovery of undisclosed stocks, the illegal hoarding of butter and cheese, and the secret slaughter of livestock.

Playing the American Card

After an ill-advised remark by Fourcade, the senior police official responsible for aliens, the Nîmes Committee[15] learned on 30 July that 10,000 foreign Jews were to be deported between 6 and 12 August 1942. The American embassy in Vichy was quickly informed. Did it respond? Nothing indicates that it did. Ambassador Admiral William D. Leahy (whom the Parisian press called the "representative of international Jewish financial interests") had been charged with maintaining good relations with Vichy: Washington wanted to prevent the French fleet and the maritime bases in northern and western Africa from falling into German hands. This was a delicate diplomatic engagement that should not be complicated by too insistent an intervention on behalf of the Jews.[16]

On the other hand, representatives of American humanitarian associations multiplied their lobbying efforts with Pétain, Laval, and their cabinet heads. Tracy Strong, Secretary General of the YMCA, was received by the Marshal and called his attention to the "unfavorable effect the deportations could have on American opinion," an argument, Strong noted, that "left the Marshal indifferent." The Marshal's secretary, Jordell, told Strong on his behalf, "it is unfortunate but we can do nothing," putting an end to the discussion; in the days following 7 August, when the first trains left for Drancy, Strong's requests for meetings were systematically turned down "because of the Marshal's heavy schedule." The time of his aides and associates was no less fully occupied.[17]

It seems justified to ascribe to this "gamble" the detention in France of thousands of persons, some internees some not, who had been waiting for, or who already had, visas to enter the United States. Almost five hundred children who had finally received visas fell victim because they now lacked the French administration's permission to emigrate. The lives of hundreds of other refugees might have been saved if the American Embassy had not, at the request of Vichy, put an end to the activity of the delegate of the Emergency Rescue Committee, Varian M. Fry. This committee, which benefited from the support of Eleanor Roosevelt, had collected a considerable amount of money in order to help German and Austrian intellectuals, artists, and politicians leave France. Fry, who had arrived in France in the summer of 1940, quickly ran into the refusal to cooperate by the Vichy government, which was, after all, responsible for turning his "clients" over to the occupiers. Fry continued his activities, now mainly clandestine, organizing escapes through Spain;[18] Vichy denounced Fry to officials at the American Embassy, who, on orders from Washington, offered no help or protection to Fry, and who even told Fry to return to the United States.[19] He refused, but eventually the French expelled him as an undesirable alien.

"Shades of Melancholy" in the Skies of France

A considerable number of accounts record the pitiless battle Vichy law and order waged against non-naturalized Jews in the "Free Zone" during the month of August 1942. Even if, here and there, some exceptions could be observed in the conduct of police officers who sought to avoid their mission, the situation remained grim. "The separation of Jewish mothers from their children, accompanied by the fact of some suicides," wrote the Italian consul to his government, "has brought new shades of melancholy to the skies of France."[20]

The testimony of the Rev. Henri Manen, pastor of the Protestant parish of Aix-en-Provence, stands out for its exceptional detail and the strength of his protest. Day after day he noted the deportation of families interned at the camp at nearby Les Milles. He is one of those witnesses who strove to make the facts known, facts that "so many people fail to grasp and whose consequences they fail to see." To sound an alarm, the pastor addressed himself to the international Protestant *Counseil oecuménique* in Geneva in September 1942. A rumor had originally alerted him: "They're turning the people at the camp in Les Milles over to the Krauts," he heard people saying in Aix. He rushed to the camp, where large numbers of police officers were already carrying out preparations for deportation in a "heavy and oppressive atmosphere." Could he at least save the Jews who had been baptized as Protestants or Catholics? No, said the chief of the Marseille police, whom he met on 8 August 1942, because in the eyes of the authorities it was a question of an "ethnic regrouping in the interests of France." The pastor then tried to save the children by persuading parents that they ought to accept separation: the expulsion order allowed children under eighteen to be exempted, so if their parents agreed, they were moved out of the camp to private homes and facilities organized by aid groups. Manen's notes for 10 August record "the unforgettable sight" of children departing: "Terrible separations. A tall, good-looking boy of seventeen or eighteen standing between his father and mother, with his arm around her neck. He is not crying. But he bends over the one then over the other, rubbing his face against theirs, slowly and gently, with all the tenderness in the world. Not a word. The father and mother continue to weep silently. . . . Finally the bus rumbles off." Manen noted the remark of an ashen-faced policeman: "I have seen massacres, the war, famine. I have never seen anything as horrible as that."

The pastor tried with next to no success to pull out the Protestant converts, slated to die because their "race" qualified them as enemies of the Third Reich: Goldschmidt, whose father and two brothers had already been shot by the Nazis in Germany; Heinsheimer, the former public prosecutor of a large German city, condemned to death in Germany—and with a son serving in the Foreign Legion. (Manen saved him and his wife at the very last moment from the cattle car they had been forced to enter.)

Hellish days: 10 August, a man and woman slash their wrists; 11 August, two attempted suicides; 12 August, ten suicides. "Distress, humiliation, disgust, indignation, loathing, infinite sadness. Ruin, trampled lives, indelible stains, inexpiable crimes" are the words Henri Manen chose to characterize the experience. For him the Jewish people had "suffered with dignity, with truth, with humility and grandeur."[21]

Since the quantitative goals had not been met and Vichy feared the anger of the Germans—or perhaps quite simply because the Pétain regime wanted to satisfy its own ambitions in the affair—the latter ordered all those previously exempt to be rounded up. This new measure affected a large number of children who had been released to the OSE and other agencies in the course of 1941; now they were interned again. "I [had earlier] left Rivesaltes," remembers Vivette Samuel, then a social worker, "after obtaining the release of the last child. . . . [But then] in August 1942, it was raids on foreigners. And the children who had left the camps, the adults who had been able to leave as workers, all of them were rounded up and brought back again."[22]

Pastor Manen wrote of the terrible night of 1 September:

What was particularly heart-breaking to see was the sight of little children. Strict orders were given at the last minute: children over the age of two were all forced to leave with their parents and the latter had no option to leave them behind with a charitable organization. Very young children stumbled with fatigue in the dark and cold, crying with hunger, clinging pitifully to their parents to be picked up and carried, but their

parents had their arms filled with packages and baggage. Poor little fel-
lows of five and six trying bravely to carry a bundle as big as they were,
then falling with sleepiness and rolling with their bundles on the ground,
all shivering in the night dew as they waited, some groups waiting for
hours. Young parents weeping silently in the face of their impotence to
alleviate the suffering of their children. Then the departure order was
given; they left the square to go to the train. The poor children kept their
place and number in the lines and followed in their parents' steps with
their sagging little legs.

Manen borrowed from the Gospels to express it: "Inasmuch as ye have done
it unto one of the least of these my brethren, ye have done it unto me"
(Matt. 25:40). And like his Lord, the pastor was not content simply to witness and testify. He judged the others and judged himself, for he was well
aware of being in the presence of something unique and monstrous. And
Pastor Manen's engagement did have results: "At certain moments," Manen
wrote, "it is difficult for me to believe that I have arrived directly at the great
bonfire of pain, but this obsession is there, and it does not leave me. How astonishing is it then that those people all around us, despite their efforts to
understand, are not able to penetrate the drama and cannot see its consequences?" He was ultimately able to dispatch a significant number of children and even adults to "Protestant refuges," in particular those in Chambon-
sur-Lignon and its surroundings.

The YMCA aid representative Donald A. Lowrie struggled to understand
the deportations as he witnessed them in the Southern Zone: "An explanation of these deportations is not easy to discover," the American writes in a
memorandum to the YMCA leadership.

> To a certain extent it may be due to Germany's urgent need for work-
> ers. . . . Since children, the aged and ill [however] are taken and since
> their destination is uniformly reported (by Laval, Pétain, the Police) as
> the Jewish reservation in Poland, the need for labor does not totally ex-
> plain this action. In view of the present transport difficulties in Germany
> it is hard to understand a German *desire* to have these unfortunates. . . .
> The best explanation we have been able to imagine is this: the general
> German plan for a new Europe includes "purification" of undesirable
> elements.[23]

The logic of events was there for those with eyes to see.

Rabbi Hirschler in the Field

Rabbi Hirschler, chaplain general for the camps, like most of the chaplains, ventured into the field when Vichy permitted present and former military chaplains access: Since "many of the threatened persons had in fact been warned in time, . . . the result of the raids was . . . meager and they were far from finding the 16,000 Jews they sought. . . . At Agen, of the two hundred persons sought, only two were found. In the Alpes-Maritimes, seven hundred and fifty persons were arrested out of 2,000." The chaplain general confirmed this lack of success when he went to Vichy on 26 August: at the Ministry of the Interior a sympathetic contact told him that the number arrested was only twenty per cent of the goal.

Trains and railway stations came under intensified surveillance. "This situation," reported Rabbi Hirschler, "had a certain number of consequences: the government had wanted the operations to be as discreet as possible. In fact, Henri Cado, Bousquet's deputy, ordered the police chiefs to carry out the raids in the early morning hours, preferably between 4 and 5 a.m. But there could no longer be any question of a secret. The general population had everywhere been witness to the hunt for people. Numerous doors were thrown open to shelter the fugitives."[24]

Between 6 and 24 August, the first phase of the operation, 4,662 internees were deported to Drancy, 1,700 of them from Gurs alone. The government ordered police chiefs to mount new raids. "Extremely urgent to compile complementary lists. Remind you of imperative to take extremely severe police measures to make planned operations effective and preclude all incident." The new operation would affect without exception all the foreign Jews in the Southern Zone who had not yet been arrested.[25]

The Law of Numbers, or "Screening"

In the internment camps in the South as well as at Drancy, social workers were confronted with the moral problem raised by their participation in "screening." The circular letters sent by both French and German authorities foresaw a certain number of exceptions (especially for the sick) when deportation lists were being drawn up. The administrators of the camps, particularly in the Southern Zone, submitted these to representatives of many Jewish and non-Jewish organizations, to the chaplains. But the "law of numbers" imposed by the Nazis and rigorously applied by the French administration required that internees exempted should be replaced by others. "Since the set figure had not been reached, the dissatisfied French authorities had all the internees assemble on the camp square and randomly loaded up a certain number of those who had succeeded in escaping the screening process the day before,"[26] according to one report on Les Milles. "But who are we to be choosing?" asked Helga Holbex, the Quaker representative at Gurs. "It seems," she wrote in a letter to her head office, "that the only thing we can do is to try to retain those whom we judge indispensable and to abandon those whom we expect to die shortly. . . . It's awful."[27]

A similar situation, putting the social workers in a dramatic moral predicament, is reported by the representative of the HICEM, the Jewish-American emigration aid organization, at the Rivesaltes camp. After three days of intense effort to obtain exemptions, "each person who had been spared unfortunately had to be replaced by someone else."[28] Georges Vadnaï, interned at Rivesaltes, never imagined that others would take his place if his name were taken off the list. "I was in the hall for those to be deported, when Abbé Gross of the Swiss Red Cross came in. I went up to him and said, 'Father, I serve God in another house of prayer than you, but I hope that this will not prevent you from lending me a helping hand." And, indeed, the camp commander ordered that he be transferred to the hall for those remaining in reserve. But at three in the morning the "screening commission" made its entry to announce, "Gentlemen! Of the forty persons who are here, thirty-eight will have to be deported. . . . We have to turn seven hundred fifty detainees over to the Germans tonight." Dragged before the commission, Vadnaï escaped the deportation by invoking the fact that he was a Hungarian citizen and thus not subject to deportation. "At 5:30 a.m. they came again to find two more of the 'reservists' in order to complete the convoy of seven hundred fifty. A few moments before the departure, the police brought up two detainees whom they had dug out somewhere."[29]

Elsbeth Kasser, another delegate of the Swiss Red Cross, had her office in the Gurs camp. There she distributed milk, chocolate, and other food that the children missed so much. The deportation day came, 20 August 1942. "The whole camp was in an uproar, the men and women separated. Why? Cries went up on every side. Is my husband one of them? Who is on the list? Help us! Hide us!" Kasser thought that her role was more than ever "to go to people, to reassure them, to act as if it was a day like the others . . . to play with the children, for their mothers were devastated." There are situations that call for decisions, for courageous choices. Elsbeth Kasser would not forget one in particular: "I brought an infant, still nursing, to the hall where the father was. The mother wanted to know: should she take the child with her? Or should she leave it there, turn it over to someone and who was that someone? The child stretched out its little hands toward its father, who cried silently in a corner. . . . And I went back out into the night and took the child back to its mother." Kasser later reflected in sorrow and regret: "I was there. I was there. I saw the last truck start up. . . . I still hear the sound." Of course Kasser wanted "to help, save, hide people, show them a way to escape." But Kasser did not do so. Why? "I was the representative of the Red Cross, it was impossible, I had no right to do anything at all that was illegal." But then this question: "Did I not have the right to lie to save human lives?"[30]

The Perverse Effects of Social Action

The deportations from the Southern Zone, where Jewish benevolent associations enjoyed legal status provided that they limited themselves to humanitarian activity, brought to light the failure in such circumstances of action of a strictly social-welfare nature. Joseph Weill, director of the OSE, experienced the same distress as Elsbeth Kasser at the same scenes of deportation. A man of action, he was not long in drawing lessons: "An act of mutual assistance," he avers, "is not truly social unless it is constructive in all the circumstances in which it is deployed. . . . There can be no void around social action; its justification is born of an insufficiency or of a social injustice. . . . It was necessary to help the internees live, but what was even more necessary was to free them."[31]

The same sentiment is shared by Abbé Glasberg, who went from camp to camp to relieve the misery of the interned of all nationalities. "In his eyes," says Grynberg, "to participate solely in the improvement of the material conditions of the internees was tantamount to explicitly accepting the camp system."[32] This attitude was consonant with an analysis made a year earlier for the Commission centrale des oeuvres juives d'assistance (CCOJA—Central Commission of Jewish Relief Work), which stated: "Today we cannot hide from the fact that the reason for the misfortunes of French Jewry in 1941 is essentially [political] and that these misfortunes were willed by the very persons who asked us to assume responsibility for the consequences of their action. It follows that to separate the politics of French Jewry from its social action, by who knows what legalist scruple, is the equivalent of suicide. . . . Action must be mounted at one and the same time *on the political level and on the social level, which today are conjoined.*"[33] The fatal effects of this apolitical and legalistic conduct soon moved other agency officials to follow Joseph Weill's example by distancing themselves gradually from the UGIF and moving in the direction of illegal activity.

Laval Washes His Hands

As a month earlier in the Occupied Zone, police reports dealing with the raids of August 1942 cite the unfavorable impression created by the arrest of innocent Jews in the "Free Zone": "The Jews are not particularly well liked, but the populace looks upon these arrests as inhumane and takes all the more pity on the lot of these foreigners because it views the deportations as of German inspiration."[34] In his memorandum, Lowrie calls early attention to one other source of misgiving: the fear of numerous officials that when the day came to settle scores they might be held responsible for the camps and the deportations.

What did those in high office think of French participation? One internal memo—probably attributable to a staff member close to Laval—identified the Germans as the principal factor: "In the Occupied Zone, we have seen an increase in German pressure over the last several months with a view to pushing the French government toward a more brutal antisemitic policy. . . . President Pierre Laval agreed to turn over the Jews in the Occupied Zone, but he limited this agreement to recently arrived stateless persons." Why did the French police assume responsibility for carrying out the raids? "According to one apologist, it was the French government that [got the Germans to confide] the operation . . . to the French police so that it might be executed with greater attention." Thus, according to this version, a large number of potential victims were able to escape because some of the police "warned the Jews." Even more hypocritical is the totally false claim that the government got the Germans' assurance that the measures would be extended "neither to children nor to the elderly." And what about the raids in the Free Zone, where German supervision was even less direct? "Unfortunately, this cutting of losses [in the Occupied Zone] was not sufficient. . . . A new concession was made to [the occupation authorities]. Another 10,000 to 13,000 Jews had to be turned over. But this measure affected only stateless persons."[35]

Throughout the whole month of August, city police, rural gendarmes, and the special forces of the General Commissariat for Jewish Questions were on high alert throughout the Southern Zone. This was an exceptional mobilization, as if law and order had no other goal. In the Occupied Zone, the French police were "formally" obliged to execute orders of the Occupation authorities. But there was no such obligation in the Free Zone. It is true that during negotiations in Paris in June and July 1942, when decisions were taken for both the 16–17 July raids and the August raids in the Free Zone with the goal of delivering 10,000 Jews to Drancy, Bousquet seemed to hesitate at the demands of Knochen and Dannecker. In retrospect, however, it would appear that the head of French police wished to give an autonomous character to the repressive measures, hoping that the anti-Jewish action would be more readily accepted by public opinion, quite hostile to everything done on the orders of the occupiers.

The "delivery" of Jews of foreign nationality to the occupiers was consonant with the spirit of the "National Revolution." But a closer scrutiny of the nature of the operation and the manner in which it was carried out clearly shows that French authorities took an extra step in the physical persecution of the Jews in the spirit of Nazi policy. Beyond their obvious ideological commitment to racist theory, one cannot but note the immoral and inhumane way in which the Vichy authorities carried out the actions. The official instructions urged the use of force to "break resistance." And so it was used. Even more telling is the use of cattle cars for the transportation of human beings. The Rev. Boegner of the Reformed (Calvinist) Church of France, who had helped the persecuted from 1941 on, wrote to Pétain himself, but without any known response: "Loaded into freight cars with no concern for hygiene, the foreigners . . . were treated like cattle." As Rabbi Israël Salzer, present in the camp at Les Milles put it, "through the openings at the top of the wagons you could see, as the train rolled by, the heads of men and women sticking up just like the heads of cattle."[36]

File under "Vichy, Responsibility of"

It was not on the orders of the Germans but following their example that Vichy treated the Jews as it did, with the intention of getting rid of them. By reducing them to the status of animals, Pétain, Laval, and Bousquet demonstrated their scorn for the lives of their fellow man. In the otherwise detailed instructions dealing with the roundup and transportation to Drancy, one notes hardly any plan for feeding the deported. On the other hand, each camp director was to provide "the quantities of straw necessary for the cars."[37]

The Jews—"refuse, trash." This is the essential characteristic of the "Auschwitz phenomenon" in the judgment of Professor Ady Steg: "Auschwitz is [still] new, in terms of the 'philosophy' of the project . . . treating people not as human beings but as *things*, refuse, trash."[38] Laval and Pétain were already thinking and acting on the logic of Auschwitz. Primo Levi, who experienced the "crime against humanity" in his soul and in his flesh, also believes that the crime began long before the first killings, in the "mass of detail . . . all aimed at establishing that the Jews, Gypsies, and Slavs were only cattle, filth, dung." And he lists among all the other details, the "trip in cattle cars that were never opened, forcing the deportees (men, women, and children) to remain for days in the midst of their own excrement" and also "the fact that no spoons were handed out."[39] We recall that during the first days those detained at the Vélodrome d'Hiver had neither bowls nor eating utensils.

Under the leadership of Pétain, France became the first country in Europe to incarcerate children behind barbed wire. From there to defining them as enemies, to forgetting that they were only children, and to turning them over to a foreign power determined to destroy them, was only a single step. In the file on Vichy responsibility, this is without doubt the most serious crime.

Did Vichy know of the final destination of their victms? The archives of the Pétain regime do not seem to contain documents employing the term "Final Solution." The author's recent research, however, has revealed in the personal archives of the Marshal some reports and notes that mention the massacre of Jews in Romania and Poland.[40] It is not impossible that one day a good deal more will be found. For example, information form the International Committee of the Red Cross leaves no doubt about the existence of the death camps.[41]

In the Marshal's office experts analyzed the newspapers and underground tracts of the MNCR and Jewish Section within the MOI. They filed them so carefully that, recently uncovered, they remain in good condition. Perhaps little credence was given them at the time, but bureaucrats checked up on the information published therein. During a visit to Vichy, Robert Kiefe, secretary general of the Central Consistory, learned that some of those he met there wanted to know more about the "massacres" that had been perpetrated in the Polish camps. For example, Jean Jardin, head of Laval's cabinet, asked him "to provide details on the massacre of 11,000 Jews in Poland by means of toxic gas."[42]

A comparison with policies carried out against the Jews in Mussolini's Italy does not reflect credit on Vichy France. Il Duce, initially rather irritated by the laxity of his administration, closed his eyes to the same liberalism after learning of the killings in Poland. He and his inner circle were already, by August 1942, aware of the mass murder of the Jews in the East. This cannot have failed to recommend to Mussolini a tolerant attitude toward pro-Jewish activities, in particular those of his minister of foreign affairs.[43] One wonders how the American Donald Lowrie, who was, however, less well informed than the men in power, could have realized simply from the sight of deportation in the South that these people were being taken to their death.

The argument that any of them "did not know" cannot serve as excuse for the men in power, disposing as they did of embassies in foreign countries, radio monitoring services, and so on, unless we are to consider them simpletons. It would have been enough to want to know, as the public prosecutor Pierre Truche said with reference to Klaus Barbie: "Can he say that he did not know the fate reserved for those he was deporting, when Radio London was already exposing the camps, and when the underground resistance press was also calling attention to them?"

The historian might well ask what happened to the daily bulletins from the radio monitoring centers of the intelligence services. In the French National Archives twenty-six boxes hold recordings of broadcasts from Great Britain, the Soviet Union, Germany (!), occupied France (!), Italy, Switzerland, and other countries. Considering that news in the underground Jewish papers and those of the MNCR about the death camps, the gas chambers, and the killings of millions had no other primary source than the BBC or Radio Moscow (picked up with the poorest of technical means), one may assume that a large number of senior officials—and why not Pétain and Laval?—found on their desks intelligence bulletins with news on the fate of the Jews. These bulletins constitute both politically and juridically irrefutable material evidence.

If such had not been the case, Laval would never have asked Higher SS- and Police Leader General Oberg in September 1942 to establish "a protocol for commentary on the deportation of Jews" in order to avoid differences of vocabulary and flagrant contradictions between Vichy's explanations and those of the Occupation authorities. It was agreed that henceforth both parties would say that the "Jews in the non-occupied territories who were turned over to the Occupation authorities are transferred to the interior of the 'General government'—the non-annexed portion of Poland—to be engaged in labor." A *language convention*—is the term they invented to describe the agreement and hide the truth.[44]

But perhaps one should consider the point from which one views the operations against the Jews in the two zones during July and August 1942: Is this point modified by current knowledge of the genocide? Even without the gas chambers, the anti-Jewish persecution by Vichy bears all the marks of an absolute crime from the moment it was adopted. The victims of the raids in Paris and the Southern Zone were delivered up to a state that demonstrated toward the Jews a hatred more ferocious than the antisemitism "à la française" that was supported by the authority of Vichy.

By no later than spring 1942, as Denis Peschanski rightly stresses, Vichy had become a partner in the "Final Solution." During the months of July and August alone the Pétain-Laval governments turned over to the occupying authorities almost 25,000 Jews who had been under their direct administration of the camps in both zones. This figure represents 33 percent of the total of Jewish deportees from France during the occupation.

In handing the Jews over to the Occupation forces, were Pétain and Laval aware that they were surrendering France itself? SS-Führer Dr. Werner Best elaborated another aspect of anti-Jewish policy at a meeting of high-ranking officials in Berlin on 27 July 1942: its function in the Third Reich's strategy for the domination of Europe. "The Jewish Question," he said, "is the dynamite with which we shall blow up the entrenchments where the last liberal irregulars are still barricaded. The peoples who turn over their Jews surrender with them their way of life determined by the false, Jewified ideal of liberty. . . . It is only then that they can be enlisted in the struggle for a new world." *Fraternité*, the organ of the MNCR in the Southern Zone, which republished this statement from the Swiss weekly *Die Weltwoche*, put it differently in their commentary: "The attitude of different nations toward the Jewish Question is viewed by the Germans as the touchstone for their capacity to resist the ideology of the conqueror."[45]

Bishops' Crosses Are Raised

The human hunt in the Southern Zone was still in progress when prelates of the Catholic Church raised public protests. The first voice was that of Monseigneur Jules-Géraud Saliège, Archbishop of Toulouse, followed by that of Pierre-Marie Théas, bishop of Montauban. Then came the declaration of the primate of the Gauls, Cardinal Gerlier, head of the Catholic Church in France, whom Pétain considered a principal pillar of the "National Revolution."

Saliège came closest to acknowledgment of the humanist tradition of France in a pastoral letter of 23 August 1942: "The Jews are men, the Jewesses are women. Not everything can be permitted against them, . . . they are part of the human race. . . . France, my beloved country, I do not believe that you are responsible for these horrors."[46]

In the same spirit shortly thereafter Théas issued a pastoral letter grounding his protest in both Old and New Testaments: "Painful, at times horrible, scenes are being acted out in France without France accepting the responsibility. I voice the outraged protest of Christian conscience and I proclaim that all Aryan or non-Aryan men are brothers because they are created by the same God. . . . The present antisemitic measures scorn human dignity. They are a violation of the most sacred rights of the individual and of the family."[47]

Finally, on 6 September Cardinal Gerlier made the protest the official position of the entire French hierarchy: "The implementation of the deportation measures currently being carried out against the Jews gives rise to scenes so sorrowful . . . that we have the imperative and painful duty of [speaking] our conscience. . . . One's heart is anguished at the thought of the treatment to which thousands of human beings have been subjected and even more by thinking of what may follow."

And yet even this declaration concludes with a reaffirmation of loyalty. "We are not forgetful that for French authorities there is a problem to be resolved and [appreciate] the difficulties that the government must face. . . . [But the New Order] can only be built, and with it peace, in the productive union of minds and hearts to which the great voice of the Marshal calls us." Though this was the most authoritative so far, one must nevertheless note that Gerlier's declaration was considerably more ambivalent than the pastoral letters of Théas and Saliège.

The Secret Letter from de Gaulle to Saliège

At the end of May 1942 Charles de Gaulle sent a top secret letter by courier to Monseigneur Saliège in Toulouse concerning the stance taken "by a portion of the episcopate with regard to the policies of the men of Vichy." De Gaulle would have "the Church dissociate itself from the Vichy regime, which [promotes the impression of] solidarity between the preferences of the clergy and the undertakings of people who have proclaimed, accepted, and aggravated the defeat of France."[48] De Gaulle's words reveal a sizable strategic objective: to deprive Pétain of one of his principal supports and perhaps one day to swing the church over to the Resistance. But why did General de Gaulle approach the archbishop? "There are reasons to believe," he wrote, "that Your Grace has understood what I am taking the liberty of expressing to him, and thus that some agreement may be reached between us." Monseigneur Saliège in the Resistance? Not in the strict sense, but the Resistance in Toulouse had had dealings with the archbishopric and other Catholic institutions in Toulouse, and even received gestures of solidarity. Monseigneur Saliège was the only dignitary of the Church later named by de Gaulle to the Ordre des compagnons de la Libération (Order of the French Resistance Fighters), the highest distinction for resistance activity. It had been, then, no mere one-time formality that on 23 August 1942 the archbishop of Toulouse was the first French prelate to voice the Christian conscience over the deportations.[49]

Théas, the bishop of Montauban, sent his pastoral letter to Police Chief François Martin (a Protestant), to notify him that it would be read in church the following Sunday. He was soon summoned to the police station, and told not to read it. "All that I can do" he told Martin, "is promise that it will not be read in your presence at the mass for the Legion." Martin then asked Théas to "give more thought to this matter." The latter had the pastoral letter read anyway. After the following Mass for Legion members, Théas admitted to the police chief that the letter had been read in all the churches of the diocese that morning, to which the police chief reportedly replied, "Your Grace, in my office I spoke to you as the Chief of Police; today, in your church, I speak as a Christian: I approve of your action and commend you for it."[50]

Despite such words of encouragement from unexpected quarters, it nonetheless remains the case that of the ninety-five bishops and archbishops in France, only five or six denounced the offence to human and Christian conscience from their pulpits during that dark month of August 1942.[51] In Resistance circles the pastoral letters (hailed, admittedly, as a turning point) did not escape criticism. Their effectiveness would be limited by the fact that they encouraged no political stand against the National Revolution or Pétain's lieutenants. And in any case a majority of the episcopate continued to support Pétain. It is in these terms that François and Renée Bédarida, historians and Catholic former members of the Resistance, later spoke of "the responsibility assumed by the hierarchy in plunging . . . into the Vichy adventure, committing body and soul at the risk of [becoming] gears in the system. . . . Events [later vindicated] the Catholic resisters, whom [the prelates] had earlier called 'dissidents' and at times even 'terrorists.'"[52]

In London those in the know saw as the "raising of the Episcopal crosses" the public stance that the bishops of Toulouse, Montauban, and Lyon adopted: "The attitude of the Church will henceforth facilitate in an invaluable way . . . the task of numerous Catholics who already find themselves in opposition to the regime and its general policies. . . . It exerts an immediate influence on those Catholics who, while repudiating collaboration with Germany, remain attached to the Marshal. . . . Even if disaffection in Catholic circles is far from general or complete, the spell has definitively been broken."[53]

Naturally the police closely followed these quite visible changes in the conduct of the Catholic Church with regard to the persecution of the Jews. The police official in charge of Jewish matters in Toulouse seems to have been quite well informed of responses to the pastoral letters and forwarded copies to Vichy. The municipal police, he noted, had not been able to prevent their open reading, he wrote, and later, despite official injunctions, they were circulated from hand to hand to avoid interception by postal workers. "Copies of these letters [he went on] have been duplicated by Jewish groups (Judeo-communists and Judeo-Freemasons) and have been sent to numerous persons in the various administrations who are known for their Christian sentiments, as well as to numerous Jews, in order that under the authority of the Church they could spread their propaganda to the French populace, always sensitive to the way in which the Church judges matters."[54] Françoise d'Eaubonne, a young poet, may have typified people "known for their Christian sentiments." Having received a copy of Saliège's text through her father, who was a personal friend of the archibishop, but having no mechanical means of copying at her disposal, she had to reproduce by hand the great number of copies she distributed.[55]

The Children of Vénissieux

In Vénissieux, on the outskirts of Lyon, a camp housed more than one thousand persons, mostly families from the departments of Rhône, Isère, and Ain. Their "referral" to Drancy, scheduled for the end of August, was preceded by a "screening" in which representatives of the OSE were authorized to participate. One of the OSE's representatives, Charles Lederman,[56] learned from one of the social workers of the possibility of getting the younger children out. Lederman alerted Abbé Glasberg, who in turn informed the Jesuit priest Father Chaillet. Together they decided to save those children whose parents would consent to be separated from them. Recounting this story we must introduce a man named Georges Garel, one of the eventual creators of the underground OSE.

Garel undertook to accompany his brother-in-law, Lederman, to Vénissieux; eighty-three youngsters under the age of sixteen would benefit from his exploitation of the dispensation for children foreseen in the screening rules. Officially remanded to the Amitié chrétienne, the children left camp in late August, accompanied by Lederman, Garel, and other social workers. They spent the night at a Catholic residence in Fourvières and were placed the next day in the Notre-Dame-de-Sion monastery or with individual families. When Police Chief Alexandre Angeli, following Bousquet's orders, demanded that Cardinal Gerlier have the children returned to Vénissieux, the latter (partly in order to protect Father Chaillet) invoked the "urgent moral obligation" to protect the foreign Jews, stressing however that "his attitude was not directed against the French government but against the German government."[57] The case of the children of Vénissieux soon took on the proportions of an affair of state. Testifying to this is the tone of the note that Bousquet's deputy Cato addressed to his superior. "The business of the Jewish children of Lyon is becoming more complicated. Following a decision made by *you* yesterday afternoon, Angeli notified the Jesuit Father Chaillet . . . that a reprieve was granted for the departure of eighty-three children [to Drancy]. . . . Since I assume that this position taken by Cardinal Gerlier, in sharp opposition to government orders, will be without delay brought to the attention of the Marshal, I believe you should be immediately informed so that *you* can get the attention of President Laval."[58]

Sensitive to reactions in public opinion, the National Police noted in a report on "anti-national propaganda," and on the Vénissieux Affair in particular, the dissemination of a tract entitled "You Will Not Get the Children!" For its part, the police denounced the "rumor" that Jewish children had been separated from their mothers and that Jews had been sent away in cattle cars.[59]

Gerlier received a hostile reaction from the Catholic right. A tract accusing him of the gravest of Christian sins, "pride," and of collusion with Britain, was distributed in broad daylight to Catholics in his diocese. "People of Lyon," the tract read "here is your master. Thirsting for glory and drunk on pride, this archbishop . . . has signed a pact with England that has promised him the pontifical crown in the event of a Judeo-Anglo-Saxon victory. . . . He has forced the priests to defend the Jews [and] fulminates against the measures taken against some Jewish aliens." The same text takes aim at Abbé Glasberg, "the Jewish convert [and] confidant of the Cardinal in the administration of the Catholic agencies of Lyon."[60]

This evolution of the Church's attitude prompted André Lavagne of the Marshal's civil cabinet to draw up a note on 19 May 1943 addressing senior officials of the government concerning "rules to be followed in matters of religious policy." Excerpts reveal the irritation felt by the Marshal's followers, perhaps even the Marshal himself, at the "adamant democratism" of the Church:

> The Church is a power with which the State must negotiate diplomatically on a footing of equality. The borderline between the spiritual and the temporal has not been clearly delineated. . . . The Church does not permit, on any account, the intrusion of temporal power into its domain. . . . It is less intransigent when it comes to its incursion into the temporal domain.
>
> The Church has a tendency to favor certain sentimentality over reason. . . . On occasion, its leaders are too responsive to political opinion and with unbecoming naïveté seek to flatter it or follow it rather than direct it. Representatives of the State must know how to refuse, and not let their lucid resolve be weakened.[61]

In reality, the lesser clergy, socially minded Catholics, and in general the mass of the faithful did not wait for authorization to express their distaste for the anti-Jewish policy of the occupiers and Vichy. A "Christian Resistance" had been born in 1941 partly as a rejection of antisemitism and racism. The first issue of their organ, *Témoignage chrétien*,[62] carried the headline, "Men and Women of France, Take Care Not to Lose Your Soul." Of this periodical the historian Léon Poliakov has written, "*Les Cahiers du Témoignage chrétien* clandestinely continued the tradition of [the humanitarian poet and philosopher] Charles Péguy, opposing the racist contagion; it surely belongs among the finest pages of the French Resistance."[63]

Was Christian resistance a defense of the Jews? Without a doubt. But it was just as much a defense of Christian morality, of a Christianity threatened by the neo-paganism of National-Socialist racism. This opposition, evident as early as the 1930s, evolved in the direction of resistance to Pétain as well as an internal force exerting pressure on the Church hierarchy. An underground text, "Mémoire de la résistance catholique," reproaches Church leaders for "making the Christian pulpit resound with praise for . . . a government almost unanimously detested."[64] In the Catholic Resistance we witness the condemnation of the traditional dogma of the Jews as deicides; the

Jewish ancestry of Jesus became for them a theme on which to found the Church's reorientation.

This rupture with the past heralded a dialogue even before widespread awareness of the scale of the genocide: Over the course of almost seventeen centuries the Church had been responsible for, if not initiator of, antisemitic expulsions, pogroms, and massacres; now the Roman Catholic Church was finally to return to the spirit of its first message: the new Catholics drew the obvious parallel between the martyrdom of the first Christians and that of Israel, a parallel evoked with the greatest compassion by such leading Catholic intellectuals as Paul Claudel, Jacques Maritain, and Georges Bernanos, as well as in the publications of the Catholic Resistance. It was perhaps a historically debatable juxtaposition, but it overwhelmed the conscience of numerous Christians and dictated to them grand acts of solidarity.

CHAPTER EIGHT

Drancy

The Last Circle before Hell

Why [have we] received no letters from the deported? Why do
we not know where they are?

J'accuse (2 October 1942)

"Drancy, the Parisian Dachau": so the camp was named in an underground
newspaper of September 1941, shortly after it was first opened.[1] The Dachau
concentration camp, established in 1933 several kilometers from Munich, the
birthplace of National Socialism, was the symbol of the horror during the period of the Third Reich. The imagination could not stretch any further. And
Drancy was the last stop before leaving France; nearly all the deported —
73,850 of them — passed through the camp.

The history of the camp can be divided into two periods, one extending
from its opening on 20 August 1941 until the first deportations on 27 March
1942; and the second lasting until the day of its liquidation, 20 August 1944.
On the day of the first deportation for an "unknown destination," the camp
underwent a change in character, no longer a place where one might bravely
endure while awaiting liberation (one was, after all, still in France). Now the
threat of deportation made people imagine themselves elsewhere, in a foreign

and still more menacing world. The second period included a date that overwhelmed the morale of camp life. At the beginning of July 1943, SS officer Aloïs Brunner made his appearance there. Brunner initiated a new set of procedures whose thrust was to classify internees into several categories of "deportables" and "non-deportables." Principally among the latter he recruited people to help in the administration of the camp, with the clear intention of making them complicit.

With the exception of this group, which numbered more than one hundred persons, internees stayed at the camp for only a few days or weeks; many had scarcely arrived before re-boarding. Others stayed for months, even longer in the case of certain privileged groups.[2] Contradictory experiences distinguish memories that differ greatly as to the degree of physical and mental suffering endured. For those who survived the death camps by dint of living for what then seemed interminable months at Drancy, what they suffered there later faded into the background. A few never experienced the horrors of deportation because they were freed or escaped directly from Drancy.

Such was the case of Szymon Fuchs, who benefited from the more liberal atmosphere that reigned during Drancy's early phase. Taken in the raid on the Eleventh Arrondissement on 20 August 1941, Fuchs was among the first Parisians to see this prison near the City of Light. He remained at Drancy a relatively short time—just under four months—and what he remembers above all is the brutality of the French police, with the exception of a few, among them Camille Mathieu, to whom he owes his freedom and his life. "The weaker we got on six ounces of bread a day and soup with no trace of vegetables, the more some of the gendarmes tormented us. . . . [When] we fell from exhaustion . . . blows with their rifle butts 'helped' us to get back on our feet."[3]

Their wives (not interned until 16 July 1942) roamed the periphery of the camp throughout the day. Some policemen accepted bribes to pass letters or small packages to the prisoners. This is how Madame Fuchs got to know the policeman Camille Mathieu, who was prepared to help her husband escape. Interestingly, the escape took place through the main gate. An epidemic and a certain number of deaths prodded the préfecture to free about one hundred internees whose health was a cause for concern. Mathieu put Fuchs' name, and those of Simon Herzberg and Alter Ajdenbaum, on the list of forty the police released between 5 and 12 November 1941 due to their grave illnesses caused by hunger and the almost total lack of sanitary facilities in the camp. Solidarité (MOI) described these scandalous conditions in an appeal to aid the Drancy internees: "Everyone lost weight, some up to 15 kilos. . . . Their only nourishment: a small cup of clear soup, a bit of bread. . . . Such is the regime installed by the French administration on the orders of the German occupation authorities."[4]

Mathieu indeed arranged for the couple to hide at his mother's in Lignières, a village of 300 inhabitants in the department of Aube. Supplied with false papers (which of course did not fool the villagers in such a small town), the Fuchs remained there without incident until Liberation. In the summers Fuchs worked in the fields, and during the winters he altered clothes. In 1979 Camille Mathieu and his mother, Blanche, were inducted into the "Righteous Among the Nations" in a ceremony at the Yad Vashem in Jerusalem.

Had the French police received orders to treat the internees brutally? Mathieu didn't recall any. "It depended on the character of the men involved, whether they were vicious or not," he said.

> We viewed the Jews who were brought to Drancy as people who were being sent to work in Germany, which didn't seem too serious to us. The most important thing was our hostility toward the Germans. They took everything from us. . . . Szymon Fuchs inspired confidence in me to the point that I asked my mother to shelter him and his wife. My uncle, a man who was more lily-livered than antisemitic, said to my mother one day: "They are Jews and we run the risk of paying dearly for it." I said then to my uncle, "You'll be sorry if anything happens to them. You'll have me to deal with." And to my mother, "If you turn them out, you'll never see me again." This was a needless warning, as she would never let herself be intimidated by her brother.

With regard to the ceremony in Jerusalem, Mathieu says, "I always experience emotion, it grabs me by the throat. It was a great honor which I had never given a thought to, nor did my mother. It was far from Drancy."[5] All the more remarkable were policemen such as this, for most others obediently carried out their orders, not a few of them zealously.

The Lawyers Take Charge

Yves Jouffa was a law school graduate who ended up in Drancy among a group of some fifty lawyers from the Paris Bar arrested on 21 August 1941, and one hundred fifty other intellectuals who had been brought from Compiègne.[6] Jouffa recalls that the lawyers soon occupied high-level posts in the camp administrative services, in what they referred to as a sort of "take over of power." Jouffa himself worked in the office in charge of "putting together the files of internees who had Aryan spouses." Whatever privileges the lawyers may have enjoyed, however, Vichy did not let them forget who they were. Jouffa recalls the visit of the president of the Paris Bar, Charpentier, who came to announce that the lawyers had been disbarred under the Second Statute on the Jews. "Men were weeping. In the barracks we talked for a long time about the visit. . . . The disbarment, because it was a French initiative, seemed more serious to us than internment, which had been imposed by the victors. This time, it was the Fatherland and their own colleagues who had abandoned them."

Did the lawyers abuse their "power"? It would seem that at first in Compiègne and then in Drancy, some of the jurists maintained a kind of "court of honor" as a check on the morality of detainees whose behavior might endanger their fellow-sufferers. Unfortunately, the documents dealing with this "tribunal" have disappeared from the archives of the CDJC, perhaps carried off by an unscrupulous "researcher" who had reason to want them to disappear.[7] The establishment of this court was not necessarily a power-seeking attempt on the part of the jurists, but there were ideological differences, which meant that not all prisoners recognized the authority of the tribunals. Although all were Jews, the Drancy internees were never able to create from within their community a supervisory body they could all recognize. Perhaps on this point, the "men of the law" committed an error of judgment.

"News" from Drancy

What documentary value do letters written from Drancy have? There can be no question of the sincerity of the writers; nonetheless, cards and letters passed through a double screening: censorship and self-censorship. What counted most for the detainee was that the letter not be blocked. The first precaution was never to complain. Then came the desire not to upset loved ones on the outside: "I'm in pretty good spirits" was the most common message that they sent home. Yet administrative and psychological filters did not sanitize letters completely, and they still offer a glimpse into the drama into which the interned had been thrust.

Thus the letter of Thomas Wajcman to his son Maurice on the occasion of the latter's bar mitzvah, a ceremony his father could not attend. Although not religious, Wajcman was troubled at missing this important moment in his son's life.

> You are going to be thirteen. This will be an anniversary that you will remember often, your whole life long in fact. You will stop being a child. . . . Despite the passage of more than thirty years I well remember my own event . . . I think with deep emotion that your memory of being thirteen will be always connected with my being in Drancy. . . . I would like to give you some advice on this occasion . . . what my father told me on the same occasion and that he repeated to me the last time we embraced. As long as I lived in his house he asked me never to forget who I am and never to hide my origins, to proudly bear my name. . . . Those who conceal their origins abdicate their freedoms and consider themselves inferior to other men. We, for whom the supreme principle is the rights of man, of all human beings, without distinction of race, religion, or color, we must always take pride in our freedom and in our right to life.[8]

And so, clearly fearful of his own impending disappearance, this inmate of Drancy managed to pass on his wish that his son resist the obliteration of Jewish identity.

A Life That Was Vanishing

Louise Jacobson, a high school student of seventeen, was arrested on 31 August 1942 by the Special Brigade of the Paris police. During a search of her residence, itself prompted by a denunciation,[9] the police found Jacobson was not wearing the yellow star.

Incarcerated in the Fresnes prison, where she was to be tried for violating the law on the yellow star, Louise killed time by writing to her classmates, her father, her sister Nadia, her brother Charles, and her mother, who had been arrested at the same time as her. The tribunal freed her, but she was soon arrested anyway and quietly sent to Drancy, where she remained from 13 October 1942 to 13 February 1943. Her letters offer a window into her inner life, her hope and despair, and her struggle to retain the memory of her previous existence, as that world vanished into the inhuman universe of the camp, a place where she nonetheless found new friends among the other interned students.[10]

Monday 8 September 1942: "At the moment I am imprisoned at Fresnes with the minors. There are about thirty of us and I have two nice friends. Mama is in the Petite Roquette [women's prison in Paris] and was arrested the same day as I was. . . . I hope that I don't need to assure you of our innocence. We were denounced. My dear Nadia, I am beginning to lose confidence in the goodness of the human race."

Thursday 8 October 1942 to her friend Monique: "To think, my dear, that I might soon be free! I'm afraid that I might not know how to cross the streets any more. But how foolish I'm being. I know very well that I would more quickly become accustomed to freedom than I ever would to imprisonment."

Sunday 11 October: "I have been released, my dears. I am perhaps announcing this a bit abruptly. Perhaps I won't get out today, I don't know. . . . It is six weeks today that I lost my freedom and now I finally regain it. We shouldn't be too overjoyed; I run a risk of losing it again, and soon. . . ."

Tuesday 13 October: "As I guessed. I'm headed for Drancy."

Drancy, 12 February: "Sad news, dear Papa. After Auntie, it's now my turn to leave. . . . My mood is good, like everyone else's. You shouldn't be too upset, Papa. . . . I was very well fed this week. As for Mama, it's perhaps better that she not know anything. . . . It's tomorrow morning that we are supposed to leave. I am with my friends. . . . I left my watch and the rest of my things with some people in my cell I could trust."

A Bundle of Yellowed Letters

A bundle of yellowed letters, some photos, children's drawings, a collection of opened envelopes with stamps bearing the likeness of Marshal Pétain, all dated 1943. These are the last records of one of the families wiped out by Vichy. Among the papers, a Star of David and the red armband of the FFI: two emblems, two destinies. The armband was the one that Denise Baumann, the only scion to survive, wore at the liberation of Lyon; the star, doubtlessly, belonged to a less fortunate member of the family.[11]

Forty years later Denise Baumann felt the distance sufficiently great for her to bear witness by publishing the letters of her father, mother, sister, and brother-in-law, most of them written from Drancy. These letters indicate something of the attitude of Jews from Alsace and Lorraine (the oldest French Jewish community), many of whom participated in the administrative routine of Drancy and some of whom seem to have underestimated, even at the end, the fact that they were no longer regarded as citizens by Pétain's France. Some of the latter saw their superior position in the camp as a natural privilege. In the Southern Zone, to which she had gone as a refugee, Denise learned of the arrest of her husband, their three children, and her sister in January 1943. "I wonder," she wrote to her father, who was still at liberty, "whether our dear ones know the dangers they face."

The failure to fully appreciate the nature of the drama in which he and his family were embroiled is what characterizes the conduct of Baumann's brother-in-law, Albert Weill, already at Drancy with his wife and their three daughters, the youngest only eight months old. The Weill family maintained as its sole community contact the UGIF representative in Nancy, Gustave Nordon, a Jew of old Alsatian stock who was quite puffed up with his office. How did they explain the misfortune that had struck them? Simone Weill, Denise Baumann's sister, writes to her parents on 21 January 1943, from the camp at Écrouves:[12] "We are charged with failing to observe the eighth regulation concerning shopping hours. . . . In that case, if it were true, why not make me alone bear the penalty instead of dragging the whole family through the filth?" The phase "through the filth" referred to internment with "people accused of trafficking on the black market, even thieves and foreigners." And scorn for the foreign Jews? Perhaps. In any case, the Weills tried to convince themselves that what was being done to foreign Jews shouldn't be done to them. They drew comfort from the fact that priority on the deportation trains was reserved for foreigners: the Fascists' technique of splitting their potential opposition achieved the desired effect here. Albert Weill's words in a letter of 5 January 1943 illustrate the point: "People are talking about leaving. *We don't think we'll be among that number, as long as there are foreigners here.*"[13] While waiting, Albert Weill permitted himself to be drawn into a post his sister-in-law qualified as "dishonourable," on the "Assignment Bureau" created by Aloïs Brunner.[14] This bureau was charged with locating in Paris the families of internees and persuading them to "voluntarily" enter the camps—under threat of deporting those already there: "Errands in the city," Albert wrote his sister Denise of this work, "where I have been for the last few days on special assignment. We leave in the morning, come back in the evening, classified as camp workers."

From 15 December 1943, Simone's last letter to Denise: "We are without doubt going to join Papa and Mama, I hope that we will be in the same camp. They are supposed to be in a new camp, near Dresden. . . . We are leaving with courage, for it's not for very long, and with a great group of people: forty camp workers, almost all from the Vosges area or people from eastern France."

Simone and Denise's parents, Léon and Renée Baumann, had been arrested on 23 October 1943 in la Ferté-sous-Jouarre, where they had taken refuge after a six-month "reprieve." In fact, the Germans had originally arrested the few Jewish families in the area on 30 March; for inexplicable reasons, they released them all on their "word of honor" that they would stay at home. The scene of the October roundup drew a crowd of more than fifty villagers, the women weeping openly. One can ask why the Jews had stayed after the March scare: more than one farmer in the departments of Marne and Seine-et-Marne had been ready to offer them shelter. "Respect for the law of the land, confidence in its government, belief in the word given by [their] future executioners"—this is how Denise Baumann explained the conduct of her family, who remained deaf to all warnings.

How naïve seems the incredible letter about his own actions that Gustave Nordon, a distinguished resident of Nancy, wrote on his arrival at the Écrouves camp as late as 5 March 1944: "Last Tuesday we were having Raymonde and Colette Picart from Malleloy to lunch and in the afternoon they up and told us while we were calmly eating that their family was being arrested." The Picart women preferred to remain with their family "rather than risk going off some place" (i.e., fleeing). Nordon did not try to talk them out of it, but rather went with them to the Gestapo. "This is how," he continued his account with touching honesty, "your mother and I were . . . suppliers to the German jails . . . , where they told me 'Come back Friday for the cases in progress' [meaning those being processed for deportation]. The next day at six o'clock, a brutal awakening. A half-hour grace period, then we were taken by limousine to Charles III [Gestapo headquarters], where we found the Haguenauers."[15]

Nordon wrote to his children, "I faced this development with my usual good humor and I cheered up all those who could be cheered up. Your mother . . . remained her usual brave self, and that evening, when we arrived in Écrouves, we had the great satisfaction to learn that police headquarters had already given instructions for our special treatment." A pathetic wish echoed in the last lines of the letter: "Our anxiety is only about what may happen to you, and we hope that if misfortune should strike, you will receive the same preferential treatment that we did." The same tone characterized the letter Nordon sent from Drancy a few weeks later: "I am convinced since things have worked out so well for us that in the event of deportation there would still be some small privileges. As I continue to think and say to your mother, thanks to all of you and to the assistance that has been shown to us, we have had happiness enough for several lifetimes."[16] Such was the utter blindness to reality that allowed some Jews to deny knowledge of their fate. The Nordons would be deported in convoy no. 71 on 13 April 1944, along with the Haguenauers and the Picarts and their parents. This convoy encompassed nearly all the Jews from Alsace and Lorraine who were at Drancy at that time. This slaughter of French Jews can be explained by the logic behind the "law of numbers." Aloïs Brunner no doubt took pleasure in filling up the convoy with people from "the reserve" even at the risk of creating chaos in the camp administration.[17]

The Spiral of Anguish

"Why no letters?" "Why do we not know where the deported were taken?" *J'accuse* expressed the generalized anguish of those still at liberty. The very destinations were unknown. "We didn't know where the trains would stop" writes Yves Jouffa:

> The day before each deportation the names of a large number of German cities would circulate But we were all sure that we were leaving for forced labor. . . . When the first convoys were assembled there were always some volunteers who were ready to leave, generally physically robust men who preferred working to vegetating at Drancy. [But] everything changed when they saw women, children, and the elderly, all incapable of heavy work, being herded into the wagons, when they witnessed the forced embarkation of mothers crazed with grief at being separated from their children and a number of suicides in which people threw themselves out of windows. (We counted a dozen . . . in the summer of 1942.) Without knowing anything at all about the means of killing, we were more and more aware that leaving meant dying.[18]

Étienne Rosenfeld, taken in the raid of August 1941, remained for eleven months in Drancy and witnessed the departure of thirty-one convoys. His letters to his wife, in which he conceals the truth, betray the increasing tension of his terrible anxiety:

25 October 1941: "Deaths are now common and are increasing in number. Leaning out my window, I chanced to see the sad procession of a little cart, pulled and pushed by two internees, on which I could make out one of ours who had just succumbed."

12 December 1941: "General roll-call. . . . Turn out on the square. . . . It is a melancholy drama that plunges the camp into sorrow when the names are called out. . . . This day, which would—alas!—end in shooting, would be terrible for our nerves, even though we could not really suspect the drama. . . .

12 June 1942: "Yellow stars that we have to wear on our clothes. Even here! . . . It's a bad sign."

2 August 1942: "Since women and children have been in the camp I haven't been allowed to remain in one place. . . . Drancy could be compared to a kind of marshalling yard, always in motion but with the difference that you don't know where you are being sent.

25 August 1942: "I no longer have any illusions about the credibility of some eventual vacation spot where they are supposed to send us to work. . . . I have the disagreeable premonition that I will not again see my friends who have left."

3 September 1942: "It is clearly not to coddle them in fine cribs that thousands of children, packed without care into cattle cars, are being hauled off, surrounded by soldiers with their weapons levelled as if these poor kids were going to jump them."

7 September 1942: "Now it seems to the internees who feel their departure for "Pitchipoi" [imaginary name] is close, that there isn't anything aside from chow and sex that warrants any interest."

13 September 1942: "Keep hoping, but don't have any illusions."[19]

Rosenfeld explains today that these words

> were not intended to express the anguish I felt at the thought of one day
> seeing . . . my family and my friends arrive in their turn. . . . At the camp
> I kept up the appearance that would inspire hope in [the] future. . . .
> But my inexperience—I was only twenty-two—did not prevent me from
> guessing that what was to come was not going to be paradise. I never let
> anything show in my letters, until the eve of my departure on 13 Septem-
> ber 1942 when I wrote a long letter that I thought would be the last one
> for a long time. For after having witnessed thirty-one convoys leaving and
> never having received any news, I didn't foresee any good coming from
> my own departure. But I found the means to reassure my wife.[20]

Moshe Rajman, interned at Drancy in August 1941, sent his wife the
usual postcards passed by the official censorship. But from time to time he
claimed recourse to a means of correspondence learned in the prisons of Pil-
sudski's Poland, writing in Yiddish with a chemical pencil on strips of cloth
which he hid in the seams of the laundry he sent. His son Simon, sole survivor of the family, preserves them with devotion. "It is impossible to know
when we will be leaving or for where," Moshe wrote to his wife, Hanele, without concealing his anxiety. "In any case, we are ready. But don't worry. I hope
to be able to hold out. But I so badly want to see you at least one more time
in this life." In a subsequent letter he asks Hanele to see that the children,
Marcel and Simon, be prevented from "hanging around" in the all-too-
dangerous streets, their favorite "theater of operations."[21]

Charles Minczeles, interned at Pithiviers, knew that deportation meant
likely death, but he reassured his wife on 26 July 1942 by telling her that they
would not kill everyone: "We are to leave today for the East and not for Co-
logne as they first said. . . . Don't be afraid, my dear, they're not going to kill so
many people." He could not hide his bitterness toward France. "And if they
send you too, after twenty years of living among the French, since we have
the children, well, we'll make our home elsewhere. I ask you not to weep for
us. Be courageous, we are still young. And to his son, Henri, "I ask that you be
courageous even if they also take you. Do not fear, the war will not last forever
and we will meet again."[22]

Gisele Lustiger understood early that deportation from Drancy meant
certain death, and managed to warn her husband and son in the letters a
policeman smuggled out for her. Her son, who went on to become a cardinal
in the Catholic Church, told the author in a 1990 interview that his mother

had dispelled their misplaced confidence in France as represented by the Vichy government, and yet, as he spelled out elsewhere, if his mother knew where things were heading, "then other must have known. . . . They knew that from Drancy they were going to their deaths."[23]

And yet reasonable people could fail to understand, as is shown in a letter of Feinstein-Wilner, a leader of the MOI interned at Pithiviers, shows. Even though a member of the camp committee, and even though warned by the MOI's Paris office ("deportation means death"), Feinstein-Wilner later recalled that "I did not think we could tell people that they were being sent to certain death [and moreover] everyone was trying to console his family. Of course no one wanted to be taken. But if we told the internees to stay on their straw mattresses and let themselves be taken only by force, no one would have listened to us and we would have been isolated from the others."[24]

Georges Wellers' excellent book categorically affirms his ignorance of an extermination plan. His *L'Étoile juive à l'heure de Vichy* (The Yellow Star in the Time of Vichy) reflects the contemporary failure to understand the significance of the deportations. According to him, even the members of the "elite" with whom he met "never spoke of systematic extermination." He names André Baur, Fernand Musnik, and Armand Katz among leaders of the Paris UGIF who "did not know the truth or, if they had heard some rumors, certainly did not believe them."[25] Now this affirmation contains an apparent contradiction. If they did not believe it, this supposes that they knew but did not retain the information. This confusion is frequent in Wellers—the witness and the historian—between two terms perfectly different, "not believing" and "not knowing," and it involuntarily distorts his point of view on the question. Jacques Darville and Simon Wichené, who remained at Drancy until the Liberation, remembered that "the radio had certainly spoken of gas chambers, of cremation ovens. But we couldn't believe it."[26] Yet information received, even if rejected, leaves invisible traces: the daily lives of the internees continuously revived premonitions of the worst. If French Jews had not had a perception of mortal danger from at least the summer of 1942, there would have been no such struggle for survival. Today the discourse is skewed because the question is generally misunderstood: witnesses believe they are being asked whether they knew an absolute truth, i.e., of the existence of the gas chambers. Between absolute knowledge and total ignorance, however, lie many degrees. In any case, no one was yet in a position to think in "images": in front of the smoking chimneys at Auschwitz even the wisest underwent an immense shock of revelation. It is the difference between being told something that absolutely defies the human imagination, and confronting it in person. Even so, the deportee could exclaim: "Oh, that, I really did not know *that* was happening!"

What did Henry Bulawko, who witnessed the deportations, know at the time? In numerous statements and in his books he claims to have been ignorant of the extermination plans before his own deportation. In his case, there is an obvious explanation, if you take into account the chronology of events, which we often forget to do. Bulawko certainly might have known something at the moment of deportation on 18 July 1943, but the secret of Auschwitz had not yet been entirely exposed. He is correct to tell us that then it was a matter more of foreboding:

> The night before . . . they collected those who were leaving. . . . The night was indescribable: lamentations, children crying, whispering. Anxiety was tangible but there was also a rumor, come from who knows where, that would have us going to Bavaria to a fruit-packing plant. Some observed, with a heavy dose of optimism: to can fruit you have to have sugar and with sugar we can hold out. [This was] a strange rumor that seems to me even madder today than it did at the time. What were the elderly and children to do there? Did we have exact information about our actual destination? No. [But] if we had had such information, it is doubtful that we would have believed it. And [even] then, what proof could we have had?

Escape: The Tunnel

After torture and interrogation in the office of the 2nd Special Brigade in the Préfecture de police and in the rue des Saussaies by the Gestapo, the majority of Resistance activists of the Jewish Section of the MOI were sent in the course of September 1943 to Drancy.[27] Idel Korman, Alfred Besserman, and Dr. Aron Bacicurinski formed a clandestine organization in the camp. They planned an escape and wrote by means of a secret network to the heads of the MOI, asking to be sent some "lemons" (hand-grenades) and "pipes" (revolvers) with which to attack the sentries, while a group coming from the outside was to attack the French policemen simultaneously. The MOI leaders disappointed them: "Your plan would require at least five hundred 'sporting types' [irregulars and partisans]. Under present circumstances this is impossible, and we must advise you to count only on your own resources." On the eve of the deportation planned for 6 October, Korman again sought to enlist the help of MOI. "François [not identified] has already written to you with the most recent useful intelligence. . . . I don't need to repeat to you that we will exploit every opportunity to get away." He set up a new leadership for the organization in Drancy, to work on "a plan for a bigger escape."[28]

Henry Bulawko comments on the question and provides an example of an unsuccessful attempt.

> Escape? It was possible to escape from the camp with the complicity (sometimes bought) of some police officers. . . . With my comrade André Deutsch (whom I would find at Auschwitz-Jaworzno and who was killed in the course of the evacuation of the camp), I hid under the false roof on one of the barracks buildings. Lying on the beams that went around the building, they would not have found us if the sun had not cast André's shadow on the ground. After they took him down, there was nothing left for me to do but to come down too. This attempted escape, which is the duty of any captive, was not the reflection of a precise knowledge of the significance of the deportation. But it was obvious that remaining in the grips of the Germans and being sent to "Pitchipoi" was enough to fuel fears that a terrible fate awaited them.

Between September and November 1943, several dozen detainees dug a tunnel beneath the camp boundaries. It was to end past the earthworks outside. At the moment Brunner's SS men got wind of it—probably after an indiscretion by one of the prisoners—almost one hundred of the planned one hundred thirty feet had already been excavated. The idea of escape had apparently originated with persons who belonged to the MS, the Drancy camp Jewish police, abetted even by the camp commandant, Robert Blum. A large number of construction and repair projects undertaken by Brunner had necessitated bringing a substantial quantity of tools into the camp, a portion of which had been hidden away by the diggers, which were divided up into three teams of fifteen to twenty. The SS identified only nineteen of the guilty internees, whom they deported on 20 November 1942 in convoy 62, after torturing them horribly. They all found themselves in the same railway car, having succeeded in smuggling some tools with them; as determined as before, eleven of them managed to jump train near Luneville.

Every escape scheme requires more than material resources and time; it calls for a considerable degree of mutual confidence and cohesiveness among the plotters. The transitory nature of Drancy made it impossible to bring these conditions together, except in the group of the temporarily "non-deportable" who were staying on for a sufficiently long period.[29]

The Jewish Administration

Before being deported, Idel Korman sent intelligence on relations between the Jewish administration at Drancy and the rest of the internees to the leadership of the Jewish Section of the MOI. He emphasized the division between the French and immigrant Jews, between the rich and the poor:

> It is necessary that you look into the "Jewish gang" that runs the interior workings of the camp and whose conduct is hideous, although it claims to be Gaullist and to be working with us. When the present departure was being organized we raised the question of saving some of our people; instead . . . , they continued as in the past to save their personal friends and especially the rich. . . . You should bear this in mind and be ready to settle scores when the time comes. I am already thinking of exposing their collaboration. I just want to name a few names for you: Captain D., head of the camp police; Colonel B., the camp commander; E., who runs the administration. The comrades who are still there will be able to give you additional details.

Those who had the power to modify the lists by favoring one category of Jews at the expense of another could be accused of xenophobia. We should recall, on the other hand, that in the camps of the Southern Zone, representatives of the Jewish agencies had refused to participate in any screening.[30] Were the detainees obliged to participate or not to participate in the administration of the camp? There are no ethical norms which would prohibit it a priori. Our answer depends on the functions they were called on to perform. At Drancy, especially after the arrival of SS-Obersturmbannführer Aloïs Brunner, the principal role assigned to the internal administration consisted of surveillance over the interned; the French police were responsible only for external security. Brunner "enriched" the camp with a new dimension. Drawing upon experience gained in Eastern European ghettos, Brunner exercised unlimited power, but assigned internal management of the camp, including the preparations for deportations, to the Jewish "leadership."[31]

Thus at Drancy, where there were only four or five Germans (including Brunner himself), more than one hundred prisoners compensated for the lack of German personnel. A "Jewish police" included a team called the "Assignment Bureau." At the head of this team stood Oskar Reich, a former Viennese soccer player. Promoted to "Camp Inspector" Reich led missions to Paris whose objective was to uncover Jews living under false identities. Internees called him *le Piqueur* ("the beater" or "the whip"). The team operated at night, and each morning the kitchen workers dished out supplementary rations to its members. Brunner must have had confidence in Reich, confiding to him such police tasks as the transportation of prisoners; Rabbi R. S. Kapel, however, spoke for the other Jews when he called him "the servile lackey of the sinister Captain Brunner."[32] The writer Laszló Javor, author of the famous song "Sombre Dimanche" that caused a veritable epidemic of suicides in Hungary and other central European countries, cut hair in Drancy. He knew Reich well for the latter used to chat with him while being shaved. "A morally flawed being," Javor pictures Reich, "a one-hundred percent antisemite." This antisemitism didn't restrain his pursuit of Jewish women, however, and he liked to be called "Bluebeard."[33] Hunted as a collaborator, Oskar Reich was traced in Austria after the war and extradited to Paris; the military tribunal condemned him to death on 8 February, 1949 for "war crimes." His appeal for clemency was rejected.[34]

Where survival from one day to the next could depend on a few supplementary rations, and where the threat of deportation was constant, joining the camp administration offered material advantages and the hope of delaying or perhaps even escaping disaster. In such a climate, there is little place for solidarity. Quite the opposite in this case: camp circumstances favor the birth of gangs and cliques with all their perverse and corrupting effects. Not long after his arrival in Drancy with his wife and four children, R.-R. Lambert had come to feel himself so betrayed by his "colleagues" from the administration of the Paris UGIF there that he asked the Administrative Council for the Southern Zone to "suspend financial aid to the Paris UGIF."[35]

Attack the Convoys of Deportees?

Today the Jewish Resistance is sometimes blamed for having failed to attack the deportation trains. When former Resistance fighters reply that this would have entailed the death of many deportees, they hear people say: "But they were all condemned to death in any case." But what if we inquired into the likely behavior of deportees in the event of an attempted escape? Were they, for the most part, capable and ready to take the risks involved? Did they understand the risks of not fleeing? According to the testimony of those who did escape, certainty that they were going to their deaths had not seized everyone: the majority, quite naturally, suppressed their fears. And, how can we fail to take into account the human composition of the wagons and cars, of the great number of the elderly, the ill, mothers with children, children on their own? And could able-bodied men abandon their families?

Even in the case of a more "favorable" composition of a convoy, escape schemes ran into innumerable difficulties, in particular the fear of those who did not wish to take part. We have abundant testimony as to the psychological obstacles: even the most resolute doubted. Jacques London later wrote that "shortly after our train pulled out we started to open a hole in the floor of the car with tools that we had paid dearly for at Drancy. But the work had scarcely begun when there were protests: some worried that not everyone would get away, others that they would all be shot. Some of them threatened to begin banging on the doors to alert the German guards . . . we had to give up the scheme."[36] Henry Bulawko had a similar experience: "A bunch of us young men got together [to pull up a plank in the flooring and jump] onto the rail-bed. Seeing us at work, our companions informed the person 'responsible' for the car, to whom the *Feldgendarm* escorting us had said that in the event of any escape attempt there would be collective reprisals. Women trying to quieten their children began to moan and to beg us to stop. . . . The appointed supervisor broke in and with the help of a couple of men put the planking back in place. I don't remember that we tried to argue with them. Did we have exact information as to our [actual] destination? No. Our attempted flight can be explained [only] by our desire to recover our freedom."[37] Yvette Farnoux and her comrades "didn't exactly know the real nature of deportation. . . . But we weren't able to make the least attempt at escape; the other deportees stopped us. They were still convinced that they were being removed in family units to work camps."[38]

And were the recalcitrant absolutely wrong? George Wellers took part in an abortive break-out on the way to Auschwitz. "This attempt was uncovered by the Germans and the sixty of us who were involved were completely stripped and in that state put into an empty car. These sixty men, naked, thirsty, seated next to each other on the disgusting floor of the car offered a terribly grotesque and revolting spectacle."[39]

The "Reserves" in the Camp Annexes

Around Drancy the German and French administrations had set up a net-work of "annex camps," of which the chief were the children's home, the vocational school on the Rue des Rosiers, and the Rothschild Hospital, with its orphanage and home for the elderly. In practical terms the sick, elderly, and very young formed a "reserve" for the convoys. The UGIF was respon-sible for the management and supervision of residents on these sites.[40]

The Rothschild Hospital and its elder hospice were converted into an internment facility in the autumn of 1942. "Inmates" were divided into two categories: internees transferred there by reason of their advanced age and "free Jews" who had been admitted to the hospital. But the distinction was based only on budgetary concerns: the former were taken over by the police service, the latter by the UGIF. The administration and medical staff were held responsible for escapes.[41]

The UGIF does not seem to have opposed this arrangement. Since the Germans had agreed that women who gave birth might stay in the hospital until their infants had reached the age of six months, the UGIF asked that they be housed in a single ward, giving an assurance that they "would take all the necessary measures to seal all exits [against] possible escape." Po-lice Chief Robert François gave his consent, "provided that the hospital administration be held responsible for the custody of the Jewish women in question."[42]

But if some staff gave evidence of compliance, others—in particular the doctors—were participants in the Resistance. Young Paulette Sliwka, sent to the Rothschild Hospital to be operated on for appendicitis, was put in contact with the outside by Dr. Lebenson, a member of the Combat Médical network of the National Movement against Racism. Through this organiza-tion, Paulette Sliwka sought to escape. Efforts to prolong her stay at the hos-pital, however, proved fruitless. Then hospital director, "Dr. H.," informed police headquarters that she was "dischargeable," and she was transferred to Drancy.[43]

Similarly, from February 1943 to February 1944, one hundred thirty-seven elderly men and women, most of them older than seventy, and some as old as ninety, were snatched from their beds and deported. The darkest day was 23 July 1943, when ninety patients including those with cancer or advanced tuberculosis, paralytics, and even postoperative patients, were piled into trucks without regard to their medical conditions. Later in the sum-mer, forty-five elderly were moved from Drancy to the hospital "because of their advanced age. In the margin of the transfer document some official wrote, "Received today, 25 August, 45 elderly for the account of UGIF."[44] The reception of cargo in good and proper form.

Drancy by itself was bad enough, and there is no denying the horrible suffering undergone by those unfortunate enough to have been incarcerated there, a French concentration camp on French soil with only one purpose: to serve as a transit point through which foreign and French Jews could be deported to the extreme hell of the extermination and other camps in the East. The name Drancy will live on in infamy as long as human memory in France and elsewhere reaches back to the 1941–44 era of inhumanity and terror.

PART TWO

1942–1944: To Resist or Submit?

CHAPTER NINE

"Night and Fog"

The Battle against Silence

. . . the Jewish Question must be resolved uniquely during the course of the war, for it must be eliminated without the whole world raising a hue and cry.

—Franz Rademacher[1]

We have given the enemy a formidable blow. We have revealed his satanic plan to exterminate Polish Jewry, a plan that he wished to execute in silence.

—Emmanuel Ringelblum[2]

The silence of the victims was one of the conditions for the success of the genocide. In France this silence was deepened by the prohibition of all Jewish publishing. This measure was followed by a prohibition against Jews owning radios. The information vacuum seemed, at first, total. But the deprivation of news, communication, and the exchange of ideas was experienced even more painfully in the nerve-wracking anxiety widespread in Paris during the great raids. In order to understand the suffering of the families facing the terrible "destination unknown," we are tempted to seek analogies from our own time. The anguish of the families of hostages? Perhaps. But here discouragement alternates with hope, a situation in fact maintained by the hostage-takers in the interests of "negotiations" or to facilitate media coverage: they *desire* to release information. Even, before the first deportations, there reigned an official silence concerning the transit camps at Compiègne and Drancy; once the trains began to depart for the East, the secrecy deepened.

Immediately after the deportations from Pithiviers and Beaune-la-Rolande in May–June of 1942, Jewish women mobbed police headquarters, demanding to be told where their husbands and sons had been taken. After the July raids carried out by the police, they learned that it was not from this source that information would be forthcoming. On the contrary, official agencies were engaged in spreading disinformation. "Before the rising emotions of the public, the [French] authorities seem to have felt a need to justify themselves," wrote the underground brochure *Témoignage*. "Without providing any exact information [they circulated] the statement that it was a false rumor that children had been separated from their parents."[3] Resistance organizations set about gathering intelligence. The UGIF of the Free Zone asked the French Red Cross whether it would be possible to contact those deported in the same fashion as with prisoners of war. The answer was affirmative, specifying that messages must not exceed thirty words and that the name and address of the sender must be given. Many families received this news through a circular letter. A week later, however, on 21 July 1942, the Vichy Red Cross announced that "as a consequence of new instructions, it was obliged temporarily to suspend the transmission of family messages destined for internees who had recently been deported to the East."[4]

Evidence from the Red Cross

At the present time, after the publication of the remarkable book by Jean-Claude Favez on the International Committee of the Red Cross (ICRC) and the deportations, there is no longer the least doubt that as early as the summer of 1942, this important organization had in its possession proof of the existence of a systematic plan for the extermination of the Jews.

At the suggestion of Leland Harrison, the American minister to Switzerland (and probably at the urging of Gerhart Riegner, the World Jewish Congress representative in Geneva), American consul Paul C. Squire visited Dr. Carl J. Burckhardt at the ICRC to inquire into reports about the mass murder of Jews in the East. Burckhardt had many contacts in Germany and was a credible witness, even though he passed on a somewhat misguided piece of information. He told Squire, "privately and not for publication," that Hitler had signed an order at the start of 1941 to the effect that "before the end of 1942 Germany *must be free of all Jews*." He had not himself seen the order, but its existence had been confirmed by two "very well informed Germans," who, Squire speculated, were officials in the Ministries of Foreign Affairs and War. "I then asked him whether the word extermination, or its equivalent, was employed, to which he replied that the words *must be Juden-frei* [sic] (free of Jews) were utilised. He then made it clear that since there is no place to send these Jews and since the territory must be cleared of this race, it is obvious what the next result would be." The "strictly confidential" report to the State Department in Washington from which these citations are taken was written on 9 November 1942.[5]

The ICRC, whose numerous emissaries were crisscrossing Germany and most of the occupied countries of Eastern Europe, had at least occasional access to the concentration camps, and had at their disposal sufficient documentation to reveal the Jewish genocide to the world. And yet the ICRC leaders did not do so. The idea of a public appeal had been discussed at the plenary session of the ICRC on 14 October 1942, but the committee decided that "such an appeal (1) would serve no purpose, rendering the situation even more difficult, and (2) would jeopardise all the work undertaken for the prisoners of war and civil internees—the real task of the Red Cross."[6] In January 1943 the ICRC became aware of a document written by Pastor Adolf Fredenberg of the Ecumenical Council of Churches. Not only did he confirm the disappearance of Jews from Berlin and from the Warsaw Ghetto, he also cited the use of gas. Still, the ICRC made no public statement.

At the same time, the UGIF in Paris was receiving a large number of postcards from deportees ostensibly in Germany for delivery to relatives still at liberty in France. But its staff worked with a self-restrained formalism and thoroughness that were worthy of an earlier age.[7] The official order permitted families to "correspond" twice a month. "We may expect," judged the UGIF administration, "to receive approximately two thousand letters or cards per month from the various camps." *Informations juives,* the organ of the UGIF, regularly published the names of those to whom this camp mail was addressed. Madame Lucie Chevalley, the Service social d'aide aux émigrants (SSAE — Society for Aid to Immigrants) delegate to the Nîmes Committee (founded by Jewish and Christian organizations in the archbishopric of Lyons in 1940 to help internees) was more skeptical. She told a 3 November 1942 meeting that because the 700 postcards the UGIF had received from Auschwitz had all been written on a single model, "the information they contained appeared to be not very credible."[8]

The postcards were part of what the Germans called the *Briefaktion*, a disinformation ploy to reassure victims and, beyond that, public opinion. "As concerned our relations with our families and friends," testified one survivor, "we had the official right to send one postcard written in German every six months, addressed to the office of the UGIF in Paris." One survivor later stated that "*It frequently happened that the authors of these cards wrote them shortly before they entered the gas chambers.*"[9] The operation was part of Berlin's strategy of total secrecy considered essential to the success of the "Final Solution." In fact, the cards falsely reassured many and thereby worked to the enemy's advantage.

The Resistance, however, reacted quickly in the newspaper *J'accuse*, denouncing Briefaktion as a diversive attempt to "[prove] to the world that all the deported Jews are not dead." The postcards all bore the same formulaic words under which the deported had only to write their names: "I am well. The food is quite plentiful. Send more workers to Germany as soon as possible." For *J'accuse* it was all "a clumsy trap, fully worthy of the cynicism and stupidity of its creators."[10]

Leo Israelowicz, the UGIF's official liaison with the Gestapo's *Judenreferat*, asked whether it was possible to obtain "certificates" for the deported, stating that they were alive. In response, Röthke reiterated the terms of Eichmann's telegram of 10 December 1942 authorizing French police authorities to release certificates stating only that "The Jew has left and his/her place of residence is not known." No reference was to be made to "evacuation" or "deportation."[11]

A few months later there was no longer any talk of "postcards from the camps" at the UGIF where, finally, they must have realized the uselessness of "looking for families" disappearing at the same rate as the departures or those who went into hiding. Total silence reigned in the UGIF about the existence of the death camps. Names like Auschwitz and Belzec—already well known—were never mentioned in the minutes of the meetings of the UGIF either in Paris or in the Southern Zone. This narrowing of their field of vision by the UGIF directors doubtlessly reflects their disposition to act only within the geographic area officially assigned them. But what was happening in Drancy and Auschwitz was so horrible that ignoring it put at risk the achievement of the UGIF's official goals.

The Consistory Knew, But . . .

The Central Consistory seemed to indicate knowledge of the extermination of deportees when it wrote to Marshal Pétain in August 1942 that "there can be no doubt as to the final destiny that awaits the deported." Their alarm may have reflected knowledge of Hitler's reiteration on 24 February 1942 of his 1939 prophecy that it would not be the "Aryans" but the Jews who would be annihilated in any European war.

The Consistory emphasized that "it has been established through precise and consistent information that several hundreds of thousands of Jews have been massacred in eastern Europe or have died there after atrocious suffering, as a consequence of ill treatment." They complained to the Marshal that "persons turned over by the French government were collected together without any discrimination as to their physical aptitude," proving that "it is not for purposes of labor that the German government is claiming them, but with the intention of pitilessly and methodically exterminating them." The letter, however, strikes the reader by its inconsistency, for it adopted a position of compromise and concluded by asking Pétain only to permit exemption of certain categories of potential deportees, and the "humane treatment" of those still condemned "to follow the path of deportation."[12]

Perhaps a better understanding of the demarche emerges from remarks of Consistory vice-president Adolphe Caen at the 20 August 1942 session that ratified the letter. "We cannot permit this to unfold without a protest from which, alas, we cannot expect much in return," he said. "It is, however, necessary to make a statement for honor and for history." More to the point, he then adds: "We might perhaps be able to attenuate the sufferings of our foreign brothers, even if it is not in our power to save them. . . . But perhaps we could spare our French coreligionists new trials."[13] Resignation to the fate of immigrant Jews, hope of saving French Jews: a tragic double perspective that must have been interpreted by the authorities as acceptance of the deportation of the immigrants.

But most surprising, indeed enigmatic, remains the fact that the Consistory under the Occupation never again mentioned in any of its announcements or communications the extermination of the Jews of France and Europe. In 1968 Georges Wormser, former president of the Consistory, gave a different version of this position: "At a date I can no longer specify, Jacques Helbronner, the Consistory president, received a Swiss copy of a letter from a German Catholic priest to the Vatican describing the atrocities committed against the Jews. I must tell you that we were completely stunned. To fulfil our

moral duty, we decided before anything else that we would have Jacques Helbronner request information from the contacts he still maintained in Vichy.
This effort resulted in neither a confirmation nor a denial." When other official and semiofficial sources could not confirm the news, it was decided
not to officially involve the Consistory in the matter, but to inform the individual members. "Our task," Wormser insists, "was to alert as many of our coreligionists as possible. Personally I broadcast the information to Free France
by way of a clandestine radio."[14]

As if wilfully disregarding the raids in Paris and the deportation of
foreign Jews from the Free Zone, in September 1942 the Central Consistory
asked the local branches to circulate a directive ("to maintain your moral responsibility"): "Whatever your bitterness, and without accepting anything of
what has put you outside common law, *submit* in regular order to the obligations imposed on you by the laws. Do not conceal your status as Israelites.
Keep informed and keep within the laws; do not conceal from yourself who
and what you are. This will only make you better Jews and better Frenchmen."[15] Here is a stunning example of the mentality that rendered people
blind and deaf to their own impending destruction. Here again is that staggering sentence on the method of being "better Jews and better Frenchmen"
by submitting to the law of the persecutors. Perhaps members of the Consistory were thinking of the ancient sacrifice of life *for the sanctification of the
name,* the age-old *Kiddush Ha-shem* adopted by the Jewish people throughout
the diaspora, in the face of the inquisitors and other persecutors, but which
had now been finally challenged even by the conservative Polish rabbis in
the era of the "Final Solution." How might one be a better French citizen by
submitting to unjust laws that exposed the citizen to the threat of death?

The Chief Rabbi's About-Face

The German occupation of the Free Zone on 11 November 1942 also did not
suffice to alter the Consistory's stand. Meeting on 28 December to respond
to the latest antisemitic legislation (the decree of 11 December 1942 mandating the word "Jew" on identity papers), the members of the Permanent
Section heard the president say that "the only counsel to be given is to submit to the new arrangements." This attitude was justified in his eyes by two
considerations: "The respect due to legal authority and because Jews owe it
to themselves to publicly affirm their Jewish identity."

The meeting was nonetheless to be the scene of a dramatic turn of events when Chief Rabbi Isaïe Schwartz made a statement that was at the very least unexpected. "There are limits which cannot be passed and it seems that today the moment has come to say proudly 'No!' . . . even at the cost of grave sanctions to which we might expose ourselves."[16] The chief rabbi at least had learned the lessons of the terrible summer of 1942. He was the only one at the time to speak out against the previous policy. For him, in any case, it meant a rupture with Vichy and an end to the suicidal policy of submission to the strictures of antisemitic legislation.

The meeting was, however, unanimous in its rejection of the chief rabbi's motion. "Can the Central Consistory," the president asked, "expose itself to sanctions that might have as result the suppression of the exercise of the Jewish faith in France?" Helbronner, thus seeking to protect the public practice of the Jewish religion, seems not to have taken account of the fact expressed as early as 1941 by René Mayer, a politician and practicing Jew: "*To save French Jewry it is first of all necessary to save the Jews.*"[17]

Thus the Consistory leadership refused to draw the appropriate conclusions from the facts. "But knowledge is sterile as long as it does not generate action," wrote Arthur Koestler, then interned in a camp in the South, in an allusion to those who did not know how to translate their knowledge of the situation into action.[18]

Revelations of a German Industrialist

The deliberate indiscretion of a German manufacturer on 29 July 1942 helped raise the curtain behind which the Third Reich hoped to complete the "Final Solution" without its next victims or world public opinion knowing of it. On 1 August 1942 Gerhart Riegner, head of the Geneva office of the World Jewish Congress, was alerted by his friend Benjamin Sagalowitch, spokesman for the Jewish community of Zurich, who said that he had received information of such exceptional importance that he could only communicate it in person and face to face. They agreed to meet the next day in Geneva.[19]

"The news was summed up in a few words," Riegner recalls. A prominent German industrialist, passing through Zurich at the end of July, dined with the Perlzweig family, who had taken refuge there from Germany. He shared with them absolutely incredible, confidential information: Hitler had decided on the extermination of all of European Jewry. He asked them to inform the Jews of the free world. The name of the factory owner was kept secret for a long time even after the war. This man, Edouard Schulte, had been the owner of a mining company in Upper Silesia that employed about 30,000 workers. The Perlzweigs had absolute confidence in Schulte, who had kept up his friendship with them, something that was rather rare among the leaders of German industry. Because of the nature of his business, he had direct connections with Wehrmacht headquarters.

True or false? This is the question Riegner and Sagalowitch asked each other during a long walk around Lake Leman. "Finally," Riegner says, "we were both convinced, although it crushed us, that we had to credit what the German factory owner had said. Because of my responsibilities, it was my duty to transmit this news to the governments of the United States and Great Britain in order to convince them of the reality of the danger."

The information was transmitted to the Department of State in Washington for transmittal to the president of the WJC, Rabbi Stephen Wise, and to the Foreign Office in London for transmittal to leaders of the British Jews on 8 August 1942, via coded telegram by the U.S. and British consuls in Switzerland. The State Department refused to forward the cable to Rabbi Wise, but the London Jews sent him the gist of its content in a separate telegram. This telegram, sent to Wise by Samuel Silverman, reads:

> Have received through foreign office following message from Riegner Geneva Stop Received alarming report that in Fuhrers Headquarters plan discussed and under consideration all Jews in countries occupied or controlled Germany number 3-1/2 to 4 million should after deportation and concentration in east at one blow exterminated to resolve once and for all Jewish question in Europe Stop Action reported planned for Autumn Methods under discussion including Prussic acid Stop We transmit information with all necessary reservation as exactitude cannot be confirmed Stop Informant stated to have close connexions with highest German authorities and his reports generally reliable Stop Inform and consult New York Stop Foreign Office has no information bearing on or confirming story.[20]

"Why did I keep Schulte's information secret," that is, why didn't I publicly announce it?" Riegner later reflected:

> Firstly, because of the censorship by Swiss authorities, which was very strict and motivated by a desire not to antagonize Berlin. On the other

hand, I was afraid that the rumor, with all that it could contain of inaccuracies, might obscure the true story. Another reason why I was obliged to observe complete discretion was that time had to be left for the American and British governments to take formal receipt of my top secret telegrams, which had been transmitted from their respective embassies. But I believe today that the responsible Jewish officials in the free world did not, at the time, give the matter of transmitting this information to Jewish communities in the occupied countries the importance that it undeniably warranted.[21]

Should We Talk about the Gas Chambers?

In the underground press of the Jewish Section of the MOI the phrase "extermination of the Jewish people" appeared as early as the end of August 1941, based in part on "the appeal of the Jewish personalities in Moscow."[22] Supported by the information about the massacres the Germans perpetrated as they advanced on the Eastern Front, the Jewish resistance movement began recommending individual and collective civil disobedience. We recall that the tract warning of the great raid of July 1942 connected the raid to the Germans' extermination plans. The MOI repeatedly warned that "deportation means death" and "not facing reality is equivalent to suicide."

Searching for the truth, attentive to all information coming from the East, in particular from Poland, in early October 1942 Jewish resistance leaders in the MOI received awful news of the use of poison gas in the camps, which confirmed that the massacres in the East were part of a large-scale systematic undertaking. In addition, the news indicated that the process of destruction was being extended to Western Europe's Jews, especially because it seemed that several thousand French deportees had already been gassed.

In a small apartment in the Porte de Choisy area of Paris on a mid-October night the five leaders of the Jewish Section of the MOI debated the news, which can be summarized in a few words: French Jewish deportees, including many women and children, had been asphyxiated by gas. Their source (a driver for the German Organization Todt, known to the underground as "the mole") seemed reliable: the anonymous comrade who had brought the information from Poland was known as a responsible person. The first reaction was identical to that of Gerhart Riegner: the information was too fantastic to stake the credibility of the group on it. And yet in the one case as in the other, these men never had the least doubt concerning the reality of the massacres in the occupied territory of the USSR. Today, we can identify a number of rational explanations for their reluctance to believe in the reports of gassing. But to limit the present discussion to feelings experienced at the time in both Geneva and Paris, only one such explanation will be offered here: the limited perception of the implicit scope of the Germans' plan for the extermination of the Jews.

To spread the news? First, the leaders of the Jewish Section had to be absolutely certain the information was true. If not, its circulation would be a crime. They worried about the negative reaction of people who would refuse to believe that their parents were no longer alive, or that they themselves were condemned to follow the same route. Suppress the news then? But did they have the right to do this? The final decision envisaged for reasons of prudence the initial publication only in *J'accuse* and *Fraternité*, which were intended for a general readership, and not in *Unzer Wort*, distributed in the Yiddish-speaking circles directly concerned. On 20 October 1942, *J'accuse* carried the headline, "Nazi Torturers Burn and Asphyxiate Thousands of Jewish Men, Women, and Children Deported from France." The paper informed its readers that "tens of thousands of Jews, men, women, and children who were deported from France have been burned alive in sealed railway cars or asphyxiated in order to test a new toxic gas." *J'accuse* was the first underground newspaper in France to report the use of gas to kill Jewish deportees.[23]

From that day onward, the search for information about the Final Solution would be a principal concern in all Jewish resistance. They actually sought news from Poland, but the Jewish Resistance in Paris was not aware of the crucial but highly dangerous work being accomplished in Warsaw by Emmanuel Ringelblum and his team. It was only after the war that they could read what Ringelblum had noted in his chronicle in autumn 1942 and see there the tragically over-optimistic appraisal of the achievements of the Warsaw group: "Our team has accomplished a great historic mission. It has alerted the world to our fate and has perhaps saved hundreds of thousands of Polish Jews from extermination. (Naturally, only the immediate future will show whether this last claim holds true.) We have struck the enemy a formidable blow. We have revealed his satanic plan to exterminate Polish Jewry, a plan which he hoped to execute in silence. We have foiled his calculations."[24] Clearly, knowledge and information were crucial, but unfortunately they were not sufficient to convince all the Jews of France.

To Know: A Moral Obligation

The obligation to know was elevated to the level of a moral imperative: this is how Bertrand Poirot-Delpech perceived it while still a student at the Louis-le-Grand Secondary School: "To seek to know becomes a duty when the little Silbermanns begin to be missing from class."[25] Poirot-Delpech spoke these strong words at the Académie Française in memory of his classmate Youra Riskine:

> A Jew from Odessa, Riskine dazzled our class at Louis-le-Grand with his gifts as a pianist, poet, clown, friend. There were no little idiots to humiliate him, as at Janson in Silbermann's time, a certain Third Reich took care of that. One morning in 1944, the student Riskine, fourteen years old, was arrested along with his mother: departure for Auschwitz! Did we not suspect the outcome? The Latin teacher, to whom we announced that Riskine's cold might last a while, lowered his eyes toward his copy of Lucretius: "No politics at school," he muttered. "Let's return to the text, *Suave mari magno.* . . . You know, 'how sweet it is when the floods are loosed and one is on firm land.'"

Poirot-Delpech stigmatized this indifference and cowardice, representative of the era: "My alarm . . . remains intact after forty-five years. If our fine culture can ignore the massacre of innocents, of what use is it . . ? To entertain the killers after work? Art has more often masked barbarity than named it and fought it! So many men of talent refused to see that the Silbermanns and the Riskines were being sacrificed. When they weren't themselves running with the pack of wolves!"[26]

The lawyer Henri Ader, in 1944 also a classmate of Riskine, recalled before another assembly of notables the disappearance of his friend. "In that class, two students, without a word to one another, vowed to themselves to recall the memory of Riskine if, some day later, they had the opportunity to make a solemn public statement," Henri Ader declared at the opening session of the Paris Bar that elected him president on 20 November 1989. "Today, before you, it is my turn to speak of Riskine, to see him again. He was so gifted, so superior in all he did, that it is certain he would have been in the first rank wherever life led him. But he was not to be a member of the Académie Française, not a lawyer, teacher, engineer, musician, or poet. But we must remember him so that things like that never, never recur."[27] Youra

Riskine was a boy among many others. His name recalls a crime commited under a veil of silence. That silence had to be penetrated and broken as much for the honor of France as for the survival of thousands condemned to death—and the commemoration of thousands more who didn't escape.

Writing: The Beginning of Memory

"Everyone was writing," Emmanuel Ringelblum notes in his chronicle of the Warsaw Ghetto. "Journalists and writers, that was only natural, but there were also school teachers, social workers, young people, even children. For the most part, it took the form of diaries in which the tragic events of that time were reflected through the prism of personal, lived experience. The texts were innumerable, but almost all were destroyed when the Warsaw ghetto was liquidated.[28] Underground writing thus appears as the first chapters on the scroll of the Shoah's memory."

The silence on the part of most Jewish leaders in France during the Occupation appears in sharp contrast to the feverish compulsion to write that seized not only intellectuals in Poland but also common people who, sensing that their world was about to be swallowed up, sought to leave written records. What had happened to all the writers of the prewar press, voicing opinions in French, Yiddish, Hebrew, and Russian, in the daily and weekly papers, in other periodicals, with all the richness and variety of ideas that reflected the dynamic and vibrant life of the Jewish community?

Zosa Szjakowski estimates the number of Jewish serial publications appearing between 1881 and 1940 at 290, of which 163 were in Yiddish and 108 in French (four others were in Hebrew, six in Russian, one in Judeo-Arabic, one in English, and five in German). Of the French periodicals, sixty-four began publication in or after 1923; more than three quarters of the Yiddish serials first appeared in that year or later, reflecting the surge in Jewish immigration from Central and Eastern Europe. From the perspective of political affiliation, fifty-six of the publications could be characterized as Zionist (thirty-five in French, twenty-one in Yiddish). Twenty-eight were communist, nine anarchist, six socialist-Bundist, and three Trotskyite. (The others were mostly liberal or apolitical.) All the papers from the left and far left were in Yiddish.[29]

Raymond-Raoul Lambert, the editor-in-chief of *L'Univers israélite,* took no steps to assure its underground publication, as if he had nothing more to say to the "Israelites" for whom the paper had been intended. He kept up his notebooks, which are of undeniable interest, but nonetheless of a private nature. Perhaps he was sufficiently conscious of the fact that to write for an underground readership, he would have to surrender the leadership of the UGIF.

What happened to the brilliant and anticonformist young editors of the weekly *Samedi*?[30] And what of Jacques Bielinky, that excellent journalist who sought a tribune in vain? The only possibility available to him was the official organ of the UGIF, *Informations juives,* published under the supervision of the *Propagandastaffel.* He refused to collaborate with them. His private diary would be discovered only after the war. As for the daily *Pariser Haïnt* ("Paris Today"), there would be no one, either among the Yiddish-speaking Zionists or among the leaders of the Federation of Jewish Associations in France, for whom the paper was the mouthpiece, who would take responsibility for any kind of underground publication. Joseph Fischer, otherwise remarkably active throughout the Occupation, seems to have forgotten *La Terre retrouvée,* the weekly of which he had been the prewar publisher.

Until December 1943, which saw the first issue of *Quand même,* a joint effort of the FSJF and activists in the Zionist Youth Movement (MJS— Movement de jeunesse sioniste), there was hardly any underground Jewish press except for that of *Solidarité,* the UJRE (the Union of Jews for Resistance and Mutual Aid), and the MNCR (National Movement against Racism), all organizations within the sphere of the Jewish Section of the MOI or the Union of Jewish Youth.

We should, however, note the publication of two issues of the newspaper *Unzer Stimme* ("Our Voice") in 1941 and 1942 before the raids of 16 and 17 July, and of a third, at the close of 1943, by the Bund, the non-Zionist socialist group. Another group, the Poalei Sion-gauche ("Workers of Zion-Left"), with Marxist leanings, began to issue a typed and mimeographed bulletin, *Arbaiter Zeitung* ("Workers' Paper"), in the Southern Zone in the autumn of 1943. These exceptions cannot modify the "desert landscape" image of the media serving a collectivity that was the first to be struck by the "law of silence." Yet few historians have tried to clarify this aspect of Jewish life during the Occupation. The hypothesis (advanced by some) that there was a voluntary renunciation of underground publication in deferral to other priorities, is scarcely credible. Otherwise the *Quand même* would not have spoken of the "torture of three years of silence." Its first editorial stated that among the multiple tortures inflicted on the Jews "that of silence is perhaps the one which most threatens our dignity. To have to remain silent [before] degenerate sadists without being able to cry out our disgust."[31]

Beginning in November and December 1943, a number of leaders (one hesitates to say it—the pleasure of rediscovered writing) expressed themselves, exteriorizing their suffering, but above all giving voice to the anger built up during the years of a silence. This was true of Joseph Fischer, Zvi Grinberg, Léo Glaeser, Henri Hertz, and Faiwel Schrager, all members of the executive committee of the FSJF. Their stage was the newspaper, brochures, and tracts of the General Defence Committee, which grouped together all the political and social organizations of immigrant Jewry. The first issue of their newspaper, *Unzer Kamf* ("Our Struggle"), had a four-page format, double the general norm imposed by the shortage of newsprint. It would eventually grow to twelve pages, each of the editors insisting that his pieces appear.[32]

Why had the passion for writing been bottled up for so long? This might be explained in the first instance by the overlap among organizations still legally permitted in the Free Zone until November 1942. Their concern to prolong their legal situation, rightly or wrongly judged essential to relief activities, is quite clear. The Consistory asked the Ministry of Information on two occasions (without success) for authorization to publish a "religious bulletin." To preserve its status the Consistory specifically declined to sponsor an underground publication. This was the terrible price to be paid, as its executive acknowledged in a motion passed in June 1941 bitterly recording "the impossibility in which the Consistory finds itself, by virtue of the anti-Jewish legislation, of responding to the persistent [antisemitic] attacks in the press, on the radio, and in film."[33]

In Gestapo and Vichy Archives

Pétain's office demonstrated considerable interest in the illegal Jewish publications, to judge from the place it reserved for them in top-secret "weekly abstracts." "The Jews are trying to create a vast movement of solidarity and resistance on their behalf," notes a special services report from 10 May 1943.[34] Was this an allusion to the appearance of the Mouvement national contre le racisme (MNCR—National Movement against Racism) and its newspapers *J'accuse* and *Fraternité*? This is likely in light of the fact that the distribution of "pro-Jewish pamphlets" is again noted in April. A review drawn up in December 1943 lists *Fraternité* under the heading "Tracts of Independent Origin," that is (in the mind of the report-writer), neither Gaullist nor communist. Under the heading "Tracts Emanating from Jewish Circles," we find the following publications: *Qu'est-ce que l'Union de la jeunesse juive?* (What Is the Union of Jewish Youth?), *Jeune Juif prends ta place dans le combat!* (Young Jew, Take Your Place in the Struggle!), *A nos frères de l'union soviétique* (To our brothers in the Soviet Union), and *Jeune Combat* (Young Struggle).[35]

The security service of the occupiers also followed the underground Jewish publications intercepted by the postal censor or seized during arrests. In the archives of Gestapo-France—now at the CDJC—one may see annotated newspapers and tracts gathered by the "antennae" of the Sicherheitsdienst in various cities.

We don't know if all such items were translated, but the archives of the office of Röthke, Eichmann's representative in Paris, contain a complete translation of the 20 November 1942 issue of *J'accuse* whose headline excerpted Georges Clemenceau's defense speech at the Dreyfus trial: "I ask that the jurors say to the instigators of this brutality in the name of the French people, you will go no further."[36] What a strange feeling today to see *J'accuse* as *Ich klage an;* what strange satisfaction to know that the Nazis were reading these papers and knew the Jewish Resistance was exposing the secret of the "Final Solution." Thus did they read in Paris and Berlin that "the Nazis are taking vengeance for their military reverses by refined cruelty toward old people and children," that "Rommel's retreat in Africa and defeats in the East of Europe are prompting them to step up their persecution," and that many Aryans households "are opening their doors to the persecuted."

CHAPTER TEN

People of the Shadows

Who knocks on the door in the silent dark?
A wind of violence is rising;
Doctor, doctor, open your house,
Open up, let me in, give me asylum.
—Louis Aragon[1]

The phenomenon had no precedent in the history of humanity: an entire category of the population, tens of thousands of all ages, condemned to live clandestinely. With what could one compare the underground life led by the majority of Jews in France from 1942 until the Liberation? The first Christians? In order to practice their faith they needed to find catacombs where they could meet, but otherwise they did not need to change their daily habits. The "Marranos"? These Spanish and Portuguese Jews formally converted to Christianity during the Inquisition but for the most part only simulated fidelity to the new faith.[2] The revolutionaries of modern times? Men and women who engaged in illegal movements or parties carried out underground activities, but generally maintained their identities, lived with their families, continued normal employment, or pursued an ordinary education. As Henri Michel observed of French Resistance fighters during the Occupation, "It was in their interests as long as possible to maintain their jobs, their place of residence . . . they went to work, lived at home. Their problem was to reconcile the obligations of a legal existence with their resistance activities."[3]

The absence of any example—one is tempted to speak of a "model"—makes it extremely difficult to grasp the phenomenon of the clandestine life of an entire civil society; but this was the life of the Jews of France during the Occupation. Until now, this human experience, this unique reality in history, has passed largely unstudied by historians and sociologists.[4]

Clandestinity: The Condition of Survival

Admittedly, there were Jews who did not go underground. There are those who wore the yellow star in Paris until the last minute and who survived, no one knows how nor by what miracle; there were those who didn't wear it, but kept their real identity papers on their persons. But for all of them survival required a change of identity, at least a partial submersion underground, while they still struggled to salvage a semblance of an above-ground life. Even if individuals arranged "complex combinations of legal and illegal resorts, intermediary and ambiguous statuses,"[5] the major factor in survival, especially after the 1942 raids, was to break with legality, which entailed partial or total civil disobedience. The diversity of situations did not result from a deliberate decision but from psychological obstacles—hesitation before the prospect of going to the logical end—or the impossibility of ideal solutions.

What did it mean to live underground, hidden, camouflaged, for entire families, infants and the elderly included? For children and adolescents deprived of their families? The material and psychological obstacles seemed insurmountable. But they had to be overcome, and quickly, as time was short.

The decision for a revolutionary involved only his or her person, and rarely involved reprisals against family or friends. His organization took the place of society or the family he left behind. The group offered a place of security. Resistance activists discovered in it a moral and material solidarity, and found experienced people who taught them the "job" of life underground. From the sociological point of view, the same difference that exists between soldiers and civilians prevailed between them and the general Jewish populace.

For the majority, the principal difficulty lay in the first decision, a decision that was so difficult because it conflicted with the social nature of human beings. Humans have a need for society, whether it be friendly or cold; in order to remain integrated within it, they must accept its laws and norms.

Beyond society, there is more than the unknown, there is the void. To the normal fear of putting oneself beyond the law then, we must add the fear of social nothingness.

Faced with the prospect of leaving home and hearth with all that they represented, tens of thousands found themselves bewildered. For many leaving home meant abandoning their means of production, their sole sources of income. Finding another roof, new and often underground employment, and a new identity of even succession of identities; getting one's children schooled; arranging health care for oneself and one's family—all this had to take place in a state of fear, desperation, and near hopelessness.

Another unknown factor was the attitude of the non-Jewish population. What would be the reaction of the "others" from whom one hoped for help and shelter? The foreign Jews, in particular, had been scarred by the xenophobic and antisemitic climate of the prewar years, a trauma that was only intensified by the antisemitic propaganda of the occupiers and their French collaborators. The surprising sympathy the Paris public demonstrated during the 16 and 17 July 1942 raids, remained, however, unknown to most Jews in the Southern Zone because of the difficulties of illegally disseminating information in 1942 and of the extreme dispersal of the affected populace.

The Hidden Face of Daily Life

From testimony drawn from the hundreds of accounts residing in the archives of the CDJC, and from interviews that I myself obtained, there emerges a "hidden face" of daily Jewish life during the Occupation. This picture records the fugitives' ceaseless invention of individual survival strategies. In all cases nothing would have been possible without the help of non-Jews drawn from all social strata.

Borwine Frenkel, a painter well known in Paris, and his ten-year-old daughter took refuge in Villeneuve-sur-Lot (Lot-et-Garonne). "On several occasions," he recalls, "we took shelter with M. and Mme Étienne Carrie. He was a plumber. . . . In 1943 we took up permanent residence with them, naturally without registering at the town hall. The presence in Villeneuve of numerous collaborators made for constant danger not only for us but also for M. Carrie and his family. In early 1944, when the militia was let loose in Villeneuve against the Jews and Resistance people, we left for the farm of M. Chansard in Casseneuil near Agen. The farmer was already giving . . . shelter to other Jews. We stayed there until the Liberation." Borwine Frenkel continued to paint Jewish motifs, but not too openly as he had to stay in "character" as a farm worker.[6]

Maurice Lewinbaum was released from the Pithiviers Camp because he had been wounded in World War I. He crossed over the demarcation line and ended up in Ussel (Corrèze), where he had to report to the lieutenant of the local police force, Puech. "As soon as I arrived, [Puech] got me an ID and a food-ration card in the name of 'Loewendal, Marcel.' Later he put me in touch with Commander Molinet of the Groupement des Travailleurs Étrangers [Foreign Workers Group] located in Neuvic and made up, for the most part, of former Jewish volunteers who had been interned at the time of their demobilization. Molinet was in the Resistance and thanks to him there were never any deportations." In the spring of 1944 Lewinbaum, with all the other internees, joined the partisans "out in the scrubland."[7]

In Toulouse, Lyon, Grenoble, Marseille, and plenty of other places people in the underground thought up all kinds of survival strategies. The testimony of D. Halter is of particular interest for the light it throws on their inventiveness.

> After the exodus from Paris [in June 1940] I found myself in Toulouse. Starting in 1941 the raids against Jews who had supposedly broken some ordinance, for example being without employment, became more and more threatening. I got to know Émile Bezombes on rue du Taur, a former clerk at a Paris department store who had gone into business [in Toulouse]. He had rented premises for a workshop, where he had given legal employment to some ten Jewish refugees from Belgium and Paris. Later, I discovered in Lyon a friend from Paris, who was also in fine leather goods and who helped people set up little workshops where they could work for a company belonging to Mme Alibert. Thanks to the latter's good relations with the police she [was able to get] work permits for at least ten craftsmen. In addition, she put her [Lyon] apartment at 19 rue du Bonnel at our disposal in the event of danger.[8]

Emmanuel Berl and his wife, Mireille, took refuge under false identities with Emmanuel Arago, a friend, who found them a safe place with the family of M. Bouyou, the postmaster of Argentat.[9] In the bosom of this extremely kind family, living in a village of close to 1,500 inhabitants amid the gorges of the Dordogue, the Berls learned to hide themselves. The vocation of their kind host made it easier for the Berls to know to whom it was safe to talk. Thanks to him they knew, for example, that "they had nothing to fear from the butcher, the shoemaker, and the baker." The cases of such persons known in their immediate neighborhood to be Jews were quite common, and confirm that there was little penchant for denunciation, even among people not free of antisemitic prejudices.[10]

Jacqueline Keller:

> How did our whole family save itself? Thanks to my father, who emigrated from Poland in 1918. He was a man who took the initiative. Freemason, radical-socialist, municipal counsellor in the 2nd Arondissement of Paris. I always remember the family meetings around the dinner table when he talked at great length about everything. He transmitted to us his faith in humans at the same time as his mistrust of the Nazis. Then, when he wrote to my mother from the Free Zone, where he had gone after the announcement of the first census, that he had arranged new false identities for us so we could join him. Now we would be the Bienvenu [welcome] instead of the Wolkom family. The name was really amusing and easy to remember.

Accompanied by a small group of Jews, the family fled surreptitiously, their group even coming under German fire at one point (one woman was killed). They arrived at the end of May 1942, establishing a new life in Creuze, where they avoided any unnecessary contact with urban life and changed their residence periodically. Key to Wolkom's strategy was "complete intergration into the style of life of the villagers":

> Harvesting grain, grapes, and other crops, we . . . did not miss out on the celebrations on big holidays and other dates that punctuated the rural calendar. Our hearts weren't always in it. . . . In each of the villages where we lived, the important people, that is, the mayor, the parish priest, the school teacher, the postman, and the policeman all knew who we were, quite simply because my father made a point of identifying himself and showing them that he was not making a mistake in placing his confidence in them. They would offer us a hospitality that they understood as the duty of protecting [the defenseless]. I will always remember the words of the woman running a course for girls in Guéret, where my father had taken me: "I won't make you pay the same price as the children of the big farmers." It did happen that I heard antisemitic remarks. But there was never any passage from words to action, such as turning us in.

The fact that her family's experience was not atypical taught Keller that the humanitarian tradition made many French immune to antisemitism and racism.[11]

An Unknown Page from the Life of Isaac Schneerson

In his function as a rabbi, Isaac Schneerson, founder of the Centre de Documentation Juive Contemporaine (CDJC—Center for Contemporary Jewish Documentation), had already demonstrated courage in the face of official antisemitism in Tsarist Russia, long before his emigration to France. In France he became a successful industrialist. In 1943 antisemitism once again forced him to abandon his accustomed life, leaving Grenoble along with his wife in December 1943 for an underground existence in Périgueux. Several months before he had laid the foundation for a center that would document the anti-Jewish persecutions in France. The first meeting took place without much discretion in his Grenoble apartment, then under Italian occupation, attended by about twenty representatives from various Jewish organizations.[12]

The Schneersons took up residence in Mussidan, near Périgueux, where Isaac had a metallurgical factory, which had permitted him, before the war, to form numerous ties with people in the region. In a letter written the very day of the Liberation he renders homage to the "good farmers" of the region who had hidden him during the war. "Today we came out of the shack where my wife and I lived for more than eight months in terrible conditions. My daughter-in-law [and granddaughter] hid elsewhere, far from us, in order to divide up the risk. The good farmers took turns hiding us while the Gestapo sought us on at least two occasions. Michel [his son] was with the partisans, and he was a constant source of worry and suffering. For months we went without news of him and believed him dead. You can understand how my poor wife suffered. Happily he survived and is now a respected personage, popular and well liked. He is a hero of the resistance."[13] Indeed, Michel was captured by a German army unit but was able to escape and continue his resistance activities until the Liberation. Elected mayor of Mussidan after the war, he died in an accident in 1961.[14]

The future sociologist Edgar Morin, then a Resistance activist, had some difficulty in convincing his father, Vidal, that he could save his life only by "diving head first into illegality." According to him, his father, like many others, "thought he was less threatened by staying within the law than by evading it." He was willing to circumvent that legality, for instance by obtaining false German papers, but he also continued to maintain his legal identity. "He saw the risk that plunging into illegality would entail," his son recalled, "but not the chance of saving himself. He thought, in a kind of eastern reflex, that the powers that be would be grateful for his submission." But after late 1942, he lived full-time under false identity: he had four false ID cards.[15]

The Void around Legal Organizations

Clandestinity assumed such proportions that official organizations like the Consistory began to observe a deep rift between them and the greater Jewish populace. We owe to Albert Lévy, an official the Central Consistory sent on assignment to the Southern Zone, a compelling description of the upheaval in the "way of life" of both French and immigrant Jews from early 1943 on. He particularly stresses the distrust toward legal organizations and people's categorical refusal to deal with them in any way at all: "In almost all the cities we have encountered . . . those of our faith who have [refused any] visible Jewish activity . . . or even [to figure] on a list of subscribers. It is almost impossible, in cities like Toulouse and Saint-Étienne, to find coreligionists . . . who are ready to serve on a fund-raising committee."

Lévy described the extreme negative attitude of Jews toward the UGIF, noting the predominant "unfavorable opinion." During an earlier trip (30 July– 9 August) Lévy had come up against "difficulties fund-raising efforts faced because of a distrust, not to say a hostility, toward the UGIF. Everywhere unfortunate rumors circulate about the institution." After the August 1943 trip he noted "the increasing spread of distrust and even hostility towards the methods of the UGIF." Several weeks of effort to create local fundraising committees met with "almost insurmountable obstacles."[16]

An unsigned document entitled "Coup d'oeil sur la situation des Juifs de France" (Survey of the Situation of the Jews of France), reflects an official perspective on the circumstances of Jewish life in the summer of 1943:

> Assuming a false identity is now very widespread. When one of the offenders falls into the hands of authorities, he is charged [but] some of the courts give a very lenient sentence. In general the church authorities, both Catholic and Protestant, are trying to outdo each other in terms of action that would save Jews, in particular Jewish juveniles. The Commissiariat for Jewish Questions, which has its seat in Paris and Vichy, has regional offices across the whole territory. The role of the

latter is rooting out Jews who have gone into hiding, identifying Jewish property now passed into the hands of Aryans, . . . antisemitic propaganda through the papers and radio, etc.

A special police force nicknamed the "physiognomy brigade" is active in tracking down Jews for infractions of the anti-Jewish regulations, and turning them over to the Germans. Only one punishment awaits them: first, the camps, then deportation.

The Commission for Jewish Affairs is greatly assisted by the policing services of the Legion, presently called the National Militia, which is the police service of the new regime.[17]

The special police service thus did not take long in developing a strong interest in the parallel evolution of Jewish response and public opinion. In September 1943 the Toulouse police, at the request of the Commissariat for Jewish Questions, carried out a raid against non-French Jews (naturalized and not), estimated at 1,300 in the census. But the operation was a total failure. "Foreign Jews arrested in the course of the raid: 100," reported the regional delegate of the Commissariat on 28 September 1943. The author tried to explain the setback as a result of various factors, most notably complicity between the local police and the Jewish population, who responded with a very active self-defense. Yet, all possible measures had been taken to obtain in secret lists of foreign and French Jews in each region. Regional delegates of the commissariat judged that they had been short-circuited by the police, who leaked the date of the raid. They formally accused the police of complicity, and the inquiry that followed made it clear that uncoded telegrams had been sent, that there had been numerous telephone calls back and forth, and that Jews had been forewarned "by numerous leaks on the part of the postal service as well."

The report is precise about the way in which Jews escaped arrest: they had been hidden on "Aryan" farms and guided from place to place at night. In the future, the inquiry concludes, the police should not rely on lists prepared in advance, but rather sudden, simultaneous operations all over France against "the residences of . . . both Jews and Aryans, with provision for exemplary sanctions against Aryans with whom Jews are found hiding." This is a radically new situation: The Jews were now less to be sought at home than in the domiciles of "Aryans."[18]

Resistance organizations such as the UJRE, MNCR, and also the General Committee for Defense (CGD), which united all the trends of Eastern European Jewry, developed their propaganda in two directions, warning Jews of the risks of visiting the offices of the UGIF, and spreading practical advice on life underground. Thus, after a brief period during which the UGIF offices in Marseille had been closed (the result of either a slackening of effort or possibly an intention to scuttle the operation), the Resistance learned in September 1943 that they had been reopened. The CGD immediately published an announcement (also spread by word of mouth among the activists): "The UGIF and its offices are a snare. Those who go to them will sooner or later be arrested and deported. Its officials claim to be helping and saving Jews; this is not true, they can neither help nor save anyone. To have your name on a UGIF list is to be under permanent Gestapo surveillance. We will do everything in our power to assist you discretely. This is a matter of your freedom and your life."[19]

At the same time the UJRE circulated a text setting out numerous practical rules, the fruits of the experience gained by Resistance operatives. "Be vigilant! Once and for all, leave your legal residences and do not return for any reason. In your illegal residences be discreet, don't bring in people whom you don't know well. Do not keep your identity papers if they are stamped 'JEW' or have a foreign-sounding name. If you have false papers, don't have anything but them in your pockets. Hide the other papers well. Don't trust people who talk a lot. Don't speak Yiddish in public places or in the streets. It would be criminal on your part to neglect these elementary security measures that will let you live to see the hour of Liberation."[20]

The Strange Underground Universe of Children

We discover an even stranger universe in the experience of children hidden in institutions or with host families, where even if their origins were known to some, they also knew to remain silent, not to refer to their old identities, in short, to behave as cautiously as illegal adults. This dimension of Jewish life in occupied France has remained largely unexplored. Without underestimating the role of the "rescuers," we must also restore to the children their role as *actors*. Their achievement: losing their memory.

The writer Georges Perec summarizes this situation in a few words: "There was no past. . . . I have no childhood memories. . . . No one asked me about this question. It was not inscribed on my program. I had a dispensation: another history, History with a large "H," had already answered in my place: the war, the camps."[21] This ostensible observance of memory covered a deliberately submerged recollection, ever latent, of the end of a world peopled by those most dear.

Denise Baumann, a Resistance activist and educator, wrote after her study of child survivors, a work that was as trying for her as for her subjects: "They had to cease being themselves, to develop another personality, to remain silent, lie. . . . They became apprentice liars, saying nothing about themselves, about their families, not replying to the questions of schoolmates except by inventing a fabricated story and sticking to it."[22] Years after the events, Baumann observed, the adults seemed to retain "a selective memory." But, given the chance to reflect without prodding, many recalled the "psychological difficulty of persevering in the temporary forgetfulness of the dear faces that they both hoped to see and despaired of ever seeing again."[23]

Albert remembers the dreadful instructions his mother gave him: "In case of a raid, you don't know me"; in public he had "to walk on the other side of the street"; if "something should happen" to his mother he must not react. Many former Resistance participants recall moments when they risked losing (or indeed lost) their freedom as a consequence of spontaneous reaction to one or another incident. Because his parents were divorced, Charles lived with his grandparents in Toulouse. They were in the Resistance and were militant communists, close to the leadership of the FTP-MOI in Haute-Garonne. At fifteen Charles had his own false I.D., which would allow him to work in a factory controlled by the Germans. Ongoing sabotage brought regular checking by German soldiers, but his disguise was so solid and his comrades considered him so trustworthy, that not only was Charles able to continue working at the factory, but he also took part in the meetings that planned the sabotage.[24]

Robert Frank, originally housed at the Lamarck children's home of the UGIF in Paris, and then transferred at the age of thirteen to the trade school on rue des Rosiers, remembers what he felt the day he changed his identity:

I can't find the words [to describe] the feeling that literally took possession of me when I understood that I would no longer have to wear the yellow star. It was in March of 1943, a few days after I had run away from the trade school, an escape that had been prepared by M. Léon, the brother-n-law of Dr. Milhaud,[25] who made a long speech to me. "Get it into your head that from now on you are not Robert Frank any more, but Robert François, Robert F. R. A. N. Ç. O. I. S. And another thing: now you are free; at the trade school it was like being in a trap; they could

pick you up at any time." . . . Each time I had to give my name as François it gave me a sense of pleasure to deceive the other person. It had
become, in a sort of way, a game.

As a child, Frank did not always understand quite how dangerous this game
was, not what freedom was or what the war meant, but life and his friends
taught him "what the word 'free' meant. I understood it when, with my pal
George Milbom, also a Jew, I listened to Radio London with the permission
of Mme Vallon [who sheltered them]. We set up little flags on a map of Russia at the places that she indicated. I discovered the larger world. . . . I was
involved in great events." Having located himself on the map, so to speak,
the boy found hope again: as he reflected decades later, "Gone was the anguish that had strangled me."[26]

Keeping the Faith

In an article entitled "La mort à cache-cache" (Hide-and-Seek with Death),
Jacques Lanzman recalls his own juvenile conception of affairs, still limited
in 1943 by "habits of the village" where the sixteen-year-old's parents had
hidden him. "My father had forbidden me to say that I was a Jew, so I hid this
carefully but also without being ashamed. I learned to say my [Catholic]
prayers in the evening before supper, I went to confession, [and] I took communion at Easter. . . . I couldn't betray either my family or the sentiments
of my foster-family who were very pleased with my attention to Christian
practice."[27]

Concealing one's Jewish identity, absolutely necessary for survival, posed
a difficult moral problem for leaders of the Éclaireurs israélites de France
(Jewish Scouts): pride in being Jewish—their raison d'être and supported
by the Consistory—was incompatible with camouflage. Moreover, lying contradicted both Jewish and scouting morality. Robert Gamzon, one of these
leaders, told another scout master, "You must try to show the youngsters that
if they have a duty to lie in order to save themselves, they must make a distinction between this lie, which is unfortunately inevitable, and their real
sense of honor."[28]

Others resolved the contradiction differently. In a "Letter to a Young
Jew" appearing as a broadsheet pasted up on walls by the Lautrec *Maquis* on
20 January 1944, the scout leader Léo Kohn seems to have taken a position

directly opposite Gamzon's; the crux was not so much anxiety over the risk of conversion as the prospect of lying to the priest:[29] "When I was told, my dear young brother, that you were calmly going to confess to a Catholic priest in order not to call attention to yourself, I asked myself whether you had [a conscience as Jew]. . . . Try to understand [the] difference between all this web of material untruths in which we are caught because a legislation of injustice and brutality forces us to it, and a lie that one would tell to a friend or to God. Well now, you are lying to God." Kohn went so far as to urge the boy to "bring this dangerous game to an end" by telling the priest "who you are and that you are tired of continuing this lie." The notion was that if the priest were kind he would help the youngster to keep his secret and remain a Jew; if not, the youth should leave and rejoin the scouts, who would find him another refuge.

René Goldman's parents were part of a group of about thirty Belgian and Dutch Jews who crossed over the demarcation line in the Jura mountains in August 1942. Happy to be in the Free Zone, they were interned under surveillance in a hotel by the French police; a few weeks later the latter conducted them to the Rivesaltes camp. René's aunt, a French national, was able to obtain the nine-year-old's release from the police, and then placed him in the Organisation de Secours des Enfants home in Masgelier. In February 1943 a woman took him to a convent near Chateauroux (Indre). Thenceforth, he was to be René "Garnier," born to a Catholic family in Chateauroux. "Never strip down to wash yourself," the mother superior told him so the other boys wouldn't notice that he was circumcised. Despite such precautions, René and three other Jewish boys discovered one another. The boys must have found some aspects of life there oppressive, for they even considered a plan to run away at one point. Overall, however, Goldman remembered that "we had it pretty good there." The practice of the Catholic rituals did not bother the young Goldman too much, indeed becoming so accustomed that he "was rather annoyed when the sister said I couldn't assist at mass with a categorical 'Oh no! no question of that!'"

René's father escaped his captors and subsequently wrote from time to time. He learned from his father that his mother had been sent to a camp in Poland. Afraid he would never see his mother again, he was nonetheless more afraid to let anyone see him cry. "No, they would have asked me why. And it was hard not to be able to talk about her. That silence, I experienced it as a betrayal." And indeed his mother never came back. His father fought with the Resistance in one of the Jewish combat groups of the MOI, but was captured a month before the Liberation. With the end of the Occupation the need to lead a double life also ended: "As if a spell had been lifted, my Catholic past disappeared from one day to the next."[30]

Real and False Baptisms

Cardinal Jean-Marie Lustiger long remembered the day in 1940 when he asked his parents' permission to convert. The thirteen-year-old's decision was not a move to evade danger—the Germans had not yet begun their persecutions—but one based on religious conviction. In the "extremely painful scene" which ensued, the young Lustiger explained to his parents that "the step that I was taking did not force me to give up my Jewishness" and indeed Lustiger remained a Jew for the persecutors. His baptism and first communion (like those of his younger sister, who followed his example) took place on 25 September 1940 in the chapel of the Orleans bishopric; he took the name Jean-Marie, but retained Aron as well. His mother was arrested in September 1942 (his father was at that very moment searching for a place to hide the family; he evaded arrest and survived the war) and interned at Drancy, whence she was deported to Auschwitz in convoy 48 of 13 February 1943, never to return.

Aron Lustiger was then catapulted into the life which was according to him "the experience of all the little Jewish children of my generation who knew the words 'persecution' and 'pogrom.'" Like so many other Jewish children, he found protection in the Catholic environment, but his was not so absolute as theirs: they for the most part had false identity papers, often showing them to have been baptized at birth. The Germans did not recognize his conversion: he remained a Jew. "I was summoned to the police station in Decazeville [where he rejoined his father]. 'Show us your papers. Come on, tell the truth. We know very well who you are.' They stamped JEW on the papers. At that moment I felt the vice tighten and I said to my father, 'We're leaving here.'" They moved to Toulouse, where he hid his father as a farm laborer under a false identity. As for the future cardinal, in the spring of 1944 he joined a group of young Resistance fighters close to the "Témoinage chrétien" group, and of course survived to become a leader of the Catholic Church in France.[31]

The shadowy world of clandestine life was always and persistently dangerous, but for tens of thousands of Jews in France no other choice existed. For them, the radical statement of J. Block-Michel describes the condition under which they were forced to live. "It took some time to comprehend that the situation of a Jew in the Resistance was safer than that of a neutral Jew [i.e., obeying the anti-Jewish statutes]."[32]

Men and women, adults and adolescents, some of the latter having painfully emerged from childhood, all of them made the leap into the unknown to live like outlaws. From there to joining the Resistance was not such a giant step, and many of them took the step. They traced a course in three stages, as Léon Poliakov describes them in chapter headings: "The Adventures of a Law-Abiding Jew," "The Adventures of a Jew in the Open," and "The Adventures of a Jew Under Cover."[33]

CHAPTER ELEVEN

Do Not Forget the Children

We must separate out the Jews as a whole, and not protect their young.

—Robert Brasillach[1]

Mothers of France! When you kiss your child at night in his bed, before his peaceful sleep, think of those hellish trains on which little Jewish children, alone, abandoned to their mortal anguish, scream with terror and thirst.

—Appeal from the National Movement Against Racism[2]

The drama of Jewish children during the Occupation furnished both Jewish and non-Jewish aid groups and organizations a tragic occasion to mobilize their forces. The image of youngsters separated from their parents, interned under abominable conditions, and then deported to the death camps undoubtedly provoked unbearable sorrow. The ferocity with which the Nazis seized children in order to send them east undoubtedly proved even to the skeptical that some sort of hitherto unknown murderous undertaking was taking place. It is this element that gave the genocide its singularity: the biological extinction of a people.

Emmanuel Ringelblum, chronicler of the Warsaw Ghetto, notes broken-heartedly in June 1942: If one excepts the pharaoh who ordered the new-born Hebrew children to be thrown into the Nile, this is without precedent in Jewish history. In the past, whatever may have been the fate of adults, children still had the right to life—in order to be converted to the Christian faith. Even in the most barbarous of times, a spark of humanity glowed in the hardest of hearts and children were spared. The Hitlerian beast is of a different nature. It devours those who are most precious to us, those who are most worthy of pity—our innocent children.[3]

And yet, as of summer 1942, perceptions in France about the fate of the deported children were less clear. But the confused premonition in Jewish organizations of a grave danger was sufficient for them to undertake to rescue children in Paris and the Southern Zone. These organizations hoped for (and often found) help for the children from non-Jewish organizations and the French populace.

Humanitarian rescue took place in a context not only of the persecution that made it imperative, but also of the evolution in French public opinion. The sacrifices Jews made toward this objective would all have been in vain in a France where the majority of the population remained anti-Jewish; this is a simple truth that must be counterposed to a certain tendency to dissociate the rescue operation from "armed or political resistance."[4] The Resistance was united by overarching goals, and its various modes of activity cannot be contrasted one to another. And yet public opinion did not simply evolve from the seeming indifference of 1940 and even 1941 to its later active sabotage of antisemitic legislation, but rather in considerable part under the urging of Resistance groups. Would public opinion have reacted as it did if people had not come to understand the true purpose of the deportations? In order for hearts and homes to open, it was necessary that public opinion be aware of the gravity of the danger hanging over the innocents' heads.

Some Jewish agencies active in rescue operations had little talent either for propaganda or other forms of resistance; most were originally apolitical by nature. Other, more militant organizations took on the job of disseminating information and sensitizing public opinion. It was inevitable—indispensable—that Jews, who were most threatened, should be present in the struggle against silence. A special place is reserved for the National Movement Against Racism, born of the initiative of the Jewish Resistance but assured of the support of French Catholics, Protestants, and atheists. This active solidarity with the threatened Jews, with the imperiled children, is to one degree or another a consistent element in the totality of the Resistance, bringing to it an "unassailable moral ethic."[5]

For the Organisation de Secours des Énfants (OSE) saving children meant first of all hiding them in its own homes (seven in the Southern Zone in 1942) while still providing assistance to families who sought its aid. The history of this great undertaking during the Occupation will in particular be the account of its desperate efforts, at times *in extremis,* to disperse the children for whom it was responsible.

In June of 1941, the OSE had a total of almost eight hundred and fifty children at its centers, three of which had been opened by the Jewish Scouts in 1939 after Paris had been evacuated because of the bombing threat. The ties then formed between the OSE and the Éclaireurs israélites de France (EIF—the Jewish Scouts) would benefit rescue operations throughout the Occupation. The scouts brought a youthful element to the OSE, one informed by civic spirit. From the summer of 1942, this cooperation, operational only in the Southern Zone, took concrete form both in the "B circuit" of the OSE[6] and in the "Sixth Division," the EI's underground structure, which established close ties with the young Zionist movement and collaborated on assisting convoys to Switzerland and Spain. The three structures were so interdependent that their separate contours are blurred; the overlap in the individual organizational accounts after the war render difficult any assessment of their individual contributions.

By January 1941 all social services of the OSE were incorporated into the UGIF. Contrary to the attestations of Xavier Vallat (commissioner for Jewish Questions) and of R.-R. Lambert (director-general of the UGIF in the Southern Zone), agencies under the aegis of the UGIF enjoyed no autonomy, even if they were in charge of their own specific tasks. After the deportations from the camps in the South in August–September of 1942,[7] the decision to close the homes and to disperse their residents lay in the hands of the UGIF, whose well-known opposition to any transgression of anti-Jewish legislation led to serious delays in the development of rescue operations and to equally serious compromises.

The contrast between the spirit of a Georges Garel, head of the B Division of the Jewish Scouts, and that of a Lambert is striking. The latter was perfectly happy and proud to keep the children around: "Saturday [2 July, 1943], I visited La Clue, *my* old people's home, and yesterday, La Verdière, *my* children's home. What great personal satisfaction to see . . . chubby-cheeked kiddies who knew and told me that they owed me their freedom."[8]

The spirit of obedience to the laws of the constituted government made some staff of the OSE hesitant to take the salutary measure of closing the official centers and going underground. They should have. On 26 August 1942, for the first time, squads of gendarmes and French public order police raided the centers and arrested a number of young people over sixteen years of age of German, Austrian, Czech, and Polish origin. They simultaneously undertook searches for younger children whose parents were in camps, on the pretext of "reuniting" families.

The Inevitable Turning Point

There are situations that brook no delay. The OSE decision on 20 August 1942 to evacuate and hide some one hundred children from the Vénissieux Camp on the eve of their deportation had to be made without there being any clear idea of where they could be taken.[9] The intensified pursuit of Jews after the Southern Zone had been occupied by the Wehrmacht, and in particular after the "cleansing" of the Old Port quarter of Marseille in January of 1943, hastened the OSE's efforts to hide a certain number of children throughout the French countryside. Also at this time the first networks leading to Switzerland were established under Adrien Benveniste and Théo Klein (one of the leaders of the Sixth Division of the EIF) in close collaboration with the Protestant relief agency CIMADE and other organizations.[10]

The clandestine EI group was formed in August of 1942 under the same circumstances as the "B circuit" of the OSE, particularly because of the danger of raids on the children's homes. The EIF ran some agricultural schools and group homes, of which the most important were at Moissac (Tarn) and La Grave (Alpes-de-Haute-Provence). Roger Fichtenberg is today the living memory of the Sixth.[11] At the beginning of July 1942, when he was turned away from the French youth labor worksites like all Jews, he had the idea of recording his daily rescue work. Naturally everything is in code: the names of his friends, the cities and towns, the children or teens to be camouflaged are designated by the name of an object in common use, which allowed him to send the supervisors messages of the following kind: "Send me the pen, book, and notebook," and so on. "For the La Grave home," Fichtenberg remembers, "it proved necessary to supply false identity papers for more than one hundred persons. . . . For the children, a food ration card was sufficient, and we had large quantities of these thanks to the complicity of the municipal offices. For the adults, we had to assemble a full deck: ID card, demobilization form, tobacco card. We evacuated the children in groups of five or six and this took three months. In March 1944 the La Grave center ceased to exist."

The year 1943 proved crucial for the OSE. An AJJDC report evokes the accelerated pace of the Nazi roundups of children.[12] In a few pages it also summarizes the whole policy of the OSE, its tireless and often desperate action to save those who could still be saved from deportation. The OSE children's homes, incorporated into the UGIF, were known, inventoried, and thus dangerously exposed to Gestapo sweeps. The children had to be placed with French families or institutions as rapidly as possible. Cited in this same report, the letters of Dr. Joseph Millner, secretary general of OSE France,[13] give some sense of the urgency of identifying a solution in the face of new decisions by the occupation authorities in the Southern Zone to "capture the children right in the homes of their benefactors." The Germans "drew up special registers," Millner goes on, "with detailed lists of information about the children's identities, and they were not permitted to leave their place of residence." Thus, the La Verdière home, near Marseille, was placed under the direct control of the Gestapo. On 20 October the entire home (with a total of almost forty children) including the director, Alice Salomon, was deported to Drancy.[14]

In November the hunt for children still in OSE centers intensified. On 4 November, Joseph Millner noted: "Each day brought new tragedies. Joseph Kogan,[15] director of our home at Brout-Vernet, was arrested along with his two children, the one six years old and the other two. . . . Nicole Weil, our social worker, was arrested in Nice when she was trying to save some Jewish families and a number of children."

Clearly the OSE was not free to act; it regularly ran into refusals on the part of UGIF officials. Millner received from Marseille "fresh news" (dated 5 November) after a meeting of the board of the UGIF of the Southern Zone: Alain Mosse of the OSE informed Millner that the decisions obliged "all sections to continue their work as in the past . . . even if the German police . . . seek to exercise strict control over all activity. The Germans demanded a complete detailed list of the children's homes, their employees and also lists of all the children with the former and current addresses of their parents." And indeed, three days later the Gestapo arrested the entire staff of the UGIF camp committees in Sisteron (the UGIF had committees for the camps in the Free Zone).[16] On 10 November, Millner noted that "we are heading into increasingly hard times. We continue our work and will so until the end. The list of our colleagues arrested and transported to Drancy grows longer every day." And he remarked yet again that "the general structure of the UGIF remains unchanged, but we have the firm conviction that maintaining large concentrations of children in the homes puts them in imminent danger of deportation. We have intensified energetic measures to counter this action."

At the close of 1943, a year and a half after the OSE had initiated evacuation and closure of its homes, some still remained open. The situation became ever more dramatic, the raids on the children more frequent. The OSE found itself in a race against time and the UGIF collaboration with the Germans. In Limoges, Julien Samuel hit upon the idea of putting the homes under the protection of prefectural authorities by the means of a ploy of a "conscription" order. The children thus passed into the guardianship of the prefecture, which was supportive of the operation.[17]

Formal Notice by Vaad Hatsala

A substantial portion of OSE funds came from Vaad Hatsala, the rescue committee of the Jewish Agency for Palestine. Vaad Hatsala was well informed about the destination of the deportees and from early 1943 warned the OSE that it would cut off its funding unless the latter distanced itself from the UGIF. Apparently in February–March 1943 the transfer of funds was in fact temporarily suspended.

Vaad Hatsala exerted continuous pressure to accelerate the shift to clandestine operations by cutting off funds to certain charitable organizations. Dr. Shmuel Scheps, head of the Palestinian Office in Geneva and liaison between France and Haïm Barlas (director of the Vaad Hatsala headquarters in Istanbul), noted on a report received in France, 3 March 1943, "I am still waiting for your response regarding *takziv* (budget in Hebrew) for the OSE." At the same time OSE France acknowledged the urgency of severing connections with the UGIF: "You insist on the fact that we should accelerate the complete separation from the UGIF. In Paris this move was already begun in 1941."[18]

The pressure brought to bear by the Jewish Agency for Palestine seems to have become so great that one of their correspondents at OSE-France thought it necessary to explain the difficulty of evacuating the homes quickly: "We agree with you . . . but we are not able from one day to the next to send three hundred children . . . to the countryside. . . . We cannot abandon the several hundred sick clients who are still dealing with official channels. . . . In several localities we have to envisage a reorganization of social assistance." But despite such concerns, the author of the communication promised that "we shall not delay for a single day our complete break with the UGIF."[19]

Alas, this was not soon enough. On 9 February 1944, Millner wrote in a new letter to his colleagues, "Sad news. Yesterday the Gestapo burst into our offices in Chambéry. Eight plainsclothes officers took part in the operation. They rounded up all the staff in a single room [and trapped] three of our aid-recipients as well. . . . The Gestapo arrested nine staffers from the OSE and three people from CAR (Committee for Aid to Refugees). The police used violence on clients who refused to say that they were Jewish." On 14 February, Millner wrote again to his colleagues. "Our relations with non-Jewish organizations have been strengthened. . . . Only two of our houses remain with a small number of children, no more than 150."[20] Considering the two numbers here—300 at the end of January 1944 and 150 remaining on 16 February—within the space of less than a month, even after the Chambéry arrests, the actions to hide the children moved 150 of them, which indicates the amplitude of the effort but also the rescue possibilities carried out in the face of catastrophe.[21]

Thirty-three men and women from the staff were also deported. Of these only four returned. Four others died in France itself: Dr. Moise Blumenstock, staff physician at the Le Masgelier Home, went underground and joined the Resistance, but was assassinated in June of 1944. Gertrude Blumenstock-Lévy, a youth worker at Le Masgelier, was later assassinated by the militia or the Gestapo. Pauline Gaudefroy, a Catholic, was arrested and tortured by the Milice, who suspected her of being Jewish; she managed to escape and joined an FTPF Resistance group in Haute-Vienne, but fell into an ambush and was shot along with other members of the *maquis*.[22] Dr. Gluck, a physician at Brout-Vernet (Allier) was assassinated in June 1944 under unknown circumstances. At this time, Francis Chirat, a Catholic Resistance activist who served as liaison between the Mouvement populaire des familles and the underground OSE, was also killed, shot at the Place Bellecoeur in Lyon.[23]

A special team composed by the OSE and the Sixth with Georges Loinger and Emmanuel Racine at its head was in charge of the clandestine movement of refugees across the Swiss border. The team exploited a network of contacts that began in Annemasse and went through a playground along the border. Associated with this activity are the names of two young women, Mila Racine (MJS) and Marianne Cohn (the Sixth). Mila Racine was caught and deported; Marianne Cohn died after being savagely pistol-whipped by the German police. Cohn left a beautiful and deeply moving poem, "Je ne trahirai pas, je parlerai demain" ("I will not betray, I will speak tomorrow"). Gerhardt Riegner of the WJC General Office estimates that the total numbers of Jewish children accepted by Switzerland during the war at 1,350, many of them saved by the OSE and the Sixth.[24]

Memories of . . . Childhood

Today there remain many UGIF "children" able to recount their experiences. Those among them who lived in the UGIF centers all remember having been the object of various "security"measures on the part of their supervisors. These they experienced as generally positive, even if they had moments of doubt.

Roger Appel, thirteen in 1943, recalled, "I often went to the office of the directress. She liked to have me read poems that I had written. She gave me advice and said: 'You shouldn't be sad, this will all end well, God will protect us.' My head was full of questions but I didn't dare talk about it. Later, after the war, I often wondered whether the staff at the home had done the right thing by not discussing with the older children the tragedy of the circumstances about which, despite everything, we all had some awareness."[25]

The memories of Robert Frank, who was fifteen in 1943, accord with Appel's. Second thoughts about the calming rhetoric of the director who ceaselessly repeated that "the danger was in the street, outside the home. The director gave us orders to be observed if we wanted to avoid internment: strictly obey the law, do not hide the star, always carry permission to leave the school, do not go to the cinema, come back before curfew."[26]

Ida Jidali recalled the same with some bitterness: "At Montreuil, they told us firmly: 'Don't run away, everything has been looked after for you; don't have any ideas about running off, and don't worry about anything.' They lulled us, they lulled everyone . . . [saying that] that we ran no risk at Montreuil, everything was taken care of. . . . In my childish mind, when they said 'everything is taken care of,' I had the impression that they already had a little place out in the country for everyone; I saw remote rural landscapes where on every farm. . . . In my mind, it was going to be like that!"[27]

In the case of Mathilde Jaffé, eighteen years old at the time of her deportation, the criticism is sharper still: "Right in the middle of rue Vauquelin, I got the idea of leaving with my sister. I was not unaware of the fact that there were resistance people who could help us to hide. But I didn't do anything. . . . Today, I think that at eighteen I was still a child, because they mothered us, coddled us even. As far as I can remember, it seems that I would never have mustered the courage to leave the home for the unknown. But, who knows, perhaps all the same . . ."[28] Jaffé poses the question of all those children and adults, who might have been able to find a path to safety on their own if they had not been the object of infantilizing programming.

The numerous testimonies about the UGIF children's homes that the historian Jean Laloum collected led him to conclude that the homes were in reality virtual internment centers. The National Commission on Deportees and Political Internees (under the State Secretariat for Veterans and the Victims of War), having received the report Laloum drew up with Georges Wellers, resolved at its session of 26 January 1988 to grant the UGIF "children" the status of "political internee"(in accordance with article L. 289 of the Pension Code).[29] The commission took into account the "danger and precariousness in which these 'sheltered' children lived." This applied, indeed, not only to those who had been under the control of the Vichy government or the Nazi occupation, but also of those who had been "free," since they had all lived under the same threat of deportation.[30]

The Protestant Plateau

Le Chambon-sur-Lignon: a site emblematic of the assistance rendered Jewish families by Protestants. We must think of all seventeen communes of the predominantly Protestant-Huguenot Vivaris-Lignon plateau when we evoke the name of Le Chambon. How many Jews found safe refuge there? The figure of 5,000 is sometimes given, but even if this is exaggerated (as recent demographic research suggests), nothing can diminish the gallantry of the population of the plateau.[31]

Here, as in all the "Free Zone," the month of August 1942 constitutes a turning point between the two eras of legality and illegality. Nor was this region exempt from the raids. The prefecture of Puy gave an account of one in a report of 30 October 1942. "According to the instructions of 5 August and subsequently, one hundred and sixty foreign Jews were located; eighty-five arrests, of whom seventy-three remained in custody; seventy-five Jews, of whom five minors, tried to escape; of these, eight, including the minors, were authorized to address Swiss Relief in Chambon; sixteen Jews have been recovered, among whom eight at the Swiss border, but five crossed over successfully."[32]

Chambon and neighboring communities experienced an influx of Jewish families or of separated children from the very beginning of the round-ups in the camps. The Reverend Henri Manen (whose efforts at the Les Milles camp to have adults and children exempted from deportation have already been discussed)[33] set up a network and direct escape route between Marseille and Le Chambon. Among the population of the "Protestant plateau," solidarity with the persecuted came as second nature: "One Sunday when we were attending the service in Tence," Marie Brottes recalls, "the pastor came and knocked on the door and said 'Three Old Testaments have arrived.' And we knew that the Old Testaments were Jews. And an old lay brother got up, an old Christian, and he said 'I'll take them.' And he took them to his farm in the middle of the meadows and hid them there."[34]

The Resistance activist Léon Poliakov, a.k.a. Robert Paul, went to Chambon on several missions. In the "evening," he recounts, "I witnessed a truly local spectacle at the Hotel May: a social worker came in with a small group of children whose parents had been deported or were in hiding in Marseille or Lyon. Frightened, the children huddled in a corner of the hall. A first farmer couple comes in. 'We would like to take a little girl eight or twelve years old,' the woman explains. Little Myriam is called forward. 'Do you want to come with Uncle and Auntie?' Intimidated, Myriam does not reply. They wrap her up in covers and carry her out to the sleigh, and off she goes to the farm."

Joseph Atlas was thirteen years old in September 1941, when he escaped to Chambon from the Gurs camp with his brother Victor. They lived there in a little apartment twenty minutes from the mayor's office with their mother, all under false papers. Joseph even went to school from 1941 to 1945. "My mother went every day to the Trocmé house where a number of children lived to work for several months altering clothing. The Trocmés provided us with false identity papers. In the summer of 1943 Mrs Trocmé found me a job on a farm where I watched over the cows. If the Pastor was the charismatic head of Chambon, Mrs Trocmé was the kingpin."[35]

The former rabbinical student André Chouraqui found refuge nearby after fleeing Limoges. Sensitive to religious issues, he later offered the following explanation for sympathy manifested by the people of Le Chambon: "There was a very old tradition of taking people in which had its origins in the memory of the Saint-Barthélemy massacre of Protestants. . . . Everyone saw in us new victims of the intolerance that had led their ancestors to settle on the heights of the Cévennes or in the valleys of the Eyrieux and the Drôme. No appeal, no request ever went without response."[36] This historical tradition generated a lasting pattern of political behavior. The populace voted for the left under the Third Republic; from the elections of 1876 to those of the Popular Front in 1936, the republican parties (radical, socialists and communist) garnered at least 90 percent of votes, at times more than 95.[37]

Even though Jews were the most numerous, all other persecuted and proscribed persons—German refugees, Resistance activists, compulsory labor service dodgers—all found a sympathetic reception. Pierre Vidal-Naquet, "placed" by his parents in the community of Dieulefit, recalls the presence of "numerous intellectuals" in his memories of this period.

> Even more than Saint-Agrève, Dieulefit was a place of refuge. . . . The granddaughter of the president of the League for the Rights of Man, Victor Basch—an eminent representative of the Dreyfusard tradition who was assassinated along with his wife by the Milice in 1944—was also there in Dieulefit as a student at La Roseraie. But in addition to the Jews on whom the most specific threat weighed . . . there were numbers of intellectuals who sided with the Resistance and who contributed to making Dieulefit a little capital of the mind. Musicians like the great pianist Yvonne Lefébure, who was staying with my aunt, writers and journalists like André Rousseau, Andrée Viollis, Emmanuel Mounier, who wrote his *Traité du charactère* [Paris: Seuil, 1946] there; poets like Noël Matthieu, a professor of mathematics and philosophy at La Roseraie, better known under the pseudonym Pierre Emmanuel. . . . [Even] the mayor, Colonel Pizot, who because he was an ardent supporter of Marshal Pétain was wrongly seen by our people as a Catholic, voluntarily closed his eyes to the veritable workshop for forged documents that the director of that operation was operating out of the town hall. Jeannette Barnier was the mayor's secretary and belonged to the Protestant community.[38]

The "Protestant plateau" also served as a marshaling yard for departures to Switzerland, an escape route extending through either Saint-Étienne or Lyon, and then Annecy, Collonge, and Salève. Mireille Philip, the wife of socialist leader André Philip (appointed Minister of the Interior of the Comité français de libération nationale in Algiers at the end of 1943), constituted the first link in a chain that joined ministers and curates and ended at the Ecumenical Council in Geneva.

Did the risk of conversion exist at le Chambon? The Jewish Consistory in Lyon was concerned and sent Marcel Bokanowski to investigate. "This region is a real fief of Protestantism," he soon reported. "The political atmosphere of the region is very favorable to our religious community," he acknowledged, and this permitted establishment of a home at Les Roches by the European student fund, and three others by the Swiss Aid Agency. Nevertheless, the rabbi called for a "specifically Jewish" solution, hopefully one that avoided the "appeal to the cooperation of agencies representing other religions." Jewish clerics in the Marseille region shared Bokanowski's concern and agreed that "This is the path that we must take, because on the interdenominational battleground, we do not have a sufficient number of rabbinical resources to fight on equal terms." His words of August 1942 bear witness to the persistence of an "isolationist" spirit, which, however, was already giving way before the imperative of saving lives.[39]

A Sanctuary for the Persecuted?

Was the refuge at Le Chambon a sanctuary more or less spared the usual repression? In Vichy the Service d'enguête et de contrôle, the police section of the General Commissariat for Jewish Questions (SEC), was interested in the "illegal activities" of the former Chambon mayor Charles Guillon.[40] In the spring of 1943 the SEC notified regional representatives that "Jews wishing to leave France are being directed to [Mayor] Guillon and Pastor Trocnic [obviously André Trocmé] as well as to other well-disposed persons in Mont Dore. Guillon has offices in Vernoux, Valence, and Albussière (Ardèche). These offices, under the cover of Protestant associations, are nothing less than illegal shops for providing false identity papers to Jews who, despite the prohibition, are flocking at the present time to the departments of Drôme and Ardèche. The offices are spreading to other departments as well."[41]

And yet this intelligence, full as it is, does not appear to have occasioned further investigations or indeed any follow-up at all. Was this due to the attitude of the prefect for Le Puy, Robert Bach? At his trial (for collaborationism) after the Liberation, no charge of treason was brought against him. On the contrary, it was established that he had been in contact with the Secret Army and that he had intervened on behalf of Jews and members of the Resistance.[42]

More complex is the case of Major Julius Schmähling, commander of the reserves for the district of Le Puy. Was he well disposed toward the Jews?

Philip Hallie, an American sociologist, in his book on Chambon would have us believe so.[43] Since his thesis has been adopted in the very fine documentary *The Weapons of the Spirit* by Pierre Sauvage (who as a child had hidden in Le Chambon), the "Schmähling Affair" has given rise to a passionate debate. The single indisputable fact is the absence of substantial raids in Le Chambon and surroundings (except for one Gestapo sweep of Cévenol College).[44] The presence of so many refugees, conscription dodgers, and Jews could not have been (as confirmed by the SEC report above) ignored by the French administration, the militia, and the German police. But no archival documentation has survived to suggest that Major Schmähling ever ordered acts of repression. Did he simply close his eyes? It is here that we enter a shadowy zone. Auguste Rivet, threw in his hand at the Le Chambon colloquium, citing "my powerlessness to answer the questions . . . which I raised a few moments ago," a prudent approach reflecting a strict respect for the available sources. In any case, the testimonies that he cites seem to indicate that Schmähling was a "moderating and conciliatory element."[45] Perhaps the role of geography, the topography of the countryside, may have been as important as that of the people in the history of the Protestant plateau during the Occupation. The average altitude of 3,250 feet, the remoteness of the communities, the absence of major lines of communication, all just as surely rendered the region of secondary interest to the occupiers.[46]

Other Rescue Organizations

From its very inception in 1942, the National Movement Against Racism aided the Union of Jewish Women (affiliated with MOI) in caring for children whose parents had been forced to leave them. In August 1942 a first inventory showed that some one hundred children had already been placed in the Parisian suburbs or surrounding countryside.[47] A Protestant village, Noirvault near Bressuire (Deux-Sèvres), with a population of about twenty, took in ten children between three and nine years of age. Not as remarkable as Le Chambon, but the same conscience and the same heart. On a return pilgrimage to Noirvault in 1984 these former "escaped children" (many accompanied by their own children) listened to the Pastor Casalis, himself a former Resistance activist, deliver a sermon on the profound meaning of the villagers' behavior then: "It is we who thank you, for it is you who taught us our vocation as human beings."[48]

In Lyon, the headquarters of the MNCR in the Southern Zone, actions to save children were mounted by Dr. Pierre Grinberg, who had established relations with the local mission of the Swiss Red Cross and the OSE. Here is another example of successful rescue actions undertaken at great risk involving the cooperation of several disparate agencies, in opposition, one must add, to the "legalism" of Jewish organization like the Consistory, to say nothing of the UGIF.

One rescue effort brought together Suzanne Spaak of the MNCR and a group of Christian neighbors who put two houses at Spaak's disposal.[49] The UGIF Center on Rue Lamarck still sheltered children whose parents had been deported. The conspirators took advantage of a rule which permitted non-Jews to take host children one day a week. The Reverand Vergara of the Chapel on rue de Rivoli later recalled how his parisioners responded when Spaak and the others warned that

> the Nazis filling out the quotas for their trainloads of deportees with children picked up by the UGIF after their parents had been deported . . . We quickly made up our minds. The next day, Sunday, 14 February, Mlle Guillemot, our social affairs staff member, contacted some thirty parishioners as they were leaving the chapel service and asked them to go to the UGIF centers over the next three days and offer to take out one or more children for the day. She would then take them to La Clairière, a Protestant children's home at 60 Rue Grenata [the center from which the children were sent to their hiding places].

In the course of Monday and Tuesday more than seventy children (according to the pastor) were thus gathered. Within forty-eight hours all had been placed with families in Paris or in the countryside. The reverend himself took in several of them.[50]

A rescue committee called l'Entraide temporaire (Temporary Mutual Aid) took part in this important operation. This network, conceived in one of the drawing rooms of Parisian high society in February or March 1941, seems to have been the initiative of Mme Chevalley, president of the Service social d'aide aux émigrants (SSAE—Society for Aid to Immigrants). Chevalley gathered a number of benefactors such as Mme Pesson-Depret, wife of the director of the Morgan Bank in Paris, and Mme Massé, wife of the future commissioner of the postwar economic recovery plan. Two more interesting "recruits" would join later: Mme Berr, the wife of the director-general of the Kuhlmann companies, and Mme Béchard, whose husband was the director of the research center of Kuhlmann. The old registry of a children's aid society created in 1921 served as cover for the clandestine bookkeeping of the group:[51] activities were retroactively dated by twenty years, and while the names of the children are given, the addresses of their refugees were not entered. The children also depended on Dr. Fred Milhaud, a physician at the trade school on rue des Rosiers, and his wife, who together arranged a large portion of the false documents they needed, which were produced by the underground labor movement. The doctor himself rescued some twenty children, "mostly boys from the trade school . . . who were placed in Catholic institutions," this despite the fact that the school's director "always hindered my efforts . . . for fear of alerting the Germans."[52]

Georges Dumas, the head of the Resistance group "Noyautage de l'administration publique" ("Infiltration of the Public Administration") in the Limoges region "accumulated" analogous missions that affected children in one way or another. Assisted by his son Roland, he helped Jews of the Limousin obtain false papers and shelter. "It seemed natural for us and was in line with family tradition," Roland Dumas states, because here republican and humanitarian values merged into the rescue actions. Winning functionaries of the public administration over to the Resistance and helping Jews were part—for the Dumas family—of the same struggle. Arrested on 24 March 1944 along with twenty-four others in the Périgord, Dumas' father was shot with his fellow resisters in reprisal for an attack on a German soldier.[53] As his son put it in 1989, no one had been thinking then of marks of recognition, "but I can't describe how I felt at Yad Vashem in Jerusalem when I was given the Certificate of the Righteous Among Nations on behalf of my father and witnessed a tree planted in his name."[54]

Simone Nathan-Ascher, then a student at the girls' secondary school in Limoges, recounts a story which illustrates the Dumas's gallantry:

> In 1943 at the beginning of the school year . . . I had an assignment to write a letter addressed to Marshal Pétain on the theme of "loyalty." My father's property had just been confiscated by the Vichy government and I could not suppress my sense of rebellion. The 'letter' was judged incendiary and did not fail to prompt an investigation. There was nothing left for me to do but leave high school; my parents asked Georges Dumas for help because he was known to be sympathetic toward Jews. Two or three days later, he came to tell us that he had found a boarder's place for me in a convent, the one attached to the hospital in Limoges.

From time to time Mr Dumas and his son came to see me. Despite all precautions, several months later one of the other boarders informed on me. . . . So I had to leave yet again. Georges Dumas helped us by getting false identity cards for my father, my mother, my brother, and me. So the four of us found refuge in the Creuse, but I had to return to Limoges to pick up the papers. He offered to put me up, which I accepted in spite of my fear of compromising him. I did not see him again. He was arrested a few days later and shot shortly after that.[55]

"With tireless zeal [he] aided the victims of racist persecution . . . hunted by the Gestapo." Not many earned the Croix de Guerre (War Cross) for this kind of heroism. One who did was Lucien Bunel, better known as Father Jacques, rector of the little school, Les Carmes d'Avon, where he gave shelter to three Jewish children under false identities. Father Jacques worked for the Direction générale d'étude et de renseignement (DGER — General Administration for Research and Intelligence), the counter-espionage service of Free France, and was liaison with the National Front. Like many other Resistance members, he aided Jews whenever they knocked at his door. Bunel was denounced and on 15 January 1944 was arrested along with the three boys, who were immediately deported. After long and arduous interrogations in the Fontainebleau Prison, Father Jacques was in turn deported to Mauthausen. He died of exhaustion on 2 June 1945, one month after the liberation of the camp.[56]

An Assessment of the War on Children

How many children were sent to their deaths? How many survived? The former numbered 10,140 under the age of fifteen. This figure represents 14.3 percent of the total number of deportees from France.[57] On the other hand, we must guess when trying to determine how many escaped. There are, however, some hard data. One statistical study carried out in the Department of Demography at the University of Jerusalem concluded that children under fifteen constituted 19 percent of the Jewish population of France (based on the census of French and foreign nationals in Paris and its suburbs in October of 1940);[58] the total was 148,024, the number of children under fifteen thus amounting to 34,557. If we estimate the total number of Jews living in France in 1939 as between 300,000 and 330,000, or to be a little more precise, as 315,000, the factor of 19 percent (children under fifteen) yields a figure of 80,000, if we subtract the number known to have been shot, who were deported, or who disappeared, we arrive at an estimate of 44,650 saved. What share can be attributed to the activities of Resistance organizations, and what to individuals and families? The statistics published after the war by charitable agencies and organizations take the population of under eighteen as a basis, which makes any true comparison impossible. In any case, in the end what counts is the result achieved through the common efforts—of organizations, families, and individuals—which mounted a partial obstruction to the criminal enterprise of pitting a military power against children.

CHAPTER TWELVE

"Intermezzo," or the Italian Reprieve

"Siamo tutte belle e ebrei."
—Edgar Morin[1]

━━━━━━━━━━━━━━━━━━━━━━━━━━━━━━━━

By 11 November 1942—a key date in World War II—Soviet resistance had stopped the German advance at Stalingrad, and the Allies were consolidating their positions in Algiers and Morocco, where they had landed on the seventh. The German reaction was not long in coming. On that day, at seven in the morning, units of the Wehrmacht in France crossed the Demarcation Line into the "Free Zone," while the Italians installed themselves in eight departments of the southeast. These changes created a new and more contradictory situation for the Jews in France. On one hand, an intensification in persecution came with the German military presence in most of the country, with new possibilities of exerting pressure on Vichy, which now lost the last vestiges of autonomy. On the other hand, a new glimmer of hope for the Jews emerged in the departments occupied by Mussolini's troops. Admittedly, the latter served fascism, and were just as certainly the allies of Hitler; but they exhibited little of the savage anti-Jewish hatred of the Nazis. In this respect Italian originality found expression in both theory and practice: their definition of race was more flexible than that promulgated by the French, leaving several loopholes; its penalties were less severe, envisioning imprisonment or internment only for specific infractions.[2]

The evolution of the military situation and the weakening of the Fascist regime during the summer of 1943 proved decisive, a period that witnessed unfocused diplomatic efforts by Rome to arrange an exit from the war toward the Western powers. We observe a desire to distance Italy from the "Final Solution," about which governmental circles—Mussolini included—seem to have been relatively well informed. Unlike Vichy, Rome attached a great deal of value to intelligence on Nazi extermination policy. As early as 3 February 1943, Dino Alfieri, the Italian ambassador to Berlin, sent Galeazzo Ciano, the minister of foreign affairs, a voluminous secret report on the "Final Solution," concluding that the "extermination of the Jewish race" was in progress. The ambassador averred "that the response of the Italian government to Berlin's demand for the deportation of Italian Jews . . . now appears reasonable. That response was a rejection."[3] The Duce was probably inclined to go along with the Germans, but Ciano's words about the mass murder taking place on Polish territory seem to have persuaded even him to close his eyes to the doings of Italian officials who subverted German pressures.[4]

After a period of uncertainty in the Southern Zone of France, Italian soldiers gave the impression of being "rather sympathetic and not at all hostile toward the Jews."[5] Both French and foreign Jews streamed toward Grenoble and Nice from Marseille, Toulouse, Pau, and Lyon. There was a to-and-fro movement between Grenoble and Nice, which favored an ongoing exchange of information, as well as contacts between the administrations of charitable and political organizations.

The German police services followed these movements closely. In April of 1943, the *Einsatzkommando*-Marseille (Gestapo) alerted Paris "that the departure of Jews [from the Marseille region] toward the Italian Occupation Zone continues."[6] Meanwhile German security uncovered "a major financial group composed of Italian Jews under the direction of Angelo Donati, the former director of the Banque France-Italie, which seems to have taken on the responsibility of 'escorting the Jews.'" In fact, Angelo Donati, who had entré to the Foreign Ministry in Rome as well as to the Vatican, would be seen by Jews as a savior, and by the Germans as a man to be eliminated.[7]

From Refuge into Trap

Thus a new chapter in the history of the Jews in France opened: that of the Italian Occupation Zone as "an enormous refuge," before it became an enormous trap. The sociologist Edgar Morin, whose father and numerous cousins, all Italian-speakers, had gathered from the four corners of France on the Côte d'Azur and in Italy, tells us how his kin "felt themselves so free that one day, sitting on the terrace of the *grand café*, on via Independenza in Modano; Mathilde replied to people at a neighboring table who had complimented her and her nieces' beauty, '*Siamo tutte belle e ebrei*' ('We're all beautiful and Jewish')."[8] But was the hope of finding refuge here well founded? Any response must take into account both the spontaneous movement of people and the policy implemented by Jewish organizations. The relative freedom that the UGIF and other agencies enjoyed in these territories encouraged immigration.[9]

Undoubtedly, racism did not animate the Italian civil and military authorities, even though Mussolini had introduced racial legislation for Italy in 1938. The first signs of Italian opposition to the application of Vichy's anti-Jewish measures came after 6 December 1942, when Vichy ordered that all foreign Jews who entered France after 1 January 1938 were to be kept at least thirty kilometers from the coast and moved to the departments of Drôme and Ardèche, which would put them under German control. The Italian consul in Nice, Alberto Calisse, speaking for the Italian representatives to the Vichy government (la delegazione de Nizza), demanded to the prefect of Alpes-Maritimes that Italian Jews be exempted. More serious in the eyes of Vichy officials was the refusal to permit the prefectural administration to stamp identity cards or residence permits with the word "Jew" in accordance with the law of 11 December 1942. The prefect of Alpes-Maritimes notes in his report to the Pétain government that this opposition was "a setback for the . . . measures legislated by the French government with regard to foreign Jews." The prefect believed that the Italian point of view was only a pretext, for in reality the Italians were acting "for political reasons," the origins of which could be found in "the Italian government's position of principle in the Jewish problem." In a word, the Italian administration separated itself from the policy followed by Vichy and the Germans.[10]

Berlin and Vichy Take Aim at Count Ciano

The same prefect indicated that the inspiration for the Italian authorities' stance derived from Count Ciano, Minister of Foreign Affairs. Whether or not he knew it, Berlin had long distrusted Mussolini's son-in-law, suspecting him of preparing Italy's withdrawal from the Axis.[11] The Foreign Ministry in Rome informed the Nice Delegation on 29 December 1942 that, "it is not acceptable in the zone occupied by Italian troops for the French authorities to oblige foreign Jews, including Italian nationals, to move to localities occupied by German troops." In the view of the Italian government it was more than a simple matter of refusing to carry out anti-Jewish measures because, as the cable instructed, "the measures for the protection of French and foreign Jews should be implemented exclusively by [Italian] agencies to which we have communicated the principles to be followed."[12] In reply to this telegram the Nice Delegation informed Rome that it had asked Vichy to annul the anti-Jewish measures, a move that provoked some resistance "dictated by the French desire to have their sovereignty confirmed." The Italian position, the prefect of Alpes-Maritimes sadly observed, "awakened sentiments of gratitude on the part of Jews."[13]

The German analysis of the Italians' behavior betrayed considerable anxiety. Röthke, head of the *Judenreferat* in Paris, observed that the latter wanted to settle the Jewish Question "after the Latin fashion," the antithesis of the "German fashion" employed in other regions of France. Röthke worried about the deleterious influence their policy would have on the French, also Latins: it was a bad example for Vichy.[14]

Within the space of three or four months Röthke would send Berlin nearly twenty reports on Italian obstructionism.[15] In Vichy the government of Prime Minister Pièrre Laval not only took the Italian attitude as an insult, but also saw in it a factor that would discredit the government in the eyes of the French. Secretary General of Police René Bousquet was ordered to meet General Guido Lospinoso, Rome's specialist on Jewish matters in the territories occupied by Italy, who refused to be swayed. He informed Bousquet that Italy would find a humane solution to the problem. All this concerned Berlin. Did not the autonomy that the Italians were exhibiting in the Jewish Question betray a tendency toward a rupture of the alliance? In the eyes of the Germans, who measured the faithfulness of friends by the degree of their adhesion to the plan to exterminate the Jews, there seemed to be no other conclusion.

In addition to the intense diplomatic activity between Rome and Berlin, Germany kept a close eye on the Italian administration on the French Mediterranean coast. Röthke personally centralized the intelligence transmitted by agents and *Vertrauensmänner* (informers), who seem to have thoroughly penetrated the offices of Lospinoso. Particular attention was paid to the activities of the banker Donati, whose telephone line was tapped by French intelligence and whose notes ended up on Röthke's desk in Paris.[16] On the basis of intercepted telephone conversations and other sources the Germans were fully cognizant of the projects to evacuate the Jews with the intervention of the Italian Army. If we are to believe Röthke, the French authorities soon would have received from the Italians the order "not to harass any Jew, even if he is in violation of French law . . . or in possession of false identity papers."[17] The information they received permitted the Germans to strike the points of concentration of Jews without loss of time when they retook the territory abandoned by the Italians in September 1943.

In Vichy, Jean Jardin, head of the Laval cabinet and a bit of a nonconformist who maintained excellent relations with Jewish friends (among them Helbronner), recommended in July of 1943 that the latter transfer the Consistory to the Italian Zone. Helbronner refused, citing such concerns as not abandoning his fellow Jews and the risk of "irritating" the German authorities, who might find in this a pretext to intensify persecution of those left behind. Even more important in Helbronner's view was the necessity of not going against Vichy's wishes: a departure of the Consistory for the "Italian Zone" would give the impression of "judging insufficient the protection of our own government and its administration in order to seek out the protection of a foreign government still in a state of war with France." The reasoning is superficially logical, but one questions what in the summer of 1943 could justify in Helbronner's mind the idea that Jews would benefit from the "protection" of the Vichy government.[18]

In any case, Jewish leaders found themselves in an increasingly complex situation in their relations with the Italians. That the Axis suffered defeats in Africa and on the Mediterranean cheered them, but also raised anxieties. This was evident each time the Italian garrison was diminished by the departure of units called to serve on other fronts. "It is terrible that each victory . . . should inspire us with divided feelings, for the collapse of Italy risks being our own loss."[19]

In order to explore all options offered by the Italians, a "policy committee" was created by several Jewish organizations in Nice to ensure smooth working relations with the Italians through the intermediary of Angelo Donati. In March 1943 Guido Lospinoso, the Italian "inspector general for Jewish questions," was sent to Nice to facilitate the move of Jews inland to save them from the Germans. The committee was composed for the most part of figures from the Federation of Jewish Societies (which had transferred to Nice) and was known as the Dubouchage Committee, after the street of the synagogue in which the group met.[20]

Twenty Thousand Jews To Be Evacuated

In July 1943 the Dubouchage Committee decided to play the Italian card to the full by elaborating with Donati a plan for the massive evacuation of Jews from the Italian Zone. On a trip to Rome at the beginning of August, Donati initiated discussions with the Badoglio Government,[21] and, at the same time, with the ambassadors of Great Britain and the United States to the Vatican. Marshal Badoglio was to have authorized the transit through Italy of Jews being evacuated from Nice to North Africa. The two allied diplomats apprised their governments. Was a date decided on? Apparently not.[22]

In Nice, Joseph Fischer, the joint representative in France and a member of the Dubouchage Committee, reported to the Consistory on the evolution of the situation. He was in constant contact with Donati, who had returned to Nice with empty hands at the end of August. Fischer recounts that when Donati came back from Italy, he reported that "the Italians were wavering. . . . I was not able to get authorization to bring the Jews to Italy, but I hope that the 3,000 persons living in assigned residences [i.e., thirty or more kilometers from the coast] will be able to enter the country.' "[23]

Meanwhile, Lospinoso and the "Committee" were confronted with an immense and urgent task: the transfer of 4,000 men, women, and children from Nice and elsewhere to Megève, Saint-Gervais, and several other small towns in the Italian occupied area. They were to live in assigned residences with a view to their eventual evacuation to Italy under the Donati Plan, a transfer rendered more urgent by the Italian withdrawal from the Departments of Savoie (Savoy) as the Germans demanded (Badoglio was still interested in appeasing the Germans). Italy was obliged to content itself with a region corresponding to the old county of Nice, situated between Var and Menton. The move to the villages of hundreds of Jews was completed by the end of April by transporting them in trucks provided by the Dubouchage Committee, thus avoiding the dangers associated with traveling by train through territory controlled by the Germans. By the end of July, when a German division arrived in Nice, it became clear that the Italian occupation era was near its end. Panic spread through the Jewish community and rumors of a mass roundup of Jews infected daily life. A few days after Italy agreed on 15 August to a reduction of its occupation zone, a ministerial meeting in Rome decided to move all the Jews in the former Italian zone to the area in and around Nice so they could be protected and eventually moved through Italy to Africa. This plan was not put into action as such, but on 6 and 7 September some Jews were moved to Nice.

"We decided," Fischer reported, "to bring the Jews from Saint-Gervais and Megève with the objective of their subsequent transfer to Italy. . . . The journey of people presently in assigned residences was delayed for eight days [because we] could not find trucks. . . . We finally obtained forty Italian army trucks, and forty *carabinieri* under an officer accompanied the convoy. . . . The trucks reached Nice on Friday [and] 1,800 persons were distributed among the hotels; . . . but by evening the armistice between Badaglio and the Allies had become public. What were we to do with all those unfortunates?"[24]

Within the Dubouchage Committee support for this evacuation plan was divided. "I didn't believe in it for a single instant," affirms Claude Kelman. "We couldn't have been more skeptical. However, Donati laid out his plan in all its detail. He was a good speaker and easily won over some members of the commission. Ignace Fink and I were against the idea of removing the Jews of Megève and Saint-Gervais to Nice. But it is no less true that we wanted to believe in it, in the absence of any other perspective in the short term. . . . Divided between [going to Nice or going to Italy], we proposed an evacuation plan not with Nice as its goal but Italy itself, in trucks with white flags driving straight toward the closest Italian border post."[25] Michel Topiol, who was also a very active official of the FSJF and in the Dubouchage group, also took a negative stance. Like many of the other members, however, he could not deny himself some degree of hope: "I was holding regular meetings with Guido Lospinoso, Rome's emissary for Jewish affairs, who, despite his official function, acted more like our protector. One of our comrades . . . came back from each visit to Lospinoso with a bunch of passes of all kinds to be distributed to the irregulars. Now pessimistic, now optimistic—such were our moods."[26]

And so between 27 August and 2 September 1943, nearly all the Jews other than those who had decided to seek an individual solution were transferred from Savoie to Nice and billeted in hotels. Even after that their numbers grew. But on 9 September, Nice, like the remainder of the Italian Zone, passed to German control.

An accurate reconstruction of the history of the evacuation and of the climate of terror that descended on the city appeared in a report published illegally by the Nice section of the UJRE in January 1944, *Cinq nuits de persécutions antijuives à Nice.*[27] The Dubouchage Committee found itself criticized for having undertaken to gather the Jews at the very moment when the entry of the Germans into Nice was generally considered imminent: "The Dubouchage Committee, still clinging to who-knows-what illusions, committed the unforgivable error of having some thousands more Jews brought to Nice, those who had been living in assigned quarters in the two Savoys. . . . The refugees arrived in Nice in veritable convoys, organized in agreement with the UGIF and under the benevolent eye of the Italian army, which two days later was to clear out of the region in the greatest haste. . . . Thus they found themselves the very next day at the mercy of the Gestapo."

About a thousand Jews eventually did cross into Italy, but the great evacuation—the project that would have encompassed more than 10,000 persons—did not take place. This is a historical disaster that to this day has not been fully explained. "It was quite simply the premature announcement of the armistice by General Eisenhower without the knowledge of the Italian government . . . which prevented the fulfilment of this rescue action," opines Angelo Donati.[28] This thesis is difficult to defend in the light of the military and political circumstances in Italy. The armistice was signed on 3 September and was to be announced 12 September, "D Day" for the Allied landing in Italy. However, mistrustful of the Italians, Eisenhower decided to land on 8 September at Salerno, south of Naples, without alerting Marshal Badoglio. It is nevertheless the case, as Donati states, that Italy had only some ten days before the announcement of the armistice and not several weeks to put the evacuation plan into action. This was too short an interval for an operation on this scale.

Viviane Forrester, an adolescent at the time, bears some bitterness toward Donati, a friend of her father who used to visit them frequently and shared some of the details of his plan: "The utopian vision of M. Donati had transformed Nice into a huge trap where masses of people destined for extermination were piled up, people who thought they would be able to escape it thanks to his plan."[29]

Flaws in Donati's plan notwithstanding, the true reason for the failure of the operation is to be sought elsewhere. What made it unrealizable was the crisis in Italy after the popular rising that overthrew Mussolini. It is plausible that Badoglio promoted an attitude favorable to an evacuation, either out of conviction or for diplomatic reasons. But, for a country plunged into a government crisis, with an army in flight, could the fate of the Jews have been a priority? Angelo Donati, plausibly motivated by sincere and praiseworthy intentions, was no doubt wrong in taking literally the promises explicit or implicit that had been made to him in Rome. This unreasonable optimism naturally communicated itself to leaders of the Dubouchage Committee and other Jewish agencies.

In the night of 28–29 July 1943 (i.e., even before the capitulation, which they knew was coming), a German division entered Nice. At the headquarters of the Fourth Italian Army, where confusion reigned, people wondered whether this meant the occupation of the city. Joseph Fischer, learning of the disarray of the Italian military, telephoned Donati in Rome: "Everything is all right," the latter replied, "the Italian border will be open for the French and foreign Jews."[30]

However, the concentration of Jews in assigned residences such as in Saint-Martin-Vésubie, Barcelonnette, and elsewhere seemed to be increasing at the end of July and beginning of August. The Italian authorities, in a spirit of complete *laissez faire,* even delegated special powers to the Jewish organizations, for example allowing them to issue passes for people en route to assigned residences. Such documents bore the stamp of the Association culturelle israélite du rite achkénaze (Jewish Cultural Association of the Ashkenazi Rite), whose synagogue served as seat for the Federation of Jewish Societies, the Dubouchage Committee.[31]

The Brunner Commando in Action

Italy surrendered on 8 September, the day of the Allied landing in the south of the country. Within twenty-four hours, the entire Italian Zone fell under German control, a transition greatly facilitated by the presence during the preceding weeks of substantial units of the Wehrmacht at strategic points— not to mention the Italian army's advanced state of disarray. Italian officers and soldiers allowed themselves to be disarmed without resistance. Aloïs Brunner, now commander at the Drancy Camp, had impatiently waited to lay hands on the Jews of the Côte d'Azur and arrived in Nice on 10 September. He was accompanied by his inseparable adjutant SS officer Ernst Brückler, along with some Jewish "lancers" of his own choosing,[32] to whom were added informers picked up on site. The latter were to receive bounties of 5,000 francs per Jew uncovered, about two months wages at the time. Brunner set up headquarters at the Hotel Excelsior, where salons and rooms became torture chambers and jail cells, turning the Excelsior into a symbol of horror for the population of Nice.

The ferocity of the German police with Brunner at their head can be explained by the desire to make the Jews pay the price for the "crime" of having struck a deal with the Italians. The entire city was combed, the hotels searched room by room. *Cinq nuits de persécutions antijuives à Nice,* gives a vivid picture of these actions: "The men of the Gestapo, supported by the militia, blocked the street, burst into hotels, and picked up everyone who from their identity cards or facial features seemed to be Jewish." Brunner, distrustful of the French police, assigned it to merely guarding access to neighborhoods that had been ringed by his men. The raids and arrests were carried out with intentional savagery: "People were roughed up, thrown brutally into trucks, and taken off without the least baggage. . . . At times machgine-gun rounds could be heard, fired at those who ran off. The people who were arrested were kept under guard in the synagogue while awaiting transfer to the Hotel Excelsior. . . . On Gestapo premises the Nazi brutes . . . subjected all the men to a hateful verification by undressing them to check whether they were circumcised."[33]

Informers became the principal weapon of the German police, since the hunted Jews learned to hide more successfully with each passing day. "To get at the Jews in a more efficient way and to identify them more easily, the Gestapo relied on a whole troop of snitches recruited especially among the members of the Parti populaire français [PPF—French Populist Party] led by Jacques Doriot. It also unfortunately succeeded in engaging several ignoble Jewish traitors, either through the promise of gain or by threats. Taking advantage of the confidence of their coreligionists, the latter facilitated the arrest of many Jews."[34]

Once the shock of the first days had passed, the Jewish populace rallied, encouraged by the same reversal in public opinion in Nice that had occurred in Paris during the great raids of 16–17 July 1942. Stanley Hoffmann, later a professor at Harvard University, shared with the author his boyhood experience of these events. He and his mother, "converted" Protestants, had immigrated from Austria at the end of the 1920s, but retained their Austrian citizenship. The year 1943 found them living in Nice, where Stanley was attending the Parc-Impérial secondary school. The previous years had been difficult because many students were from pro-fascist families, but the teachers subverted the antisemitic regulations, and other boys were friendly. However, "the climate after the arrival of the Germans quickly became unbearable."

Hoffmann's best friend, a Hungarian Jewish immigrant, was arrested, one of the factors motivating the Hoffmann's flight to Lamalou-les-Bains, a village in Hérault; one of Stanley's teachers fabricated their false papers. In the countryside Stanley and his mother "never felt that we were in danger in the village, where the 'locals,' hotel- and shopkeepers, knew perfectly well who we were and were as friendly as possible toward us." This was the France that undermined the genocide the Germans planned and Vichy abetted, a France personified in Stanley's teacher and his wife: "In my most personal memory [remains] the teacher who taught me the history of France, gave me hope during the worst days, dried my tears when my best friend was deported with his mother. This man effaces all the bad moments and humiliations, and the terror. His gentle wife and he were not heroes of the Resistance, but if there exists an average Frenchman, it is this man who represents his people."[35]

The prefect of the Alpes-Maritimes, Jean Chaigneau, had earlier perceived a certain antisemitism in public opinion, but in his report for July–August 1943 (i.e., after the Occupation) observed a reversal in the political climate: "The arrival of the German occupation troops in Nice very rapidly provoked a complete turnaround in the mental state of the populace. In the face of raids that occurred day as well as night in the apartment buildings of all parts of Nice, in the street themselves, at the railway station, and on highways leading out of the city, an atmosphere of veritable terror soon descended." Despite his official position, he expressed concern at the behavior of members of some parties, such as the PPF, "who do not hesitate to serve as hired informers for the German police." This behavior, he worried, would increase "mental turmoil."[36]

Others were jubilant: the local delegate of the Commissariat for Jewish Questions informed his superiors in Vichy that "the city of Nice has lost its quality of ghetto since the arrival of the German troops; the Jews are no longer circulating in the city; the synagogues are closed and the Promenade des Anglais offers Aryan strollers many chairs that until now had been occupied by Jews."[37]

But the scale of the assistance by the city populace to the hunted Jews made the German agencies anxious: "The arrest of Jews in territories until now occupied by the Italians is encountering great difficulties because of the fact that nearly ninety percent . . . have false papers and are hidden in the villages and mountains. This is why capturing them is only possible with the assistance of local informers."[38]

The Agencies Caught Unprepared

The Jewish relief agencies, comfortable under the relative security Italian policy had offered, were caught unprepared by the reversal of the situation, even though numerous signs had pointed up its precariousness: only the local section of the UJRE continued during the entire Italian period to conduct its operations underground. It may be true that the French communist analysis of Italian fascism is deficient in its failure to distinguish between Mussolini and Hitler. What confirmed them in their error was the repression communists experienced along with all the other Resistance forces by the Italian secret services. But their erroneous analysis discouraged illusions and ironically saved the UJRE from making other errors, in particular that of exposing itself. After the fall of Mussolini on 25 July it was consequently wise enough to warn against the demographic concentrations in the Italian Zone and to call for an end to the illusion of a presumed security to which many still clung.[39]

Other organizations discovered to their great cost that underground activities could not be improvised instantly. Time was required to learn the craft and become hardened by experience. The UGIF, the Dubouchage Committee, and the OSE closed their offices at the beginning of the raids. The young Zionists judged the attitude of the "adults" severely: "Everything collapsed at once and the responsible leaders who had freely chosen that responsibility either ran off or hid."[40] Only the OSE succeeded in continuing its activities, looking after children, the elderly, and the sick. In liaison with the Jeunesse sioniste (Zionist Youth), the OSE sought to move as many children as possible to Switzerland. The "independent" activist Maurice Loebenberg (a.k.a. Cachoud) prepared false papers for them (and later headed counterfeiting for the MLN, the Movement for National Liberation). Léon Poliakov, in Nice on the eve of the Italians' departure, remembers Loebenberg confiding that there were 25,000 Jews in Nice then—one-eighth of the population— and that if they were to stay then it would be necessary to produce false identity papers for all of them.[41]

Funding was furnished by André Bass, the friend of Maurice Brener (treasurer for France of the American Jewish Joint Distribution Committee, which out of prudence avoided directly financing underground activities). Bass also established contact with Georges Spolianski on the underground Nice Committee of the UJRE. Attracted by the dynamism of their organization, André Bass (unbeknownst to Maurice Brener), transferred "funds of a certain quantity" to the communists.[42]

The passage from legal to clandestine action proved a difficult one. Social workers struggled to maintain ties with clients, often meeting them at secret rendezvous. The SEC ("Jewish police" of the CGQJ) followed their movements as closely as they could. On 9 September, for example, they managed to infiltrate a Jewish informer into a meeting of several hundred Jews sponsored by the illegal Committee for Cultural Assistance, learning that money and hotel vouchers were being arranged for the refugees. We don't know how accurate the information was, but the authors of the report wrote that "the transportation of the Jews by truck is reputed to have cost a million francs."[43]

The situation grew more perilous by the day. The efforts of the OSE and UGIF to restart in September their official work after a period of inactivity (the OSE had continued to function clandestinely) ended tragically when the premises of the OSE, after having been open for some ten days, were occupied by Brunner's police, which arrested the staff and all callers: the trap drew other victims. Social workers posted surreptitiously at each end of the street tried to warn people "who looked Jewish," but success was limited: some seventy Jews fell into the net. The UGIF resumed its work on the express orders of Brunner, who demanded that the Jews themselves finance the food costs of those imprisoned in the Excelsior. At its head Brunner placed the well-known local arrestee, Guggenheim, provisionally freed for this purpose. After operating for several weeks, the offices were in any case closed, and Guggenheim and his family were deported. This, in brief, ended the history of the UGIF, whose right to exist had ultimately been determined by the requirements of progress toward the "Final Solution." In Nice, Brunner pushed this cynicism to its extreme limit.

Jewish Youth React

On streets infested by thugs and combed by informers, young Zionists and Jewish Scouts suffered numerous blows. Falling into the clutches of the Gestapo were Jacques Wister (Weintraub), who was preparing the departure of a group of children for Switzerland; Jacques Gutman (Griffon); Rabbi Prunner; Germaine Meyer, Donati's secretary; and Hilde Helman, Kelman's secretary.

The Nice Committee of the UJRE was also badly hit. It lost its two principal officials, the lawyer Joseph Roos and the teacher Georges Spolianski, as well as the young Raymond Fresco. According to a UJRE statement, "Roos and Spolianski were savagely tortured for three successive days in the Hotel Excelsior. . . . The Gestapo [unsuccessfully] demanded the names of their Resistance comrades as well as the Jews whom they had helped." The martyrs died of course but "in the certainty that hundreds of their brothers and sisters would take their places in the battle to avenge them, to save the Jews of France from extermination."[44] The Jewish Section of the MOI replaced them with Suzanne Band and Bella Blaustein: women traveling by train on clandestine business were not subject to the "physiological" checks (i.e., checking to see whether men were circumcised) the fascists carried out in trains and train stations to render false identity papers ineffective. The author of the Zionist youth document cited above concluded from the fiasco of the "Italian parentheses" that the principal error of Jewish leaders had been their persistence in the legal mode of operation: "It is quite evident that at the decisive moment the Jewish organizations were not at all adequate to their task, for . . . an official body cannot transform itself from one day to the next into an underground organization."[45]

For analogous reasons Joseph Fischer wrote the Consistory that "we decided to distribute aid not through the intermediary of the UGIF but through private channels." In his opinion the UGIF "ought to disband because its officials risk becoming the forced collaborators of the Gestapo." Léo Glaeser, the secretary of the FSJF and its General Defense Committee, formulated the lessons learned from what he called the Hourban-Nice (the disaster of Nice) in a circular letter to members of the federation leadership. He confirmed the existence of different opinions among the FSJF leaders on the policy of concentrating Jews along the Riviera. "We have witnessed, in a manner all too concise, the tragic results of the exodus to the South. We have seen with great anxiety the resurgence of dangerous illusions. We missed too many occasions to distribute statements and notices on the subject, which was our political, moral, and material responsibility, to counter the dreams of certain individuals or groups."[46]

Testimony of the First Escapee from Auschwitz

In July 1943, when Nice was still under the Italians, a man who identified himself only as Salomon came to the Committee of the Federation of Jewish Societies at the synagogue on Boulevard Dubouchage. He said that he had lived in the Marseille area before his deportation and that he had escaped from the Koziel Camp near Auschwitz. This elicited general suspicion, which dissipated at the sight of the number tattooed on his arm. Moreover, he asked for nothing more than to be heard and to be given some kind of identity document. A meeting with Claude Kelman and other federation leaders, including Michel Topiol and Ignace Fink, was arranged.[47]

The facts of the industrialized extermination of the Jews in the "factories" of Auschwitz were incredible, beyond belief, but Claude Kelman got the man's story to London through the Resistance, even if his doubts had not been entirely laid to rest. "If I were forced to believe it [Salomon's words],

I would have gone mad," Topiol said. The news spread quickly in Nice. Georges Spolianksi of the UJRE asked Salomon to tell his story again. *Notre voix* published extensive excerpts in its 1 August 1943 number under the title, "The Massacre of Jews in the Camps of Poland: Two Witnesses Testify."[48] This horrible news added to the tension, anxiety, and general stress suffered by the Jews along the Riviera at the end of the Italian occupation. Thirty thousand Jews had temporarily found some protection during the "Italian reprieve." Unfortunately, only about a thousand of them found refuge in Italy.

CHAPTER THIRTEEN

Jewish Perceptions of the War

You say 'collaboration!' Unfortunately, at the present time, people don't want to collaborate with us. Now it is only a matter of supplications.

—Rabbi Zalman Schneerson

———————————————————————————————————

In the midst of the massacre of the people they wished to rescue, two men had the same dream: to create a Jewish state under the auspices and with the aid of Nazi Germany. One of them, Rabbi Zalman Schneerson, wanted a "Jewish state" that would have neither territory nor borders but would be separated from the "world" by the spiritual bonds uniting its "citizens."[1] The other, Paris lawyer Itzhak Kadmi-Cohen, was a Zionist extremist who hoped for a Jewish state in *Eretz Israel*.[2] To achieve this, according to him, it was necessary to drive Great Britain out of the Middle East and to ally the Zionist cause with—Germany. Dreams? Eccentric projects rather, although elaborated in great detail and having their origins in constants of Jewish history.

A Jewish State without Territory

Rabbi Schneerson did not turn to Turkey, the Russia of the tsars, or France as Theodor Herzl did in his time,[3] but directly to the anti-Jewish regime of

Vichy, and indirectly to Hitler's Germany, already embarked upon its own solution to the "Jewish Question." Schneerson entitled his text: "What I Propose to My Jewish People." Copies were sent in August 1943 to the secretary general of the Vichy government, to the prefects of Isère and Gers, and to Cardinal Gerlier. Today a reading of Schneerson's text leaves an impression of pathetic irreality, but in the author's mind it was doubtless as realistic an attempt as any to save what could still be saved of the Jewish people. It was the ancient and eternal dilemma that the powerless have often had to debate: to prevent the executioner from swinging his axe, do we fight him or beg him to stay his arm?

To judge by the evidence, Rabbi Schneerson made his choice: his texts are addressed to the man with the axe. One should read them in context: it is difficult to imagine him explicitly condemning Vichy outrages and Nazi atrocities in a letter to their architects. Schneerson wished to be a realist, which precluded neither a certain amount of sincerity nor a dose of cunning, whether or not it appears ridiculous from the perspective of today.

The Jewish state that he proposes is a "State of Jewish Religion," one "whose existence does not depend on the possession or retention" of a territory. The principal idea of the new prophet Schneerson can be summed up in this premise: the Jewish people should retire forever from the political life of other peoples, a scheme that, as it happens, corresponds to the classic requirement of antisemites, a kind of *apartheid* before the fact.

To Rabbi Schneerson the political circumstances of the hour seemed favorable to the realization of his project: "The foundation and center of the State of Jewish Religion can occur, at the present time, in Europe . . . where the question of the resolution of the Jewish problem as Providence dictates is intimately connected with all the other problems, where [there is] a whole range of governments united among themselves [i.e., the Axis], on whose will depend the recognition and guarantee of the rights of the State of Jewish Religion among other peoples."[4]

Schneerson's suggestion was not merely tactical. The vehement fashion in which he attacks those Jews who would oppose his project, a kind of Jewish Vatican without the Rome, can leave little doubt as to his sincerity. The Zionists who "want to organize a state in Palestine" are characterized as "Jewish nationalists," their opinions as "fatally" dangerous. The misfortune of the Jewish people, he says, is in emancipation.[5] Even more harmful, in Schneerson's eyes, were the "assimilationist" Jews who "based the destiny of the Jewish people on the outcome of the struggle between other peoples," the Jews who cried "Long live liberty!" But, the rabbi exclaimed, if liberty means assimilation, it is still a "threat no less dangerous for Jews than the terrible situation in which we presently find ourselves in Europe." Schneerson was weighing his words, for he was certainly aware in July and August of 1943 of the massacre under way in the East. In fact, reference to the disaster surely appears where he writes: "I am ready to kneel before Europe, before Germany, and to beg them to spare what still remains of the Jews of Europe, to spare the women, the children."

Léon Poliakov, in his memoir of resistance activism, recalls the episode of Rabbi Schneerson's project. It was he who put the text into good French, since he was the rabbi's secretary from 1941 to 1943. "A prophetic flame," writes Poliakov, "ran through certain passages, animated by a limitless love for the people of God. We were walking along the avenue of beeches that led to Le Manoir Château."

"But in the final analysis, who is this project intended for?"

"That scarcely matters. For Berlin, if you like. Think of the millions of brethren in Poland for whom an atrocious fate awaits."

"Berlin will never accept a solution of that kind as long as the war continues. Are you aware that, basically, you are playing the German card?"

"German card, British card. . . . What are these shopkeepers' calculations? Do you think that you are going to save our people with your forged papers?"

Knowing to what kind of criticism he was exposing himself, he declared to Poliakov, bringing the discussion to an end: "You say 'collaboration!' Unfortunately, at the present time, people don't want to collaborate with us in Europe. Now it is only a matter of supplications."[6]

All this is worthy of pity, but the era was pitiless for the Jews. And Schneerson, whatever his visions, could not escape it. In vain did he brandish his religion and expound a virulent anticommunism. Here he moans in a letter to the prefect of Isère after the 22–23 March 1943 arrests of children who had received a religious upbringing at his center, Le Manoir, near Grenoble:[7] "Neither the French government, nor the German government, nor any other government (save perhaps the Soviet authorities) has any cause to destroy this religious school." Plaintive, trying to convince the adversary that they have a common enemy in the USSR, arguing with the regime in favor of a state in which the Jews would cease to be citizens and remain only as an excluded community of believers, trying to save lives with arguments ill-suited to the drama then unfolding, the prophet of the new Jewish "state" advocated a return to the ghetto, voluntary exclusion, in the hope, no doubt, of protecting those who had not yet perished. But the time of the ghetto, even of the yellow star, was completely past for those promoting the "Final Solution": for them the gas chamber offered the definitive means.

A "Greater Israel" with the Aid of Nazi Germany

Kadmi-Cohen, lawyer and right-wing Zionist, believed a German victory likely. In the months that followed the Germans' entry into Paris, he circulated a tract in which he set out his idea of an alliance with Hitler's Reich for the conquest of Palestine. "M. Kadmi-Cohen," writes the anonymous author of the "Inquiry into the Situation in the Occupied Zone," "transmitted to Paris chief rabbi Julien Weill a study on the prospects for the creation of a Jewish state in Palestine that the German victory would open to European Jewry."[8] The chronicler Jacques Bielinky noted on 16 October 1941: "The lawyer Kadmi-Cohen was just interned at Compiegne. He wrote a brochure about Palestine and hoped that the Paris censor would authorize its publication." Kadmi-Cohen was part of a group of Jewish lawyers who were disbarred and arrested in mid-September and interned at Compiègne. His disbarment was, however, annulled by a Vichy decision of 2 January 1942, when he was released from the camp.[9]

His ideas became more concrete and elaborate in the course of a series of lectures that he gave at the Compiègne camp. At the end of the twelfth and last lecture, on 22 December 1941, Kadmi-Cohen announced the creation of the Massada movement,[10] which counted only a dozen adherents among the internees. At that time the majority of the interned were French Jews and hostile to the idea of a Jewish state.[11]

Freed from Compiègne just before the first deportation in March of 1942, Kadmi-Cohen hurried to Vichy,[12] he was accompanied by a priest named Catry, a friend of André Lavagne, head of the Marshal's civil cabinet. Catry, like Lavagne, said that he was a "Christian antisemite," and saw in the Massada movement the chance of a nonviolent solution to the "Jewish Question." In touch with the Germans at a relatively junior level, he discerned—to his credit—the real nature of the "Final Solution." He wrote André Lavagne, to whom he also introduced Kadmi-Cohen, "that in the event of a complete victory, the two components of Hitlerian dogma, viz., no Jews in Europe and no Jewish state, would be implemented. This was tantamount to saying that the Jews would be suppressed, the supposed ghetto of Poland [being] then only be an enclave where the Jews could be put to death."[13] In his eyes this prospect justified the objectives of Massada and the search for a solution in a moderate antisemitism.

Intimately linked to an extreme nationalist current of Zionism, Kadmi-Cohen's movement recognized only a single enemy, the power blocking creation of a Jewish state: Great Britain, the mandatory power in Palestine. His strategy of an alliance with Germany, which was at war with Britain, was inspired by the principle that the enemies of my enemies are my friends, and it was perfectly logical, save one point: this same Germany was at the same time the most terrible enemy that the Jewish people had ever known. Kadmi-Cohen was not the only one to fall into this abyss. In Palestine his political friends who belonged to the Stern Group (the "Stern Gang" in British parlance; in Hebrew *Lohamei Herut Israel,* or *Lehi*—Fighters for the Freedom of Israel), from whom he had been cut off after the defeat of France, actively pursued the same goals. Founded in June 1940 by Abraham Stern after Zionist authorities in Palestine had decided to suspend military action against the British, the group sought to enter into contact with the Axis powers. (The British Palestine Police shot him during a raid on 12 February 1942.)

One of the officers of the group, Naftali Lubentchik, went to Syria in December 1940 to establish relations with the Germans. In early 1941 he met Otto Werner von Hentig, an envoy of the German Ministry of Foreign Affairs, who had come to study the situation in the Near East. Lubentchik gave him a memorandum that advocated an agreement with the Nazis in which it was suggested that if Hitler promised a Jewish state within Israel's historic borders, the Stern Group would engage to fight on the side of the Germans for the liberation of Palestine. The memorandum also says that the group was close to the *Weltanschauung* (worldview) of the Axis, and claims that the Jews of Palestine were being persecuted not only by the British but also by Jewish socialists. But von Hentig gave Lubentchik to understand that Berlin already had a well-defined policy with regard to the Jews; he did not think that his government could adopt a special position with regard to the Stern Group.[14]

At the close of 1941 the Stern organization despatched another emissary to Syria, Nathan Frydman-Yélin, but he was intercepted by the British. By trying to obtain the support of Germany for the Zionist cause, the Stern Group took a stance opposed to Vladimir Jabotinsky, founding father of the "revisionist Zionist" current, whose heirs they claimed to be. In fact, Jabotinsky, despite his sympathies for Mussolini's ideology, did not hesitate to place his bet on an Allied victory. He went to the United States in the summer of 1941 to plead the cause of a Jewish Legion that would fight on the side of the British, thus adopting the same position as his political adversary Ben-Gurion.[15]

Vichy and the Zionist Cause

Kadmi-Cohen sent his vision of the "Jewish Question" to the Marshal in a handwritten manuscript on 28 June 1943; there is no indication the Marshal ever read it.[16] At the outset Kadmi-Cohen observes that the policy implemented in France during the last three years with regard to the Jews "can hardly find a justification in either the defeat of France or Franco-German collaboration." The observation was true, though perhaps irrelevant given the context. And yet as Kadmi-Cohen pointed out other countries that had been defeated by or were allies of Germany—Belgium, Holland, Italy, Hungary—had found it possible to refrain from practicing the same "passionate anti-semitism." Whatever the case, Kadmi-Cohen pointed out, the persecutions have "generated a desire for vengeance" bolstered by the ease with which Jews could denounce their "executioners" as "traitors to France." He then presented himself as capable of diverting rebellious Jews from the Resistance and of averting a long-term danger then only *apparently* insignificant: This was the danger of an eventual civil war, in which Jewish participation might be precluded only by allowing the Massada movement to re-orient "Jewish dynamism in a nationalistic sense" by "concentrating the Jewish people in a Jewish state." Kadmi-Cohen was at pains to assure the Marshal that the movement he was advocating "would be implemented under such control that all threat of conflict with the occupation authorities . . . would be precluded."

Attached to the memorandum is the sketched map of the Jewish state, whose borders extend substantially beyond those of the Greater Israel claimed even by ardent Zionists. Thus, the northern border passes close to Saïda in Lebanon and south of Damascus; all the Sinai Peninsula and part of Saudi Arabia to the west, as well as Transjordan, which is extended in the form of a corridor ending in Iraq, are to be found within the frontiers of the proposed Jewish state.[17] Kadmi-Cohen's ambition was to win a monopoly position for his movement in occupied France. He attacked the UGIF and the Consistory, the only Jewish organizations officially tolerated, albeit in rather different ways. How did he see the organization of French Jewry?

The fate of the UGIF, against which he voiced no explicit criticism, was dealt with in a few words: The agency was "only an expedient" to begin with, and therefore had no chance of lasting. The fortress to be destroyed was the Consistory, a "Napoleonic" creation giving refuge to "the old principles of the Revolution." Its officials are "the supporters of the Ancien Regime [i.e., ironically, the Third Republic] and it ought to be abolished." Thus Kadmi-Cohen's ideas on the French monarchy and 1789 paralleled those of Vichy's "National Revolution."

But, as significantly, the hatred he directed toward the men of the Consistory came from his exacerbated nationalism, founded on an isolationist principle that rejected any integrationist current among the Jews of the diaspora. "No prize for assimilation!" he cries. This is why the measures of persecution and exclusion do not seem to trouble him so much. They represent only a stage to be left behind after the realization of the national aspirations of the Jews. "The negative and destructive [i.e., assimilationist] politics followed in France," he opines, "can be excused and absolved only [as the] inevitable, and preliminary clearing of the way . . . to the positive and constructive second stage, that of the autonomous national renaissance of the Hebrew idea." His conclusion suggests more of the degree of his folly: "You want no part of us; we have, indeed, been destroyers and parasites. We shall leave on our own. Give me a free hand and I shall rid you of the Jews!" In the rush of his rhetoric and immoderate ambition he ends with an offer to be the Marshal's "attaché for Jewish affairs."[18]

For a "Christian Antisemitism"

In Vichy, Kadmi-Cohen's ideas seem to have caught the attention of André Lavagne, a fervent Christian who was considered in Consistory circles as "pro-Jewish," although it would be more correct to characterize him as a moderate antisemite. His interest in the Massada project indicates the state of mind of individuals in Pétain's entourage who were concerned about the negative consequences of the anti-Jewish persecutions on public opinion, and, increasingly, on the credibility of an already shaky regime.

Where did this interest, clearly exaggerated, in Kadmi-Cohen's projects come from? A clue appears in a brief that Lavagne prepared for the Marshal on 6 February 1943.[19] "For France to take the initiative in this movement [i.e., the Massada project] would permit it to discharge the terribly onerous mort-

gage that too violent an antisemitic policy has caused to weigh on the nation."
He took the occasion to remind the Marshal that of all the countries of Europe, "*it is France, along with Germany, that most persecutes the Jews.*"[20] This was
a policy that risked, in his opinion, "generating a profound hatred of France
in America"; Italy (according to him) was not risking this, and had given "evidence of the greatest humanity" with regard to the Jews. With this note Lavagne expressed the reversal in the state of mind of numerous Vichy officials
who, foreseeing the German defeat, hoped to improve the image of Pétain's
government in the Allied countries. The same spirit animated those who may
have wanted to explore prospects for a separate peace between the Western
Allies and the Third Reich.

Lavagne advanced another argument as well: "The creation of the Jewish state will be a powerful antidote against communism, and the Bolshevik
messianism of the dispersed Jews would cease immediately." Here he borrows Kadmi-Cohen's contention that Zionism could be a "rampart against
the radicalization of the Jewish masses."

With or without the Marshal's agreement (we do not know), on 9 April
1943 Lavagne asked Henri Cado (deputy of police chief Bousquet) to grant
a certain number of privileges and immunities to Kadmi-Cohen. Residence
in Vichy and its surroundings being denied to Jews, Lavagne hoped that the
government would authorize his protégé's family (his "Aryan" wife and three
children) to live in Bellerive or Cusset, a few miles from the capital. He further hoped that Kadmi-Cohen would be authorized to travel by automobile
seven days a week, including Sundays. Even more interesting was Lavagne's
request for a safe-conduct that would permit his protégé "to move about,
accompanied by a Jew as his guide": all the prominent Jews were in hiding, and only a Jew informed of their hiding places "would be in a position to lead Kadmi-Cohen to them." To all this Lavagne added a request
for authorization—at least informal—to circulate the brochure in the camps
and places of "supervised residence" under the gaze of the authorities, for
which purpose Lavagne requested a complete listing of interned Jews. In effect, Lavagne was seeking the establishment of a Jewish organization at a time
when this was legally precluded.[21]

For Kadmi-Cohen the "assimilated" Jews of the Consistory had lost the
"living and fertile Hebrew vigor," and thus were unsuitable for his project of
reconquering the land of Israel. Nonetheless, at the urging of Lavagne (who
was on friendly terms with Helbronner), Kadmi-Cohen agreed to meet the
president of the Consistory in early March. Helbronner, however, squarely

refused. In any case, Kadmi-Cohen had been interested only in possible financial support; at the collapse of this plan he reassured Lavagne that "Massada will succeed without the financial aid of Jewish plutocrats."[22]

The brochure "Massada" was printed probably in Roanne. There is nothing to prove, however, that its distribution was ever begun. We know only that Kadmi-Cohen complained to Lavagne that "a package had been broken open and a number of brochures were missing."[23] In August or September 1943 Kadmi-Cohen left Vichy for Paris, though the exact nature of his mission remains unknown. Was he disappointed with the meager results of his undertaking in the Southern Zone? Did he hope to get a more favorable hearing from the Germans? He seems to have been encouraged by the fact that some months earlier Goebbels, the German propaganda minister, had spoken in favor of a "Jewish state." Kadmi-Cohen had told Lavagne about this even then.[24] Now, having asked Abbé Catry to sound out the Germans, Lavagne learned that indeed "certain German agencies have already shown in their attitude that even if they would not support Kadmi-Cohen, they would be ready to encourage him unofficially or, in any case, to close their eyes."[25]

When Kadmi-Cohen was arrested and again interned in the autumn of 1943, collaborationist circles in Paris took a discussion of his initiative as a pretext to debate "practical solutions" to the Jewish Question—as if it had not already been by that time almost "resolved." On 18 February 1944, the Aryan Club at 5 boulevard Montmartre hosted a meeting of the "cream" of antisemitic Paris whose participants indulged in a kind of one-upmanship as to who could offer the best plan. The German observer, who rendered a report on the meeting, must have been laughing up his sleeve.

Taking part were current CGQJ head Louis Darquier de Pellepoix, the "ethnologist" Professor Georges Montandon (author of the book *How to Recognize Jews*), Serpeille de Gobineau (grandson of the theorist of modern racism, Count Gobineau), and a certain Saïda Ivatry, a pro-Nazi Iraqi woman. The chairman of the meeting, the poet and anti-Masonic propagandist Robert Vallery-Radot, presented the project of Kadmi-Cohen and the Massada movement, whom he characterized as "Jewish national-socialist," declaring that "if I were a Jew myself, I would think as he does." He cited the support of two clerics, Abbé Catry and Father Berthelot, known in Vichy as advocates of Massada, and circulated to participants a brochure reproducing the speeches that Kadmi-Cohen had given during his internment in Compiègne.

But others had their say too, and Kadmi-Cohen's dreams went without concrete support. The German observer reported the "suggestions" of other participants, for example Montandon's proposal "to concentrate all the Jews on the island of Cyprus, under the surveillance of torpedo boats that could crush any attempt at flight from any part of the island"; the professor recommended "[excluding] all Jews from European society by imposing on them a special passport so that they would appear as Jews and not as French, British, or German." More suggestive, given the dual contexts of what was happening to the Jews in Europe and of Kadmi-Cohen's proposals for Palestine, were the words of Saïda Ivatry, who stated her opposition to any solution that involved granting the Jews a homeland on Arab territory: "If Palestine were under the control of the Wehrmacht and if the Arab people were given a free hand with regard to the Jews, the Jewish Question in Palestine would be resolved."[26]

Polemics on the Nature of the War

The fact that Zalman Schneerson and Kadmi-Cohen's "projects" involved primarily only their authors does not excuse the blinkered character of their authors' ideas. It was quite a different matter in the case of a document—coming from a Resistance group—in which an erroneous understanding of the singular nature of World War II led to a no less unrealistic response to the circumstances of the war. In Toulouse (the greatest center of the Resistance after Lyon), a broadside entitled "Les Juifs et la guerre" (The Jews and the War) was circulated in the autumn of 1943. Although it was not signed, its content indicated well enough that its authors were to be sought in the ranks of right-wing Zionists called "Revisionists."[27]

The Jewish Section of the MOI, whose leadership had transferred in early October from Paris to Lyon, judged the text questionable and challenged it in a public criticism that circulated in its own ranks and beyond. Taking as its title "Les Juifs dans la guerre" (The Jews *in* the War), its author initially takes pains to state the difference between the two attitudes and to point out that his reflections are situated *within* the war and not at some distance from it as is suggested by the "and" in the title of the Zionist document.[28]

"The Jews and the War" took as *its* point of departure a speech by the Soviet writer Ilya Ehrenburg who, on his return from the front, had suggested to the Jewish Antifascist Committee in Moscow[29] the publication of a work glorifying the contribution of Soviet Jews to the war effort, their heroism, and their sacrifice in terms of human lives, which was proportionally greater than that of other nationalities. Ehrenburg conceived the idea after having noted on his frequent trips to the front that the troops were ignorant of the contribution of Soviet Jews.

Ehrenburg's speech was interpreted by the Zionists—and not without reason—as irrefutable proof of the survival among the populations of the USSR of traditional Russian antisemitism. For communists the idea appeared unimaginable, convinced as they were of the virtues of the Soviet regime. But our interest in the controversy lies in questions raised by the Zionist document: "What guarantees have the Jews that the blood they spill will not prove without effect?" the author asks. Why anticipate, he wondered, that facts to appear in the collection proposed by Ehrenburg would exercise a greater effect than information presented in *The Book of the Slain,* published by the Jews of Germany at the end of WWI, showing that the twelve thousand Jewish soldiers who died defending Germany represented a higher percentage of the total war dead than the Jews' percentage in the population generally. The Zionists' answer was that despite the German Jews' sacrifices on behalf of Germany then, or their terrible persecution now, many Germans were asking why the Jews "are suffering less than we are"! British, Canadian, South American, and Australian Jews were currently fighting and falling on land, at sea, and in the air, and yet "there are individuals in Britain who ask, 'Why don't we see any Jews at the front?'" "In all these countries, a great deal has been done to uproot antisemitism. People have been educated in equality, and hatred for man has been banished along with hatred for Jews. Jews had been granted equal rights and all doors had opened for them. They had been promised the possibility of assimilation. The USSR was in advance of all the other countries in this respect. . . . But when the world upheaval occurred, when dark hours fell on humanity—man is vicious in the hour of his misfortune—suspicious, accusatory, hateful looks were turned toward the Jews." In a word, the one thing that nothing had accomplished was "to resolve the Jewish Question."

As in the majority of the publications of the Jewish Section of the MOI, "The Jews *in* the War" gives a picture of the drama that was being played out in Europe. "The very existence of Jews in the majority of European countries is threatened by unleashed Nazi barbarity. Of the three million Jews who inhabited Poland before the war, there remains today, it would seem, only 500,000. Also led to the slaughterhouses in Poland were tens of thousands of Jews . . . from France, Belgium, Germany, Romania, and so on. . . . And at present, at the moment when the rout of Hitler's forces has begun, the danger of new killing becomes more evident."

The skepticism as to "the absence of guarantees in the event of victory" that is sensed in the Zionist document is viewed by the MOI as the expression of a "spirit of resignation, expectation, and passivity." And yet, "where would we be today," ask the communists, "if the Soviet Union had not made that enormous sacrifice of blood? Would we still have been able to resist without the example of that fierce will to triumph?" The heroic participation of Soviet Jews at the front and in the partisan movement was a source of inspiration and courage. What was important in the eyes of the MOI was that "the Jewish community [should have] a clear and unambiguous policy of salvation." This salvation was to be gained by the defeat of Hitlerism, without which "no solution can be envisaged . . . unless it is complete extermination."

Given this, "guarantees" about a Jewish homeland could not constitute a prior condition for Jewish participation in the war and in the Resistance. The communist text points out that the mainstream Zionists thought similarly, stressing that "Ben Gurion has just publicly declared that the Jews of Palestine would fight in the ranks of the Seventh Army, although until now he has not obtained from Great Britain any guarantee as concerns the Zionist claim."[30]

With or without guarantees, the survival strategy demanded Jewish engagement in the war against Nazi Germany. For the Jewish Resistance in France the right of the Jewish people to a national homeland in Palestine was inscribed as an objective of the war in the summer of 1943. This goal was taken up by all political currents among the Jews of foreign origin. The participation of Jews in the war effort would constitute the major argument validating their claims after the war.[31]

Translating Perceptions into Strategy

A review of various newspapers, brochures, and other tracts published by the Jewish organizations of the MOI illuminates the evolution in the analysis that they made of the nature of the war. A lack of information slowed that evolution, which arrived at global generalizations only later in the execution of the extermination plan.

From Hitler's accession to power—even before—it was understood that if he some day launched a war it would be an ideological war (even if an important motive was simple revenge for the defeat of 1918 and the Treaty of Versailles). The ideological character of World War II, with its objective of installing the Germans' "New Order" in Europe (and beyond), constituted the war's first characteristic. This fact may have been confused in the mind of communists during the period of the Stalin-Hitler pact. The threat that ideological war posed to the fundamental values of humanity did not yet signal, however, the mass murder of "inferior" races. The place that the French authorities occupied in the persecution of the Jews after June 1940 left room to hope, at least initially, that persecution would not exceed the framework of "traditional" antisemitism. In addition, the fact that the persecution was phased in gradually made it difficult to grasp at the time its passage to the "Final Solution" itself. That the mass murder was taking place far away from France, not to mention the rupture in communications and the exceptional secrecy surrounding the killing sites, made it harder to know what was actually going on.

The summer of 1941 showed to all, however, that this war was unlike all others. The massacres of Jewish men, women, and children in the occupied territories of the USSR by the Einsatzgruppen marked the beginning of a new phase in the Nazi program. The immediate effect of the August 1941 "Appeal from Moscow"[32] was to raise the question of whether the same was possible in the West. The analytical and editorial pieces from the "Jewish Section" bearing on the entirety of the situation show that if "extermination" was an objective of Germany's war, this did not necessarily mean that the fate of the French Jews would parallel that of Soviet Jews. It was only in the spring of 1942 that the first deportations established the definition, "deportation equals death." Yet even then the supporting evidence was unavailable.

The deportation of children from July 1942 onward furnished further proof that the disappearance of the Jewish people was one of the objectives of Hitler's war.[33] The rapidity with which the Polish ghettos began to be emptied at the end of the summer and in the fall of 1942 illustrates the Nazis' determination to achieve total extermination as quickly as possible. Under the title "Hitler Wishes to Complete the Extermination of the Jews in 1943," *Notre parole* wrote in February 1943: "Hitler, seconded by Himmler, the head of the Gestapo, announced the destruction of 30% of the Jews in 1942. The diabolical plan of these thugs is the destruction of the Jewish populace in the course of 1943."[34] Henceforth, it is possible to discern the existence of two rhythms in the conduct of the war: the pace of military operations and that of operations aimed at the annihilation of the Jews, and thus of two parallel but separate timelines: that of the Jews and that of everyone else. This idea now assumed a central position in the political thinking of the Jewish Section of the MOI and determined its strategy.[35]

CHAPTER FOURTEEN

1943

By the Light of Flames from the Ghetto

Our only morality: to kill him who is killing us.

—Mark Edelman[1]

Citing as pretext an attack on German soldiers, Himmler himself gave the order to raze the old harbor area of Marseille and to comb the rest of the city for undesirables, characterized as "riff-raff," that is, communists, illegal aliens, prostitutes, and others including Jews of all nationalities. Operation "Sultan" got underway on the night of 21–22 January 1943. The code name suggests that Berlin had the North African Theater in mind: the loss at El Alamein made it vital for the Wehrmacht to secure its rear at a time when the Resistance was taking on alarming proportions in Marseille, a very important transit point. The Germans may have been seeking to test Vichy by demanding its cooperation in a reprisal against a French community, and that in the former Free Zone, where the government's autonomy was theoretically still intact. In reality, despite the assurances of Berlin, Vichy's maneuvering room had been considerably restricted after the entry of German troops. Plans for the raid were prepared in fine detail by German security with the invaluable assistance of Bousquet, who knew the terrain well.

Starting in the early morning hours, raids and arrests got under way throughout many Marseille neighborhoods. The purge should have been predictable, for public order police had been arriving by train and in personnel carriers from Toulouse, Lyon, Nancy, and even Paris. Jews were arrested during identity checks, forced to show their stamped cards. In the course of Saturday, raids were extended to the downtown commercial areas, long the home to many of the city's Jewish residents, the majority native. A certain number of UGIF officials were among those arrested, despite the "legitimacy" their posts had ostensibly guaranteed them.

By Saturday morning news had spread that a trainload of 1,500 persons, about eight hundred of them Jews, had left for the camp at Compiègne. More than four hundred were French-born or Algerian Jews (i.e., French subjects). Entire families were sent, in conformity with the principles of the "Final Solution."[2] "We have just lived through several days and several nights from which we emerge worn down as if from a serious illness," noted the refugee Lucien Vidal-Naquet in his diary for 25 January 1943, "several days during which the French police, obeying orders from Berlin, proceeded with massive house searches and arrests intended to supply the Nazi Moloch. . . . One youngster was taken with his schoolbooks by the French police [without ever making it home]."[3]

Raymond-Raoul Lambert, whose office was in Marseille, feverishly intervened at police headquarters and in Vichy in order to "bring help to the unfortunate and assure them of spiritual and moral aid through the presence of chaplains." In Vichy, rumors soon had it that the train for Compiègne might soon turn back.[4]

Was there in fact any possibility of freeing the French Jews? Helbronner seemed to think so. He asked Bousquet to receive the lawyer Robert Kiefe in order to review ways to "assure our unfortunate fellow-citizens of the protection to which they have a right from the authorities of their country."[5] Received on 13 February 1943 by Martin, principal secretary in Bousquet's office, Kiefe learned that a "screening" operation, led by the French, had been in progress in Compiègne for the last three days. Bousquet was himself in Paris, "negotiating with the Occupation authorities the modalities of repatriation. But no one would be freed before the completion of the screening operation, and that could take some additional time." None were released. All eight hundred Jews from Marseille were ultimately sent to Auschwitz (on 23 and 25 March 1943). None is known to have survived.[6] The intervention by Kiefe on behalf of the UGIF officials who had become victims of the raids had also yielded nothing: "No one knows where the Germans transferred the people who had been arrested nor what they are charged with. The Gestapo is so centralized that those carrying out orders are sincere when they reply that they don't know anything; orders come in direct line from Paris, and more often than not from Berlin."[7]

On the political level, the Marseille raids sounded the death knell for the "Free Zone," which would thenceforth be simply the "Southern Zone." By multiplying their efforts to intervene with a hypocritical and in any case powerless Vichy, official Jewish leaders were not only wasting their time, but encouraged the false hopes of some French Jews that the marshal might be concerned about their fate.

The Raid on Rue Sainte-Catherine in Lyon

"The Gestapo will seek out the Jews where it knows they are," said Serge Klarsfeld: "in the offices of the UGIF."[8] Ill-informed about the UGIF in the Southern Zone, the Gestapo had asked Paris, through the intermediary of Israelowicz, for a list of all the regional committees, including the names of the staff. This list was intended—the Gestapo specifies—"to inform the *Aussenstellen* (local branches) about 'union' officials and their activities, in order to avoid in the future the kinds of difficulties that have already arisen."[9] The difficulties referred to here were presumably the escapes of Jews, and others, due to lack of complete information on the part of the Gestapo.

In fact, on 9 February—some ten days after the Marseille raid—the authorities conducted a sweep of the UGIF offices, where the OSE medical clinic and FSJF were also located, at rue Sainte-Catherine in Lyon. Eighty-four persons were arrested, most of them officials of the OSE, the FSJF, and associated groups who had taken to gathering there, a habit particularly risky because some of them were already carrying counterfeit identity papers. The German police had set a trap by forcing the switchboard operator to arrange several ostensible meetings for the same day, which explains the number of persons caught. All those arrested were sent without delay to Drancy.

Some escaped by luck, some by miracle. Jean-Pierre Lévy, the founder of *Combat,* was warned about an immanent Gestapo sweep of the FSJF premises and stayed away. He also alerted his friend Victor Sullaper, a young Zionist resistance activist, but the latter tempted fate anyway: "He warned me of the danger of going to the UGIF offices, which we used for our meetings," recalled Sullaper, who paid no attention because he was meeting his elder brother, Rachmil, there. The latter was a highly visible official of the

Zionist-Socialist Party. Rachmil, who, worried his accent would give him away, had not obtained false papers identifying him as a native of France, was deported to Auschwitz. Victor just barely escaped: "Weapons in their hands, the SS lined us up with our arms in the air, facing the wall, and no visitor who came into the place was allowed to leave. After our papers had been checked, I was among three persons who were detained separately. Interrogated through an interpreter, I explained that I had come there by mistake. Then I heard them say this sentence, which I understood: *'Verfluchtes Land, man kann nicht wissen wer Jude ist'* ('Damned country where you can't tell who is a Jew!'). It was an unheard-of chance and my false papers allowed me to get out of the trap from which so few escaped."[10]

Faiwel Schrager, a Bund official and an escaped prisoner, had gone underground and was carrying false papers. He showed up at rue Sainte-Catherine in the afternoon for the "meeting" of the board of his organization. "I hardly had time to see what was happening when the door was yanked open and a group of toughs burst in and forced everyone who was present to gather in a neighboring room. . . . Unfortunately ignorant of all this, other Jews kept coming. Thus, one after another all the militants of the Bund arrived."[11] Schrager was finally released when his "papers" passed the test, while his comrades were arrested and deported.

The FSJF had earlier, in June 1942, opted for "technical" cooperation with the UGIF—against the urging of its president Marc Jarblum, and soon the federation was operating under the UGIF's aegis. After the attack on the FSJF headquarters "there could no longer be any doubt as to the danger from that quarter [the UGIF]," the memoirist Schrager later recalled, and "those who escaped agreed that [our] activity could no longer be conducted in Lyon." They decided to go underground and to "transfer the headquarters to Grenoble, in the Italian Zone."[12] However, the very unusual situation there—the unwillingness of the Italian authorities to go along with the Germans and with Vichy's persecutions of the Jews—retarded the passage of some Jewish organizations into complete clandestinity, who proceeded too slowly with plans to go completely underground. Amazingly, the administration of the UGIF resumed activities in Lyon after the raids, creating a supposed regional grouping that would be capable of "normal operations." It is hard to see on what their optimism was founded, unless Lambert judged that the danger had come from association with the "foreigners" in the FSJF and the OSE. And indeed, recruitment of the group was carried out only among French Jews. For its part, the Resistance understood that the raids, directed in effect by the Gestapo, meant the end of any "Free Zone." An MNCR tract entitled "The Attack against the Jewish Population of Lyon Has Begun" made it clear that among the people rounded up were "French Jews of old stock, veterans, girls, children of fourteen who did not even have the time to warn their families or to take any clothes with them." All had been kept for a few days in a "Nazi military prison" and then "deported to Germany."[13]

The Warsaw Ghetto Uprising

On Monday 19 April 1943—the eve of Passover—an armored column of SS troops invaded the Warsaw Ghetto. It was met with a rain of incendiary bombs thrown from the windows and roofs. This was the beginning of a rising which constitutes one of the great events in the history of the Holocaust. Some ten days would have to pass before the "Free World" learned that the last Jews of Warsaw—30,000 out of the 400,000 crowded there in 1940— had refused to die without fighting. Theirs was a desperate revolt, but it was the first in occupied Europe. The BBC reported it in several languages at the end of the month, but left to the Polish-language broadcasts the burden of following the event over the next days. It is by this means that the news could be picked up in France on the night of 30 April–1 May by the Jewish Section of the MOI. Once the emotional impression had been absorbed, these activists, despite the danger represented by the surveillance of the FTP-MOI by the Special Brigades of the Vichy police, judged dissemination of the news the highest priority. In Paris nine news-sheets and tracts were disseminated in May and June, along with one discussion paper; much the same occurred in Lyon, Toulouse, Nice, and Grenoble.

The rising was perceived as a tragic end to the history of Jewry in Poland. Were there still any doubts as to the scale of the extermination? If there were, Warsaw dissipated them irrevocably. And all evidence suggested that the same fate awaited the deported Jews of France. Initially without reliable numbers (the underground press spoke of Poland transformed into a "slaughter-house," and of "two million exterminated" there), the editors relied instead on images of the battle where the heroism of the fighters was the equal of their tragedy. "Can you hear the screams of our brothers and sisters in the Warsaw Ghetto?" asked the underground papers. It was vital, in the face of the imposed news blackout, to make sure the Jews' uprising achieved the maximum resonance: exhausted, starving, the Jews had successfully challenged the Wehrmacht, a rebellion the Germans had hoped to crush without making too much noise.

One cannot ignore today the relative ignorance of such matters on the part of the Jewish organizations in France. There is no mention at all of the ghetto in the publications of the major resistance movements. Given the frailty of their intelligence capacities, however, it is unlikely that the multitude of underground organizations (several hundred) even picked up the BBC broadcasts. Were they uninterested? Did they underestimate the event's significance? The latter seems more likely. Decades later at a colloquium on "The Impact of the Rising of the Warsaw Ghetto," Germaine Ribière, one of the publishers of *Témoignage chrétien* (Christian Witness), regretted having ignored the event: "We did not know, we could have known, we should have known."[14] We are aware that at least some leaders of the Resistance knew at the time. Vercors (Jean Bruller) recalls his meeting with François Mauriac at the latter's residence on avenue Théophile-Gauthier in Paris at which both listened to the BBC. "We first had to listen, through all the static, to 'Les Français parlent aux Français' (The French Speak to the French), then news from the various war fronts. Then came the atrocious and staggering news of the [last] 35,000 Jewish survivors of the Warsaw Ghetto: having seen 400,000 disappear convoy by convoy, they had sworn to resist to their last drop of blood. And to reduce them the Germans had had to have recourse to artillery and air strikes, crushing the ghetto . . . until nothing was left over a surface as great as a Paris city district but a mountain of rubble."[15]

The feelings of these two did not necessarily predominate at the upper levels of the Resistance, even the Jewish. No echo has been found among the records of the Consistory, the Jewish Scouts, or even the "Jewish Army."[16] Can this fact be explained by a lack of interest in intelligence work? This may be the reason that they were not constantly waiting for the next Allied broadcast about Poland or the death camps. Surely the exclusively French vision of the "Jewish problem" in Consistory circles contributed to the general ignorance. In the case of the Jewish Army, where Polish Jews were numerous, the failure to react may be explainable by the fear at the time "that what one could have said would only have terrified people and perhaps pushed them to commit suicide."[17]

Did one have to be a "Polish Jew" to be interested in the rising? One is tempted to think so. Yiddish-language circles such as the Bund and the Poale Sion disseminated information. The news bulletin published by the Poale Sion in Grenoble reproduced an appeal from the ghetto fighters to the Zionist organizations of Palestine that concludes with a cry of despair: "When you receive our appeal it will perhaps be too late. We shall be no longer." But Paris Jews too were inspired by Warsaw; activists of the Union of Jewish

Youth (UJJ) also disseminated information about the event. Jacques Adler, then sixteen, took part in the distribution of an underground newspaper (through the front of a furrier's shop catering to the Wehrmacht); he later recalled that "the reactions of our readers, immigrant Jews for the most part, were very warm, and their contributions were the largest that we had ever received. Everyone was very eager for information. All of us in the organization felt that our relations with them had been transformed." During a visit to a canteen run by the Bund shortly thereafter, Adler noted that "most people had heard [and were] both devastated to learn that the Jews [of the Warsaw Ghetto] had been massacred, and proud of the struggle that they had waged there."[18]

Uprisings in Jewish History

A new enthusiasm for armed resistance; a sharper sense of unity with all the still vital forces; and an intensification Jewish identity conditioned the turning point experienced by the Jewish Resistance of the MOI in the days following the Warsaw Ghetto Uprising. The armed struggle and the role of the Communist Party as the apex of the Resistance would more and more be perceived as a duty toward the fighters of the ghetto and their memory, a duty inflamed by the need for vengeance. At the same time the ghetto's flames illuminated a closing of ranks, a natural but also ancestral reflex coming from the depths of collective memory.

A declaration signed "The Jewish Communists" published in June 1943 inscribed the revolt in the history of the Jewish people and interpreted it as both a continuation and a new departure. On the one hand, it was linked to the time of struggle for the independence of ancient Israel, and on the other it was taken to symbolize a break with the submissiveness practiced during centuries of exile: "After the revolt of Bar Kokba,[19] the struggle of our brethren in Warsaw represents the greatest battle in the history of our people."[20] The Lyon edition of the newspaper *Unzer Wort* saw a rupture with the time when martyrdom equated to heroism: "The uprising is . . . the symbol of the new spirit which today animates the Jews of the entire world. Yes, undergo martyrdom, die for the Sanctification of the Name (*Al Kiddush Hashem*) like our fathers and grandfathers, but in a different way. . . . Today, Jews are dying while sanctifying the Name, but with weapons in their hands."[21] At the same moment a young Zionist resistance fighter was uttering analogous words 1,250 miles away in the Bialystok ghetto during preparations for a revolt there: "For the first time in my life, I am a participant in a meeting about death. [Our goal is not] to write history but to die with dignity, as is suitable for young Jews of our times. . . . And if someone should write this history, it would be different from that of the Spanish Jews who leaped into the flames, *Shema Israel* ("Hear, O Israel") on their lips."[22] This stunning similarity in responses by people sundered by the near total communications blackout may appear to some almost mystical; but others will perceive in it manifestations of a common historic culture that transcended ideological and geographic diversity.

In numerous publications of the Jewish Section of the MOI, information and reflections were expressed, naturally, with a great deal of emotion, reflecting a double perception of events, both political and plaintive. Thus, this appeal, for example:

> Rise up for the last combat against the Nazi barbarians! Hear the cries of millions of our brothers tortured in the camps of Poland and in the ghettos! The day is near when Hitler's horde will have to account for all its crimes. So much blood can never be appeased! Nor will the innocent dead be silent. The spectre of defeat haunts the Nazi bandits. It appears to them in the faces of millions of their victims who rise from their graves, issue from the flames and the death factories. They mobilize like a powerful army, and behind them march the living, all the persecuted, all humanity, in order to efface from the surface of the earth for ever all trace of Nazi barbarity![23]

In other Jewish circles in France, deprived of all information and cut off from the exterior, the impossibility of contact with Jewry abroad created a climate of palpable anxiety. We are entitled to ask whether the Jews of the Free World were any more conscious of the situation and whether they fulfilled their obligations according to its actual gravity.[24]

Paradoxically, the news circulated in only one direction: from occupied Europe toward the countries of the Free World. The Warsaw ghetto fighters made superhuman efforts before and especially during the uprising so that the world would learn of the disappearance of Polish Jewry. On the other hand, no world Jewish organization tried—very probably underestimating the prospects of a Jewish resistance—to put into place any kind of arrangement to communicate with the resistance groups, so utterly cut off from the rest of the world.[25] And yet whether it is a question of the World Zionist Organization or of the World Jewish Congress, world Jewry was relatively well informed. Independently of diplomatic sources, they had access to the daily bulletins of the Jewish Telegraphic Agency which, thanks to its vast network of correspondents, was at this time almost entirely devoted to the unfolding of the extermination plan and to action in the free countries to alert governments and public opinion. On the other hand, little space was given to the resistance that the Jews were putting up, with the exception of abundant information on the participation of Jews in the Red Army or in detachments of Soviet partisans.[26]

Still, even a small increase in the quantity and character of the information transmitted in the direction of the Jews of occupied Europe could have constituted a source of courage and, above all, would have been a symbolic sign of the moral unity of the Jewish people, something that it so lacked during this crucial period.

Reorganization of the "Jewish Section"

During a meeting of the National Board of the Jewish Section in Paris on 27 May 1943,[27] it was decided (on the initiative of Jacques Rawine, responsible for the Southern Zone) to regroup into a single organization the various branches (in particular, Solidarité, L'Union des femmes, and trade union groups affiliated with the CGT). The new grouping would be called the Union des Juifs pour la résistance et l'entr'aide (UJRE—Union of Jews for Resistance and Mutual Aid). The political aspect of this restructuring was by far the most important. In Lyon and Grenoble first contacts were already being made with the Zionists and socialists (Bund), as well as groups around the FSJF. The objective was to reconstitute the unity of Eastern European Jewry, from which the communists had been practically exiled after the Ribbentrop-Molotov Pact in August 1939.[28] The UJRE translated the widespread desire for an umbrella organization to gather all those Jews in the Resistance irrespective of ideology. No distinction was to be made "French or foreign, workers or middle class, Zionists or communists, atheists or believers," for all were "simply Jews," that is, people condemned to extermination.

The raid by Barbie's men on the premises of the FSJF in February 1943 had hastened the transition to underground activity of those remaining at liberty. Jacques Rawine now had a green light to contact them. He approached Faiwel Schrager, a Bund official whom he knew from the time when Schrager, then a militant communist, had been one of the most prominent leaders of the Jewish organizations of the MOI.[29] But the first communist proposals for a unity pact received a unanimous negative response from the Coordinating Committee that had formed around the FSJF. Attitudes changed at the beginning of the summer of 1943. In his memoirs, Schrager credits the Warsaw rising with a determining role in the unification of the immigrant Jews.[30]

The UJRE was represented at negotiations by Jacques Rawine and Adamicz (Henri Braun); the Coordinating Committee by its secretary general, Léo Glæser; the left by Faiwel Schrager (a Bundist and thus non-Zionist) and Joseph Fridman (a Zionist); and the FSJF by Ruwen Grinberg, president after the flight of Marc Jarblum to Switzerland. Agreement was reached in early June on a "unification program" centered on three objectives: to organize the defense of the Jewish populace; to assure material relief to the needy; and to establish relations with other resistance forces against the common enemy. The Coordinating Committee would henceforth be called the Comité général de défence (CDG—General Committee for Defense), and would meet in either Grenoble or Lyon.[31]

Through the establishment of committees in Lyon, Toulouse, Marseille, Nice, and elsewhere, the CDG was able, despite its underground circumstances, to get close to the "grass roots" and to attenuate the consequences of the dispersal and fragmentation of the immigrant Jewish population. The foundation of the CDG was noted by the prefect of the Rhone, who observed that it was made up of Polish, Hungarian, and other immigrant Jews who had come to France as refugees, with differing opinions but united by their will to defend their rights. The prefect noted the initiative of the communists and the numerous difficulties that had lain in their path.[32]

The UGIF: To Be or Not to Be

The UGIF remained the prisoner of its initial options, which prevented any global approach to Jewish problems. A new law of 5 June 1943 introduced an official tax on the revenue of the UGIF (instead of the philanthropic dues which very few people paid regularly); this raised a storm of challenges with the UGIF Administrative Council for the Southern Zone because it obliged the UGIF to furnish the General Commissariat for Jewish Questions the list of "taxpayers" and to inform it of any changes of address.[33] Lambert submitted to the demands of the authorities but then came in for violent criticism from members of the council. But the most vehement criticism came from another source: André Weil, "the Young Turk of French Jewry"[34] and the treasurer of the Consistory, who had already called attention to himself by

categorically refusing Vallat's invitation to join the administrative council of
the UGIF.

At a conference in early June in Aix-les-Bains, about which we know too
little, Weill delivered a violent attack on Lambert. Théo Klein (Alexandre?),[35]
a member of the administrative council, was visibly shocked by Weill's indictment. He shared his feelings with Lambert: "The UGIF, a German creation,
is a moral ghetto while we wait for the geographic ghetto. The law of 5 June
has made it an instrument of police searches by constraining it, under . . .
the authority of the General Commissariat for Jewish Questions, to furnish
lists that make it possible to track down those who have changed domicile
and to turn in the indigent." Klein asked Lambert whether he now shared
Weill's views and how he planned to protect the dignity and safety of those
whom they assisted. The board must not delay too long, he added, in "alle-
viating the torment of our consciences."[36] We do not know specifically how
Lambert responded, but his subservience served him little: in late August,
he, his wife, and their four children were arrested and sent to Drancy, from
where they were deported in December 1943. He had crossed paths with
Röthke once too often.

Lambert's deputy, Gaston Kahn, left his position in September and went
underground. Activity at the Marseille office was reduced to a minimum, a
situation which continued until January–February 1944. Was the institution
to be scuttled in 1943? A report on a UGIF meeting in Paris notes: "The question had already been discussed within the Union on the occasion of a plenary session of the Administrative Council, held in Paris on 25 October 1943,
which decided against it, invoking the usual motives of a fear of aggravated
persecution."[37]

Recognition of Failure

On 6 October 1943 officials of the Central Consistory and the UGIF met in
Lyon. Helbronner, Meiss, and Kiefe represented the Consistory; the UGIF
delegation included the lawyer Raymond Geissman (Lambert's successor as
director for the Southern Zone) and Robert Gamzon (head of the Jewish
Scouts). At issue was the future of the UGIF. The crisis consisted of three related problems: financial difficulties, a lack of members, and most important,
doubt as to the very reason for its very existence.[38]

Gamzon wanted the Consistory to help reinvigorate what was now a
"skeletal" UGIF council. The vacuum was due not only to arrests. The last

influential members of the council were leaving. "Messieurs Seligmann and Wormser have gone underground," said Gamzon. "Wormser has left without a forwarding address. As for Seligman, all we know is that he is somewhere in France." Finding prominent figures who would agree to sit on the UGIF was practically impossible under these circumstances. Only Gamzon had the nerve to ask the fundamental question that was on everyone's mind: "Should we try to hang on?" Helbronner and Meiss assured the others of the Consistory's desire to maintain good relations with the UGIF but evaded specific commitment. Did Helbronner sense that closing down the organization risked drawing the authorities' wrath? After all, as far as Vichy was concerned the UGIF was a "public institution" and therefore part of the state apparatus. Was not advocating its disappearance the equivalent of an illegal act? In the event, Helbronner argued that the UGIF ought to continue its work: "You cannot abandon the unfortunates who must be assisted," as he put it. But Gamzon pointed out in reply the cost of this assistance in human lives, recalling the raids and arrests. "Yes, that is true," he continued, "but do not forget that the very premises of the UGIF have often served as traps. Is that in the interest of the unfortunate?" Helbronner could only suggest that assistance be delivered in people's homes.

The Gamzon-Helbronner confrontation grew more adversarial as Gamzon backed Helbronner to the wall by asking him to prove by his actions that the Consistory really wished to prevent the foundering of the UGIF, and to propose new appointments to its council. Helbronner, who was not unaware of the state of mind of those close to him, none of whom wanted to compromise himself, sidestepped the question by arguing that the Consistory did not intend to usurp "your responsibilities; it would be better that you yourselves proceed with the selection of candidates." Gamzon understood that it was futile to rely on the Consistory. Had he counted on this response in order to make the failure of the UGIF a recognized fact? "I agree, at all events [prospective] candidates would fear a loss of honor by agreeing to become members of the UGIF Council." He knew that he was at a turning point, and that it would not be long before he joined the Resistance.

Meiss, visibly irritated by Gamzon's attitude, despite the latter's verbal precautions, in frustration told the scout leader, "It is difficult to deal with you when we don't know exactly in whose name you are speaking."[39] To put an end to discussion, Helbronner, who knew that the rump UGIF delegation would be meeting the Germans in Paris, advised it to insist that Baur and Lambert be allowed to return, "for without them there is nothing to be done." Unfortunately, as far back as anyone could remember the SS had never released an arrested Jew. It is possible that at that very moment the fate of the most emblematic figure of French Jewry under Vichy was already being decided in Paris or Berlin: In fact, the president of the Central Consistory himself would be arrested in November.

Vichy's Last Hope: The Milice

The day after the Marseille roundup (30 January 1943), Laval, either on his own initiative or at the behest of German security, authorized the creation of a "parallel" police force to bolster the maintenance of law and order. The country seemed to be in a state of latent civil war. The prefects and the postal monitoring service called attention in their reports to a growing loss of public acceptance of the regime. The new "Milice" was to be composed of volunteers, coming for the most part, like their commander Joseph Darnand, from the fascist Legion Française des Combattants' Service for Public Order. It was to function both as political police and a paramilitary organization. Conceived as an instrument in the service of the state, the Milice would have the juridical status of an "association of recognized public utility" and would have as its president Laval himself, with Darnand as secretary general.

The prime minister, who was anxious about the possibility of "a partisan war as in Yugoslavia," gave the Milice the task of rooting out the *maquis* (partisan underground).[40] In January 1944 Laval would go so far as to make Darnand part of his government,[41] overlooking the fact that the latter had had to swear allegiance to Hitler in summer 1943 in order to accept appointment as honorary SS-Sturmbannführer. Pétain did not condemn the crimes the Milice soon began to commit (notably the murder of former cabinet minister Georges Mandel) until August 1944, too late to distance himself from them.[42]

The Milice was completely attached to National Socialist ideology and to collaboration with the Germans; it regarded the Resistance as the Jews and vice versa. Its intelligence service relied on informers and spies specialized in the hunt for Jews in the underground, an ongoing effort aimed at capture or assassination. The regular police were becoming ever less reliable, and it was through the Milice that the program of the "Final Solution" would be advanced in France, under the indulgent eye of the heads of state and government.

New Methods for Jew-Hunting

Capturing Jews became increasingly difficult. Helmut Knochen, head of the German police in France, was obliged to draw up for his Komandos detailed instructions better adapted to the new circumstances.[43] All Jews, immigrant or native, were targeted. All family members found at a residence were to be picked up during an action, and policemen were to remain behind to wait for any absentees—until then this practice had been used only against Resistance operatives.

New actions were going to be aimed at Jews both in hiding and still officially living at liberty. All foreign Jews from the labor camps or serving prison terms were to be transferred to Drancy. "It is important to search through the penitentiaries and jails," according to Knochen, "because foreign Jews are getting themselves arrested and condemned for slight infractions in order to find shelter from German measures."[44]

Since instances of escape en route to Drancy were still frequent. Knochen ordered that "the Jews be bound together by the hands with a long rope." This was the idea of a very irritated policeman indeed. Surveillance measures were to be stepped up at Paris stations when trains for Drancy came in. "In each of the buses there should be four Jewish supervisors who will look after luggage at the station so that the escort need only look after the Jews, thus excluding all possibility of flight."[45]

The German security service doubtless put the number of persons gone underground quite high since they ordered the seizure of "authentic" documents as well as false identity and food ration cards to stop them from circulating in the Resistance. In order to make the hunt more successful, following instructions from Berlin the service recommended the introduction of a bounty on "hidden or camouflaged Jews," to be paid from "Jewish funds" and turned over to the informer "on the spot." As Knochen explained, "we must utilize the greatest possible number of persons . . . if we really want the territory to be cleansed of Jews." This all was, in fact, an explicit admission of failure, for anti-Jewish propaganda was no longer paying off and the occupiers were obliged to turn to the corruption of bribery.

Himmler: Put an End to the "Foreign Jewish Resistance"

During the months of May, June, and July 1943, the Jewish organizations of the MOI suffered extremely grave losses in Paris. Police commissioner Paul

David's "Special Brigade" had established a system of patient and prolonged surveillance (teams might shadow individuals six or even nine months), a program completely subordinated to the instructions of the occupiers.[46] By late July nearly the entire Jewish leadership had fallen, with the exception of Sophie Schwartz, Roger Aronson, and Adam Rayski, as well as Léon Chertok, one of the officials of the MNCR.[47] Sixty other members of the Jewish Section network—among them Idel Barszczewski (Korman, Rayski's deputy) and other significant Resistance figures—were caught in the meshes of police surveillance. At the same time, the Second Detachment (of the Paris FTP-MOI) was dismantled: its leader, Meir List, was arrested along with his deputy, Boria Lerner, and the youngest fighters, Roger Engros and Henri Tuchklaper, aged seventeen.[48]

It was only after the summer's disaster that the few leaders who had escaped or been left "in reserve" by the police as leads for a new round of surveillance were authorized by the French Communist Party to leave Paris in order to reconstitute the national headquarters in Lyon. The episode pointed up the differences in immediate priorities between Jewish leaders and the Communist Party,[49] which judged the situation in reference to its own global strategy and required its maximum strength in Paris. What was important for the Jewish leadership was to minimize its distance from the majority of the Jewish population, most of which was now spread throughout the Southern Zone. "Like fish in the water?"[50] Not really, for the deportations were drying up the river.

If the Second Detachment had ceased to exist, most of its fighters, among them Marcel Rayman,[51] were reassigned to other detachments with various responsibilities. By October the net had closed in on the entire military contingent of the MOI, a coup facilitated by the treason of Joseph Dawidowicz, its "political commissar," responsible for the rank and file.

The assassination of Julius von Ritter on 28 September 1943 was experienced in Berlin as a humiliation. Von Ritter had been the representative in France of Fritz Sauckel, responsible for the recruitment throughout Europe of forced laborers for German industry. After the assassination the hunt for Jewish Resistance fighters became a matter of state, to such a degree that Himmler himself followed the progress of repression against the FTP-MOI. Herbert Hagen, one of the Gestapo's top men in Paris, conveyed this point to Laval in Vichy. In the words of Fernand de Brinon, Vichy's ambassador to the Occupation and the man responsible for conveying the message, "He pointed out that of one hundred two persons recently arrested as guilty of terrorist attacks, fifty-two were foreign Jews. He added that his police services had received from Reichsführer SS Himmler very precise orders that foreign Jews should henceforth be rendered incapable of doing further harm."[52] Laval later sought Hagen's recognition for "our recent success in combating the Jewish terrorists who executed Sauckel's representative in France."[53]

The prestige of Germany required an immediate response, and von Ritter's funeral was conducted with great pomp in the Church of the Madeleine. The sumptuous ceremony, with the participation of dignitaries from Berlin, became almost a national day of mourning for the Occupation and even the Reich. The Special Brigade then initiated the last phase of its long hunt. Along with Missak Manouchian, who for the last two months had replaced Boris Holban at the head of the armed branch of the MOI,[54] seventy-two men and women were arrested in the space of some ten days, frontline fighters and others from the various support services. From among them were chosen the twenty-three "Resisters" for the spectacular show trial which would be the origin of the notorious "Affiche rouge" ("Red Poster"). The twenty-two men were shot on 21 February 1944 at Mont-Valérien.[55] Olga (Golda) Bancic was beheaded in Stuttgart on 10 May 1944, her twenty-fifth birthday. Her last thoughts were of her daughter, then three years of age: "Your mother is writing her last letter, my little dear. Tomorrow at six in the morning, the 10th of May, I will be no more. . . . Darling, don't cry, your mother is not crying either. I am dying . . . in the conviction that you will have a happier future than your mother and that you will no longer have to suffer. . . . Be proud of your mother. I have your image always before me. . . . Little one, your father will also be a mother to you, he loves you a great deal, and you will not feel the absence of your mother."[56] Forty other resistance fighters, Jews for the most part, were deported. Joseph Epstein ("Colonel Gilles"),[57] a regional officer of the FTPF arrested at a rendezvous with Manouchian, was shot after a summary trial along with twenty-nine other French Resistance operatives on 25 April 1944.

In March of 1943 a German poster depicting ten of those who had been shot at Mont-Valérien in order to stigmatize the "criminal army" of Jewish and stateless "terrorists" appeared in thousands of copies on walls throughout France. Red in tint so as to be symbolic of the bloodshed, the poster stimulated, contrary to its intended objective of arousing xenophobic and antisemitic sentiment, a new state of public opinion that reacted with admiration to the deeds of the Resistance fighters.[58] "If the Germans had not thought up that poster," Manouchian's widow, Mélinée would later say, "France would perhaps have forgotten the heroic sacrifice of these men." In answer to the poster the UJRE published in March 1944 its own "Declaration" on the Red Poster: "Why do they struggle, why do they die?" It challenged its readers with the question: what were the motives of the "ten immigrant workers who, weapons in hand, made life difficult for the mortal enemies of our country"? "Hunted and pursued in their countries of origin," the declaration explained, "these immigrant Jews had come to France to breathe the air of liberty. *They fought and are dying because they are sons of a people whom the enemy of France and of the Jews is in the process of exterminating* [author's emphasis]. There is another reason that calls Jews into the ranks of the Resistance and that turns Jewish youth into bold soldiers in the army without uniform. *There is not another people in the world that has suffered so much.* More than two million Jews have been murdered, asphyxiated in the gas chambers, burned alive in the synagogues, or buried alive."[59]

The tally of the Franco-German police frenzy against the Jewish resistance—as both Jews and members of the Resistance—was a very high one. At Mont-Valérien alone a total of eighty activists from the Jewish organizations of the MOI were shot, to whom it is appropriate to add the name of Abraham Trzebrucki, which does not figure on the list because he was condemned and guillotined by the French fascists.[60]

From the Perspective of the End of the War

At the moment when the executive organs of the Jewish Section of MOI and the UJRE were reconstituted in Lyon in October of 1943, their members found themselves at the head of regional organizations with solid structures and good roots in the Jewish communities of the cities in the center and South of France. Even though a large portion of the Jews lived illegally, their concentration in cities like Lyon, Grenoble, Toulouse, and Marseille was substantial. Work life called for the maintenance of old ties. The example of Lyon is interesting. Here a number of fine leather-working and knitting shops served the city and surrounding communities. This required in turn suppliers of raw material (or ersatz substitutes) and retailers. Thus emerged a network of more or less durable relations.[61]

Doubtless, the morale in these underground enclaves, both dispersed and concentrated, differed little from that of the citizenry as a whole. At the close of 1943 one certainty prevailed: Hitler had lost the war. The year had seen the surrender of Field Marshal von Paulus at Stalingrad, the arrival of Allied forces in Tunis, the liberation of Corsica, the Anglo-American landing in Sicily, the capitulation of Italy (August), the retaking of Kiev (in November), and so on. These triumphs of the Red Army won general admiration among the populace and reflected a new esteem for the communist resistance.

Morale improved and also the will to fight. Terror bred hate, leading numerous Frenchmen "to move progressively from passive resistance," as a Vichy report put it, "to a formidable activity that will swell the camps with labor dodgers, rebels, and terrorists."[62] This feeling became so palpable in city and countryside that the atmosphere (both political and human) became more breathable for the harried Jews. The number and variety of underground organizations grew with the desire to fight back. Jews could join a Jewish resistance, while others joined the predominantly Gentile groups; so eager were they to fight that initiates rarely asked many questions about an organization's political coloration.

From the permanent game of hide-and-seek with the repressive apparatus (itself a form of individual resistance), entry into the organized Resistance was only a short step. The prospect of coming victory bolstered people's courage and strengthened their determination. The new mood spelled new recruitment opportunities for the MOI in Lyon, Grenoble, Toulouse, Marseille, and other localities thanks to the important concentrations in these places of Jewish units in the MOI. This also affected the Jewish Scouts and the Jewish Army, less inclined to the idea of large-scale or rapid recruitment.[63]

The Marcel Langer Brigade

In Toulouse and environs the Marcel Langer Brigade of the FTP-MOI would earn its place among such major units of the Resistance as Mouvements unis de Résistance, (MUR—United Resistance Movements), Armée Secrète, (AS—Secret Army), and others. Marcel (Mendel) Langer, a veteran of the International Brigades of the Spanish Civil War and head of the Toulouse FTP-MOI, was condemned to death on 21 March 1943. During his detention he was often visited by Rabbi Nathan Hosanski, a member of the Armée juive (AJ), who passed on messages, including the last letter from Marcel Langer to the UJRE of Toulouse. The rabbi accompanied him when Langer was being led to the guillotine. Marcel Langer was avenged on 10 October 1943 by comrades who assassinated the Toulouse public prosecutor, Lespinasse. From July 1943 on Rabbi Hosanski chaired the General Committee for the Defense of

Toulouse, uniting the various currents among the immigrant Jews. Arrested himself by the Milice in January 1944, the rabbi was turned over to the Germans,[64] who deported him to Estonia. He never returned.

After the Liberation the Marcel Langer Brigade was recognized by the Fifth Military Region (Haute Garonne) for its numerous resistance actions between 1942 and 1944. If its activities did not play a tremendous role in 1942 and 1943, by 1944 it ever more frequently carried out direct attacks on the Milice and on units of the Wehrmacht. For Serge Ravanel (named Companion of the Liberation), a former commander of the Free French Forces of the Interior (FFI) the "MOI was an elite assembly. . . . In Toulouse the Langer group played . . . a decisive role. . . . We were staggered by the number, effectiveness, and audacity of the actions undertaken."[65]

In the Toulouse city center, as in the suburbs, commemorative plaques bear witness to the important place occupied by Jews and Jewish organizations in the Resistance. Appearing on these plaques are the names of Rosine Bet, Jacob Insel, Jacques Kramkimel, Zeff Gottesman, Boris Frenkel, David Freiman, and of course Marcel Langer; the names of Ariane Knout (née Scriabine, wife of David Knout) and Thomas Bauer (both assassinated by militiamen who discovered their hideout at 11 rue de la Pomme) also appear on a plaque noting simply "killed 22 July 1944."[66]

Combat Groups in Lyon

Formed simultaneously in Lyon and Grenoble at the close of the summer of 1942 under the leadership of Henri Krischer, the FTP-MOI groups (including antifascist Italians who had been in the region for years) recruited a considerable number of young Jews who had evaded the great roundup in Paris (most of these had lost parents to the deportations). One example is Simon Frid, who without specific ideological motivation became, like his twin sisters, a member of the Union de la jeunesse juive (UJJ). He always wanted to "do more" and asked to join the combat groups of the UJJ and, later, the FTPF.[67] Simon Frid was guillotined on 4 December 1943 at the age of twenty-one. In reprisal, his comrades, led by Eizer Najman (Gilles), assassinated Faure-Pinguely, president of the special court that had condemned Frid, in his home on 12 December 1943.[68]

Integrated among the Jews of Lyon and Grenoble, the FTPF publicized accounts of sabotage and assassinations without giving away any vital information. Secretive, they identified themselves to prospective comrades they wished to recruit. When Dina Krischer met Jeanine Sontag, she let her guess that she belonged to an armed combat group. The latter, a young woman of twenty already active in "Combat," told her the FTPF was too centered on words: "It's not enough for me to make propaganda, I need to fight." In July 1944 Sontag fell into the hands of the enemy along with several other Resistance fighters. All were executed at Saint-Génis-Laval on 20 August.

Léon Pfeiffer, one of the fighters in the so-called "Carmagnole Batallion," became part of the history of Lyon, the capital of the Resistance on 27 July 1944, just one month before the liberation of the city. On the orders of Klaus Barbie he and four other resistance activists were taken out of the fortress of Montluc and executed in broad daylight at the Place Bellecoeur. Their bodies were left for horrified passersby to see until curfew. The French police were on orders to prevent any attempt to remove the bodies and to suppress any manifestations of sympathy. Immediately after Liberation the city raised a monument on the site. Engraved alongside the name of Léon Pfeiffer are those of Albert Chambonnet, Gilbert Dru, Roger Bernard, and Pierre Chirat.[69]

The fate of Pfeiffer's family illustrates in condensed form the history of the Jews of France. His mother, convinced that the Paris roundups threatened only men, made her husband and three sons leave for the Southern Zone. She was taken in a raid, however, and her husband was arrested at the demarcation line. Both were deported and did not come back. Maurice, the youngest son, crossed the Pyrenees and joined the Forces françaises libres (FFL — the Free French). He would participate until the day he met his death in November 1944 near Belfort. Léon and Élie joined combat groups of the Lyon UJRE, and then transferred after a few months to the FTP-MOI. Only Élie survived.

No exhaustive summary of the actions carried out by the FTP-MOI in Lyon and Grenoble is possible here; in 1944 these actions included direct attacks on German military units. On 24 August, a large group of FTP-MOI activists waited in a garage in Lyon near the Brotteaux Railway Station for an arms delivery by French gendarmes who had gone over to the Resistance; they were attacked by a mobile unit of the Wehrmacht passing nearby. Retreating to Villeurbanne, the Resistance fighters were received by the overwrought populace like FFI liberators. This was the beginning of the Lyon insurrection, which precipitated the city's liberation even before the entry of American units.[70]

Where did the idea come from in the summer of 1943 to create combat groups associated with the UJRE? The leader responsible for the Southern

Zone, Jacques Rawine, explains it as a result of the high demand among the young for direct action.[71] If the FTP-MOI detachments were already seasoned by more than a year's experience, training was still necessary for the new recruits. Their apprenticeship took place in combat groups, which had objectives of a less military nature, although they were still asked on occasion to lend their support to the FTPF. It is nonetheless likely that the creation of combat groups was intended to provide the UJRE its own armed branch, but it also offered a new kind of fraternity for the oppressed: "Joining a combat group," says Fernand Kohn, "was not only the expression of our sorrow and our anger, but also offered the possibility of finding a family again."[72] From the list of their countless actions we may mention here the execution in Lyon of Milice leader and former regional director of the General Commissariat for Jewish Questions, Carrel-Bellard (May 1944); the rescue of six Jewish children under the care of the UGIF at the Antiquaille Hospital Lyon (June 1944); and the armed break-in to the offices of the UGIF office on the Montée des Carmélites Lyon to spirit its files to a safe place (January 1944).

In Grenoble, "you slept all winter with all the windows open so that you could hear the crunch of braking tires," in anticipation of police raids.[73] There the UJJ (mostly children of deported families) and its combat units were continuously targeted by the Gestapo and the Milice, yet wrote pages of exceptional courage, inspired by motives both ideological and Jewish. Twenty-four-year-old Charles Wollmark, who succeeded Juline Zerman as head of the UJJ after her cowardly assassination by militiamen or the Gestapo, soon met his own tragic martyrdom. Arrested in May 1944 by the Germans, he disappeared. His wife, Marguerite, retrieved his tortured and nearly unrecognizable body in the small town of Charniècles, twenty miles from Grenoble. The inhabitants had discovered it next to that of Isaac Baumol (nicknamed "the Lombard"), a veteran of the International Brigades in Spain.[74]

The lives of Charles Wollmark and his friends can serve as models for coming generations. Their ideological engagement may pass with time, but what remains is the example of Jewish youths who faced adversity and became heroes.

CHAPTER FIFTEEN

Jews, French and Resistant

The Jews have a religion of justice. . . . Their Messiah is
none other than the symbol of eternal Justice . . . which
may doubtless quit the world for centuries but cannot fail
to reign there some day.

—Léon Blum[1]

I experience as a Frenchman the insult done to me as a Jew.

—Lucien Vidal-Naquet[2]

Can one place an equation sign between "Consistory" and "French Jews"?
Officially, the former spoke for the latter, even if it was often ignorant of
their opinions and feelings. Nevertheless, its loyalist opinions did not correspond to the state of mind of the active minority of French Jewry that condemned from the start Vichy's policy of collaboration and its antisemitic legislation. Thus, critical judgments we make on the Consistory do not apply to
French Jewry generally.

The men of the Consistory were obstinately convinced that they and
those whom they spoke for would be protected against deportation. Was this

attitude not founded on the hope, not explicitly voiced, that persecution would remain limited to foreign or recently naturalized Jews? This is a hypothesis that should not be discarded: statements made during meetings of the Consistory Council suggest as much. Thus in August 1942, after having observed that "nothing can be done in Vichy to save the foreign Jews," its vice-president, Adolphe Caen, thought it possible "to spare [our] French co-religionists from new trials."[3] The ambivalence of the occupiers' policy with regard to native French Jews, plus the timing of the stages of persecution, encouraged such illusions.

Vichy's Intentional Ambivalence

The Free French in London understood that Pierre Laval was trying to give the country "to understand that he is obliged to surrender the foreign Jews in order to save French Jews."[4] As that excellent and always well-informed chronicler of the era Pierre Limagne noted: "Laval has 'released' to the Germans the Italians and Spaniards in France, the last 'foreign' Jews."[5] At the Hotel du Parc the Vichy government continued to feed the lie as long as possible. However, the Occupation authorities were becoming less solicitous in their relations with Vichy as they once had been. In November 1943 they dryly announced that they "would no longer entertain interventions on behalf of Israelites." De Brinon, the Vichy envoy to Paris, informed the Marshal that "efforts on behalf of even prominent personalities or veterans with outstanding service records were of no avail."[6] There could be no doubt that in the eyes of Berlin the French Jews no longer had any citizenship and had become just so many more "stateless" people whom Germany might dispose of as it saw fit.

Not all the Consistory's leaders were taken in. In February 1943, Chief Rabbi Isaïe Schwartz had a meeting with a senior official in the French police, who told him that "the increase in arrests affects only foreign Jews and has been necessary in order to protect French Jews." The chief rabbi rejected this assertion, remarking that "the latter had never been consulted on the matter of whether they hoped for that kind of protection." He could not have been more clear, but his language is new: "It was his duty to protect [the foreign Jews] to the full because their suffering was due to their Jewish origin, and all the more since there was no certainty that French Jews were actually being protected."[7]

Abandoned by Their Brothers?

The chief rabbi's stance was not widely known because the Consistory did not make it public. But even if it had done so, it would not have much altered immigrant Jews' opinion that French Jews scorned them. This feeling did not derive solely from the experience of the prewar years, when they had been called "Polacks" and accused of provoking antisemitism; now they suffered the daily experience of persecution which seemed to strike them alone. The impression that the French Jews were being privileged revived the suspicion of their lack of solidarity.[8]

Marc Jarblum viewed the Consistory this way: "The Storia family [the codeword for the Consistory] is also of very little interest, especially for foreigners," he told to the World Zionist Organization in Geneva. "This family has learned too little; it remains almost as it has always been." He did not despair, however, of one day reconciling French and foreign Jews.[9]

Jules Jefroykin, Maurice Brener, Robert Gamzon, and others whom one would not suspect of any prejudice against the French Jews, did not hide their irritation over the latters' "xenophobia" and "antisemitism" after a May 1943 meeting with the leaders of the UGIF-Paris. They observed that the Consistory Council members for the Northern Zone were divided into two factions: "the leaders, more or less xenophobic, more or less anti-Semitic and opposed to Zionism; and those more or less favorably disposed to the foreigners, philo-Semitic and Zionist." The two factions remained enclosed in "their ivory tower. . . . Some of them receive solicitors with hostility, in particular if they are foreigners."[10] Abbé Alexandre Glasberg, having attended an April 1942 audience granted by Cardinal Gerlier to Father Chaillet and Jacques Helbronner, recounts that the latter called the cardinal's attention to the untimeliness of protesting on behalf of the foreign Jews; Helbronner feared, according to Glasberg, "that they might adopt analogous measures later against French Jews."[11] Some French Jews employed a xenophobic vocabulary to set themselves apart from their alien cousins. One of Helbronner's correspondents denounced the aspiring "luxury Jews" and their "recently imported additions." This complainant worried that after a victorious war these might predominate in France's Jewish community, and he expressed the hope that their triumph would remain "modest."[12]

On the other hand, the OSE leader Julien Samuel cast a critical eye on the relationship of many Alsatian Jews to their foreign brethren: "Our common roots in the earth of the old Alsatian communities caused in me, too, a revival of that proud xenophobia that we are displaying toward foreign Jews," he self-critically confessed. But at the OSE he had met foreign Jews and made the "astounding discovery of men of a quality and temper both unsuspected and exceptional."[13] Camille Dreyfus, another Alsatian Jew, reasoned similarly (though only after having been uprooted from his home): his new status as "wandering Jew" brought him closer to the refugees from Eastern Europe. "The Jews of Alsace had become progressively rigidified in their own culture, and had comfortably withdrawn into themselves. But the Second World War made pariahs of them, condemned to the wandering of the eternal Jew whom they had sought to forget. . . . The Jew of Alsace was precipitated into a history that . . . made him brutally aware of the common destiny which tied him to the foreign Jews cast with him onto the paths of exile."[14] Dr. Fred Milhaud explained the reasons for the silence of his fellow French Jews on the lot of the foreigners as "a cowardly propensity to disinterest themselves." He, instead, was persuaded that "the German projects affect all Jews."[15]

Pierre Dreyfus, who after the war became a senior manager at Renault, did not believe in Vichy's protection: "I was convinced that Vichy would go on right to the end. I knew who Alibert (Vichy minister of justice and author of the first anti-Jewish legislation) was because I had been with him on the Conseil d'Etat. I know that Pétain believed that Colonel Dreyfus was guilty."[16]

From Mistrust to Resistance

The number of French Jews who early realized that the process of isolation, persecution, and deportation would not ease after the foreign Jews had been removed from France was considerable. Among them, as Jean-Pierre Azéma points out, were such republican Jews of long distinction as René Cassin (member of the Council of Defense of the Empire), Maurice Schumann (diplomat and later minister of foreign affairs), and General Georges Boris (of the Central Consistory).[17]

One could add many more examples. "Le Mouvement Petites Ailes-Vérités (The Little Wings–Truth Movement), then Combat, had at its head-quarters—from its very birth—perhaps the largest single share of Jews in the Resistance." Claude Bourdet (one of the leaders of Combat) lists more than twenty names of founders of movements who were Jews, among them Colonel Blum (called Baudricourt), Léo Hamon, Françoise and François-Gérard Seligmann, Benjamin Crémieux (who along with Marc Bloch and Georges Friedmann signed the declaration on the UGIF), and the latter's son Francis.[18] Others such as Valentin Feldmann, Georges Politzer, Jacques Solomon,[19]

Pierre Villon (Ginsburger), Maurice Kriegel-Valrimont—some of them communists at the beginning of the war, others being converted by the end—
would make their contribution to the history of these times. The two last-
named, along with Vaillant (Jean de Voguë), headed the FFI's Comité
militaire d'action (COMAC—Military Action Committee)—charged with
preparation of the national insurrection.

Among the 1,041 Resistance members decorated by de Gaulle with the
Order of Companions of the Liberation were fifty-one Jews, or about 5 percent. If we assume that the percentage of Jews in the Resistance generally
was the same (global statistics are not available), this would mean, since Jews
made up only 0.75 percent of the French population, that they were over-
represented in the Resistance by a factor of more than six.[20]

Lucien Vidal-Naquet: A Bourgeois Republican

Lucien Vidal-Naquet, according to his son Pierre, was a peculiar type created by the Third Republic, a "bourgeois republican." He was a lawyer whose
middle-class career was destroyed by the antisemitic laws. Idleness weighed
on him and he sought to cope by keeping a diary starting on 15 September 1942.

> I want to try to express . . . the interior monologue that is gnawing at my
> spirit, to free myself from it, so to speak. . . . We have seen France, after
> having deserted on the battlefield, shake hands with the executioner. . . .
> We have seen France accept collaboration with the enemy who has never
> hidden his will to destroy her, . . . profaning the most glorious memories
> of her history. . . . As long as they were the acts of the enemy, I bore them
> in silence; I experienced a certain exaltation to think that for the enemy
> of my country I was myself the worst enemy; but the bullets that struck
> me most deeply are not shots from the Germans but from the French.

If we compare Vidal-Naquet's diary with positions taken by numerous other
prominent Jewish figures, we shall discover the same catechism: a sense of
patriotic honor, fidelity to the "pact" between the Jews and France. Bourgeois
republicans denied the France that "shook hands with the executioner." The
parallel between the Jews and the others stops there, for many in the establishment resigned themselves to accepting the Vichy regime perhaps in the
interests of social order; Vidal-Naquet did not hesitate to choose the Resis-

tance: "I think very firmly today, since we are distinguishing between 'us' and France, that France *was* us and it was terribly wrenching to turn away from her."

This "bourgeois republican" entertained no illusions about the regime of Marshal Pétain, whose crimes, he underlines, included sacrificing the foreign Jews who had come to France seeking asylum. If France survives, Vidal-Naquet opines in early 1943, it is not thanks to Pétain but to de Gaulle, who "from the dark days of June 1940 has incarnated that faith which will not die." Inevitably, his reflections turn to the attitude of the authorities toward the French Jews. Did not Vichy claim to "protect" them? Did it not argue that "by turning the foreign Jews over to the Nazis it was paying a 'tribute' to sate the appetite of the occupiers"? Did not many French Jews cling to the vain and degrading hope that the deportation trains would not stop at their station? Lucien Vidal-Naquet replies with lucid, biting scorn: "Some who push prudence to the point where it becomes cowardice to continue to declare that it is only a matter of 'normal' measures that have affected only foreigners. This is completely and utterly wrong. I wonder in what way we have been saved because Mme Arn, Jacqueline Lang, and young Mlle Rosenblitt have been arrested and thrown to the German beast." So much for the lucidity. For the contempt, a few lines suffice. Even if this were true, he observed, "the crime would be no less glaring." Vidal-Naquet's moral revulsion eschewed any compromise with the pseudo-"realism" then still current. "In the last several days I have experienced the most horrible wound that bleeds from my heart." These words, as those above, are references to the mass roundup in January 1943 carried out in the old port of Marseille.[21] Vidal-Naquet first aided the Resistance group in the Musée de l'Homme (Museum of Man) in Paris, and later in the National Front. On 15 May 1944 he was arrested along with his wife and deported from Drancy to Auschwitz two weeks later.

The Jewish Identity of Marc Bloch

The great historian and founder of the Annales School, Marc Bloch, and Professor Georges Friedmann, two men whose ties to Judaism were scarcely perceptible but who were gravely affected by the anti-Jewish legislation, reacted both as Frenchmen and Jews. Their conduct epitomizes that of all French Jews who chose early between "legality" under the France of Pétain, and illegality alongside the other France, the true France, the France of the Resistance.

We have already noted the highly visible stand taken by Marc Bloch in the UGIF affair.[22] Barred from the university, Bloch was permitted to continue teaching (in Montpellier) by the dispensation of the Ministry of Education. This "favor" did nothing to dampen his hostility to the Pétain regime. His refusal to accept the military defeat—he had already expressed it with great force in his work *L'Étrange Défaite*, written in 1940 but only published in 1946: "I will be frank," he affirms, "I wish under all circumstances that we still had blood to shed, even if it were that of those who are dear to me." This foreshadows his own future destiny. "Marc Bloch, like many other French Jews, saw in persecution a supplementary reason to affirm his Frenchness," writes Stanley Hoffmann in a preface to the work.[23]

By the close of 1942 Bloch had accepted a seat on the administrative committee of the Mouvements unis de Résistance (MUR), along with Georges Altman and Jean-Pierre Lévy, founders of the underground newspaper *Franc-Tireur*, around which MUR crystallized. Jean-Pierre Lévy would say of Bloch: "The eminent professor came with modesty and simplicity and put himself under our orders."[24] Arrested in the spring of 1944 along with a number of other MUR leaders, Marc Bloch was imprisoned in the fortress of Montluc, where he underwent terrible torture. On 16 June 1944 he was forced into a truck with other detainees. The execution took place at the edge of a field near Saint-Didier-de-Formans.

Conscious of the fact that he could be killed at any moment, Bloch wrote his will while in the underground. In it he makes an explicit point of his Jewish heritage. Bloch echoes the *kaddish*, the Jewish prayer for the dead "whose cadences . . . accompanied to their final rest so many of my ancestors and my father himself." Yet he asks his wife and children not to recite the prayer at his own grave, for he wished to remain true to his life as a non-practicing Jew: on his tombstone he wanted them to inscribe only the words *Dilexit veritatem*—"He loved the truth." Unwilling to affirm "an orthodoxy whose credo I in no way recognize," Bloch felt it would be worse still "if anything that resembled a cowardly denial were to be seen" in his abandonment of the Jewish religion: "I was born Jewish [and] I never sought to hide the fact." He concludes with a profession of his own faith: "In a world assailed by the most atrocious barbarity, the generous tradition of the Hebrew prophets, which Christianity took up in its purest form in order to enlarge upon it" remained for him a wellspring of "reasons to live, to believe, and to struggle." Attached to his country by a long family tradition, Bloch faced death knowing that "I have loved France greatly and served it with all my strength."[25]

Georges Friedmann: The Shock of October 1940

Professor Georges Friedmann, mentioned earlier in the context of his common initiative with Marc Bloch denouncing the UGIF, refused to allow himself to be isolated. A "marginal Jew" is how he described his relation to Judaism. In October 1940, he received "a first shock in discovering the staggering consequences the fact of being labelled Jewish could have." The secretary of state for education offered him the possibility of "begging the indulgence of preferential treatment" so that he might "continue to exercise his professorship." He refused the "favor."[26]

The "blow to the heart" brought in its wake a true identity crisis, "shaking the foundations" of Friedmann's personality. He viewed the legislation as a shipwreck in which his faith in France foundered. It was through his friends and teachers, "who treated him as if nothing had changed," including Marc Bloch and the historian and *annaliste* Lucien Febvre, that Friedmann rediscovered his faith in France, finding the means to "situate" the events in their "context."

Most important for Georges Friedmann, as for all the French Jews, was to refuse to let themselves "be excluded from France." They could express this refusal in two ways. The first was by clinging to the hope that Vichy would give some sign of recognizing their Frenchness. The second was resistance— Friedmann joined up with Combat in January 1941, adopting the nom de guerre "Gaston Fromentin." Here was a France "from which all racial discrimination had been swept." Neither a practicing Jew nor a Zionist, Georges Friedmann's relationship to France was founded on that of the country itself to its Jewish children. It was this criterion that determined his choice between de Gaulle, who accepted the Jews, and Pétain, who abandoned them. But his view of the Polish Jews whom he judged so different from "us" was transformed by events: "I did not at first feel 'interdependent' with these men and women from the Polish ghettos, as I do today after the cruel experiences and reflection, with the handful of them who have survived."

Whether they placed themselves within the cultural or social organizations of Jewry or not, all French Jews experienced the same trauma when the racist legislation put back into question the fundamental achievement of emancipation: integration into the nation. "That leaves a mark," said Pierre Dreyfus, who long remembered the moment when a Vichy functionary asked him: "How long has your family been parked in France?" "Parked!" Thus "insulted," he joined the Resistance.[27]

Dominique Schnapper, the daughter of political theorist Raymond Aron, has kept as a relic the decree of October 1940 which removed Aron from his position at the University of Toulouse. Her father-in-law, a participant in the Resistance from the very beginning, was deported after having been betrayed by a fellow Frenchman. "Like all Jews of my generation I have forgotten nothing that the Vichy government did."[28]

"Israelite" and Jew: Denise Baumann and Other Rebels

Denise Baumann was born into an Alsatian Jewish family and lived her Jewishness with difficulty, self-conscious and ashamed, until she met other Jews in the Resistance. Having joined cousins in the Southern Zone in early 1942, Baumann freed herself of family tutelage and her parents' conformist acceptance of the Marshal and Vichy. She had originally planned to assist at a rural women's center under a false identity, but allowed her father to caution her away from breaking the law.[29] She soon found herself working on the staff of an OSE preschool preparing to "fade away into the landscape" with the help of the underground network "Garel."[30] In Lyon she met Charles Ledermann, who recruited her in late 1943. Denise was soon charged with responsibilities in the MNCR, where she focused her efforts on rescuing children. Later still she collaborated with Ledermann when he became a national official with the UJRE. At his side she helped publish the underground paper *Droit et liberté*.

With the passage of time, maturing from one action to the next, the young men and women transformed themselves. Many experienced a kind of gradual mutation of identity. "For the first time I heard Yiddish spoken," Baumann recalled, "and discovered a culture of which I was ignorant. I discovered the folly of struggling against what I belonged to. . . . My Jewishness was part of my being, just like my French culture. It gave me deep roots and additional strength."[31]

Rabbi Samy Klein, chaplain of the Jewish Scouts, believed that to serve France he must go beyond his spiritual work with the young, so he joined a group affiliated with the Free French Forces of the Interior (FFI). "To our surprise," writes Frederic Hammel (a chemistry professor who established a farm where children could live), "one of the leaders of the Scouts, Samy, informed us that he had contacted an underground unit of the Secret Army in Haute-Loire and that he did not intend to join the EIF [the Scouts] underground."[32]

All such French Jews felt the same way: all wanted to fight the enemy with deeds instead of organization alone: René Cassin, Daniel Mayer, Pierre Mendès-France, Louis Kahn, Raymond Aubrac, and Jean-Pierre Lévy— to cite only a few—all joined the Resistance in its early days. In the words of the historian André Kaspi, they "set aside the notion of 'Jew' to retain only their identity as 'French citizen.' "[33] But this fails to take into consideration the cultural and political traditions of French Jews, for whom civic engagement, according to a consecrated formula, was made on an individual basis. In any case, there could be no question for them as political people of turning toward the Jewish organizations which were nearly all social assistance agencies, excepting of course those connected to the Jewish Section of the MOI; welfare agencies could offer no framework for action against Vichy, even less for action against the Occupation forces. Moreover, under the umbrella of the UGIF, the agencies were quite defenseless against surveillance by the German and French police. Their choice was also inevitably motivated by the republican and patriotic tradition to which they belonged, and this explains the considerable number of Jews among the founders of the major groups in the Resistance.[34] The patriotism of these French Jews was only intensified by the laws seeking to purge them from the nation; they allied themselves with the France that did not deny them membership, the France of the Resistance. The directors of the Consistory, on the other hand, thought they might defend the gains of emancipation by appeasing the France of Pétain, which in fact wanted nothing to do with them.

Stanley Hoffmann suffered under Vichy France as a child, and is now one of its finest analysts. Cutting through some of the debates today over secondary issues he writes: "There can be no question that it was the sacrifice of men and women like Marc Bloch, moved by the same ideals if not the same faith (Christian or communist), that made it possible for France to raise itself up again and to freely question its past."[35]

The MOI: A Hand Outstretched to French Jews

From the spring of 1943 on, the Jewish Section of the MOI showed increasing attention to the situation of the French Jews. In its declaration of principles, the UJRE affirms: "Anti-Semitic persecution is addressed against all Jews in general. Leaving aside some purely verbal declarations whose purpose was only to put our vigilance to sleep, no distinction is being made among

Jews, whoever they are: French, Polish, German, Turkish, etc., all are consigned to the same fate, extermination."[36] The UJRE, under whose umbrella all the Jewish organizations of the MOI had gathered, was seeking to intensify contacts between French and immigrant Jews; this in itself was part of an effort to extend the influence of the UJRE to social groups heretofore not well connected with the Resistance. Illegal publications of the UJRE and MNCR aimed at French Jews denounced the "protection" Vichy claimed it was affording them. "It is certainly comfortable to live with such illusions," wrote *Notre parole*, but the French Jews were warned against the "awakening" that awaited them when the Nazis began taking them too "to the slaughterhouse."[37] In the MNCR's summons, "A tous les Juifs français," appears the first mention of poison gas as the Nazis' principal instrument: "Mothers, their infants in their arms, are being asphyxiated in gas chambers. . . . What has become of the thousands of French Jews torn from their country and deported with the complicity of Laval and Darquier de Pellepoix"[38]

Among the Alsatian Jews illusions as to the attitude of Vichy and the effectiveness of the Consistory's interventions were as or more widespread than among French Jewry generally. Persistent rumors of raids in the Clermont-Ferrand region, where the majority of Alsatian Jews had gathered, made it vital to give those likely to be affected reliable information. "Do not passively await the day when misfortune will strike us down," urges a tract published by one group of Alsatians. "Let us take preventative measures today to avoid falling into the hands of the beasts. . . . Let us go underground. And first of all, let us save the children and elderly from the enemy's appetite for blood."[39]

The general roundup in Marseille at the end of January 1943 showed that the native Jews could no longer expect anything of Vichy: the occupier made the law. The change gave the UJRE, at last, a hearing among Marseille Jews. The leadership of the local section would soon have a native French majority. At the head of the Marseille UJRE stood Maxime Crémieux, the descendant of a family that before coming to Marseille had lived in the Comtat Venaissin for centuries. After the Liberation he would become the UJRE's president. Speaking at the first UJRE public meeting at the end of August 1944 Crémieux declared his democratic convictions which were motivated by his Resistance experience and family tradition: "The Jew is not only French or a foreigner of a different confession, but, rather, identical with all his brothers. . . . My grandfather, like all the grandfathers who lived through the sad years of the Dreyfus affair, told me when I was only a child: "The Jew can only be in the vanguard of democracy and, if he remains passive, does not defend those who defend him . . . he prepares his own subjugation for the morrow."

In other leadership positions appeared men who once would have found little in common with the MOI, men such as Henri Cohen,[40] Séraffino, and Misrahi, the latter responsible for the MOI combat units. On the list of Resistance fighters who fell during actions or were executed, one finds next to the names of Maurice Korzec and Armand Wassermann those of Roger Carasso, Ben-Sadoun, Maurice Dubray, and Pierre Joël.[41] These French Jews knew how to appeal to their French brothers by salting their language with local color and making repeated reference to the Republican traditions of the community. For example, tthe Bouches-du-Rhône UJRE newspaper *Résister* published an article about Gaston Crémieux, a "native son" condemned to death after the failure of the 1871 Marseille Commune, in which he played an important role. "Crémieux's life . . . is a wonderful synthesis of the qualities of a great patriot. . . . To speak of Crémieux is to speak of the life of a man of the people, a poet and a republican."[42]

How Vichy Is Ruining French Jews

After the 19 August 1943 arrest of Lambert and the departure of his deputy Gaston Kahn to the underground, the UGIF found itself in a crisis that put the very purpose of its existence in doubt. In mid-October a Jewish combat group raided the UGIF's Marseille offices and forced the employees to turn over the card index and the files on the recipients of assistance. The combatants destroyed the index cards because the information they contained represented a threat should they be confiscated by the authorities. On the other hand, about one hundred of the files were preserved, mostly those of French Jews. These now constitute important documentation on the material distress of those applying for aid, the victims of the anti-Jewish legislation. In April of 1944, the Marseille section of the UJRE published an underground study based on this documentation. Its title was *La Mort par la misère. Comment Vichy ruine les Juifs français* (Death by Destitution: How Vichy Is Ruining the French Jews).[43]

As a preamble, it offers this comment on the ambiguity of Vichy policy with regard to French Jews: "In order to calm public opinion and to appear quintessentially French, the Vichy government hastened to establish a distinction between foreign Jews and French Jews. The former were quite simply handed over to the Gestapo; the latter, on the other hand, fell under the 'protection of Vichy' and, according to an official declaration, were not to be 'personally harmed' How much hope and illusion did this Vichy magnanimity not stimulate?"

The study deals with forty-five persons belonging to the most varied social strata, from manual laborers to senior government officials. All applications enumerate the services rendered to the state, on the battlefield, or in civil life, some including the service of parents, grandparents, and even great-grandparents. Thus, M. F. adduces proof that his great-grandfather received the Saint Helen Medal. The fact that this information appears in requests for aid highlights the mental distress of applicants who appear to be relying on the same arguments they would have used with the Vichy administration even though they were actually applying to a Jewish (albeit semi-official) agency. Excerpts from a few of them offer us today a window onto the material consequences of successive laws directed against the Jews:

M. A.: Forty-seven years of age. Streetcar driver for twenty-one years. Relieved of his duties in conformity with the statute. Was receiving a pension of eleven francs per day until September 1942. Thereafter bereft of all resources. Monsieur A. receives a small grant from the UGIF.

M. L.: Fifty years of age. Former student at the École des Chartes. Graduate archivist-paleographer. Expelled from Alsace in July 1940, retired after seventeen years of service. Looking for work of any kind.

M. F.: Forty-four years of age. Former student of the École polytechnique. Mentioned in military dispatches (5 June 1940). Father a graduate in engineering in 1878, grandfather a graduate of the St. Cyr military academy, great-grandfather, recipient of the St. Helena Medal.

D. J. E.: Forty-five years of age. Police inspector. Volunteer's Cross, two wounds. War Cross, 1914–1918, four campaigns. Receives a monthly grant of 500 francs.

R. G.: Fifty-four years of age. Civil servant at the Ministry of Finance. War widow, 1914–1918. Dismissed. Receives a pension of 250 francs per month. The UGIF assumes responsibility to provide a grant of 200 francs per month.

F. F.: Thirty-eight years of age. Teacher at the X secondary school in Paris. Master's degree. Looking for work in one of the trades he practiced while a student (engraver, café manager, copper foundryman).

M.: Forty-four years of age. Astronomer with the B. observatory. Lecturer in the faculty of sciences at the university in the same city. Pensioned off as a consequence of the statute. Receives a grant of 800 francs per month.

K. A.: Thirty-five years of age. Medical biologist, former assistant at the École practique des hautes études in Paris; author of numerous research publications. Looking for a position as a pharmacist's assistant.

L. L.: Forty-three years of age. Professor of philosophy, married, father of two children. Dismissed. With the redundancy compensation now finished, the family is without resources. Receives 1,000 francs per month.

K. H.: Fifty-eight years of age. Of French descent with family dating from the Revolution of 1789. Examiner at the Conservatory of P. Knight of the Legion of Honor, first prize in piano at the Hague Conservatory, first prize in violoncello in Paris.

C. R. E.: Thirty-eight years of age. Actor at the Gymnase Theater, the Variétés, Palais-Royal. Redundant. Cares for mother. Receives 800 francs per month.

F. M.: Eighty years of age. Physician, Knight of the Legion of Honor for services rendered in the hospitals during the War of 1914–1918. Since his savings are deposited with the Paris bank and cannot be transferred to the Southern Zone, he is obliged to apply for aid.

These are just a very few examples, a tear drop in the ocean of devastating suffering experienced by Jews in France. They could be multiplied by tens of thousands.

Days of Joy and Sadness in Algiers

In Algiers, liberated on the eighth and the ninth of November 1942, the Jewish community experienced one of the more perverse ironies of the war. More than two hundred and fifty young people were members of a resistance organization grouped around Raphaël Aboulker and supported by figures such as Professor José Aboulker, who in turn was in contact with Emmanuel d'Astier de la Vigerie and René Capitant, de Gaulle's undercover emissaries. While waiting for D-Day, they drilled and readied their plans for the Allied landing, namely "the occupation of sensitive civil and military sectors and the neutralization of the authorities."[44] The operation was launched on 8 November at 12:30 a.m. and successfully concluded by 11 the same morning. The prefect was surprised and confined to his office, and the landing points were secured by the Resistance fighters. "A military success" it was, Jacques Zermatti testifies, but from the political point of view "a fool's errand. . . . We thought that we were fighting for a Free France but in actual fact we found ourselves, with the blessings of the Americans and through the intermediary of [Admiral François] Darlan, [still] under the flag of Vichy."[45]

Though a number of works treat the situation of the Algerian Jews during the war years, one contemporary source has until now not been explored, the *Bulletin* of the Federation of Jewish Associations of Algeria (FSJA).[46] The exploits of the Jewish Resistance fighters were passed over in silence by the new Allied administration. Thus, in the official review *Les Cahiers français* (published in London), the account of events makes no mention of the Jewish partisans, a fact noted immediately by the FSJA bulletin. "We abstain," it wrote, "from analyzing the reasons, for we have a duty to calm the very legitimate resentment of fiery youth which, having bravely accomplished the task to which it had dedicated itself, having seen two of its members fall, struck dead, wish to protest [and] lay claim to some honor."[47] There were opportunist considerations behind the official failure to recognize these "worthy descendants of the Maccabees," however, and the Jewish community would suffer further insult.

To be sure, the annulment of the anti-Jewish legislation was not long in coming. But the same was not true of the Crémieux Decree of 24 October 1870, which had granted the Algerian Jews French citizenship. The Pétain government had been quick to abrogate this law on 7 October 1940, only a few days after the promulgation of its other anti-Jewish legislation. And now General Henri Giraud (who had become Allied Commissioner for French Africa after the assassination of Darlan) feared any action that might provoke hostile reactions by the Muslims; therefore the new government decided to maintain Vichy's abrogation of the Crémieux Decree, thus keeping alive the spirit of Vichy's anti-Jewish legislation. The FSJA recalled Giraud's personal debt, for he had been hidden by a French Jew upon his escape from German internment in 1942. "A leader takes it on himself to abrogate a decree that has stood for seventy-three years and that granted citizenship to an element of the population that is honest, loyal, and worthy, and that paid the price of citizenship with the most sacred of sacrifices . . . blood shed on the field of battle."[48]

Henri Aboulker, president of the Comité juif d'études sociales (Jewish Committee for Social Studies), and Armand Karsenty, head of the lawyers association, became the spokesmen of an indignant community, publicly condemning this outrage:[49] "At the moment when . . . justice restores to the French Jews of Algeria the rights of which they had been illegally deprived, they cannot try to take back a portion of these rights. . . . The French Republic made Algerian Jews French citizens and its will must remain sovereign." The Jews of Algeria were aware of the situation of the native Muslims, and they were not claiming special treatment. What their declaration emphasized was that "France's traditional policy with regard to autochthonous populations has never been a levelling toward the bottom, but a more generous and humane one of raising peoples toward its own civilization." The Jews complained more bitterly still that the corollary of failing to restore the decree was that, as "non-citizens," they were being excluded from military service— and this at a time when "liberation imperiously dictates the deployment of every will and all energy."

General Giraud's policy prompted a campaign in the press and even protests among the Free French in the United States. Jacques Maritain, shocked, did not mince his words in a thunderous letter to the editor of the *New York Times:* "But if an attempt were made to justify the abrogation of the Crémieux Law merely as a measure of appeasing the anti-Semitic feelings developed by German propaganda and by the servility of the Vichy regime toward Nazi Germany, such an argument would deserve only to be branded as unworthy of the cause for which the free peoples are fighting."[50]

It was not until 21 October 1943 that de Gaulle reestablished the Crémieux law. His position on the French Committee for National Liberation, which he had co-chaired with his long-term rival Giraud, had solidified only after the latter—unpopular with the Allies and with the rank and file—had been eased out of his political role in August and Roosevelt had recognized the Provisional Government of the French Republic.

History's Lesson

Having witnessed the scorn that many French Jews felt for the immigrants, Théo Klein and Jean Kahn, both natives, shared the following reflections several decades later. (As chance would have it, the one succeeded the other at the head of the Representative Council of Jewish Institutions of France in 1992.)

Klein, a member of the Jewish Scouts and of the "Sixth" Resistance Group, spoke frankly of the "lesson" taught him at the time by a comrade of foreign origin:

I got my first false papers, I believe, at the close of 1942. It was Otto Gi-
niewski (Toto) of the MJS who gave them to me in Grenoble. . . . Giniew-
ski, a fierce opponent of assimilation, gave me, a French Jew, a lesson
that in tone was more like a bawling out: "You, you French Jews, you're
not worth people's concern. You detest your immigrant brothers and
think, in addition, that you are going to be spared, but you are wrong."

These words, I meditated on them often during the war. They gained
in significance with the worsening in persecution, affecting ever new categories of people.[51]

Kahn seconded Klein's feelings on the matter: "I would say that for French
Jews the Vichy legislation was a veritable lightning bolt that brought them
back to realities about which they did not wish to think. The French Jews had
not understood that foreign Jews were their brothers and, very often, they
judged themselves sheltered from persecution for the simple reason that
they had been citizens for two centuries or almost. Today I would like to express the regret that I feel as a French Jew for so frequently disregarding the
situation of Jews who had come from abroad."[52] It is clear that most, if not
all, of those French Jews who survived learned the lesson. It is equally clear
that they learned it too late, a fact not forgotten by many foreign Jews in
France who also survived. The matter was not one of "resistance and death,"
but "resistance or death moral and physical."

CHAPTER SIXTEEN

The Jewish Scouts Take Up Arms

Timid "little Jews" were transformed into men sure of themselves.
—Robert Gamzon

‡━━━┿━━━┿━━━┿━━━┿━━━┿━━━┿━━┿

The Éclaireurs israélites de France (EIF—Jewish Scouts of France) were officially dissolved in January 1943, although the decree was actually implemented only later that summer.[1] From that time onward, the national leadership undertook the disestablishment of the rural affiliates that had become too easy targets for the police. "The situation of the lads from eighteen to twenty-five, even of those who had taken cover and were working in the countryside, was not safe."[2]

As we have seen, the founder of the EIF, Robert Gamzon, left the UGIF Council, on which he had served since its establishment in December 1941. According to his widow, Denise, he stopped attending UGIF meetings in October 1943, immediately after the joint meeting with the Consistory in Lyon on 6 October 1943, the session at which he had urged the UGIF's dissolution.[3] For the scouts the time had come to join the Resistance, to take to the *maquis,* much as the large cohort of Parisian Jewish teens and young adults who had joined the Second Jewish Detachment of the FTP-MOI in July 1942.

The leadership of the Jewish Scouts noted the decline in morale among its members as a consequence of their long period in hiding, which prompted

259

in them "a kind of inferiority complex."[4] Large numbers "dreamed of defending themselves weapons in hand." As a result of their own efforts, before too long, Robert Gamzon was able to note that "thanks to an excellent diet, intensive training in hand-to-hand combat, grenade throwing, and running, the timid 'little Jews' had been transformed into men sure of themselves. . . . The youngsters, submachine guns and rifles on their shoulders . . . had the feeling . . . that they were no longer slaves being hunted down."[5]

The first maquis of the EIF were formed in November 1943 in Lamalquière on an abandoned farm. The region was both mountainous and Protestant, two factors that favored the establishment of the *maquis*. The group was incorporated in the Second Company of the Corps Franc Libre-10 (CFL— Free Irregulars), commanded by General Maurice Redon ("Durenque"). From the military point of view, the underground Jewish Scouts had no autonomy and their military objectives were not separate from those of other Jewish Resistance movements, for example those of the MOI.[6] Eventually they lost some of their Jewish character through the recruitment of a considerable number of young non-Jews from the region.

The complement amounted to a mere ten members at the beginning. In March and April of 1944 its numbers swelled with the arrival of almost twenty scouts from Toulouse and due to recruitment among the young farmers of the area. The latter remained with the scouts long enough to learn the essentials of handling weapons. A liaison system was established to speed their mobilization on D-Day. "Relations between the farmers' sons and the fighters were excellent," General Redon tells us, even if the former had little understanding of the "Jewish factor," and even if "occasionally . . . one or another expressed surprise at not being allowed to take part in the evening gatherings—despite the fact that these did not include prayers. These were minor matters that did not harm the profound comradeship among the *maquis*."[7]

Led by "Lieutenant Roger" (Roger Caen), the Lamalquière Group split in May, after their number had grown; there were now about eighty, including a large component of non-Jews.[8] The two groups of Jewish Scouts were placed under the direct responsibility of Robert Gamzon, who adopted the nom de guerre of "Lieutenant Lagnes." The pages Gamzon's memoirs assign to his underground period seem as if written by a different man than that one who a few months earlier had still been a leader of the very official UGIF. In his memoirs he scarcely speaks of it. Denise Gamzon explains this silence by his wish to record "the encouraging moments rather than the thorny discussions."[9] On the other hand, he overflows with enthusiasm when he recounts life in the underground. We sense him expand into the figure of Lieutenant Lagnes. He traversed the region by motorcycle, recovered parachute drops, trained fighters. "I believe that Robert," Denise Gamzon remembers, "got caught in the cat-and-mouse game that he was playing with the Germans. But once he joined the *maquis* he felt himself much safer. There he could resume the role of leader and educator that was so dear to his heart." There is no doubt that Gamzon had found himself out of place when he became aware of the risk which the UGIF was causing Jews who applied for assistance. When leaving his legal functions, Gamzon could choose between two illegal branches of the scouts: the "Sixth," which concentrated on hiding children, and the armed resistance; Gamzon preferred military action. Even though he never spoke of his personal motives, we must not assume that he discounted the work of the "Sixth." For Gamzon, it was a matter of signaling, in both a personal way and as head of the Jewish Scouts, the patriotic engagement of Jewish youth, its presence at the front in the spirit of the finest traditions of French Jewry. He thus came to serve the France of the Resistance, and not the Vichy legality he had respected for a time.

Gamzon was attracted by those who burned to tangle directly with the enemy. Thus he sketches a particularly laudatory portrait of a girl called "Jojo" who appeared more emancipated and open than the other girl scouts.[10] She came to the EIF from a communist background in Toulouse and proved one of the most energetic organizers of the underground. It was she who first went from boy to boy saying: "It's all very fine, hiding out, the false papers, but other people are fighting and you are hiding. The communists are fighting, the Catholics are fighting, and we, the Jews, all we do is camouflage ourselves. It's necessary, I agree, and it's also dangerous for those who do the work, but we have to fight too." An impressed Gamzon recalled how Jojo went around with "her hair tousled, ardent, impetuous; and the boys, moved by her impassioned words (and her pretty face) said to themselves, 'Look at her, the girl has more energy than most men!' And she didn't just talk; she transported weapons and took part . . . in a good number of 'strikes' that her communist friends carried out in the city."[11]

On 8 August 1944 a German column attacked the positions of a number of Resistance fighters near the site, including the "Patrick Company," led by Lieutenant Gilbert Bloch. Superior in numbers, the enemy succeeded after a fierce firefight in gaining the upper hand. Bloch was killed along with his adjutant Roger Godechaux, as were Rodolphe Horvitz, the Spaniard Idelfino Cavaliero, and three French Resistance fighters, Gabriel Sicard, Henri Bernard, and Victor Célestin. All were between eighteen and twenty-four years of age. It is worth noting that most memoirists and historians of the Jewish maquis do not mention the names of the non-Jewish Resistance fighters who fell with Bloch, seemingly zealous to downplay facts that could dilute the Jewish specificity of this underground group.[12]

The "Haguenau" Platoon of the Jewish Scouts (named for Marc Haguenau, assassinated by the Gestapo) was regularly assigned the recovery of parachute drops—quite frequent in that sector—at a site nicknamed "Virgule" (the Comma) near Lacaze. The most celebrated exploit of the Hagenau Platoon was without doubt its participation in the capture of a German armored train between Mazamet and Castres on 19 and 20 August 1944. Among the several descriptions of this remarkable feat the most accurate seems to be that of the commander for the region, General Redon ("Durenque").[13]

> At 1900 hours, the train left Mazamet on the Castres line and hit a first break in the track. It started up again after repairs, going very slowly, preceded by a soldier on foot.
>
> At 2130 hours, this man was hit by our sniper, while an explosion stopped the train. Both sides immediately opened fire. The Germans kept our forces at a distance thanks to four 20 mm artillery pieces firing from a platform. The exchange of fire continued until 2330 hours without decisive result. Then Segonzac (Commander Hugues) regrouped his people and kept watch overnight with frequent patrols.
>
> At 0800 hours on 20 August three 60 mm mortars were set up. Until then they had been supporting a diversionary attack that had taken place the day before right in the middle of Castres against the Kraut garrison.
>
> At 0805 hours a first shell made a direct hit on the train; very accurate fire was loosed; at 0825 hours the white flag was raised and the train's escort surrendered.
>
> During this time, one of our officers, Captain Dumoulin, initiated negotiations with the German garrison in Castres. Seventy-one officers and 4,200 men were included in the surrender of Castres. Segonzac had two hundred and fifty men around the town. The Jewish Scouts were under his command and were notable for their determination and courage.

We can imagine the emotion of the latter, for whom the event represented not only a baptism by fire but an opportunity to say to the officers and soldiers of the defeated garrison: *Ich bin Jude!* "I'm a Jew." This pride in having engaged the Germans directly was well expressed by Lucien Lazare: "I was assigned to knock out the locomotive with a grenade . . . and I must say that I felt a great exaltation in doing that job as a Jew. . . . Two years earlier I had returned to Judaism and I saw in the combat which took place on the Sabbath, preparation for which had been made the night before, a powerful symbol: I was living to the full the exceptional case foreseen by Judaism which allows fighting on the day of the Sabbath when there is a risk of death."[14]

In any case, the Haguenau Platoon never became a pole of attraction for the Jewish Scouts as a whole because of the geographic limits of its operations.

The Origins of the Jewish Army

Only a few months after the occupation of France, David Knout, a Russian poet and right-wing Zionist, had circulated a voluminous notebook among his friends in Toulouse and Marseille. Its title was *Que faire?* (What Is To Be Done?) and Knout's answer was "armed resistance." Until now the original of the notebook has not been found. However, its author reproduces some excerpts in his memoirs, published immediately after the war.[15] His friend Jules Jefroykin recalls in a commemorative article that Knout gave him a copy of *Que Faire?* in November 1940 in Marseille. And he remembers that "the idea of armed resistance was very poorly received by the constituent bodies of French Jewry."

In his analysis Knout gives proof of a premonitory perception such as only a poet might have: "The Jewish people is imperilled as never before in its long history. . . . A numberless and powerful enemy wages on us a war without quarter. . . . The extermination of the Jewish people is already in the course of realization."

As a follower of the right-wing Zionist Vladimir Jabotinsky,[16] Knout arraigned assimilationism as a frequently proposed solution to the "Jewish Question." He is unsparing with regard to the directors of the agencies who assigned welfare activities the status of survival strategy: "It is not bureaucratic philanthropy that will remedy the ills of our people. You can't fight catastrophe with donations; in that way you only teach the stricken a lesson in resignation, that great school of cowardice." Knout's organization *Ben David* ("Sons of David") proclaimed itself "a revolutionary and national movement, the militant vanguard of a people that will recover its independence."

In the summer of 1942 David Knout sought refuge in Switzerland and he did not take part in the formation of the Armée juive (AJ), whose principal organizers were Lucien Lublin and Abraham Polonski. Both of these men were Zionists, but they belonged to diametrically opposed currents. The former was a socialist, the latter (like Knout), a follower of Jabotinsky. Paradoxically, neither Knout's great inspiration nor his breadth of view can be found in the Jewish Army.[17] New recruits, on the other hand, had to swear an oath during a ceremony to which they were brought blindfolded: the "movement" was thus arguably reduced to the level of some kind of secret society. The organization changed its name from Jewish Fortress to Strong Hand, and then to Jewish Army or at times Jewish Legion; finally in the spring of 1944 it settled on Organisation juive de combat (OJC—Jewish Combat Organization). The grandiose names, quite unrelated to the real strength of the organization (except perhaps for the last), reflect more than anything else the romanticism of Abraham Polonski.

At the head of the Jewish Army then stood a heterogeneous Zionist leadership. The Mouvement de jeunesse sioniste (MJS—Zionist Youth Movement), represented by Lucien Lublin and Simon Levitte, consisted mostly of socialists affiliated with the French section of the moribund Second (Social-Democratic) International, and even some of the more radical Marxist communists. Following his personal penchant for secrecy, Polonski assigned great importance to ritual, which in his eyes was a guarantee of discipline and fidelity. Yet, as Lublin pointed out, "the members of the MJS who joined the Jewish Army rarely took the oath, which, moreover, was supposed to be sworn on the Bible. We were all secular people."[18]

The "Blue and White" Squadron

The Armée juive (AJ), often confused with the Jewish Scouts despite the difference in name, had only a single armed group, at Biques, near Albi (Tarn). In late 1943 this was incorporated into the noncommunist and not specifically Jewish group called the Armée secrète (Secret Army).[19] The AJ, called the "Blue and White" because its members wore a blue and white bar on their clothes, the colors of the Jewish Star of David flag, was primarily involved in arranging the escape of young people to Spain, whence they might emigrate to Palestine. It would seem, according to the statement of a veteran, Saïa Voldman, that its creation was due to chance: "One day," he testifies,

we received a group of Dutch Jews who had succeeded in escaping. How were we to put them up, feed them, occupy them? In the end it was thanks to Commander Roger Mompezat, a former cavalry colonel who commanded a maquis unit of the Secret Army, that we resolved the question; he took our little troop into his own underground unit. And thus was born the legendary Jewish resistance underground. In actual fact, our organisation, I must repeat, did not think of the struggle in terms of armed combat. The maquis units, made up essentially of men, was less important to us than the day-to-day survival of everyone: men, women, and children.[20]

"We were a truly Jewish maquis unit," says another former Jewish Army leader, "completely out of touch with any Jews in Castres or elsewhere. . . . Our problem was to school and train young people and to get them on their way to Spain so that they could join the Jewish Brigade" of the British army in Palestine.[21] At this time the Blue and White Squadron's leader, Pierre Loeb ("Pierrot"), accepted the military discipline of Mompezat's unit.

Later, in July–August 1944, when the maquis in the southwest were harassing German units retreating toward Paris or Normandy, circumstances sidelined the Jewish Army's Blue and White Squadron and Mompezat's unit, which de Gaulle's non-leftist resistance had recently absorbed along with several other resistance organizations. On Monday, 24 July 1944, the order to move was given to the squadron for reasons of security. Apparently the squadron's recent recruits had not received sufficient training to enable the group to attack the Germans who were carrying out punitive strikes as they retreated. The recruits, "two-thirds of the complement" (nine men) of the Blue and White Squadron, went to Toulouse, where they were to remain until "the call over the radio" came. Between 24 July and 18 August the rest of the squadron moved in stages toward Labastide in order to join the Corps franc de la Montagne noire (CFMN).[22] The course of this move brought them near the sector held by the Haguenau Platoon of Jewish Scouts under the leadership of Gamzon ("Lagnes").

Contrary to the impression given by some testimony, no meeting took place between Pierre Loeb and Robert Gamzon, which supports the fact that little coordination existed among various Jewish resistance groups. Loeb notes that, from Friday the 11th to Monday the 14th of August,

I was in the sector of Commander Dunoyer de Segonzac (Hugues). I thought that it was proper to establish contact and I showed up at his command post on Saturday the 12th. The meeting was otherwise of no great interest. As I knew that the Gamzon (Castor) group was nearby, I tried to meet him, probably on Sunday the 13th or Monday the 14th of August. I have no memory of meeting Castor during those days. I believe that he himself was absent so that I only spoke with his adjutant Roger (Caen). Our meeting was very friendly but certainly very informal. Castor's group did not belong to the [CFMN] and did not plan on joining it, while I, for my part, had the very precise mission of proceeding as well and promptly as I could to join the CFMN."[23]

Pierre Loeb continued according to plan and reached the headquarters of the CFMN by 18 August.

"Cooperate and Infiltrate"

Grey areas still cloud the subject of relations between the Jewish Scouts and the Zionist Youth Movement's (MJS) military wing, the Jewish Army. Between 1943 and August 1944 the two principal components of the non-communist Jewish Resistance appear to have reached two or three agreements with a view to their unification. The agreements, however, remained a dead letter.

The first effort at unification took place in late 1943. Leaders of the MJS and Jewish Scouts sought to unify the "living forces of Jewish youth in France" by adopting a common discipline and common operations;[24] nevertheless, there could be no question of a fusion of the two movements. In fact, one document of the period reflects the scouts' critique of the ideology of the Zionists. This was a proposed reorganization of the scouts, who would "be grouped in two branches according to the ideological thrust of the units, a non-Zionist branch and a Zionist branch."[25] Of all the documents relative to the unification issue, the most explicit seems to be the agreement (signed on the eve of the Normandy landings, i.e., late May or early June 1944 by Lucien Lublin for the Jewish Army and Robert Gamzon for the Jewish Scouts)[26] limiting cooperation to the military domain, the army's sphere of competence, while the army undertook not to involve itself in the "political, spiritual, and religious life" of the scouts. This phrasing remains inexplicable, especially given the excellent military structure of the scout maquis in the Tarn, not to mention the competence in that domain of Gamzon himself or of Gilbert Bloch, then a student at the Polytechnique. The scouts were to take the Jewish Army oath, which did not imply—Gamzon was careful to explain—"any lack of subordination to the regular French army."[27] Thus he gives evidence of distrust with regard to the Zionist objectives of his counter-parts and of prudence in not laying himself open to the charge of "double allegiance," the specter that haunted French Jewry.

By far the most numerous grouping of Jewish youth, the scouts represented a considerable reservoir for Zionist recruitment. The objective of the later was the "Zionization" of the scouts, as can be seen in the "platforms for cooperation" that were worked out during the Occupation. The testimony of Denise Gamzon confirms this:

> Between 1942 and 1944 there were a number of contacts between leaders of the Jewish Army and those of the Jewish Scouts but there was no fusion between the combat elements, for two reasons: the Army was openly Zionist and the Scouts were "pluralist." They accepted the option of the Aliyah in Eretz-Israel but did not make it an obligation; at the beginning the Army's maquis was rather a screening and training center to make up groups of young people who were to cross the Pyrenees and by way of Spain to get to Eretz-Israel. One may be surprised, and with good reason, that these two maquis units, only some twenty-five miles distant from each other, did not join forces. But their long-term goals were different.[28]

The Jewish Army consequently sought to infiltrate its ally. A document called a "Report on the Inn,"[29] dated 25 June 1944 and written by an "observer," noted that the maquis unit he visited included about twenty boys who would have to be considered "anti-Army" (i.e., not Zionist):

> They are fighting for France and, if need be, for the destruction of certain antisemitic prejudices. There is only one Zionist among them. But [even] in him the team spirit is more important than Zionist ideals.
>
> The author advises that: "We have to *recruit* and *infiltrate*, bind people by oath, and send some Jewish Army leaders there. Perhaps we could even regroup here everyone who is AJ, since its maquis seems to be poorly based in consideration of the topography. The danger would be minimal because it is not a plateau here but very hilly, and such a group, if by chance surrounded, could well be a couple of miles distant from a brother group.[30]

Alain Michel, the historian of the Jewish Scouts, unsympathetically confirms the presence of a Jewish Army "eye" in the organization.[31]

The Visionaries of the Jewish Army

The leaders of the Jewish Army were thinking big while the Occupation tottered (as they had in 1941 when they adopted the name Armée juive). As victory approached they foresaw creation of a Jewish Legion outside the FFI. To this end, they sought direct contact with either Allied headquarters in London, or, at a minimum, the British War Office.

An ostensible contact appeared on 6 May 1944, when the AJ leader Henri Pohorylès met a certain Charles Porel in Marseille (through Porel's mistress, a Russian Jew named Lydia Tcherwinska, who claimed to be a Resistance activist). Porel passed himself off as an agent recruiting on behalf of British Intelligence.[32] In reality, Porel was Karl Rehbein, an officer in the Abwehr, German military intelligence.

Without losing a moment Porel sought information: How many of you are there? What are your plans? Pohorylès' reply: "Can't give figures but ready to admit visit to our units of technician for arms and equipment." Porel pursued his idea: "Agreed, as concerns inspection; but we want to integrate your groups into the general plan on the landing day. What do you want exactly?" To which Pohorylès replied: "Weapons, equipment, money." The Abwehr agent could not have been more generous: he rattled off a long list headed by Thompson submachine guns with a supply of 20,000 rounds of ammunition, machine guns, and, if necessary, antitank guns. And in the same rush, this enticing offer: "I propose to have you enlisted as of this moment in the British Army, [to get] you regimental numbers from them, military record books, salaries corresponding to your rank paid in gold sterling." Such promises should have awakened Pohorylès' distrust. And indeed throughout the discussions with Porel, the Jewish Army leader made no mention of plans for future cooperation with the Jewish Brigade attached to the British 8th Army.

In the course of another get-together in Toulouse, to which Porel came in the company of a second man in a car stuffed with weapons and equipped with a radio set, it was agreed that two emissaries from the Jewish Army would leave for London in order to finalize the agreement. A meeting was scheduled for early July in Paris. In the meantime, D-Day came and the Allies established themselves in France. This did not, however, move the Jewish Army to reconsider its idea of seeking out the leaders in London. The two emissaries were Jacques Lazarus (Captain Jacquel), one of the most famous leaders of the Jewish Army, and Rabbi René Kapel. The latter remembers the anxiety of Alexandre Kowarski, a member of the administrative committee of the Jewish Army, whom he met before leaving for Paris. Kowarski was suspicious of Porel, but no one else shared his distrust.

Arriving in Paris on 2 July 1944, Lazarus and Kapel, through Lydia Tcherwinska, resumed contact with Porel. The meetings took place at the Hotel Montpensier (near the Palais-Royal), where several other leaders of the Jewish Army were also staying. "The telephone rang without stopping," wrote Rabbi Kapel, and this of course worried him.[33] With the agreement concluded, the departure for London was set for 17 July. "At six in the evening," Lazarus recounts, "we were at the café de la Régence; Charles Porel introduced us to the man who was to guide us to the rendez-vous, at the Michel-Ange-Auteuil Station. There a car was to come to pick us up and take us to the airport."[34]

Once the car started up, one of the "guides" pointed his pistol at the two resistance figures and said, "Hands on your heads!" Then the car stopped in front of 180 rue de la Pompe, headquarters of a French group working for the Abwehr.[35] The trap had closed on Lazarus and Kapel, and a few hours later it closed on twenty other members of the Paris organization of the Jewish Army, who very imprudently regularly met at near full strength in an apartment at 90 boulevard de Courcelles.

The apartment was rented and occupied by Lucien and Rachel ("Patricia") Rubel-Rabier, both members of the Jewish Army's Paris unit. According to "Patricia," who was in charge of intelligence, the team specialized in identifying informers. Despite the group's abilities and experience, they permitted the apartment to become a trap set by the staff from the rue de la Pompe, who managed to arrest the twenty or so militants. The Rubels, who had left Paris before the meeting, were arrested when they returned. "We were greenhorns . . . our leaders lacked caution," says Rachel Rubel today with great bitterness.[36] For example, the telephone number was given openly and also served as a password, not the most secure way of operating a clandestine organization.[37]

Charles Mandelbaum, a member of the "Alerte" irregulars, a Paris combat unit of the Jewish Army, explained what happened at the apartment due to sloppy security arrangements: "On 18 and 19 July my whole group was to meet. . . . Someone slipped into our group, a kid called Emmanuel Herbein [actually Rehbein]; he had the names of practically everyone; arrests began in this apartment on the evening of 18 July and continued until the next day."[38] This effectively destroyed the Alerte group, but worse was to befall the National Liberation Movement (MLN) as a whole.[39]

The Collapse of the MLN

After the arrest of Kapel and Lazarus, the arrest of other resistance operatives followed almost immediately, notably that of Maurice Loefenberg (Cachoud), who had been a member of the Jewish Army before becoming head
of the large MLN service producing false identity papers. According to documents from the archives of the MLN, however, Cachoud was arrested only
on 21 July 1944, at the close of an "immense" operation against it.[40]

Under the title "Alert, alert—urgent, urgent, urgent," the general secretary of the MLN sent out a belated call on 20 July, based on news from
his intelligence service had given him on the 18th, according to which the
French police, who now had a list of one hundred and eighty-five people,
would launch a huge dragnet at 6 a.m. on 21 July. A second note, dated the
21st, announced that "Cachoud has just been arrested along with several
comrades." Since documents had been found in Cachoud's briefcase, the
order was given to "clear out immediately" and to break off all dispensable
liaison with the counterfeit document service.

Cachoud was savagely tortured at the Gestapo facility in the rue des Saussaies. He did not speak and his killers finished him off. As head of the false
identity service of one of the most important movements of the Resistance,
he represented an exceptional catch for the French and German police.
Some idea of the scale and diversity of the activities of this service—virtually
a complete quartermaster unit—can be had by consulting the voluminous
correspondence between Cachoud and "Dominique," a leader of the Centre
d'action et de défence des immigrés (CADI—Center for Action and Defense
of Immigrants), an umbrella committee affiliated with the MOI.[41]

With his fertile imagination and energetic initiative, Cachoud often for-
got the elementary rules of security. "Permit me," wrote the head of CADI
to Cachoud on 26 June 1944, to "beg you . . . in the future not to call us to
rendez-vous in uncoded messages." Another note from the 29th is even more
categorical: "No member of our service will go to a rendez-vous that has been
named in uncoded written form."[42]

Why Go to London?

Excessive ambition? Mistaken political objectives? Or perhaps simply unrealistic idealism? Whatever the motive, the objective of the leadership of the
Jewish Army, to have the group recognized by the War Office, was doomed

to failure. Weren't the leaders aware of the hostility of Great Britain to admitting Jewish nationals of other countries to the Jewish Brigade?[43] Moreover, the AJ leaders did not need to deal with a virtually unknown person—more promising routes were open to them: going through the Jewish Agency in Geneva was one, or they could have made contact through Jules Jefroykin (one of the AJ's own founders, after all), who had been in Lisbon since the spring of 1944.

The initiative appears even more paradoxical when we recall that the "contact" was already within reach, in the maquis of the Tarn, whither numerous British agents had already parachuted. In the Jewish Scouts maquis there was even a British captain who shared Gamzon's nom de guerre, Castor (he was called *le Castor anglais,* "the English Beaver").[44] More to the point, the Black Mountain irregulars (CFMN), of which the Blue and White squadron was an integral part, were supervised by a British major, Richardson, who was in direct contact with the Special Operations Executive.

The fact that the Zionist leaders in France were also not informed of the proposed delegation can only be explained, it seems, by the lack of understanding the latter evinced for armed struggle. "Our projects of a military nature," explains Lucien Lublin, one of the principal leaders of the Jewish Army, "did not enjoy the approval of certain representatives of the World Zionist Organization in France. I think, for example, of Joseph Fischer, who remained quite reserved about the engagement of Zionist youth in the armed struggle. Marc Jarblum, on the other hand, encouraged us. But he left France for Switzerland in early 1943. He was a politician on the grand scale, with the temperament of a revolutionary. We felt that we would never be understood by those who succeeded him."

In any case, the AJ never got the chance to present its plan for British recognition to any British agency. Gamzon's Jewish Scouts carried out their resistance actions as effectively as could be expected under the circumstances. But they returned to their civilian status as the Occupation, and then the war, finally ended for their tortured country.

CHAPTER SEVENTEEN

The Jewish Resistance in All Its Variety

In the ghetto she had suffered hunger, cold, exhaustion, but she felt her many souls blend together. The woman, the Jew, the Zionist, and the communist had been fused into a single Line who had a single enemy.[1]

Primo Levi

A single thought, a single passion, and the weapons of suffering.[2]

Paul Éluard

Why and how did they become members of the Resistance? The testimony of a very large number of men and women, young people and adolescents, coming from very different backgrounds, reveals a dominant common characteristic: it was the tragic reality of the Jewish situation that served as the common soil from which the Jewish Resistance erupted in all its diversity.

Jacques Adler was fourteen when in May of 1941 he went to the Pithiviers camp in the vain hope of exchanging a few words with his father behind the barbed wire. He never saw him again.[3] This traumatic experience would lead him about a year later toward the Union de la jeunesse juive (UJJ—Union of Jewish Youth), affiliated with MOI. At this time there was no other organization in Paris for young Jews. In the shop where he worked, almost all the young people belonged. Adler writes,

I remember too deciding that the time had come to tell my mother that I was a member of an underground organization. That was early in 1943. She opened her arms to me, and with tears in her eyes told me to "be careful." There was no question why, no attempt to dissuade me, and no probing about what I "did." It was not ignorance that explained her response. Every Parisian and certainly every Jew knew of the terrible reprisals against resisters and their families. Everyone saw all-too-frequent black-bordered posters on the walls of Paris announcing executions. My mother's silence was a defiant answer made with the full understanding of the risks involved. I later asked some of my underground comrades, the few who still had a living parent, what the reaction had been in their homes, and each had met with a similar reaction. Were we an unusual assortment of people? Perhaps. But of one thing I am certain: though our actions may have been limited to a comparatively small group, the sentiments that motivated us were shared by many more.[4]

Annie Kriegel belonged to a very typical family: French, Jewish, petitebourgeois. The day of the 16 July raid in 1942, when she witnessed the horrible scenes on her way home from school, she experienced an irresistible urge to act: "It was a raid, clearly. Still, I went on my way, when at the corner of rue de Turenne and rue de la Bretagne I heard screams rising to the skies. Not shouts and cries like you hear from a noisy and excited crowd, but screams like those you are used to hearing in the delivery room. All the human suffering that life and death can bring. A garage there was being used as a local collection point and they were separating the men and women." Kriegel's parents decided to flee Paris. "It is certain that the spite and sense of humiliation provoked in me by our slipping away in what you had to call flight contributed to advance the moment when I would make the decision to join the Resistance and the armed struggle."[5]

From a background similar to that of Annie Kriegel, Jacques Lazarus locates his decision to join the Resistance to the date when he was dismissed from the military. Since he had not succeeded in getting across Spain to join the Free French forces, and while waiting for another opportunity, it was a completely chance meeting—as it was for so many others—that determined his involvement. "In August 1941," Lazarus writes in his memoirs, "a notice from the Minister of War informed me of my discharge from the army. It was heartbreaking for me, scarcely compensated for by the joy caused by the wonderful letters of young soldiers who assured me of all their sympathy. . . . The 11th of November 1942 brought me to a saner conception of reality.

This violation of the conventions of the armistice was a very hard blow for numerous Jews who had come seeking refuge in the Southern Zone after all kinds of hardships." One morning in February 1943 he met a childhood friend, Ernst Lambert, who made him "understand that a courageous Jew could do more and do better." One month later he became a member of the Armée juive (AJ).[6]

For Catherine Winter ("Varlin"), the irresistible feeling of a need to act against her persecutors led her to contact a Zionist group:

> Events and the trials of my family had made me discover that I was Jewish. One rarely makes a similar discovery in adolescence without drawing a radical conclusion from it: I became a Zionist on the spot. During the school holidays I attended a Zionist training school. There, very quickly, the debate among participants centered on the essential alternatives: should one fight at once beside the non-Jews against the Nazis, or should one, deep in the underground, prepare oneself with weapons and baggage to get to Palestine as soon as possible? I chose the first option; I then almost immediately joined the first Jewish combat groups in Toulouse, and then, naturally, the FTP-MOI.[7]

"Was there a scale of values where you could situate yourself as a hunted Jew, communist, French patriot or, quite simply, a kid of twenty who should be registering for the STO [compulsory labor service]?" wonders Henri Krischer. "In 1942 when I became a member of the Communist Party, did I do so out of ideological conviction or out of admiration for the Russian people who stubbornly defended their country and who stopped at no sacrifice to defeat our common enemy, or because in France the communists were the spearhead of the Resistance and because they took us in, immigrant Jews, without restrictions, and immediately gave us the opportunity to quench our thirst for vengeance? Are we really obliged to choose among the labels for the one we would first stick on the bottle from that macabre pharmacy?"[8]

The Common Ground of the Jewish Resistance

Unlike other movements, the Jewish Resistance had little need to create new structures in order to organize. Various movements, political groupings, and social-aid agencies that had existed from before the war constituted its framework, even though the borderline between the agencies and the political wings was not always clear. This can be observed particularly in the case of the Federation of Jewish Societies, which could not regain its popular base in the aftermath of the Occupation. On the other hand, the leaders and militant members of the Zionist-socialist movement closed ranks rapidly around their leader, Marc Jarblum, who was also president of the FSJF. And it was also around this entity that in the winter of 1940 a Coordinating Committee comprised of the left Zionists and the socialists of the Bund was constituted.

The OSE became the pole around which rescue and camouflage networks would coalesce in late 1942. Thus, cooperating with the OSE were the "Sixth" (the section of the Jewish Scouts charged with the rescue of children), the Zionist Service for Evacuation and Resettlement (SER), and others.[9] The Jewish Scouts represented, after the various Jewish branches of the MOI, the most numerous and best-structured organization, welding together between 1,000 and 1,500 teenagers and young adults.

The historian cannot ignore the existence of "two spaces," each with its own political conditions: persecution and the implementation of the "Final Solution" proceeded at differing paces in the Occupied and Free Zones. One fact in particular had many negative consequences, namely that the Jewish administrations, the decision-making centers, the spiritual, political, and intellectual elite were mostly in the Free Zone. As a result, they were not in a position—even if they did receive reports—either to know well what was going on in Paris (where almost all the foreign Jews were grouped) or to recognize the full and true nature of the general peril. Another factor was the long-time inclusion in the UGIF of all the agencies and groups located in the Southern Zone and the consequent illusion of the possibility of legal operation could only have a retarding effect on the perception of the reality of life in the Occupied Zone. It would not be possible to write the history of the Jewish Resistance without taking into account these factors of "space and time," unless for partisan reasons one wishes to maintain a vagueness that distorts and falsifies that history.

From the geographic and political points of view, the principal aspect of the Jewish Resistance in the North is the early presence in Paris of only one of its constituents, the MOI, joined later by leftist Zionist youth (the Hashomer Hazair, or "Young Guard," integrated into the Amelot Committee); the Amelot Committee, a creation of the FSJF, began its clandestine rescue operations only in June and July 1942.

In any case, quite aside from the issue of the attitudes of various organizations, there was the conduct of the Jews themselves. All in all it was here that the drama was played out. Confronted with the horror of the raids, the execution of Jews as hostages, the internments, the transit camps, and the deportation even of children, the Jewish populace—especially in Paris—nearly foundered in fear, despair, and resignation. Nothing happened by itself: It is true that human beings all have hidden resources, reactions of self-preservation, but these reactions must not be delayed—feelings that might paralyze the will have to be neutralized quickly. This is the principal role of organized forces. As in any collectivity, a minority of men and women rose to the occasion. They came from all backgrounds and the resistance they organized was pluralist, reflecting the complexity of prewar community from which it sprang.

Rewriting the History of the Resistance?

Decades later the Jewish organizations of the MOI found themselves on veritable trial for ostensibly having neglected specifically Jewish concerns (the trend then was toward unification with the rest of the Resistance).[10] In 1973 a polemic of extreme virulence arose in the Jewish press. Despite its rhetorical tone and its stated objective—the retroactive excommunication from the Jewish Resistance of the strongest of its constituents, the communists—this debate seemed mean by comparison with the actual events, when the life and death of the Jews of France, indeed all of Europe, was being decided. Consider the particularly outrageous statement of Arnold Mandel, a well-known writer and thinker: "[The communist Jewish resistance] was not born of the recognition of Jewish distress and solitude."[11] Is it necessary to reply that the Jewish communists were human beings—not monsters—who suffered and wept like everyone else? Wladimir Rabi, whose contribution to Jewish thought has been no less enriching that Arnold Mandel's, subsequently protested such outbursts with a call for greater dignity: "Let us abstain from making judgments, condemnations, exclusions. . . . The rift that we currently observe within the Jewish community of France is, to speak frankly, scandalous." Rabi cites Mandel in particular as an example of "sectarianism and fanaticism."[12] Were he still alive, Rabi would hold the same opinion of the current status of the debate: the detestable theme of exclusion has not disappeared.

In rather repetitive fashion commentators have recently pointed to the "non-Jewish" character of the military operations of the MOI: the attacks against the Wehrmacht "did not serve the immediate interests of the Jewish population."[13] They reproach the Jewish resistance fighters of the MOI for not having attacked the deportation convoys (not posing this criterion, by the way, for the other groups in the Jewish resistance). This objective would not have occurred to anyone at the time; and in practical terms it would have been unfeasible. Even if there had been a clear awareness in Resistance circles of the nature of the camps in Poland, an attack against a train would have cost the lives of most of the deported. No one knew the attitude of the deportees themselves, but even they would not—could not—believe in their certain deaths. This is why they themselves frequently opposed such initiatives; it was not for the Resistance to risk their deaths. In any case direct attacks were not practicable because no resistance group had the capacity to directly engage forty or fifty well-armed convoy guards. This would have been an operation of an entirely different scale than the derailment of a train, an action in which the operatives would be long gone before the event.[14]

Moreover, the same process of exclusion depends on the concepts of Jewish "specificity" and the "purity" of the various groups. The example of the Armée juive is cited, yet the latter was very much part of the Black Mountain irregulars, as were its own irregular groups, which were completely merged with those of the MLN. The Marc Haguenau Platoon of the Jewish Scouts was also part of a Secret Army maquis unit and had as many Gentile farmers from the region as Jews. The scouts and the AJ were under the orders of the maquis command and participated in operations with "non-Jewish objectives."[15] Any analysis which contrasts a purely "Jewish resistance" and the MOI would appear to be based in ignorance of the other movements, in particular the Zionists and the Jewish Scouts: to this day their history has not been written except for a few works which depend essentially on oral histories.[16]

It is no accident that Jewish partisans in France (Zionists, Bundists, communists, and others) faced the same choices as in all of occupied Europe. In Poland those who escaped the ghettos joined whichever partisan units were willing to accept them. Jews in the partisan detachments of the Red Army numbered some tens of thousands.[17] Haviva Rajk, a member of Palmach (the combat units of the Haganah), parachuted into Slovakia to join the armed Hashomer Hazair, led by Edith Katz; the group was part of the "Stalin" detachment under the command of Neumann-Nowak, an FTP-MOI fighter sent from Paris by Artur London (head of Czechoslovakian group in the MOI).[18] Hana Senesz and her teammates parachuted into Yugoslavia to join Tito and aid Jewish partisans "to spread fire and blood behind the German Front." In reality, however, nowhere (except in the ghettos) could there have existed a separate "Jewish" resistance. This fundamental condition alone calls into question the projects of the historical "reconstructionists" who would retro-actively "ghettoize" Jewish participation in the French resistance. The same applies for neighboring Belgium, where the Jewish resistance of the MOI and that of the left Zionists were integrated into the general resistance movement.[19]

The Various Functions of Armed Struggle

What was the real function of armed combat? According to Henri Michel, "partisan warfare was the logical end of the underground struggle"—i.e., it was primarily *political*.[20] A relatively voluminous underground literature that the Jewish Section of the MOI sent out to the armed groups and the resistance generally shows that from its perspective political effect took prece-dence over military results. On the first anniversary of the raids of 16–17 July, the leaders of the UJRE addressed Jews in the FTPF, evoking the "hell of the Winter Velodrome and Drancy" and informing fighters about the situation in the camps in Poland, site of "the collective assassination of our brothers." In the context of a call to commemorate the raids by acts of resistance, this appeal combined direct action and emotional propaganda. Purely ideologi-cal motivation, decisive for the founders of the first armed groups did spread to the second cohort of joiners but may have been unimportant to the later arrivals, in particular the young people arriving after the summer of 1942. "Avenge all our tortured and assassinated brothers, avenge the innocent blood"—such are the words motivating the fighters to correlate their action with the tragedy. They were encouraged to keep in mind that their actions would inspire broader layers of the Jewish population to struggle on many fronts: "We are convinced, dear comrades, that with your courage and self-denial you will serve as examples to the Jewish masses, and in giving the purest expression to their will to fight . . . you will lead them to an even fiercer struggle."[21]

It was hoped that the armed resistance would effect a transformation in mentality. A declaration from the MOI leadership dated April 1944 under the title "Aid to the Jewish Partisans" develops this theme: "In the fire of the battle which the partisans and Jewish masses are waging for their existence, a new kind of Jew has been born. It is a Jew who has definitively freed him-self from every complex of inferiority, a Jew in whom the feeling of weak-ness has been replaced by a feeling of strength and confidence, and who stands by all his brothers throughout the entire world, faithful to his people and to the country for whose liberation he is fighting."[22] We have already seen the same idea expressed by Robert Gamzon.[23]

It is not without interest, finally, to consider the objectives of the Armée juive—in the minds of some the model of "Jewish resistance"—as formulated by one of its leaders, Jacques Lazarus. Challenging the view of Saul Friedländer, who refers to "the passion which the French and immigrant Jews felt for France,"[24] Jacques Lazarus objects that "for many Jews their passion for France had experienced a rude shock." It is for precisely this reason, says Lazarus, that many were eager rather to join the ranks of an organization such as the Armée juive. He specifies: "The military option, chosen at the outset by the founders of the Armée juive, with its ultimate goal the creation of a Jewish state in Palestine, better matched their conception of a Jewish resistance."[25] A noble objective, no doubt, but limited, one that could only be a part—to be judged according to one's personal involvement—of the global strategy for the survival of the Jews of France.

If one were to set an absolute criterion to evaluate the role of this or that current of the Resistance, it would be the current's relationship to the choice which all Jews in France had to make between submission and refusal, legality and clandestinity, turning inward or allying with the broader uncorrupted forces of the country. Organizers progressively reinforced this idea among the Jewish populace. The varied activity of the MOI from the moment of the first internments in 1941 had as its chief objective assisting the Jewish community to make the right choices, and beyond that, to motivate the indispensable solidarity of non-Jews.

The world-renowned historian Yehuda Bauer also questions the legitimacy of the charge brought against Jewish resisters of the FTP-MOI, declaring, "Protagonists and other witnesses who have stated that these Jews were not active within the armed Resistance in their capacity as Jews but as communists or Frenchmen seem to me more concerned with rationalizing these episodes than being faithful to the psychological truth of the matter."[26] Moreover, it should be recalled that the law to create Yad Vashem, the supreme institution of Jewish memorialization, refrains from all discrimination among Jewish resisters by stipulating that the "Remembrance Authority" would commemorate "the heroism of Jewish servicemen, and of underground fighters in town, village, and forest."[27] Annie Kriegel put it somewhat differently: "If, in fact, the choice of communism was a deplorable one on the global scale . . . it was, on the more limited scale of the times and under those circumstances, a pertinent choice, one which was almost self-evident, once it became a question of life and death, or more precisely, of the survival of an identity [that was] being lost."[28]

When all is said and done, the polemic against the role of the Jewish organizations of the MOI—beside the fact that it disregards the minimal ethical rules applying to debates over such a tragic period—has proven sterile because of its thirty-year fixation on one and the same theme, one moreover purely speculative and thus ahistorical. The polemic has not advanced research either on the highly complex problematics of the Jewish resistance or even on the history of its other constituents, which remains to be written.

The Weight of the Past

Beyond its political side, the debate resonates with Jewish history itself, in the millennial debate over the choice between the "sword" and the "spirit" as strategy for survival. Faced with persecutions whose essential objective was the eradication of the religion, the response had to be spiritual; against overwhelming numbers physical resistance would have been hazardous if not suicidal. This absence of an alternative generated not only a specific behavior pattern, but a specific kind of Jew, one who abhorred violence as a defense. This is the mentality that is still found today in some uncompromising religious circles, notably among the Haredim, who are still content with the image of the Jew bowing before his enemy. Heroism is death, submission is life. This is what a recent text from a Haredi source seems to be saying: "From Greece and Rome the western world has inherited the symbol of the hero preferring death to slavery. But we, we have learned from the mouth of God, 'And you shall choose life.' It is not the dead who will celebrate the Lord, even if they have met a hero's death. That is why we have become as supple as the reed, why we have bowed our heads before each new wave. We have left to others the crown of the courageous combatant dead on the field of honor." From this to a condemnation of the uprising in the ghettos was but a single step. "The defiance launched against evil and the forces of impurity—against Hitlerism—. . . drove us to lose the better part of our brothers."[29]

In 1942 André Chouraqui, a student at a rabbinical school, experienced the painful tension between these two kinds of behavior: "I was enraged by my imprisonment in a condition from which I could escape only 'vertically,' in *Elohim*. I was giving in to the image I had of myself, powerless, immobile in my infantile cowardice, busy storing up encyclopedic knowledge while the world was dying in misery. . . . At the rabbinical school we continued to live as if what was going on was a 'chance mishap,' despite everything we heard, knew, or wished not to know of the atrocious truth."[30] A profound believer, Elie Wiesel felt the same internal conflict, and set it out in this dialogue between a peasant and his neighbor, old Abraham: "I can't understand you. You have a son and you want him to live. Why don't you teach him to survive?" Abraham replies, "But I am teaching him. How do you think my people has survived exile if not through study?" To which the peasant replies: "You ought to teach him to run faster than a hare, to hide himself at the first alarm; you ought to teach him to disguise himself as a Christian; that's what a good father ought to be teaching him."[31]

The survival in France of a substantial portion of the Jewish population, thanks to the alternative that was offered by the favorable human environment, risks deflecting attention from the large Jewish communities of Poland and the occupied territory of the USSR, which almost entirely perished. Of the millions of victims of the Holocaust, these regions supplied the largest contingent. And people nonetheless rush to condemn their passive attitude, even their "anticipatory submission."

The weight of history, in the opinion of Raul Hilberg, was at the origin of the Jews' failure to resist. "Caught in the straitjacket of their history," he writes, "they hurled themselves physically and psychologically into the catastrophe."[32] Yet Eastern European Jewry has also known rapid changes in modern times and it was swept by the ideologies and movements of the external world. In integrating them, it also gave them an expression of its own, as Zionism and the socialist Bund show. Moreover, large segments of the common people and a portion of the intelligentsia supported communism. Divergences of an ideological order did not hamper the emergence among the vital forces of all of Eastern European Jewry of a new spirit favoring a reconciliation with the moral legitimacy of political violence. During the Revolution in Russia and with the arrival of Zionist pioneers in Palestine, we discover Jews, descended from a people that had not borne arms for seventeen or eighteen centuries, who revealed unsuspected military potential. The importance Hilberg assigned to centuries-old historical attitudes must be relativized because they do not provide an explanation for the behavior of the Jews.

The genocide is analyzed by Hilberg—and this is astonishing—in military terms, as if it were the encounter between two forces organized as states. "The destruction of the Jews of Europe by Germany," he writes, "was an amazing accomplishment, and the rout of the Jews in the face of German aggression was a patent demonstration of defeat."[33] Imagine, at the front, the presence of the families of the soldiers, most of whom, moreover, have no weapons. Is this army still an army? A similar situation was created by the decision of Nazi powers to proceed with the "concentration" of Jews. In Poland, for example, the concentration phase, that is, the creation of the ghettos, had already come to an end by December 1941. Seen retroactively, this part of the German plan proved the most decisive for the extermination enterprise. Thus, the fate of the Jews was sealed as of the moment they were locked into the vast concentration camps: the ghettos of the twentieth century, which of course had little in common with those of the Middle Ages except the name. The refusal to be locked up provoked an immediate physical response. Is it because they suffered so much that one, a posteriori, demands the impossible of the Jews?

In late 1942, when the tides of war had not yet turned in favor of the Allies, when all over Europe resistance had only barely begun, the extermination of the Jews, in particular those of Poland and the occupied territories of the Soviet Union had already been more than 80 percent completed! The men, women, and youth of these imprisoned communities harbored—and all those familiar with the Jews of Eastern Europe know this—a rare potential for heroism. The Warsaw Ghetto Uprising and many other revolts furnish the proof. But in this region, this potential had neither the time nor the opportunity to realize itself, as it would in France and Belgium. The surprise and the speed of execution of the genocide holds the explanation of the success of the Blitzkrieg—for it was one—against the Jewish populations. Any objective reflection on the behavior of the Jews in the face of the Nazi enemy must take into account this fact.

Portrait of a Jew in the Resistance: Vladimir Jankélévitch

At times coming down the rue de Metz or the rue d'Alsace (in Toulouse) I would see a man who was still young, with fine features, a sharp glance, mischievous and sad at the same time, his forehead crossed by a lock of hair which was, at that time, of the finest raven black. . . . But Vladimir Jankélévitch, like the other Jews of France, was a persecuted man. I heard him speak a few times at a place near the Capitole about the romantic composers among whom his soul sought refuge in order to escape, if only for a few moments, from the surrounding nightmare. And he would entertain us in the evening with accounts of the recourse to silence and to "refreshing shadows" in which this brother of Chopin, of Schumann, of Fauré—and especially of Baudelaire—also found respite from the ills of living in the real world, pitiless toward poets and the just.[34]

This is how the celebrated writer Claude Vigée, then a young student at the University of Toulouse, remembered Vladimir Jankélévitch. The year was 1940. He gathered his students, driven from the university because they were Jews, in secret in a room at the Café Conti on the place du Capitole. Claude Vigée could not know that this brother of Chopin and Baudelaire was in no way fleeing the "nightmare," but facing it, attacking it more and more courageously. These meetings to "philosophize" with his students, this was already the "pre-resistance," even if Jankélévitch was still acting alone. Reflective thought, in the face of current events and those that his deep knowledge of the "Teutonic" soul anticipated, seemed insufficient. The Marxist-Leninist principle of no revolutionary theory without praxis, no revolutionary praxis without theory, he bore in his inner being—yet he had never been a follower of Marx, because for him putting his ideas into practice was an imperative of an ethical order. If Lyon was the capital of the Resistance, Toulouse was surely its cradle, at least as concerns the Southern Zone. The city had intensely lived the events of the Spanish Civil War, and then witnessed the internment camps for refugees from Spain and subsequently for tens of thousands of Eastern- and Central-European Jewish and non-Jewish refugees as well, camps that sprang up like fungi, but which sensitized public opinion to the misery of others. The first networks facilitating escape from these camps benefited from the support of Jean Cassou and a group of friends, one of whom was Vladimir Jankélévitch.

In the summer of 1942 Dr. Stéphane Barsony created a Toulouse section of the Mouvement national contre le racisme (MNCR). He secured the collaboration of Jankélévitch (called André Dumez). The thinker thus entered the active Resistance on the same footing as all the others. He would retain an indelible memory of those times: "Four years of struggle and misery, the ever-present danger, suspicious rendez-vous with a stranger in front of the Narbonne town hall, the doorbell ringing at six in the morning—and your heart stopping its beating—the precarious, hunted, underground life that people were beginning to call *clandestinité*."[35]

From his very first meetings he made the acquaintance of admirable men who, one is tempted to think, were already waiting for him. University circles were, for the most part, already prepared to act on behalf of the persecuted Jews; the people had already begun to suspect that not only their liberty but their very lives were in danger. An important center for resistance to the barbarity was established at the Catholic Institute of Toulouse, with the rector, Bruno de Solage, at its head. Later de Solage would be deported. At his side was a young faculty member, Georges Papillon, who began his "career" in the Resistance by helping Jews. He was shot on 17 August 1944 in Paris as one of the leaders of the "Ceux de la Résistance" (Those of the Resistance) movement led by Léo Hamon.

Solicited by Jankélévitch, D. Faucher, then dean of the Faculty of Letters, recalled later the activity of Papillon: "He came to ask me for my help . . . he was gathering friends, grouping people, from the rector of the Institute and the Archbishop to the Protestant minister, from the minister to the rabbi, no one could resist his desire to protect, support, respond to the appeal of the persecuted. He took on himself the most thankless of tasks; he went toward the most unfortunate. He hid, he camouflaged, he organized flight."[36] Léo Hamon, then in Toulouse, also remembers these "university people, professors and students, priests and lay people, who organized the committee to aid the Jewish students, giving expression at one and the same time to the protest of Christian conscience and French conscience against racism."[37]

Vladimir Jankélévitch took his place in what the historian Henri Michel calls the "war of words." He weighed the serious consequences entailed by submission to the law of silence imposed by the occupiers and Vichy on the whole of France and on her Jews in particular. He wrote for *Fraternité* and drafted tracts in Russian for the MOI to distribute to Soviet prisoners who had been conscripted into the Wehrmacht. In the summer of 1943 Jankélévitch got the MNCR to publish an anthology on racism, then finding expression in the unparalleled persecutions of the Jews. Étienne Borne and Dean Faucher also contributed to the booklet, which was printed in 5,000 copies and appeared in November–December 1943. The analyses that we owe to Faucher ("Race and Racism"), Borne ("Racism and Christianity"), and Jankélévitch ("Psychoanalysis of Antisemitism") still retain their freshness and topicality.[38]

Dean Faucher averred that "No apostle of racism will convince us that the Mediterranean or the Semite has contributed less to enrich the human patrimony than the Nordic." Faucher highlights the moral values of the Church as against racist ideology: "Legitimate and permissible in racist orthodoxy are: sterilization, the extermination of Jews." This is a remarkable observation for the time—the year was 1943—when it had as yet occurred to few (outside some of the Nazis) to connect euthanasia and the extermination of the Jews. Étienne Borne stigmatized those who chose neutrality in the struggle between "the God proposed to us by the Gospels" and "the God who justifies the most bloody violence." Was this an allusion to the silence of the Vatican?

In the last chapter, "Psychoanalysis of Antisemitism," Jankélévitch has recourse to his preferred weapon: murderous humor. Here is what he has to say about psychoanalysis: "Camp life, the folly of dazzling uniforms, a certain Helleno-Nietzchean ideal of masculine beauty . . . Hitlerian pseudo-virtue must be seen as the revenge of an inverted virility on the voluptuous feminine civilization of France."[39] With the premonition characteristic of the very sensitive, and because his status as a Jew in the Resistance steeped him in the tragedy, Jankélévitch perceived the singular nature of the crime: "For the first time perhaps, people are being officially hunted not for what they do; they are expiating their *being* and not their *assets,* not their acts, political opinion, or profession of faith . . . but the fatality of birth." One finds in this thought the basis of the future definition of "crimes against humanity."

This thought also encapsulated the premises of Jankélévitch's entire intellectual approach to the Holocaust, including his personal actions at the time: the principle of the unpardonable, the unforgivable. Thirty years later he would write, "No, it is not for us to grant a pardon for the children tortured by those brutes for their amusement. The children will have to grant their own pardon. And so we turn toward the brutes and toward the friends of the brutes: ask the children yourselves for forgiveness." Voicing the unspeakable suffering of the martyrs, he adds: "We shall reflect deeply on the agony of those who were deported, never to have a final resting place, and of the children who did not return, for this agony will last until the end of the world."[40]

CHAPTER EIGHTEEN

CRIF

Constructing the Future in the Shadow of Death

> And he looked, and, behold, the bush burned with fire, and the
> bush was not consumed.
>
> —Exodus 3:2

Beyond its original objective of unifying all currents of Jewish resistance, the Comité général de défense (CGD—General Defense Committee)[1] established through its very creation a new relationship between immigrant Jews and the Consistory. From then on the CGD would represent in the eyes of the Resistance the vital forces of the community. The Consistory, nonetheless, persisted in its policy of maintaining a "presence" in the government, even if it seemed to distance itself somewhat from Vichy as the latter began closing the few remaining half-open doors.

In the fall of 1943 it became evident even for the blindest that it was the Resistance that incarnated the France of tomorrow; people's relations with the Resistance would be decisive for the place they would occupy in a liberated France. But even at the moment when Hitler's defeat became certain—the fall of Mussolini was the portent[2]—and as de Gaulle's place as leader of the future France was becoming increasingly clear, the Consistory still hesitated to make an opening toward the Resistance in the interior and toward London.

We find in London and in Algiers many French Jews in positions of responsibility, but none was charged with representing the Consistory to General de Gaulle. Even René Mayer and Louis Kahn, members of the Consistory's Administrative Council who reached London at the close of 1942, did not have any mandate and spoke only for themselves. The Consistory had to be concerned by its increasing isolation from French Jewry and the Resistance. Joseph Fischer, the sole immigrant Jewish leader to maintain contacts with Consistory circles (in particular Léon Meiss, more open than Helbronner), closely followed the crisis that the august body was undergoing as its leaders faced a difficult choice: when to abandon their last hopes of working within the Vichy order. The CGD, informed by Fischer, saw the possibility of salvaging something from the Consistory and achieving the unification of French and foreign Jews. Still, it was only after the arrest of Helbronner in October 1943 that the Consistory took the biggest turn in its history by agreeing to meet representatives of the CGD, primarily Jews from Eastern Europe and including the communists. Under the direction of the Consistory's new leader Léon Meiss a new spirit would animate the centenary institution, so much so that we might well speak of a "Consistory II."

Vichy Does Not Respond

On 1 and 2 August 1943 Robert Kiefe, the Consistory's secretary general, responsible for relations with the Vichy government—that is, the few high officials still prepared to meet him—found himself at first denied an audience with Jean Jardin, Laval's chief-of-staff. His notebook furnishes an account of his last two days at the government's office in the Hôtel du Parc and at the same time gives a sense of the atmosphere that reigned inside ministerial bureaus, where there was no longer any doubt about eventual German defeat.[3] Finally, he did see Jardin briefly. "1 August, at Jardin's office [Kiefe transmits the now customary message from Helbronner]: I have found it necessary to insist in the most vigorous terms on the evolution in the state of mind of the Jews. . . . Until now President Helbronner and the Central Consistory have directed all their efforts to keeping their coreligionists obedient to the law, but now they feel overcome by events; . . . we can no longer bear responsibility for the discipline of French Jews."

Jardin tells him that he is tired, wishes to leave office, that he is seen as pro-Jewish; if he stays on, it is only to prevent excesses.

2 August: I went to see [General Jacques] Campet, the head of Pétain's military cabinet. I was with him only ten minutes but I insisted on the point that there were new facts to consider: the aggravation of the situation; the new deportations that were projected, and the arrest of André Baur.[4] He assured me that he would do whatever was . . . within his power, but he did not hide from me his skepticism as to the outcome.

Immediately after this meeting, I went down to see Jardin. I waited for two hours and I was finally received by [Jardin's secretary] Mme Vinatier. She told me on behalf of Jardin that he had done a great deal for the Jews, even to the point of compromising himself, but as of the moment we were no longer discreet,[5] he could no longer do anything. I viewed this information as the definitive rejection, the more so because it was the second time he had refused to see me. J. [Jardin] is quite simply afraid of the Germans.[6]

And at the office of Bousquet's collaborator Martin: "Very friendly reception, as always. He read attentively the documents I turned over to him and promised me that he would brief [Henri] Cado [Bousquet's deputy] but he did not hide the fact that he did not believe the Ministry of the Interior could intervene. . . . The Germans were getting more and more vicious, and were making arrests by the dozens in all circles; we would have to expect, in his opinion, a doubling of severity in the Jewish question."

Kiefe's notebook ends here. For the Consistory, this day marks the end of its policy of maintaining a "presence" in Vichy.

Orders from Berlin: Arrest Helbronner

On 28 October 1943, the German police seized Jacques Helbronner and his wife at their home. The occupiers could not have struck higher or harder. When Léon Meiss was subsequently summoned to the Gestapo, the secretariat of the Central Consistory held an emergency meeting to decide whether he should obey. The question was evaded by Chief Rabbi Schwartz, but in moving terms he bespoke the Consistory's new attitude: "We have deliberated but it is not our intention to try to influence your decision. If you decide to go underground, we shall understand; . . . if you decide to obey the Gestapo, may God protect you." After having consulted his wife, Léon Meiss went to the potentially fatal meeting. There he was told by the officer, "we were obliged to arrest Helbronner on the orders of Berlin. We here did not take the initiative."[7]

Paradoxically, the Central Consistory's reaction to the arrest (followed by internment in Drancy preparatory to deportation) of its president—officially the leading figure of French Jewry—was limited to a few letters, without the least hint of protest, to Laval, to the Garde des Sceaux (whose role was like that of a lord chancellor), and in particular to the vice-president of the Council of State. The letters did, however, call attention to the fact that Helbronner was honorary president of a department of the Council of State and a commander of the Legion of Honor. There was no letter to Pétain, in whom Helbronner had invested so much hope. To what avail? the Consistory must have wondered. Nonetheless, a delegation did go to the prefect's chief administrator, where it learned that the latter planned to protest to the German authorities:[8] but everything took place at a low level, not even ministerial. Sad times! The Vichy press, of course, did not breathe a word of the arrest. The only newspaper to mention it was the underground paper *Fraternité*, the organ of the MNCR, which on 15 November 1943 printed a headline that ran: "Monsieur Helbronner, president of the Lyon Jewish Consistory, former vice-president of the Conseil d'État, [arrested] at age seventy-two as Gestapo hostage."[9]

What kind of message was being sent by the seizure of the president of the Central Consistory? It was clear: All Jews are foreigners, there are no French Jews; their fate is no longer with the Pétain government but depends solely on the Germans. The Consistory faced a total rupture of all contact with Pétain.

Rare are the documents that echo the growing crisis within the rabbinate and the Consistory, aggravated by the psychological impact of Helbronner's deportation. In his memoirs René Kapel, camp chaplain and Resistance activist, records a particularly crucial debate at a meeting of the rabbinate in January 1944 on whether to close the synagogues.[10] The question was more political than theological, for no religious stricture forbade such a measure if human life depended on it. Opinions were nonetheless divided, in particular because it would have precipitated the Consistory into illegal status. Kapel writes: "Five [including Kapel] were for closing down; four voted against it: Chief Rabbi Liber, which didn't surprise me at all; Rabbis Jacob Kaplan, Samy Klein, Israël Salzer were of the same opinion. As for Rabbis Nathan Hosanski,[11] Moïse Poliatchek, Max Sal, and Georges Apeloig, they voted to close."

At the end of the meeting they reached a compromise solution that, despite its ambiguity, contained a political analysis, the pertinence of which still impresses. It stressed the danger to the faithful of "maintaining public offices, which is far from serving the spiritual interests of [our] religion and favors the undertakings of the enemies of Judaism who, behind the façade of supposed respect for the Jewish faith, strike day after day at the life and liberty of our coreligionists." It was this sense of false security deriving from the legal status still acknowledged by Vichy that the Resistance ceaselessly denounced in calling for dissolution of the UGIF. The motion authorized each rabbi to propose the closing of his synagogue to the Central Consistory. It explicitly challenged the Consistory's appeals for obedience to Vichy law as long as the regime continued to practice tolerance in the sphere of religious practice.[12]

The Outline of the Postwar Community

One of the first to take the initiative for a union between French and foreign Jews was Marc Jarblum, leader of the Zionist-Socialists and president of the FSJF. In a letter to Helbronner after the roundup of July–August 1942, Jarblum stressed the urgency of unification if French Jewry were to defend itself "before it is too late." The Consistory's reaction to the raids was far from adequate in Jarblum's opinion, and he did not hide "his painful surprise at the lack of reaction from Jewish organizations. . . . The catastrophe has struck Jews of foreign origin in particular, but it threatens to destroy a great portion of the Jewish population of France."[13] This protest had no immediate effect, since Jewish leaders were not quite ready for a shift in direction.

In September 1943 the leadership of the Jewish section of the MOI in Paris made public its program for "true representation of the Jews of France."[14] This text reflects the perceptions of the Jewish communists, who founded their initiatives on the reality of the situation. They recounted three years of persecution beginning with the Pithiviers internments and continuing through the execution of hostages, the roundup of 16–17 July 1942, the deportations, and "the assassination of tens of thousands of Jews of France, among them children of all ages, in poison gas chambers."[15] They called for unification around a program of three points. Most important, coordination in the struggle of the Jewish organizations against deportation had to take precedence. The other two points concerned the program to be brought forward on the liberation of the country and before international bodies once peace negotiations had begun. An expression of the unity of immigrant and French Jews, this new representative body would, in the MOI view and in contrast to what had been practiced in the past, encompass all the working class and general populace that had been systematically kept out of representative bodies.

The CGD also put creation of a representative body comprising all Jews at the center of its planning. In the first issue of *Unzer Kamf* ("Our Struggle," November 1943), it argued that a representative organization "reuniting all the Jews of France [would be able] to formulate our just claims with reinforced authority and effectiveness."[16] In France, unified representation would ensure respect for "our rights as human beings and as citizens, would dress our wounds, and would exact material and moral compensation for our suffering." These claims were also to be formulated at the global level, along with other representations of the Jewish community at such a time "when the liberated peoples will lay the foundations of a new political edifice that will regulate the friendly relations of one people to another."

Would union with the native-born French Jews be well received by the immigrants to whom *Unzer Kamf* was addressed? Perhaps not, and this required that the question be addressed frankly, all the more so since the *folksmensch* (man of the people) did not care to be spoken to in any other language. "There are many among us," the editorial continued, "in whom there is the deeply engrained idea that there is an unbridgeable gap between *us* and *them* and that *they* have but the single thought of getting rid of *us*." These feelings, as regrettable as they are legitimate, are the result of "relations between two groups of people who are distinguished by their social and economic structures, by their language, customs. Precisely because they are brothers, the tensions generate in the weaker of the two a painful exasperation." On a rare light note the author conjures a meeting "between a highly placed Jewish official or a prominent banker and an Eastern European Jew. On the face of the one are all the marks of his superiority, while the other stands before him visibly fearful and, in addition, stumbling in his French." Yet times have changed: "At present . . . the leaders of French Jewry express their regret and dispute the existence of such a rift." The author may have been overly optimistic, but envisaging the project required a positive light.

Beyond official contacts between the CGD and the Consistory, multiple discussions proved necessary. Unanimous in its wish for unification with French Jews, the CGD came to negotiations in less-than-closed ranks, since its diverse constituents did not share the same point of view on the question of a homeland in Palestine. While the Bund stood by its doctrinal anti-Zionist position, the communists were evolving toward recognition of the right to a national homeland in Palestine. Joseph Fischer, a leader of the Organisation sioniste de France (Zionist Organization of France), attached particular importance to securing the support of Jewish communists for his draft charter for the unified body. He was no less eager for the support of Léo Glaeser, secretary of the CGD and a non-Zionist, who accepted the necessity of rescinding the British "White Book,"[17] but hesitated to include in the charter any call for a Jewish state. A meeting between Glaeser and the MOI's Rayski in Fischer's presence achieved the beginnings of a rapprochement but not a common platform. Glaeser would be the only one not to see the fruition of the project: he was assassinated along with six other Jewish hostages on the orders of Paul Touvier (right hand of militia chief Darnand) on 29 July 1943 at nearby Rillieux-le-Pape.

It was subsequent to these events, in mid-November, that Fischer organized a meeting with Meiss, interim president of the Consistory, and Rayski in an apartment on the quai de Tilsitt in Lyon, close to the synagogue. Meiss "did not hide his belief that in Rayski he was dealing with a 'Jewish extremist,' and could not see why Jewish communists organized themselves separately from the general movement."[18] The desultory conversation turned from one subject to another, but Fischer was reluctant to pull his draft charter from his pocket, aware as he was of the Consistory's categorical opposition to supporting Zionist objectives. After an hour or an hour and half that hardly resembled negotiations among participants representing totally incompatible views, the meeting broke up, leaving a feeling that a representative council would soon be established. This, in any case, was Fischer's conclusion.

Seven Versions of the "Charter"

As witness of and participant in the foundation of the Conseil représentatif des Juifs de France (CRIF—Representative Council of the Jews of France),[19] I was long convinced that my memory of events was faithful. I devoted several articles to the subject; in the absence of archival information on the subject, these provided the ground for future study, although they were doubtless inadequate.[20] Archival research restored the complexity of the situation, though the first efforts were meagerly rewarded: at the CDJC and YIVO in New York only two versions of the charter and no other testimony. Jacques Adler uncovered a version at the Institut Maurice Thorez in Paris that originated with the UJRE. The Consistory archives rendered nothing: they were still inaccessible. Then, during my third or fourth visit to Jerusalem's Yad Vashem Archives in 1989, chief archivist Bronia Klibanski turned up a voluminous and hitherto uncatalogued file: Joseph Fischer had brought it from Paris and deposited it as one of the founders of the Yad Vashem.[21]

This file contains a large number of drafts of the charter, among which seven basic variants can be identified. Some bear handwritten notes and corrections. One dated 25 April 1944 is found in several copies, suggesting it served as a working document for participants. Even more instructive is the jumble of scraps of paper with amendments introduced at various working sessions. Some are signed by Meiss, Adamicz, Glaeser, and Fischer. Only when they have been deciphered is it possible to discover which topics were litigious and to find an explanation for the length of the negotiations.[22] Things did not, in fact, go smoothly. Can we draw the hasty conclusion from this that the founders of the CRIF were not showing historical responsibility? This is a matter of personal judgment. Only full knowledge of the file will aid in grasping the difficulties encountered in the "conference."[23]

The various versions of the charter are for the most part undated, making any chronological classification impossible. But from one amendment to the next, the texts fill out and begin to draw closer to (or at times distance themselves from) the final version.[24] It seems that initially there were three "agreement proposals" in circulation: one offered by Fischer in the name of the World Zionist Organization, one by Adamicz (Braun) on behalf of the UJRE, and a very different one from the Consistory. The authorship of the Consistory's version is attributed to Chief Rabbi Liber, who proposed not a "representation" but a "delegation of the Jews of France," which, less permanent-sounding, seemed to him less political. But the idea of a mere delegation was soon dropped, only to recur in attenuated form: the Consistory's determination to reassure its leadership can be discerned. The Consistory's version that then resulted is titled "Central Consistory and the United Jewish Associations." It was around the Consistory, not to say behind it, that "representation" was to be constituted, the statement reserving three of the six seats for the Consistory, one of the others going to the Zionists and two to the "Defense Committee," with the stipulation that at least one native and one foreigner be included. This draft seems to bear Fischer's mark.[25] Article 7, on Palestine, accounts for at least a third of the whole. This iteration of the Zionist program would later serve as a basis for the debate on a Jewish Palestine.

Subsequent drafts amended the preamble to take into account sometimes four, sometimes five "undersigned organizations." The name of the Alliance israélite (Jewish Alliance) appears at one point. Was it a fight over seats? Apparently.[26] From the beginning to the end, the proportion of seats claimed on the council by immigrant Jews remains about one-third: they seem rather reserved, as if the number of seats were secondary to the simple fact of their inclusion (could this have expressed a certain inferiority complex?). The communists asked only for one seat of six, or two of nine, as the case might be. In the end it was decided that the council would be composed of thirteen members: six for the Consistory, five for the Defense Committee (which would include two communists), one representative of the Zionist Organization of France (Fischer), and one of the Comité d'action et de défense de la jeunesse juive (CADJJ—Committee for Action and Defense of Jewish Youth), which had both Zionist and communist adherents.

The Transformation of Israelite into Jew

More bitter were the discussions on fundamental questions. The meeting of foreign and French Jews, which both wanted, required a profound change in the attitude of both, but much greater for the French. What separated them, in the final analysis, was the fundamental difference in their ideas of Jewish identity in France. For the French Jews this was identification through religion; for those of Eastern Europe, it was the double principle of an ethno-religious community. If for the one "national" meant French, for the other the term signified the unity of the Jewish people.

For the Consistory, Jewish identity had been shaken by exclusion from the French nation, on the one hand, and by the new currency of the concept of a "Jewish people" among the unified representatives of the Defense Committee, on the other. After investing a century in becoming French *israélites*, the French Jews were forced during a brief period to travel the opposite route from *israélite* to Jew.[27] This determinating moment was captured by Robert Badinter in a striking observation: "Among many other . . . unfortunate and pitiful victims, the anti-Jewish legislation had a conceptual victim. It killed the French Israelite; the Jew took his place."[28]

Debates on the crucial problems of a worldwide Jewish representation and a "national homeland" in Palestine would bring into play the cultural traditions of the Consistory, enclosed in its traditional vision of a Jewry encompassed by French national frontiers. But worldwide representation related to problems beyond religious practice presupposed support for the idea of a Jewish *people*. Thus the new notion of a "body representative of the

Jews of France" dictated a break with the principle of the individual presence in the political sphere, and signified recognition of a collective presence in civic life. More to the point, "a Jewish homeland in Palestine" implied a double allegiance: might this not threaten the gains of emancipation and integration? Behind all this could be sensed the danger of becoming again — something absolutely unthinkable in the modern tradition of French Jewry — a national minority, a role deeply rooted only among the Jews of the East. To better understand the Consistory's hesitation, one must bear in mind that the promulgation of the anti-Jewish legislation was originally experienced (until people became aware of its ultimate purpose) as a legislative act reducing them precisely to . . . a national minority.

Amendments, notes, phrasings are the only signs that bear witness to the tensions that marked the wrangling that concluded with the final agreement on the charter, achieved less than two weeks before the liberation of Lyon. Apprehensions about the postwar future of the Jews coursed under the surface of the debate, which focused after all on the proposals of the Zionists. Joseph Fischer saw no other rationale for a Jewish representation than the premise of a Jewish state; ironically the idea gained ground faster even among the communists than in Consistory circles. Fischer took pains to justify his proposals in a "statement of motives" of great emotional force, although some considered it "too political." This statement would be suppressed in the final text, but is worth quoting here: "The Jewish representation of France judges that satisfaction of this claim [i.e., to a national homeland in Palestine] will cancel in fair measure the debt contracted with us by all humanity, which for centuries has witnessed with . . . indifference the great tragedy of Israel, forgetful of its contribution to the civilization and culture of all peoples among which it has lived, counting as naught the sacrifices offered by Jews on the altars of their respective fatherlands, in particular in the course of the last two world wars."

Some initial common ground emerged in the proposal to denounce the "White Book." The draft's ambiguous phrasing suggested that Fischer was hoping that the "representation" would support the World Zionist Organization. Other voices contradicted Fischer's optimism: "We want to concern ourselves with all the Jews in Palestine as well as elsewhere." "The British will decide, the Palestinian government will act, and not the Jewish Agency for Palestine." "The Jewish Agency is a Zionist organization!" "White slave trading!" In self-defense Fischer interrupted, "The Jewish Agency is a real government!" Another voice: "If, for example, the Jewish Agency decreed that the Jewish language [?] is the only language of the country, we could not accept it." "We should have liked to see the Zionist question deferred, because it lies beyond the defense of the Jews according to the CRIF program." A cooler head seems to have been seeking to restore priority to interests of the current moment by identifying a least common denominator that would permit all to agree on the question of postwar Palestine: "The Jewish Agency for Palestine is an instrument of the League of Nations. It is acceptable to non-Zionists."[29]

Yet another question elicited differences of opinion: the admission of youth organizations into the representative council. The Resistance was above all the work of young people. Nonetheless, some persisted in the traditional attitude of distrust toward youth, resisting its autonomous representation. Chief Rabbi Liber was particularly hostile, considering that the adults could speak for the youth under their tutelage. Two "youth committees" proposed their own candidates, each claiming to be the legitimate representative of all "Jewish youth." The first was the Comité directeur de la jeunesse juive (CDJJ—Administrative Committee of Zionist Youth), created on the initiative of the scouts in 1941, with the participation of the traditionalist group Yeshurun and of the Mouvement de jeunesse sioniste, or Zionist Youth Movement. The other was the same Comité d'action et de défence de la jeunesse juive (CADJJ), formed in Lyon at the close of 1943 by the MJS and the leftist Union de la jeunesse juive (Jewish Youth Union, with links to the MOI). In the agreement reached between Zionists and the communists (their "charter for unity"), the movements sanctioned two objectives: the "defense by every means of the Jewish masses and the coordination of "relief and mutual aid among Jewish youth."[30]

For those who spoke in the name of the CDJJ, time seems to have stopped, which is confirmed by the near anachronistic terminology they used: the Occupation period is called a "the period of armistice"; their service activities are designated as "social service, spiritual growth, and vocational training"—all terms from the UGIF statutes reflecting the official duties Vichy delegated to Jewish agencies. There is no allusion in the text to resistance.[31] In part for this reason, in the end the Youth Committee for Action got the seat on the CRIF.

All the differences deadlocked the drafting of the charter. The communists, impatient, finally submitted a declaration to the participants at the end of June: "Discussions . . . have been going on for seven months, and for the last three they have been in an active phase, but we must recognize with great regret that they are still far from successfully concluded."[32] The difficulties did not come from the Zionist program as such, the communists acknowledged, but from those who made it a condition that "the CRIF lend its support to the World Zionist Organization." In the communists' opinion, "the basis for any solution in Palestine is in an agreement with the Arab population. With that population with which the Jews of Palestine have an interest in living in peace, and not on a footing of war, solutions could be found."[33] Reminding everyone that "unity is not a fetish, but a means," the communists urged setting differences aside for the duration of the war, for common action was "dictated by the hated enemy who wishes to *unite* all the Jews in a common grave," for "the Jews, in the face of the cataclysm beating down upon them, prefer to *unite* to defend themselves, to live."

The New Face of the Community

The declaration also contains a passage highly indicative of the evolution then under way within the Jewish community:

A reconciliation is being effected between French Jews and immigrant Jews, and between the latter and the French nation. At the same time . . . favorable conditions are being created, thanks to the participation of immigrant Jews in the struggle to liberate France, for them to become French citizens. The new generation, these young people with their attachment to Jewish origins, their love for our cultural patrimony, their pride at being both Jewish and French, do they not prefigure the Jewish community of tomorrow? Thus, everything dictates that the CRIF move to the front rank its concern to guarantee French Jews their rights as human beings and to guarantee immigrant Jews equality in treatment and admission to French civic life.

One of the copies of the "draft agreement" has a rather long marginal note by Adamicz (Henri Braun, the UJRE delegate), intended as an amendment, a note which surely reflected the sentiments of many at that time:

Grant of the right of citizenship to all foreign Jews (and to their families) who fought as volunteers in the wars of 1914–1918 and 1939–1940 and to all those who took part in the combat squads for the Liberation of France. . . . Grant of the necessary funds for the temporary support and resettlement of all Jews who on their return from deportation find neither home nor equipment for work nor salaried employment. . . .

Grant of a pension to every repatriated person who at the conclusion of deportation is unsuited for the exercise of vocational activity. . . . Grants of funds for the creation of children's homes and other institutions which would facilitate the reception of the children of deportees and repatriated children who are unable to locate their parents.

This point was followed by a paragraph calling for the "punishment of all those who inspired, ordered, and executed the anti-Jewish measures or helped the Hitlerites in their policy of extermination of the Jews."[34]

Such proposals would be omitted from the final charter (the motives for this are not entirely clear), even though they reflected essential concerns of the Jewish organizations as they contemplated the moment of Liberation. Perhaps they were too concrete for a charter intended to proclaim general principles. However, even that could hardly justify excluding a demand for the punishment of the criminals from the charter, still an issue fifty years later. Paradoxically, neither "the extermination of the Jewish people" nor any other explicit reference to the tragedy figures in the charter, lending the latter a certain "dryness," a failure to resonate in true accord with the amplitude of the drama. Admittedly, the vocabulary reflects the current state of understanding of the objectives of the deportations, still uneven, still partial. But it is possible that this is equally to be explained by a certain tendency—to be observed in the leaders of the Consistory and as was the case during the Dreyfus Affair—for an "elegant" and cold (read "modest") language when speaking of the plight of the Jews.

Essentially conceived as a postwar project, was the CRIF to begin operations immediately after agreement had been struck? Some delegates thought so. They wished to see in it an executive body that would immediately undertake "all action useful for the defense of the Jews of France against the extermination policy of the Hitlerites," as in Adamicz's proposal, supported by the CGD. But the proposal was not retained.[35] The Consistory did not see how to reconcile its legal status (by which it continued to set such store) with support for the actions of the Resistance, then moving into the phase of armed struggle. This same prudence had prompted it to revise the phrasing put forth by the CGD. The proposed expression, "the CRIF pays homage to the resistance of the Jews," became in the adopted version "to all Jewish activities," to which there would in any case be added the words "having contributed to the liberation of the country."

Nevertheless, immigrant Jews saw in the new body the chance for the representation to which they aspired, and a good reason to recognize the his-

torical legitimacy of the Consistory, if not its religious dimension. Through
its decisive contribution to the CRIF, the Consistory translated the evolution
of its thought into fact, in particular in its commitment to a collective Jewish
presence asserted in the context of world politics. Admittedly, it did not renounce the primacy of the spiritual, which it incarnated by definition, but it
thus recognized at the same time the other dimensions of Judaism. The notion of a "multidimensional" Jewry was thus incorporated into the fabric of
the CRIF. To challenge this fact today[36] is equivalent to dismantling its foundations in a Jewish identity both ancient and new, one forged in pain and
grief—and in the Resistance.

The final version of the charter was passed during the course of the first
meeting of the CRIF in liberated Lyon on 5 September 1944. Formulated
in terms of "claims," the charter was understood as an action program to be
implemented immediately, conscious as its authors were that nothing would
be won without struggle. It was important, first, to obtain "constitutional
guarantees against any attack on the principles of equality of race and religion [and to restore] the civic, political, economic, and nationality rights to
Jews through the abrogation of all exclusionary laws." Likewise the charter
demanded the "re-establishment of institutions and Jewish social, cultural,
and economic agencies that had been closed, suspended, or prohibited by
reason of anti-Jewish policy." The charter expressed the CRIF's support for
the Jewish Agency's denunciation of the "White Book" and its demand for
free immigration to Palestine, adding only the formulation of the left Zionists and the communists that promised "the establishment in the broadest
democratic spirit of the most complete accord between the Jewish and Arab
populations of Palestine." The Consistory contributed its specific understanding that "the national status of the Jews of Palestine will in no way affect that of the Jews of other countries nor the ties that attach them to their
fatherland."

Should we be surprised at the difficulty of the new community's ges-
tation? At the passionate character of the discussions? Perhaps not: the as-
perity of the debate never actually challenged the basic agreement forged at
the first sessions. Besides, the circumstances themselves permitted only a few
months to close the gap between native and immigrant Jews that had opened
centuries earlier. Having regained their liberty, the Jews of France created a
new framework for community life, an exceptional institution whose emergence from the depths of suffering and heroism conferred on the CRIF a historical rootedness that could bear up to the challenges of the future.

CHAPTER NINETEEN

A Time for All Fears and All Hopes

I know very well that hard times await us, and the worse it gets
for *him*, the harder it will be for us. With the difference that, for
us, it will get better and better.

—Daniel Finkelstein[1]

On New Year's Day 1944, Laval appointed Joseph Darnand Secretary of State
for the Maintenance of Order. Maintenance of order? This was the France
consigned to fire and blood by the Milice and the Gestapo. In their fury the
losers struck at the maquis and Resistance fighters, perhaps to delay the end
of the Occupation, surely to make the inevitable defeat as costly as possible.
And the Jews? The sweeps and deportations had slowed because it was increasingly difficult to find Jews, so now the security forces began to undertake
simple assassinations, transferring to France some of the open terror practiced in the occupied territories of the Soviet Union. From the assassination
of Victor Basch and his wife Hélène in January 1944 to the summary executions of Rillieux-le-Pape at the end of July, the Milice made its bloody mark.

In Lyon the Jewish Resistance learned very quickly of the murders of
the Basches. Emotions in the MNCR, some of whose operatives used to visit
them, ran high. An MNCR tract appearing in mid-January denounced Darnand and the militia he had recruited from the underworld for the abomi-

nable crime: "On 11 January in the suburbs of Lyon two bodies riddled with shots were discovered. . . . the corpses of Victor Basch and his wife. Who assassinated the eighty-year old couple who for the last three years had lived in retirement in the country, ailing, sick, and broken? There can be no doubt: it was the Milice." The charge was well founded. Somewhat later, people learned of the report of the local gendarmes who discovered the bodies near the Lyon-Geneva highway. A note had been pinned on Victor's coat, the visiting card of the criminals: "Terror against terror. The Jew will always pay. This Jew paid with his life for the assassination of an anti-terrorist nationalist. Down with de Gaulle! With Giraud! Long live France! Signed: National Antiterrorist Committee, Lyon Region."[2]

The Crime at Rillieux

On the morning of Wednesday, 28 June, Philippe Henriot, secretary of state for information, was assassinated in Paris by MLN activists. In reprisal Paul Touvier sent the Second Service (militia action groups) on a hunt that ultimately led to the arrest of seven Jews. During the course of roundups in the streets of Lyon, the Milice and Gestapo had recourse to a method called *déculottage,* a shakedown involving lowering the trousers: since most of the Jews were carrying false identity papers, checking to see if a man was circumcised offered an alternative means to determine if a suspect was Jewish.

Early in the morning of 29 June, after a militiaman pinned cards on their backs with their names, the seven hostages were loaded into a truck with their hands tied behind their backs. On Touvier's order, their gentile cellmate, the FTFP fighter Louis Godard, had been separated from the group. It was as if Touvier had wanted to signify (as in the case of Basch), that it was "for the Jews to pay." There could be little doubt that he bore the Resistance fighters the same hatred he bore the Jews. Still, it was not the Jews who shot Henriot. The Milice leader had carried out a "racial" selection. The victims were then taken to a cemetery in Rillieux where they were lined up along a wall and gunned down one after another: Léo Glaeser, secretary general of the Jewish Defense Committee; Schlisselman of the Lyon committee of the UJRE; Krzyzkowski, a former member of the LICA; Benzimra, Zeizig, and Prock, about whom little is known; and the seventh, an unidentified man. On the day of his arrest Léo Glaeser was supposed to have meet Dora Braun-Adamicz, who was going to give him some documents for her husband.[3] He was not at the rendezvous, nor was he ever to be seen again at meetings of the CRIF, where he was sorely missed for his qualities as mediator. He was the only founder not to have the pleasure of participating in the solemn CRIF Council meeting of 5 September 1944 in liberated Lyon. Touvier's direct responsibility in the Rillieux executions has been established: "The testimony of former militiamen that is preserved in the archives," reports Jacques Delarue, "leaves no doubt as to the conception, organization, and execution of this crime."[4]

The Massacre at Guerry

In the afternoon of Friday, 21 July 1944, the Bourges Gestapo arrived in Saint-Amand (Cher) to carry out nearly six hours of raids that culminated in the massacre of several dozen Jews.[5] At 10:30 p.m., when people were at home because of the curfew, about fifty Germans and a similar number of French militiamen began their invasion of the remaining Jewish homes. According to one survivor's account, "A woman of eighty-two who could not find her stockings was told: 'You old witch, shut your trap or I'll break your head with my rifle-butt.' Monsieur Janklowitsch of Vierzon, whose left side was paralyzed after an accident, did not come down the stairs promptly enough for the Germans and was thrown on his back and dragged by the feet to the truck."

The seventy-one Jews they nabbed (twenty-seven men, thirty-five women, and nine children, the youngest a ward of the state whose father had fallen at Amiens in 1940) were temporarily concentrated in a cinema. They were thence to be loaded into trucks and taken to Bourges for incarceration until the twenty-fourth. At four in the afternoon on that day,

> the men were piled into a small truck. Beside the driver was Paoli, the head of the Milice, in the uniform of a German lieutenant, and a militiaman in civilian clothes. Behind the truck was a car with five German officers. They stopped at Kilometer Nine on the Nevers Road and then plunged into the woods and drew up in front of an abandoned farm. Every few minutes, soldiers came and got men in groups of six. Those who remained in the truck heard nothing because of the sound of the motors. When his turn came, Krameisen moved to the left as the column turned right and he had time to cover some fifty yards, skirting the wall of the house, before the soldiers began firing.

The women and children were still at the prison. On the evening of 8 August, eight of the women and a girl of sixteen were taken away, never to be heard from again; nor do we know what subsequently became of those who were left behind.

After the Liberation a search turned up a pit hidden in the middle of some briars on the abandoned farm. Discovered there were the unrecognizable bodies of several women, among them the naked sixteen-year-old Mlle Strauss. The bodies of twenty-five men were found in another pit. The coroner concluded that the victims had been thrown into the pit while still alive. Among the men were the eighty-six-year-old M. Dreyfus and M. Strauss, father of the murdered girl. The operation had been under the command of Joseph Lécussan, then head of the Lyon Milice. At his 25 September 1946 trial Lécussan was condemned to death; it was confirmed that (among his other crimes) he himself had shot the Basch couple.[6]

The Testament of Samy Klein

Rabbi Samy Klein, chaplain of the Jewish Scouts, was summarily executed by the Gestapo one month before the Liberation. He was arrested on Wednesday, 5 July 1944, at the small railway station of Saint-Étienne-Carnot, just before departure to join an underground group of the Secret Army in Haute-Loire. His cousin Édith Klein was waiting for him at the station to give him a knapsack with a few personal things. Beside her were her brother-in-law Henri Klein and her cousin Touly Elbogen, also preparing to go underground. They were not speaking, so as not to reveal that they were together. Suddenly Édith saw a "big, strong, handsome fellow" come up to Henri and yell at him "Your papers!" At that she got up unhurriedly and went toward exit so that she could warn Samy at the streetcar stop where he was to arrive. This interminable wait came to an end when she saw the three men leave the station under police escort—Samy had arrived by a different route. The fascists seized the false papers he was to have distributed to his companions, as well as the Old and New Testaments that were part of his disguise as a Protestant cleric.[7]

The martyred bodies of Rabbi Samy Klein, Henri Klein, and Touly Elbogen were found by farmers in a field near Saint-Genest-Malifaux not far away. After the Liberation it emerged that the execution had taken place two days later (16 Tamouz 5704).[8] Marguerite Klein identified the bodies. And the "big, strong, handsome fellow" who challenged the group at the station? This was "Freddy," whose full name was Alfred Guggenheim, a hired agent of the Gestapo and the terror of the Jews and the Resistance around Saint-Étienne in 1943 and 1944.[9] Arrested after the Liberation, Guggenheim was sentenced to death by military court and executed on 28 September 1944, the day after Yom Kippur; he is reported to have refused the services of a rabbi.[10]

On 24 May 1944, Samy Klein had drawn up a moral testament, perhaps moved by a premonition of his impending martyrdom, perhaps haunted by the consciousness that his own father had died at his same age, twenty-nine.[11] "Life hangs by only a thread in these times," he worried, "the younger you are, the sooner you risk dying . . . at the whim of the occupiers or one of their accomplices." His first wish was for his two daughters to be brought up as Jews and as Frenchwomen: "When Israel and France are together suffering the most terrible martyrdom of history, is it not normal that a French rabbi pay his tribute?" Klein believed in an almost mystical tie between Jewry and France, seeking to remain its apostle in death as he had been in life.

The Charnel Pits of Bron

On 26 August in Lyon, over the sound of German artillery fire on the Villeurbanne District, where an uprising had broken out three days earlier, people could not hear the chattering of machineguns on the airfield of Bron. Here more than fifty prisoners (forty-nine of them Jews) brought from the Montluc Fortress to fill in craters left by the American bombing were executed at the end of the day in front of the last two gaping holes. Among them was thirty-six-year-old Robert Kahn, regional head of the MUR. Today his daughter describes his final moments:

> The men come over with some difficulty and approach the craters. They are approaching their graves. . . . As they march forward who knows whether some of them did not understand what was going to happen. . . ? [Soon forty-nine Jewish prisoners are] standing around the holes, their hands empty because they had just been ordered to put down their shovels and pickaxes. They felt a little awkward and looked worriedly at each other: What had [their captors] thought up now to humiliate them a little more? And suddenly the Germans take up position four paces off, pull up their machineguns, [and] spray shots straight

ahead in a fusillade whose echoes reverberate in the distance, rolling across the hills and down into the city.[12]

In Paris, Brunner Liquidates the UGIF Children's Centers

News of the arrival of General de Gaulle on French soil on 14 June stimulated feverish expectations everywhere. After the capture of Cherbourg on 1 July, Parisians were certain that the days of the Occupation were numbered. All who were not indifferent soon heard the rumblings of the uprising already being prepared.

But that July, a month of great hope, was marred by what was unquestionably the most tragic episode for the Jews of France. Between 21 and 25 July, the six children's homes and two centers for adolescents, in other words all the institutional shelters of the UGIF in Paris, were emptied of their residents on the order of Aloïs Brunner, head of the Drancy Camp. The hunt for people gone underground was no longer producing results, or very few; to raid apartments the collaboration of the police was required, something the Germans could no longer count on. All that was left for Brunner were the UGIF children's homes. The children caught in the raids were condemned to death because of their extremely young ages and because they were housed, against all common sense, in obviously Jewish places.

On the night of 21–22 July alone German police burst into five centers, excepting only the preschool center in Neuilly, whose clearance would be delayed by three days. On Saturday morning Brunner could register the arrival in Drancy of 242 children and adolescents (not to mention 30 adult staff members): from the Secrétan center, 80 children, the majority evacuees from rue Lamarck (damaged in an Allied air-raid); Montreuil, 25; Louveciennes, 50; the trade school, 8; Vauquelin, 32; Saint-Mandé, 20. Another sweep took place Saturday night and Sunday morning at La Varenne, carrying off 27 more children.[13]

Georges Edinger, leader of the UGIF-Paris after Baur's arrest on 21 July 1943, informed the commissioner for Jewish Questions on 27 July that "the children in the Neuilly home have been the object of an administrative measure by the authorities at the Drancy camp, on Tuesday the 25th, sixteen in number. We must deplore any measures aimed at our personnel in that home." Edinger did not count on an intervention by the commission on behalf of the Jewish internees, but only for the "Aryan" employees: these had been arrested too and interned along with their wives (!); while a few were quickly freed, a certain number remained at Drancy, though their subsequent fate remains obscure.[14]

Mathilde Jaffé was one of the girls at the rue Vauquelin center, where the UGIF had gathered girls over sixteen. They had been insulated there from news of outside events, certainly with the intention of making them oblivious to the drama that loomed around them, but leaving them ill-prepared when the time came to protect themselves. She remembers,

> The night of 21–22 July, about one o'clock in the morning, shouts in German made us start up. Soldiers burst in, with levelled machineguns. They shouted 'Quick! Quick!' We weren't given time to get dressed. In our nightgowns we were pushed outside and made to get into trucks. A few hours later we found ourselves at the Drancy camp.
>
> Goodbye to our dream of being warned in advance, of jumping over the wall to hide with the nuns of the convent next door. Once we got to Drancy—and I was not the only one to ask myself these questions—we realized that this hope had been based on absolutely nothing. It was irresponsible, very irresponsible to have let us believe it. And why weren't we instructed to leave the home and disperse? Despite our isolation, we would have found somewhere to go. But we didn't want to blame it on the directress. Wasn't she sharing the same lot as all the rest of us? Moreover, the camp administration allowed her to go back and get our things, which she did with a great deal of care.[15]

The children and adolescents picked up by the German police in the UGIF homes left for Auschwitz a week later (31 July) in convoy 77. A convoy to hell. And hell already existed on the train. To the extent that statistics can measure the degree of horror, let the numbers speak: of the seven children less than three years old, two were less than two and one less than a year old. Sixty-four were between four and seven years, one hundred and forty between eight and twelve, fifty-seven between thirteen and fifteen, and the rest either sixteen or seventeen years old. Most of the deported children were between four and twelve years of age. They totalled 299.[16] Two who survived, Jacques Darville and Simon Wichené, later wrote about events: "The littlest ones . . . toddle along, whimpering, cheap little toys in their hands. They go every which way, stopping, coming back; the soft and firm hand of a supervisor brings them back in the right direction. The supervisors! One could say so much! For a week now they have been on guard, scarcely sleeping, their eye always on the acts and gestures of their children. Human tenderness was never more fully developed than in these so tragic circumstances. They knew what 'departure' meant."[17]

"All my memories of that terrible 'trip'," testified Mathilde Jaffe, "are overshadowed by just one. At Drancy I saw the arrival with the children from Neuilly of a little three-year-old boy whom I had taken care of in the nursery. He was so happy to find his "mama" again, a joy that I shared. In the train he did not leave my arms. When we arrived at the camp, the SS, who because of my age would not accept that he was my child, sent him to one side and me to the other. Our column set off. The child looked at me with eyes where I could see nothing but surprise and reproach. It was a look that I shall never forget."

Inquest into the Drama

If this roundup constitutes the most monstrous of Brunner's crimes,[18] it remains too one of the most painful of the era generally. After the liberation of Paris on 30 August 1944, a commission of the Jewish Resistance, appointed by the Comité général de défense conducted an inquest under the direction of Jacques Rabinowitch, UGIF counsel to first determine the facts, then the responsibility of the UGIF leadership. Dr. Kurt Schendel, member of the UGIF office answerable to the Jewish Service of the Gestapo after the arrest of Israelowicz, was the principal witness.[19]

Summoned to Drancy on Thursday 20 July by Brunner, Kurt Schendel was charged with furnishing him, on the spot, with the list of all the shelters and their residents. This should not have surprised Schendel because even though Brunner had all the information, the German practice was to implicate the UGIF as much as possible in the conduct of its deportation program. Schendel was accompanied to the UGIF offices on rue de Téhéran, where, after having pretended not to be able find the lists, he was finally obliged to take the list on Secretary-General Edinger's desk—"hoping that the disappearance of the list would attract his attention," he stated, so that the latter might warn the intended victims.

Schendel was kept under close guard at Drancy until late Saturday to prevent him from alerting anyone. Brunner did allow him to phone his wife that he was "temporarily" detained at Drancy, but not one word more. It seems that Schendel's wife did not inform anyone, fearing to cause him some harm. Edinger, having noticed that the list was missing, contented himself (according to Schendel) with "bawling out the orderly and the housekeeper."

But the disappearance of a list that was kept in the open anyway, and of which the Germans already had the contents, did not trouble him any more than that.

After the war former UGIF officials also sought to evade responsibility by reproaching the Jewish Resistance for not having taken the children to safety. Supposedly they had suggested this to the CGD, urging a series of staged "abductions." It was the Resistance, they claimed, that had been slow to act. What is the real truth of the matter?

It is true that the UJRE-Paris had continued to hope for a general closure of the UGIF children's shelters. This was its general policy, one often reinforced by such actions as that in February 1943 under the direction of Suzanne Spaak and Pastor Vergara of the MNCR, and another at the Antiquaille Hospital in Lyon.[20] However, carrying off the children against the wishes of the staff of a particular shelter seemed inappropriate: one can well imagine the reaction of the personnel and the panic of the children if they had tried. To get the children out, then, it was necessary to "negotiate" with the UGIF. And this is just what Gaston Griner, UJRE delegate to the Paris CGD, proposed to Edinger and Juliette Stern, head of UGIF social services: the planned closure of the centers.

Frédéric Léon (father-in-law of Dr. Milhaud) heard of the proposal while working with Entraide temporaire (Temporary Mutual Aid). Also a member of the CGD in the Occupied Zone (representing Bordeaux), Léon had become acquainted with Gaston Griner. According to Léon, Griner apparently had one or two meetings with Edinger and Stern; Edinger, it seems, hesitated to take a stand, but Stern replied in the negative, invoking the standard argument of the likelihood of provoking government reprisals against the tens of thousands of Jews still in Paris and environs.[21]

Albert Akerberg, representative of the "Sixth" (the underground branch of the Jewish Scouts responsible for saving children) in Paris, is categorical: "In the face of the UGIF administration's determination to stay in line with the occupation authorities, we were obliged to limit ourselves to isolated acts." At the very most he succeeded in getting the consent of Juliette Stern to have children spirited away one at a time. This "kidnapping" would typically take place during a child's visit to the dentist on boulevard Murat; the staff member who accompanied the child would close her eyes at the appropriate moment. According to Akerberg only five or six children were ever saved this way.[22] This method of individual removal is confirmed by Charles Mandelbaum, a member of the clandestine Resistance group "Alerte" in Paris. A younger sister of his fiancée was in the Montreuil home, but only after protracted bargaining with the director was it agreed that Mandelbaum might "nab" the child on her way home from school.[23]

If it is true—as she affirmed after the war—that Juliette Stern had set up a parallel network for hiding the children, we have a right to ask why the UGIF relied on the Resistance when it would have been much simpler to work through their own network. What seems even more incomprehensible is that the adolescents—and their number was not inconsiderable—were not encouraged to seek refuge on their own.

The only credible explanation comes from the administrative council of the Paris UGIF itself. Even before its charter was approved, the CRIF established a commission in Lyon in May 1944 at the demand of the CGD, charged with considering the dissolution of the UGIF. When the opinion of the CGD (represented by Ruwen Grinberg and Adamicz) in favor of wrapping up the UGIF prevailed over the arguments against that were put forward by the lawyer Geissmann (who had replaced Raoul Lambert after the latter's deportation), Léon Meiss announced as chairman of the commission the consensus that the UGIF ought to terminate its activities. He nevertheless agreed to hear the advice of the leaders of the Northern Zone. "In a secret session held on 17 July 1944, the leadership voiced strong opposition to the dissolution of the UGIF in the Southern Zone for fear of reprisals that might be undertaken against the population in both zones."[24]

Thus, the old "threat of reprisals" was invoked by Edinger in Paris and Geissmann in Lyon. Reprisals? What worse could have happened? The closure of the centers did not occur, but the children's disaster did. The last word on this tragedy goes to Serge Klarsfeld who, citing a letter of thanks that the Jewish commandant at Drancy sent to the Jewish police and to other services the day after the deportation of the children, cries out in anger: "Macabre buffoons who were still playing Brunner and the SS's game on the eve of the Liberation! Those who let the children be arrested, those who assured their departure to an atrocious death with the satisfaction of duty done, those who by giving in saved themselves from what they most feared, deportation."

Suicidal Behavior

Why did they continue? Why did the UGIF never take the decision to involve itself in any kind of opposition? Even if some of its staff individually went over to the Resistance, why did it not dissolve itself after it had clearly become a trap for staff and clientele alike? All the more was this refusal paradoxical after they had received the coded directive from R.-R. Lambert, interned at Drancy, to scuttle the operation in order to save the children from deportation.[25]

The answers are complex, since the UGIF was not just any Vichy body. In a sense all Jews were slated for extermination, with the "due date" varying according to the category. All those who made up the UGIF were men condemned to death in the "Final Solution." Their role gave them, in effect a reprieve; but this should not have deluded them, and certain key events should have signaled that the time had come to abandon the enterprise. The period following the deportations in the summer of 1942, marked as it was by raids on the UGIF's offices, shelters, and nurseries, under the circumstances should have been the turning point. But, despite all the evidence, the leaders sustained the institution: to understand their several reasons the observer must make a special effort to put him- or herself in their shoes.

To what extent were they aware of the overall function and the final destination the Nazis had assigned them? If they were aware, they would appear to have been in some sort of denial. For one thing, because there were — or there seemed to be — French officials between them and the Germans, there was — or there seemed to be — a French government; and it was, after all, Vichy, via the CGQ J, that set their operating rules. Their legalist mentality should not be underestimated. Second, because they were implicated in an administrative structure, they rapidly became its prisoners. Driven by its logic, their operations were transformed into ends in themselves. This is the well-known bureaucratic drift which causes agents to forget their initial intentions.

It was through the corresponding kind of thought mechanism, in which the initial intentions to assist the needy were still present, that UGIF officials created their raison d'être, the letters patent that authorized them to hang on to their structure. There was also a more pedestrian everyday reality, unavowed but nevertheless experienced: the officials of the UGIF were "privileged" Jews, protected along with their families by their government ID cards. They benefited from employment, the use of the telephone, the possibility of shopping at hours that were forbidden to other Jews (in the Occupied Zone), and so on. In short, their yellow stars may have appeared to them a little less yellow than those of the persecuted group to which they belonged. This motivation, even if it is surely not the determining one, must not be excluded.

And this is why they could not escape the fateful mechanism that entangled them in fear and hope. Not the fear and hope of the Resistance fighter, afraid of dying but hoping for victory. No, rather the insidious, paralyzing fear of one day sharing the lot of the victims, with the hope only of delaying the day when the note would be called in. The feelings are all too human, and they explain both weakness and blindness. But they do not exempt the men of the UGIF from being focus of debate because their organization was a trap not only for those who ran it but also for those who came to it seeking help. The debate on their role emerged with the birth of the organization and continued until the Liberation, proof that the critical analysis was not the historians' creation, but a reality experienced on a daily basis during the war.

The majority of the UGIF leaders (and a portion of the French Jewish establishment generally) were not only the hostages of Vichy and the Nazis but also of their own mentality, of their incapacity to see beyond the walls of the ghetto into which they had let themselves be enclosed. It was for these reasons that they persevered, some right to the point of death. But in the name of what on earth did all of them put their families in a such a defenseless situation? While nearly all children of members of the Resistance of every persuasion survived, the officials of the UGIF would be deported with their families.[26] Confidence in the virtue of "legality"? Or, as seems more likely, fear of committing a subversive act by hiding those nearest and dearest to them? In any case, their example suggested to Jews generally, and not only to those who had dealings with them, a model of suicidal behavior.

The End: "Remove your stars!"

During the evening of 16 August 1944, Drancy internees noticed signs of feverish activity in Brunner's offices. Light came from the kitchen windows, soon followed by smoke. The Germans were clearly burning their records, and the internees anxiously concluded they would soon liquidate the camp. But how? Were they going to evacuate the seven hundred remaining internees?

Aloïs Brunner was in a hurry to flee, and, though he thought only of saving his skin, he did find time to couple to his train a wagon with fifty internees for hostages, mostly fighters of the Jewish Army and the FTP-MOI. Happily, almost all succeeded in escaping: "At the Laon station, the rail line was cut and the train had to back up," Jacques Lazarus later recounted. "The car with the hostages, which until then had been hooked up behind the locomotive, was put at the tail end of the convoy and it was easy to escape."[27]

Brunner had left Drancy on the afternoon of the seventeenth. "Finally, around four-thirty . . . a cry of triumph went through the camp: '*Remove your stars!*' The shock was so great that many refused to believe what was happening."[28] The captain of the French gendarmerie remained, continuing, more or less, to supervise the camp. But he found himself facing a new power as the internees formed a committee to demand immediate release of all—with the exception of "some informers" to be held over for subsequent judgment. "A representative of the Swedish Consulate-General [as a neutral, Sweden was one of the few powers with an embassy in Paris]," recount Jacques Darville and Simon Wichené, "came to attend to the formalities of liberation, by virtue of an agreement reached with the German authorities"; the latter urged the prisoners to be patient until a date could be set for their release. "But nothing could deny the camp committee's insistence on immediate liberation."[29]

An FFI group from the now coordinated Resistance movements, with Drancy Deputy Mayor Gibrat at its head, took charge. Releases began on Friday, 18 August, with former officers of the French Army, non-coms, and veterans leaving first, rushing to get back to Paris by the eve of the planned uprising. The clearance of Drancy was completed on Sunday. Almost six hundred persons were ultimately transported in Red Cross trucks and located at reception centers in the Paris region.

In the capital city, the battle was still under way. Young Jews of the MOI, the Young Zionists (MJS), and hundreds of others who came out of the shadows to join them assaulted the first barricades. Soon the majority of these would form the new Marcel Rayman Company. In liberated Drancy, as in Paris, the yellow star, the emblem of those condemned to death, disappeared. Yet for several thousand Jews who had been deported from France with the active complicity of the Pétain-Laval government—now gasping its last in its shabby German exile—the crematory ovens continued to smoke.

CONCLUSION

The Weight of the Present
and of the Future

In Bialystok, where I grew up, there was an old cemetery abandoned for several generations. A little more of its wooden fence disappeared each winter, severe in that part of Europe, as the poor carried off bits and pieces for firewood. In the summer, the locals would graze their goats there. They thus transgressed against a principle of the Jewish religion: that respect for the dead takes precedence over the convenience of the living.

One day at the end of Sabbath services a famous *maggid,* or moral preacher, sought to move our congregation to undertake the repair of the fence. With a striking power of suggestion, the *maggid* painted a picture that made everyone tremble, me included. His words are inscribed in the child's memory. "Think of the day of resurrection. All those who lie in the old cemetery, in their trampled graves, with their cover of earth scraped aside, will rise up to sing the glory of God. But it will be a march of cripples, one without legs, another without arms, a third without eyes." The sobbing coming from the women's gallery intensified the images, as if the gruesome procession were already winding its way through the synagogue.

Twenty-two years later, in May 1943, I wrote in an underground publication one of the first accounts of the Warsaw Ghetto Uprising, essentially announcing to the world the end of Polish Jewry—an idea as yet nearly inconceivable—when the terrible images evoked so long ago by the *maggid* returned. And from my pen there issued another vision in which "millions of

313

victims rise from their graves, from out of the flames and the death factories [while] behind them come the living." This was not a vision of the resurrection expected at the end of time, but of a much closer day, the day of victory.[1] Memory was already there. And then it was the evening of 18 May 1948; I had taken the floor at the Winter Velodrome, filled with assembled survivors to celebrate the independence of Israel. Abruptly, images of the past, of that place in 1942, superimposed themselves on the present: the feeling that "the victims are all here" conquered me. I abandoned my prepared text, but with a voice cracking with emotion, I associated with the victory celebration "those who lived no longer, but who in that great moment joined us."[2]

In the aftermath of the destruction of the Temple, that other great disaster in the history of the Jews, the rabbis wondered whether the people would have the spiritual strength to bear so heavy a sorrow.[3] They considered lightening the liturgy by reducing the litany of tragedies. Thousands of years later in France some insisted on stressing the accounts of the revolts, even when these were not crowned with success. The philosophy of history that has prevailed in Jewish tradition, however, was that of an endless cycle of sin-punishment-redemption: the inevitability of martyrdom connected with the certainty of salvation.[4] We know that this idea is of great comfort to believers; it establishes reason for those who think they know why the Jewish people suffers and even discover in tragic events a logic which may otherwise escape reason.

But it seems to us that the "lachrymose conception of Jewish history"[5] as one composed uniquely of suffering does not enlighten historical research or make Jewish history a fertile field of inquiry. And the question was not born in the aftermath of the genocide: it already counted heavily in the past, when it dictated the attitudes adopted by Jews in various circumstances, including those of the Holocaust. Every manifestation of Jewish resistance, collective or individual, first called for a rupture with fatalistic conceptions, be they of a theological or secular order. Unquestionably, the Resistance wrote itself into the warrior tradition that was no less present in the history of the Jews.

It is important to record the conduct of the majority of "victims" who defended themselves, resisted, fought. This book has sought to do this for the Jews of France by addressing the poorly known phenomenon of clandestinity, "people going underground"; and to a lesser extent to do this for the Jews of Poland by posing the limits of their possibilities for self-defense.[6] Let us recall the Germans' strategy of Blitzkrieg, the extreme rapidity with which the Nazis executed their plan for the extermination of the Jews of Eastern Europe. The chronology of the genocide illuminates a fact that historians often fail to bear in mind: the statistics of Raul Hilberg, solid and trustworthy, establish the fact that 76.5 percent of the murdered Jews (3,900,000 out of the total of 5,100,000) had been massacred before the end of 1942.[7] A more realistic and balanced conception of the attitude of Jewish communities facing the greatest military power of the time should replace the obsessive fixation on martyrology. This would enhance understanding of the victims in their multiple dimensions without ceasing to interrogate the conscience of humanity; if some of the victims were passive, it is unjust to reproach them all because the majority were not.

Finally, we cannot leave aside a question which raises among survivors of the camps a terrible anxiety, one so great as to be of concern to many more people: what memory will survive after they have passed away? The question is legitimate, for they are the only ones to have lived the genocide in their flesh and soul. Many of them find meaning in their survival precisely in the obligation to bring to the world's knowledge their experience of this greatest of crimes against humanity. There are historians who are aware of this, who respect this feeling, and know how to listen to witnesses. Others seem distrustful of personal testimony, convinced that it reflects the "deficiencies" of human memory. To which survivors object that the label "historian" is no guarantee of objectivity, rigor, or even intellectual integrity, as is confirmed when historians unleash partisan and passionate polemics, often to their own discredit. Be this as it may, anguished witnesses should find comfort in the fact that their contribution to knowledge of the Shoah, if published or made available in public repositories, has and will continue to have its place in the sources historians must rely on as much as they rely on other forms of documentation of this period.[8] With the contradiction between witnesses and historians in mind, François Bédarida expresses a wide consensus among contemporary historians when he writes of "the degree to which this testimony brings to life the reality of the genocide in dramatic and irreplaceable fashion, generally from the perspective of the victims but sometimes also from the perspective of the killers."[9]

I should like to conclude by returning to the question formulated in the introduction, why if France was "the country which along with Germany most persecuted the Jews," it was at the same time a country where nearly three-fourths of the Jews survived. There were two divergent forces at play. The first was statist, and its ideology with regard to the Jews drew upon xenophobic and antisemitic French sources; it easily assimilated murderous National-Socialist racism. The second force (it found expression after a brief eclipse) was the French republican tradition. The majority of the French eventually found their ideological home here. French *identity* could never be on the side of the Vichy regime. There could be no confusion between a state whose servants betrayed and murdered humanity, and the true France which sheltered, concealed, and saved it.

The Twenty-First Century

On the clock of history, the hands advance more quickly for
the Jews than for other peoples. The time of the others was
not our time.

It was with this reflection in the summer of 1942 that I summarized all the
uniqueness of the Jewish condition in Europe and in France, in particular
the rapidity of the extermination program as compared to the Germans'
prosecution of their war generally. The perception that the pace of the war
against the Jews differed from that of the overall war demanded a more
rapid mobilization by the Jewish Resistance and objectives that could not be
assumed by the Resistance in general. The latter coordinated its action with
Allied strategy and considered that victory over Nazi Germany would ipso
facto put an end to the suffering of the Jews. This might have been true if
the war Hitler had declared on the Jewish people had not been such an urgent priority for the Nazis.

The matrix of the Jewish Resistance, pluralist by virtue of its diversity,
consisted of the prewar organizations and social agencies, in particular those
of the Jews of Eastern Europe. Depending on whether it was operating in the
Free or the Occupied Zone, the Jewish Resistance in France experienced an
uneven development. In the Free Zone, to which almost all the organization

and agency officials withdrew, priority was initially accorded humanitarian action inside the numerous camps, special concern being devoted to getting children out and into homes run by the OSE. But the political climate, at first relatively liberal, encouraged illusions as to Pétain's intentions and delayed adoption of an underground existence, *clandestinité*, the first condition for effective resistance activity.

In Paris, where persecution was administered by the occupiers and the Pétain regime in concert, the Jewish Resistance organizations affiliated with the MOI, well rooted in the working-class neighborhoods of Paris and supported by such Zionist youth groups as Hashomer Hazair, launched an intensive activity. However, in the face of the census and the registration ordinance of May 1941 leading to internments in the Loiret camps and to the roundups of August 1941, no call to civil disobedience was issued. It was not until the community had suffered the first blows that the Jewish Resistance in the capital hammered out a survival strategy and disseminated it through its underground press. This strategy placed each and every individual before a grave and dramatic choice: respect the law, including the anti-Jewish legislation, of the Vichy regime, or go outside the law by joining the underground.

The abandonment of legality was first implemented on a wide scale in Paris on the eve of the great raids of 16–17 July 1942. In an appeal distributed in Jewish neighborhoods a few days earlier—the underground was informed of the plan but not its timing—the Resistance urged people, "Don't wait at home. . . . Make every effort to hide yourselves, and first of all your children, with the help of sympathetic members of the French population." More than 13,000 Parisian Jews thereby succeeded in escaping the clutches of the French police, in charge of the roundup. This was the greatest single "rescue" action undertaken by the Jews themselves. Though under the circumstances the plan could only be implemented on an individual basis, and for some in total solitude, the Jews were thus adopting the behavior of a collectivity.

In this sense, the days of 16 and 17 August mark a decisive turn in the history of the Jewish Resistance. First, the Jewish Resistance found its composition modified by the entry on stage of a new player, the Jewish "masses," an actor largely ignored since by historians. It became apparent that the only means of escaping deportation was life in clandestinity. Second, the *maquis* where Jews "hid" was not a physical location "out in the scrub" but the human social environment, a French civil society which increasingly recovered the Republican and Christian values at first swept aside in Pétain's "National Revolution." Public opinion gave proof of a surge of solidarity, confirming its rejection of Vichy. The completely clandestine daily existence of a large part of an entire minority was a phenomenon without precedent in human history: even the early Christians had been obliged to hide only during prayer and services.

If relations between the "organized Resistance" and the enormous mass of those living underground were of necessity sporadic, in particular because of the extreme dispersal of the Jews (more than eight hundred cities, towns, and villages in the two zones afforded shelter to Jews in hiding), the underground press in Yiddish and French played a liaison role. It provided accounts of the major events affecting the Jewish population, and beginning in October 1942 it disseminated the (admittedly scant) information on the Germans' extermination program. Thanks to this, deportation thus came to be equated with death, at least for those capable of believing the unbelievable.

The organized Resistance found a reservoir of human resources in this underground population which, driven by its desire for vengeance, was now prepared to take a further step. This readiness found expression in Paris in armed action by Jewish fighters of the FTP-MOI (let us not forget the "Red Poster"), and in numerous cities and towns of the Southern Zone in the form of the creation of Jewish combat groups, underground units of the Armée juive (the Zionist Youth Movement), and the Jewish Scouts. We see the expansion of efforts to rescue children, hidden in the countryside or smuggled into Switzerland. The Jewish Resistance gained in unity as persecution intensified. In the aftermath of the Warsaw Ghetto Uprising, which was experienced with deep shock, Jewish immigrant organizations of all shades formed the General Defense Committee. This new group worked for rapprochement with the officially tolerated Central Consistory of the Jews of France. In the spring of 1944 Le Conseil représentatif des Juifs de France was born of the hope to unify the efforts of those in the underground with those who had so long continued to try to work within Vichy law; it still exists.

Although channeled into Jewish structures, the Resistance did not allow itself to be ghettoized. Its links with the general Resistance in activities of all kinds were numerous and indispensable on both the political and practical levels. The pages written by the Jewish Resistance correct the image of France as "the country that along with Germany most persecuted the Jews" (the words belong to the head of Pétain's cabinet): this was also the country where more than three-quarters of the Jews (220,000) escaped deportation, thanks not only to their own courage but also to the solidarity they found in the "other" France, patriotic and republican. The Jewish Resistance and the active solidarity of the non-Jewish population would not have been conceivable in a France where a majority were loyal to Pétain.

At the first symposium organized by the United States Holocaust Memorial Museum in October 1994, I concluded my presentation with a reflection on the future of the history and memory of the Shoah. It expressed some concern, but pointed to a new field of research—the resistance of the Jewish community—that had long lain fallow: "It is true that the history of the Jewish people cannot be recounted without tears. However, it must not be lachrymose, in the words of Salo W. Baron. Has the time now arrived to restore to the millions of victims, by means of scientifically rigorous and documented research, their status as combatants who were vanquished during an entirely unequal combat? Through this research, we will serve historical truth and help new generations to conquer the trauma while keeping memory intact."[1]

Since the end of the war, thanks to the enormous efforts of actors, witnesses, survivors, and historians, the memory and the lessons of genocide are constituent elements of today's Jewish identity in the diaspora. This identity remains fragile. Always required to define itself against the pressures of the political, cultural, and sociological environment, it cannot define itself solely in reference to profound injury. Only a global approach to the Holocaust highlighting the resistance of Jewish populations will be able at the same time to affirm the reality of the years 1939–1945 and also offer sources of pride, courage, and moral strength.

INTERVIEWS AND TESTIMONY

Jacques Adler, member of the Resistance, professor at the University of Melbourne, Australia

Albert Akerberg, member of the Resistance, administrator with l'Action sociale par l'habitat

Roger Appel, escapee from a UGIF children's home

Joseph Atlas, refugee in Chambon-sur-Lignon

Lucie Aubrac, member of the Libération-Sud Resistance

Denise Baumann, member of the Resistance, OSE, and MNCR

Claude Bourdet, member of the Resistance, leader of the Combat movement

Henry Bulawko, member of the Resistance, deported, vice-president of the CRIF

Daniel Darès, survivor of the Vélodrome d'Hiver roundup, director of the Théâtre Antoine, Paris

Jacques Delarue, member of the Resistance, police commissioner, historian

Roland Dumas, member of the Resistance, Ministry of Foreign Affairs

Hélène Edelman-Kuperman, survivor of the Vélodrome d'Hiver roundup

Roger Fichtenberg, member of the Resistance, councilor for the 11th city district, Paris

Robert Frank, student at the ORT trade school

Anne Frenkel, and her father the painter Borwine Frenkel, who went underground

Szymon Fuchs, escapee from Drancy

Denise Gamzon, member of the Resistance, widow of Robert Gamzon

René Goldman, survivor, professor at the University of British Columbia, Vancouver

Stanley Hoffmann, survivor of Brunner's roundup in Nice, professor at Harvard University

Mathilde Jaffé, deportee

Yves Jouffa, member of the Resistance, president of the League for the Rights of Man

Jean Kahn, president of the CRIF

Pierre Kaufmann, member of the Resistance, Jewish Scouts underground group

Jacqueline Keller, executive director, CRIF

Claude Kelman, member of the Resistance, honorary president of the Memorial to the Unknown Jewish Martyr

Édith Klein, member of the Resistance

Théo Klein, member of the Resistance, former president of CRIF

Fernand Kohn, member of the Resistance, Jewish combat groups, Lyon

Henri Krischer, military leader of the Carmagnole-Liberté batallion

Pierre Lœb, leader in the Jewish Army underground group

Lucien Lublin, member of the Resistance, leader in the Jewish Army

Jean-Marie Lustiger, Cardinal-archbishop of Paris

Charles Mandelbaum, member of the Resistance, Alerte irregulars, Paris

Camille Mathieu, gendarme at Drancy, decorated along with his mother with the Medal of the Righteous among the Nations at Yad Vashem

Henri Minczeles, son of a deportee, journalist

Simone Nathan-Ascher, saved by Georges Dumas

Maurice Redon, General "Durenque"

Gerhard Riegner, vice-president of the WJC, Geneva

Étienne Rosenfeld, deportee

Rachel Rubel, member of the Resistance, Jewish Army

Sophie Schwartz, member of the Resistance, official with the Union of Jewish Women, MOI

René-Samuel Sirat, Chief Rabbi of France

Jean Sirchis, member of the Resistance, Jewish Army

Michel Topiol, member of the Resistance, vice-president of the Jewish Agency for Palestine

Claude Urman, member of the Resistance, 35th Marcel Langer Brigade

Maurice Wajcman, son of an internee at Drancy

Ida Zaïontz, survivor of the Vélodrome d'Hiver roundup

ACRONYMS OF AGENCIES, ORGANIZATIONS, AND MOVEMENTS

AA   Auswärtiges Amt (Reich ministry of foreign affairs)

ACIP   Association culturelle des israélites pratiquants (Cultural Association of Practicing Jews)

AJJDC   American Jewish Joint Distribution Committee

AHPP   Archives historiques de la Préfecture de police (Historical Archives of the Prefecture of Police)

AIU   Alliance israélite universelle (Universal Israelite Alliance)

AJ   Armée juive (Jewish Army)

AN   Archives nationales (French National Archives)

AS   Armée secrète (Secret Army)

BBC   British Broadcasting Company

BCRA   Bureau central de renseignement et d'action-"France libre" (Free French Central Service for Intelligence and Action)

BDIC   Bibliothèque de documentation internationale contemporaine (Library of International Contemporary Documentation)

CADI   Comité d'action et de défense des immigrés (Action and Defense Committee for Immigrants)

CADJJ   Comité d'action et de défence de la jeunesse juive (Jewish Youth Committee for Defense and Action)

CAR   Comité d'aide aux réfugiés (Refugee Relief Committee)

CC   Consistoire Central (Central Consistory)

CCOJA   Commission centrale des œuvres juives d'assistance (Central Commission for Jewish Relief Agencies)

CDJC   Centre de documentation juive contemporaine (Center for Contemporary Jewish Documentation)

CDJJ   Comité directeur de la jeunesse juive (Administrative Committee for Jewish Youth)

CFL	Corps franc libre (Free Irregulars)
CFLN	Comité français de libération nationale (French Committee for National Liberation)
CFMN	Corps franc de la Montagne Noire (Black Mountain Irregulars)
CGD	Comité général de défence (General Defense Committee)
CGQ J	Commissariat général aux questions juives (General Commission for Jewish Questions)
CGT	Confédération générale du travail (General Confederation of Labor)
CNR	Comité national de la Résistance (National Committee of the Resistance)
COMAC	Comité militaire d'action (Military Action Committee)
CRJF	Conseil représentatif des Juifs de France (Representative Council of the Jews of France), presently CRIF, Conseil représentatif des institutions juives de France (Representative Council of Jewish Institutions of France)
DGER	Direction générale d'étude et de renseignement (General Administration for Research and Intelligence)
EIF	Éclaireurs israélites de France (Jewish Scouts of France)
ET	Entraide temporaire (Temporary Mutual Aid)
FFI	Forces françaises intérieures (Free French Forces of the Interior)
FFL	Forces françaises libres (Free French Forces)
FSJA	Fédération des sociétés juives d'Algérie (Federation of Jewish Associations of Algeria)
FSJF	Fédération des sociétés juives de France (Federation of Jewish Associations of France)
FTPF	Franc-tireurs et partisans français (French Irregulars and Partisans)
FTP-MOI	Military branch of the immigrant Resistance; see FTPF and MOI
GTE	Groupement des travailleurs étrangers (special camps for immigrant workers)
ICRC	International Committee of the Red Cross
IMT	Institut Maurice Thorez
IS	British Intelligence Service
JOC	Jeunesse ouvrière chrétienne (Christian Worker Youth)
JTA	Jewish Telegraphic Agency
JTS	Jewish Theological Seminary
LICA	Ligue internationale contre l'antisémitisme (International League Against Antisemitism)

MBF   Militärbefehlshaber in Frankreich (German military command in France)

MJS   Mouvement de jeunesse sioniste (Zionist Youth Movement)

MLN   Mouvement de libération nationale (National Liberation Movement)

MNCR   Mouvement national contre le racisme (National Movement against Racism)

MOI   Main d'œuvre immigrée (Immigrant Labor Association)

MS   Militärsicherheitsdienst (Jewish police at Drancy)

MUR   Mouvements unis de Résistance (United Resistance Movements)

NAP   Noyautage de l'administration publique (Infiltration of the Public Administration [Resistance group])

OJC   Organisation juive de combat (Jewish Combat Organization), name adopted by Jewish Army, May 1944

ORT   Organisation reconstruction travail (Organization for Reconstruction through Labor)

OSE   Oeuvre de secours aux enfants (Children's Relief Organization)

PPF   Parti populaire français (French Populist Party)

RG   Renseignements Généraux (General Intelligence, Vichy newsletter)

SD   Sicherheitsdienst (Security Service)

SEC   Service d'enquête et de contrôle (Service for Investigation and Control of the General Commission for Jewish Questions, CGQJ)

SER   Service d'évacuation et de regroupement (Zionist Service for Evacuation and Resettlement)

SFP   Service des faux papiers (False Documents Service), MLN

SOE   Special Operations Executive (British)

SOL   Service d'ordre de la Légion (Order Service of the Legion, Vichy paramilitary)

SSAE   Service social d'aide aux émigrants (Society for Aid to Immigrants)

STO   Service du travail obligatoire (Compulsory Labor Service)

UGIF   Union générale des israélites de France (General Union of Jews of France)

UJJ   Union de la jeunesse juive (Union of Jewish Youth)

UJRE   Union des Juifs pour la Résistance et l'entraide (Jewish Union for Resistance and Mutual Aid)

USJ   Union des sociétés juires (Union of Jewish Associations)

WJC   World Jewish Congress

WZO   World Zionist Organisation

YIVO   Yiddisher Wissenschaftlecher Institute (YIVO Institute for Jewish Research)

YMCA   Young Men's Christian Association

NOTES

Introduction

1. Salo Wittmeier Baron, *A Social and Religious History of the Jews* (New York: Columbia University Press, 1937), 1:30 f. Here the term "national" refers to the Jewish people.

2. André Lavagne, head of the Marshal's civil cabinet.

3. "The final solution must be achieved before the rest of the world raises a cry," as one highly placed Nazi official would put it. See chapter 9.

4. Reference is to what was called the "Pétain trunk" (*la malle Pétain*), which accompanied him to Singmaringen and was brought back to France on his return.

Prologue

1. The president of the federation, Marc Jarblum, was a member of the Socialist International and was on the executive of the French Section of the Workers International.

2. Later, during the resistance and under the name of Édouard Kowalski, he was one of the leading figures of the MOI (Main d'oeuvre immigrée), the reception agency within the French Communist Party for foreign workers.

3. The allusion is to the *Saint Louis*, loaded with refugees from Germany, which was turned away from one port after another. It then turned its course toward France in the hope that authorities would grant asylum to a certain number of the passengers. In fact, the *Saint Louis* docked in Boulogne-sur-Mer in late July 1939, where a few dozen families with young children were allowed to disembark.

4. Cf. David H. Weinberg, *Les Juifs de Paris de 1933 à 1939* (Paris: Calaman-Levy, 1974), 248. Remarkable for its objectivity and scholarly quality, this is the only book as of this writing to deal with the history of the Parisian Jews on the eve of the war.

5. "Unter di schtechldrotn" ("Behind the Barbed Wire"), no. 7 (14 July 1939), Saint-Cyprien Camp (David Diamant archives).

Chapter One. The First Anti-Jewish Measures: Dark Forebodings

1. "La France au palmarès hitlerien de l'antisémitisme," in *Témoignage chrétien, 1941–1944,* facsimile edition of the complete text, with a preface by Renée Bédarida (Paris, 1980).

2. In Germany, two successive laws had been drafted in haste, on the occasion of the congress of the National Socialist German Workers Party that met in Nuremberg in September 1935. Passed by the Reichstag on 14 November of that year, they defined as a "Jew" any person having at least three Jewish grandparents. Membership "in the Jewish religious community" determined the Jewish identity of the grandparents.

3. Centre de Documentation Juive Contemporaine (hereafter CDJC), doc. no. LXXV-71, cited in Joseph Billig, *Le Commissariat général aux questions juives (1941–1944)* (Paris: Éditions du Centre, 1955), 1:27.

4. Ibid.

5. Ibid., 28.

6. Undated German memorandum from the same period (August–September 1940) (CDJC, LXXV-70).

7. CDJC, LXXV-278.

8. The 36-page typed document covers the period from September 1940 to the spring of 1941. On the basis of the ideas presented and the vision of events, the author can be situated among the Zionist-Socialists grouped around the Amelot Committee (named after the street address where meetings took place. Fédération des sociétés juives de France (archives in the CDJC, DLXXXIX-1).

9. Ibid., p. 2.

10. The first German newsreels shown in Paris can be viewed today in the military film theater at Vincennes.

11. Thus, when Quirinus, the Roman legate in Syria (which included Palestine), decreed the census of people and inventory of goods and properties in the years 6 – 7 C.E., the Jewish people were filled with dark forebodings (S. W. Baron, *Histoire d'Israël,* 1:33 f.).

12. Amman, first minister of the Persian king Assuerus (fifth century B.C.E.), envisaged assuming power by exterminating all the Jews of the capital, Suza. His plot failed thanks to the intervention of Queen Esther. Although the historicity of the event is doubted, before Hitler the name Amman symbolized the most atrocious enemy of the Jews.

13. Henri Michel, *Paris Résistant* (Paris: Albin Michel, 1982), 27.

14. Anonymous, "Étude sur la situation des Juifs en zone occupée," 2. For Paul Valéry's funeral elogy, see Archives of the Consistoire Central, box 5.

15. From the tables published by Jacques Adler in *The Jews of Paris and the Final Solution: Communal Response and Internal Conflicts, 1940–1944* (New York: Oxford University Press, 1987), using materials in the Department of Demography at the Hebrew University of Jerusalem.

16. See Zosa Szajkowski, *Analytical Franco-Jewish Gazetteer, 1939–1945* (New York: privately published, 1966).

17. The Central Consistory of the Jews of France did not establish a regional delegation in Paris until the summer of 1943, when it was represented by the rabbinate. At the end of 1941, the Consistory in the Unoccupied Zone had regional delegations in seven cities: Lyon, Marseille, Toulouse, Grenoble, Clearmont-Ferrand, Brives, and Pau. See documentation in the Archives of the Central Consistory, Alliance box 16.

18. Jewish workers' mutual assistance organizations had existed in France since the end of the nineteenth century. Most of these were organized by "language," but in 1923 the French Communist Party (PCF) established a reception service for foreigners, initially called the Main d'oeuvre étrangère (Foreign labor force), and later renamed Main d'oeuvre immigrée (MOI—Immigrant Labor Association). In fact, the PCF used the phrase "language groups" in order not to say "nationalities," a juridical term that had no standing in Jacobin France.

19. Compared to other political currents in Jewish life, the Jewish Section of the MOI acted as an autonomous party, whence the frequent general use of the name "Jewish Communist Party."

20. "Étude . . . zone occupée," 35.

21. For the collaboration of police forces, see the conference paper by Jacques Delarue, at the Institut de l'Histoire du temps présent colloquium, Paris, 11–13 June 1990, printed in *Le Régime de Vichy et les Français* (Paris: Fayard, 1992).

22. Report of 25 August 1940 (CDJC, XXIV-4).

23. The reports of 7 and 28 October 1940, and of 10 January, 11 February, 8 March, and 17 March 1941, contain analyses and extracts from the newspaper *Unzer Wort* and from political tracts. In the absence of the collection of original texts, which disappeared during the arrests and apartment searches in the spring of 1941, these extracts, even though selective in nature, illuminate the thought of the editors of the paper (CDJC, LXVII-7, LXVII-15, LXXV-238). See also the holdings of the Bibliothèque nationale (Res. G 1472) (133). In the catalogue of underground publications, *Périodiques clandestins en France,* p. 189, appears the following remark: "Tendentious excerpts of German origin." It should also be noted that the numbering of the newspaper's issues began in October or November 1939, which explains how the 29 September 1940 issue has number 23.

24. Yad Vashem Archives, P7/1 and the report of *Renseignements généraux* ("General Intelligence") of 8 May 1941.

25. Ibid.

26. *Renseignements généraux* (CDJC, LVII-7).

27. This issue, like those to be cited in the following, is quoted from the archival holdings of the *Renseignements généraux* of the Prefecture of Police and was appended to the earlier cited police report of 8 May 1941.

28. Ibid.

29. CDJC, XXIV-33.

30. "Étude . . . zone occupée," 12.

31. The Einsatzgruppen were operational units of the SD charged with repression in general and more specifically with anti-Jewish actions. The Reinhard document is printed in Jewish Historical Institute of Poland, *Faschismus-Getto-Massenmord* (Warsaw, 1961), 37 (CDJC, CCCXVII-11).

32. Theodor Dannecker, "Judenfragen in Frankreich und ihre Behandlung," report in CDJC, XXVI-1.

33. See chapter 3.

Chapter Two. The Consistory between Religion and Politics

1. Observant Jews resented the absence of most of the rabbis as a desertion. "Étude . . . zone occupée," 16, and CDJC, DLXXXIX-1.

2. Archives of the Central Consistory, box 9. At this writing, the Consistory has not yet opened its archives for the period 1940–43, with the exception of six boxes that may be consulted at the Alliance israélite universelle (AIU) library since May 1991.

3. Cited in Jean-Pierre Azéma, *De Munich à la Liberation, 1938–1944* (Paris: Seuil, 1979), 106.

4. *Activités des organisations juives en France sous l'Occupation* (Paris: Éditions du Centre, 1947), 19.

5. CDJC, CCXIV-6.

6. Cf. J.-M. Chouraqui, "Patriotisme et judaïsme: la France dans le regard des Juifs français (1789 à nos jours)," *Pardès* 7 (1989).

7. French National Archives, 2 AG 617. This unpublished document was mentioned for the first time at the CDJC colloquium, "Il y a 50 ans: le Statut des Juifs de Vichy," Paris, 1 October 1990; see the proceedings published by the CDJC as *Actes du colloque* (Paris, 1991), 33 f.

8. The fully acculturated Jews whose families had been resident in France for generations preferred to call themselves *Israélites*, reserving the then slightly pejorative term *Juifs* for more recent immigrants. Interaction between the two terms is also apparent in the names of organizations and agencies. (Translator's note.)

9. It is thus that the objective of the anti-Jewish legislation is defined in the official communication which thereby sought to play down the severity of the law.

10. During the period between the wars, "invasion" is Charles Maurras's favorite word to designate the arrival of Jews from abroad.

11. Helbronner's document is not included in the portion of Central Consistory archives that is presently accessible.

12. Arthur Koestler, *La Lie de la terre* (Paris: Calmann-Levy, 1947), 260. First published in English as *The Scum of the Earth* (London: Hutchinson, 1941).

13. Robert Badinter develops this point with intelligence and flair in his closing address on the occasion of the colloquium on the bicentenary anniversary of Stras-

bourg: "We must always bear in mind that the emancipation of 27 September 1791 cannot be dissociated from what constitutes its foundation."

14. Archives of the Jewish Seminary of New York, box 14, and CDJC, XXXI A-48. The motion carried some forty names of members of the council of the Central Consistory. In the margin of the first page is a note by an official of the General Commissariat for Jewish Questions: "Submitted 30 June 1941 by Monsieur President Helbronner. To be filed."

15. 18 May 1941 session of the Council of the Consistory (Archives of the Central Consistory, box 5).

16. The handwritten text of the motion of confidence in Pétain carries the annotation "P. V., p. 9." It also figures as a separate item in box 5 of the archives of the Central Consistory along with a handwritten note by G. Leven.

17. Pastoral letter, 3 July 1941 (Jewish Theological Seminary, New York, box 14).

18. Ibid.

19. Created on 29 July 1940, it had Pétain as its president and its mission was to "promote the national revolution, defend it, and, if need be, impose it."

20. A Jewish member of the Legion, Léon Argoutine (card No. 2928 23), wrote to the head of the Legion to express his astonishment over the poster. He preferred to believe it resulted "from an omission." (Letter of 31 March 1941, Consistory Archives, box 16). It is not clear how he, as a Jew, joined the legion.

21. CDJC, XXXI-41.

22. Maurice Moch and Alain Michel, *L'Étoile et la francisque* (Paris: Éditions du Cerf, 1990), 84f.

23. Yad Vashem, P7/11.

24. *Journal officiel,* 19 July 1942 (CCXIV-6).

25. Private collection of Claude Urman.

26. CDJC, XXXI-42.

27. *Renseignements généraux,* Vichy, 29 May 1941 (CDJC, XXXI-47).

28. *Mémoire pour les dirigeants JOC* [Jeunesse ouvrière chrétienne—Christian working youth] *et la Conférence des travailleurs chrétiens* [Conference of Christian workers], undated.

29. Report from 29 May, 1941 (CDJC, XXXI-47).

30. Archives of the Central Consistory, box 67.

31. Ibid.

32. Author's emphasis.

33. Archives of the Central Consistory, box 9.

34. Ibid.

35. His brother Paul was a director with the iron and steel works (Société des forges et aciéries) in Pompey near Nancy.

36. See below, chapter 15.

37. Archives of the Central Consistory, AIU Library, box 9.

38. René Cassin, *Les Hommes partis de rien, le reveil de la France abattue* (Paris: Plon, 1974). See, too, Cassin, "Carnets—Journal de 1940" in the Cassin Archives,

38 Q AO 27. The remarks are cited by Claude Singer in "Des universitaires juifs dans la Résistance," a paper presented at the colloquium *Les Juifs dans la Résistance et la Libération* (Paris: Scribe, 1985), 71.

39. Jean Lacouture, *De Gaulle*, vol. 1, *Le Rebelle* (Paris: Seuil, 1984), 737.

40. Pierre-Louis Blanc, *De Gaule, au soir de sa vie* (Paris: Fayard, 1990), 117. A sizable group of fishermen from the Île de Sein had reached London by July of 1940. De Gaulle held them in high regard. The population of the island would be collectively named to the Order of Companions of the Liberation (L'Ordre des Compagnons de la Libération).

41. Daniel Cordier, *Jean Moulin* (Paris: J-C. Lattès, 1989), 1:41.

42. See, in this regard, Eliézer Yapou, "Pétainistes sans Pétain," *L'Arche* (July 1982).

43. Albert Cohen had important duties at the European office of the World Jewish Congress in Paris from 1938 to 1940. He left Paris during the exodus and took refuge in London (Archives of the World Jewish Congress, Geneva; the letter is reproduced in *40 années d'action, 1936–1976* [Geneva: Éditions du Congrès juif mondial, 1976]).

44. Message to Maurice Perlzweig, secretary general of the World Jewish Congress in New York, "through the good offices of the British Consulat General," New York (CDJC, exhibition, *Les Juifs dans la lutte contre le nazisme*, panel no. 1).

45. CDJC, CCXIV-104 (France libre, file B2935/1).

46. CDJC, exhibition, *Les Juifs dans la lutte contre le nazisme.*

47. Poster published in 1942 by the Institut d'étude des questions juives; reproduced in *La Propagande sous Vichy, 1940–1944*, a work published under the editorship of Laurent Gervereau and Denis Peschanski (Nanterre: BDIC, 1990), 193.

Chapter Three. Preliminaries to a Massacre

1. SS Obersturmführer Theodor Dannecker, "Les questions juives en France et leur treatment" (CDJC, XXVI-1).

2. On 29 April 1940 in Warsaw the Nazis gave the order to construct a wall around the ghetto.

3. Dannecker, "Questions juives."

4. Ibid.

5. The ORT and the OSE had been founded in Russia at the beginning of the century, the former for manual vocational training among the poor, the latter to promote health and hygiene. The Amelot Committee was responsible for the social activities of the Fédération des sociétés juives de France (FSJF—Federation of Jewish Societies of France) and had been created in the 1920s to unify a multitude of associations constituted along lines of national and local origin (Yiddish *landsman-shaften*): immigrants from Poland, Lithuania, and Bessarabia who had organized themselves by their original town or village (*shtetl*). The FSJF was within the Zionist-socialist

sphere of influence; its president from 1936 onward, Marc Jarblum, was one of the leading figures of the Second, or Socialist, International.

6. Szajkowski, *Analytical Franco-Jewish Gazetteer.* The Parisian Jews coined the phrase "little brown Jews" (*broïne yiddelech*), an allusion to the Nazi Brown Shirts, to designate Israelowicz and Biberstein.

7. Ibid.

8. The chief rabbi exposed himself to criticism for having, in a way, legitimized the paper by his message ("Étude . . . zone occupée"). The agreement of the Paris Consistory to assume responsibility for forming the coordinating committee was severely deplored by the Central Consistory of Lyon, which held the view that "it had cut itself off from the Parisian Jewish masses." (Szajkowski, *Analytical Franco-Jewish Gazetteer,* 53, n. 229).

9. Alliance israélite universelle library, P/150–P/151.

10. Dannecker, "Questions juives," (CDJC, XXVI-1).

11. Szajkowski, *Analytical Franco-Jewish Gazetteer,* 41, n. 183.

12. H. J. Kaufman, *Under the German Occupation in France* [in Yiddish] (Paris, 1964), 38. The manuscript of Bielinky's diary resides at the YIVO Archives in New York.

13. *Informations juives* 4 (9 May 1941) and 8 (6 June 1941).

14. On an order given by Aloïs Brunner, Austrian Jews would be deported beginning on 1 February 1941 to camps in Poland. Each convoy consisted of 1,000 persons, according to Simon Wiesenthal, *Le Livre de la mémoire juive* (Paris: Robert Laffont, 1986).

15. *Informations juives* 6 (23 May 1941).

16. Letter of 4 February 1942, cited by Bernard Friede, *Une mauvaise histoire juive* (Paris: Ramsay, 1991), 129f.

17. Billig, *Commissariat général,* 1:49f; and CDJC, V-63.

18. "The creation of the CGQJ is typical of all the essential acts of collaboration: the government publicly assumes an attitude of independence while carrying out a project imposed by the occupiers which, at the same time, fits conceptually into the logic of the French state regime." Billig, *Commissariat général,* 57.

19. A visceral antisemite and friend of the writer and the founder of the radically anti-Republic Action Française, Charles Maurras, he had always been on the extreme right as a deputy, and was characterized by his violent attacks against Léon Blum, whom he called alien to France because Jewish. He founded the Légion des combattants français before his appointment to the commissariat.

20. CDJC, XXIV-40.

21. CDJC, XXIV-15A.

22. CDJC, CXCV-184. *"J'accuse"* would, a year later, become the title of an underground newspaper.

23. Adler, *Jews of Paris,* ix.

24. Szajkowski, *Analytical Franco-Jewish Gazetteer,* 42, n. 188.

25. YIVO, Ug i-13. See, too, the report of the German police of 4 August 1941 (CDJC, LXXV-238).

26. On this subject, cf. Maurice Rajsfus, *Une terre promise* (Paris: L'Harmattan, 1960).

27. Letter of 19 June 1941 to the Marshal's civil cabinet from General Hutzinger, government delegate to the occupation authorities in Paris (AN, AG II-617).

28. Code name for the invasion of the USSR.

29. *The Black Book,* ed. Ilya Ehrenbrug and Vassili Grossman (Jerusalem: Yad Vashem, 1980); from the preface by Yitzak Arad, x.

30. Psalms 118:17, in Hebrew in the committee's text.

31. *Unzer Wort* 4 (1 September 1941), published in the unoccupied zone, reproduced in *Dos wort fun Widerstand un zig* (The Voice of Resistance and Victory), pref. A. Rayski (Paris: Éditions Renouveau, 1949), 43 f.; this is an anthology of underground journalism in Yiddish. The American press, particularly that in Yiddish, devoted considerable space to the action of the Einsatzgruppen on the basis of information transmitted from Moscow by the Jewish Telegraphic Agency. Cf. David S. Wyman, *L'Abandonnement des Juifs* (Paris: Flammarion, 1987), 39, where the author proves that those who wanted to know, knew.

32. Cf. Philippe Burrin, *Hitler et les Juifs. Genèse d'un génocide* (Paris: Seuil, 1989), 106 f.

33. Bulletin of the Jewish Telegraphic Agency, ca. September 1941.

34. Ibid.

Chapter Four. The Creation of the UGIF, the "Compulsory Community"

1. Primo Levi, preface to Jacques Presser, *La Nuit des Girondins* (Paris: Maurice Nadeau, 1990).

2. In his text "What Are We To Do?" which served as a manifesto for the Armée juive; see below, chapter 16.

3. CDJC, LXXVI-16; see also Billig, *Commissariat général,* 211–14.

4. Ibid.

5. Lavagne would play an influential role after the war as the legal counsel for the French episcopate; he was intimately involved in the defense during the "Touvier Affair." See *Paul Touvier et l'Eglise,* the report of the *Commission historique* instituted by Cardinal Decourtray and under the direction of René Rémond (Paris: Fayard, 1992).

6. Raymond-Raoul Lambert was an editorial writer with *L'Univers israélite* during the 1930s, the organ of the Alliance israelite universelle, and was similarly engaged in the activities of the CAR, created in 1934 to receive refugees from Germany.

7. Szajkowski, *Analytical Franco-Jewish Gazetteer,* 130.

8. Notes taken by the lawyer Lubetzki (FSJF) during a meeting with "Monsieur X" on 14 February 1942 (Yad Vashem, 09/22–3).

9. 24 October, 1941, meeting of the Commission centrale des œuvres juives d'assistance (CCOJA), created in Marseille on 30 October 1940, on the initiative of Rabbi Hirschler (CDJC, CCXIII-73).

10. "Rapport du Consistoire central. Sur la création de l'UGIF," in Szajkowski, *Analytical Franco-Jewish Gazetteer,* 128, and CDJC, CCXIII-10.

11. This summary is based on the report of R.-R. Lambert, "Mes voyages à Vichy," in Szajkowski, *Analytical Franco-Jewish Gazetteer,* 125.

12. Szajkowski, *Analytical Franco-Jewish Gazetteer,* 130.

13. The "solidarity funds" would come from Aryanization and economic despoliation.

14. Letter to Pétain, 8 December 1941 (Archives of the Central Consistory, AIU Library, box 5). In fact, the Dalloz legal dictionary defines "public institution" (*établissement public*) as follows: "Entity in public law possessing a juridical identity and charged with the administration of a public service activity within the limited framework of its specialization."

15. CDJC, CDX-8. One notes that René Cassin always disputed the legitimacy of the Marshal's legislative actions, contending that the National Assembly could not legally delegate plenary power to him (see Jean-Pierre Azéma, *De Munich à la Liberation, 1938–1944* [Paris: Seuil, 1979], 83).

16. CDJC, CCXIII-10.

17. R.-R. Lambert writes that André Weil, "the Young Turk of the Consistory," called him "Vallat's Quisling": *Carnet d'un témoin, 1940–1943* (Paris: Fayard, 1985).

18. *L'Activité des organisations juives en France sous l'Occupation* (Paris: CDJC, 1947), 205.

19. 1 February 1942 (CDJC, XXVIIIa, 220).

20. See Jean-Louis Couveliez, *Histoire du mouvement Combat en Haute-Garonne* (master's thesis, Université de Toulouse-Le Mirail, 1987).

21. Among these may be mentioned Benjamin Crémieux, an author; Dr. Max Aron, of the University of Strasbourg; Paul Grunebaum-Ballin, honorary member of the Conseil d'État; Marcel Lisbonne, professor in the University of Medicine in Montpellier; and Raymond Milhaud, former president of the Order of the Bar in Nice. For the complete list, see Marc Bloch, *L'Étrange défaite* (Paris: Gallimard, 1990), 319–21.

22. "*France libre,*" 1 May 1942, File B/2935/1 (CDJC, CCXIV-75).

23. For the trajectory of these men in the Resistance, see below, chapter 15.

24. CDJC, CDX-8.

25. André Chouraqui, *Cent ans d'histoire. L'Alliance israélite universelle et la renaissance juive contemporaine, 1860–1960* (Paris: Presses Universitaires de France, 1965), 278.

26. The subject of the letter: "Bank deposits of the Alliance israélite." Handwritten notes in the margins give the following: "in the Banque de Paris, 1,500,000 francs; in the Comptoir d'Escompte (for the agricultural training school in Tunisia), 1,500,000 francs; and 1,225,000 for the École normale in Vallat coupons." The nature of the last mentioned is not known, unless it was a sum "borrowed" by the commission against vouchers signed by Vallat.

27. Chouraqui, *Cent ans d'histoire,* 278.

28. *La France continue* Collection (Archives de la Seine). Paul Petit, a friend of the writers Paul Claudel and Max Jacob (himself a Jewish convert to the Catholic Church who died in 1944 as a result of the sufferings he underwent in Drancy), was one of the first "socially-minded Catholics" to denounce collaboration and the persecution of the Jews.

29. See Jean-Louis Crémieux-Brilhac, "René Cassin et la France libre," *Les Nouveaux cahiers* 92 (spring 1988).

30. Yad Vashem Archives, 09/29. The text has three sections, whose headings speak eloquently of the author's concerns: "Aspects of Governmental Antisemitism," "Its Consequences," and "Deportations from Compiègne." Louis Kahn was born in Versailles in 1895. Chief engineer in the French navy, from 1928 to 1938 he led the Technical Department of the Ministry of the Air Force. Forced out of the Navy by Vichy, he joined de Gaulle in London in summer 1942. De Gaulle appointed him director of naval construction.

31. This is a line of reasoning that still maintains its vigor in the face of revisionist arguments that seek to exculpate the French and shift responsibility for the Holocaust in France onto the Germans alone.

32. The first convoy left Compiègne on 27 March 1942 with 1,112 men and included 550 Jews who had been arrested on 12 December 1941, a reprisal for certain assassination attempts against German occupation officers.

33. Recollection of his son Pierre, Paris, January 1990.

34. Federation minutes (Jarblum Papers, Yad Vashem). "Some even believe that it is neither more nor less than the continuation of the *kehillah*." Cf. Henri Minczeles, *Vilna, Wilno, Vilnius—la Jérusalem de Lithuanie* (Ph.D. thesis, École des hautes études en science sociale, Paris 1991). Subsequently published by Éditions la découverte, 1993.

35. Yad Vashem, P 7/4; and CDJC, CCXIII-54.

36. Yad Vashem, M. 20/85.

37. *Le Pilori*, an ultra-collaborationist and antisemitic publication, effectively called for the establishment of a "central Jewish committee." *Das wort fun Widerstand un zig*, 65.

38. *Unzer Kamf*, undated (YIVO Archives, New York).

39. Ibid. The American Jewish Joint Distribution Committee (AJJDC or "Joint") was created in the United States in November 1914 to aid Jewish communities in Europe suffering from the war. From 1939 to 1945 it spent a total of $78,878,000 in occupied Europe.

40. Szajkowski, *Analytical Franco-Jewish Gazetteer,* 132.

Chapter Five. The Yellow Star: Stigmatize, Humiliate, and Isolate the Jews

1. Personal diary ("Carnet intime") of Daniel Darès; see below, n. 8.

2. "Instead of emigration there now appears a further possible solution [to the Jewish Question], after the prior authorization of the Führer, viz., evacuation of the Jews

to the East." Minutes of the Wannsee Conference (copy sixteen); reproduced in Hans-Jürgen Döscher, *Das auswärtige Amt im Dritten Reich* (Berlin: Siedler Verlag, 1987), 231.

3. This was the first issue of *J'accuse,* which after September 1942 became the organ of the Mouvement national contre le racisme (MNCR—National Movement against Racism), created by the Jewish Section of the MOI during the July 1942 round-ups. A copy of the paper seized by the police on the rue de Vaugirard in Paris and transmitted to the Minister of the Interior in Vichy was recently rediscovered by Denis Peschanski in the Tasca Archives, Feltrinelli Foundation, Milan (cf. Stéphane Courtois, Adam Rayski, et al. *Qui savait quoi? L'Extermination des Juifs, 1941–1945* (Paris: La Découverte, 1987).

4. Weekly reports in the *Renseignements généraux,* henceforth *RG,* Historical Archives of the Paris Prefecture of Police (AHPP).

5. Ibid.

6. Knochen to Reichs Security Main Office, 16 June 1942 (CDJC, XLIXa-90).

7. *RG,* 15 June 1942 (AHPP).

8. Daniel Darès, manuscript, "Carnet intime," undated. It is no fluke that those former children saved by the Union des Juifs pour la résistance et l'entraide (UJRE—Union of Jews for Resistance and Mutual Aid) or the Mouvement nationale contre le racisme (MNCR) should have chosen him [Darés] as president of their association, L'Amicale des Anciens des Foyers de la Comité Centrale de l'Enfance, founded in 1988 with about two hundred members.

9. Report from Paris to the Federation in the Southern Zone, unsigned (CDJC, CCXIV-5).

10. *Brodati,* "the bearded one" in Polish. The reference is no doubt to David Rappoport, head of the Amelot Committee.

11. Pierre Limagne, *Éphémerides de quatre années tragiques* (Paris: Editions de Candide, 1987), 1:593.

12. Protestant Federation, 11 June 1942 (CDJC, XXII-12).

13. Ibid.

14. Vercors, *La Marche à l'étoile* (Paris: Minuit, 1943), 71–72 (new edition, Paris: Minuit, 1992.)

15. Limagne, *Éphémeridas,* 1:584. The note is accompanied by the following commentary: "The Frenchman can rightly be recognized by a certain way of taking the side of the persecuted against the persecutors."

16. Archives of the Central Consistory, box 6.

17. Ibid.

18. *La Documentation catholique,* 42:124 f.

19. "Note sur le problème juif," undated, Archives nationales, 2AG 495.

20. Letter of 27 November 1942, written in German. The letter contains the names, dates of birth, and addresses of the persons in question. Authorization was given three days later (CDJC, XXVa-166).

21. Request submitted on 7 September 1942; positive reply on 23 November (CDJC, XXVa-167).

22. The letter appears to have provoked Dr. Ménétrel, head of the personal secretariat of the Marshal, who annotated it with the following in large letters, heavily underlined three times: "A Jew typical of the race." Is this notation a response to the ingratiating politeness Jean S.'s letter to Pétain's wife?: "I place at your feet, Madame, the expression of my most respectful homage." The antisemites despised all Jews to be sure, but certainly the obsequious still more. (Archives nationales II-82.)

23. Report of 28 February 1942, printed in Serge Klarsfeld, *Vichy-Auschwitz*, vol. 1 (Paris: Fayard, 1983–85), 1:196.

24. At the beginning of spring, 37,000 boxcars and 1,000 locomotives were withdrawn from the rolling stock of France. (CDJC, RF 1218.)

25. The figure was set by Eichmann and Dannecker on 11 June in Berlin (Klarsfeld, *Vichy-Auschwitz*, 100).

26. Minutes taken by Hagen (CDJC, XXV-b 49).

27. Abetz telegram to Ministry of Foreign Affairs in Berlin, 2 July 1942. (CDJC, XLIXa-41).

28. The first convoy included 550 French Jews, the second about 100.

29. Archives nationales, III 1A2–7.

30. Laval's observations in the "handwritten notes" appended to the minutes of the meeting of the Council of Ministers on 3 July 1942. (Archives nationales, III 1A2–9.)

31. Michael R. Marrus, "Vichy et les enfants juifs," *L'Histoire* 22 (April 1980).

32. Circular letter no. 173–42, signed by Hennequin, superintendent of municipal police. (Original in the private collection of Claude Urman.) Émile Hennequin was sentenced to eight years' imprisonment after the war.

33. Ibid.

34. Jacques Bielinky, "Journal, 1940–1942," manuscript in the YIVO Archives, New York.

Chapter Six. July 1942: The Great Roundup and the First Acts of Resistance

1. Yad Vashem, 09/6-1.

2. CDJC, XXVIII-31a.

3. *Dos wort fun Widerstand un zig*, 105.

4. Claude Lévy and Paul Tillard, *La Grande rafle du Vél' d'hiv'* (Paris: Robert Laffont, 1967), 30.

5. Interview with Henry Bulawko, August 1990. The Amelot Committee was not informed by the UGIF but, after learning that its staff was working on the preparation of numbered labels, they suspected that raids were forthcoming (see also Adler, *Jews of Paris*).

6. Israël Belchatowski, *Fun a lebn was is mer nicht do* ["From a life that is no longer"] (Tel Aviv: Édition J. L. Peretz, 1975), 159–72; also quoted in Klarsfeld, *Vichy-Auschwitz*, 518.

7. Daniel Darès, excerpt from his unpublished *Carnets intimes*.

8. Belchatowski, *Fun a lebn*, 159–72.

9. Lévy and Tillard, *Grande rafle*, 30.

10. Ibid.

11. Clandestinely published by Solidarité and the MNCR in August–September 1942, the first account of "Black Thursday."

12. Darès, "Carnets intimes." [Editor's note: The word "raifen" does not exist in German; Darès must have mistaken it for something else.]

13. Report from the *RG* (historical archives of the Prefecture of Police; also in Klarsfeld, *Vichy-Auschwitz*, 261 f.).

14. Report of Heinz Röthke, CDJC, XXVb-80.

15. A. Rayski, *Nos illusions perdues* (Paris: Balland, 1985), 94. See also Léon Chertok, Isabelle Stengers, and Didier Gille, *Mémoires d'un héritique* (Paris: La Découverte, 1991), 84 f.

16. *Presse antiraciste*, 47–53.

17. Archives Nationales, 2 AG 495.

18. Testimony of Sarah Lichtsztein in Serge Klarsfeld, ed., *Letttres de Louise Jacobson* (Paris: FFDJF and CDJC, 1989). Sarah and her mother, denounced as underground activists in May 1944—two months before the Liberation—were deported to Auschwitz, but did survive.

19. Written testimony, Paris, 10 December 1963 (CDJC, DLXXVII-7a).

20. Lucie Aubrac, "De l'engagement instinctif à la mort apprivoisée," in *Le Courage. En connaissance de causes* 6 (Paris: February 1992).

21. The actors here are the wife and son of the author: see Rayski, *Nos illusions perdues*, 96 f.

22. Written testimony, Paris, 9 January 1964, unsigned (CDJC, DLXXVII-7c).

23. Written testimony, Paris, 17 January 1964 (CDJC, DLXXVII-7b).

24. CDJC, CCXIV-5.

25. Testimony of Mathilde Jaffé, January 1990.

26. Handwritten report in Yiddish (original document at CDJC, DLXIX-8).

27. Interview, August 1990.

28. Röthke's report (CDJC, XXVB-80).

29. Prefecture of Police, municipal police headquarters, note of 20 July 1942. AN, CJ 447, cited in Klarsfeld, *Vichy-Auschwitz*, 1:271 f.

30. Testimony of Madame X, former supervisor at the center on Rue Lamarck, who chose to remain anonymous.

31. Testimony in Denise Baumann, *La Mémoire des oubliés* (Paris: Albin Michel, 1988). Denise Baumann, who died in August 1988, left a manuscript of a play devoted to the life of Larissa Wouzek.

32. August–October 1942 report, from the *RG*, Historical Archives of the Prefecture of Police (AHPP).

33. Report by the Prefecture of Police, 17 July 1942 (AHPP).

34. August–October 1942, Weekly reports from the RG (AHRR), 19 July 1942.

35. Ibid.

36. *Unzer Politik* ("Our Policy"), document in Yiddish, August 1942. See *Dos wort fun Widerstand un zig*, 117–24.

37. *Le Patriote résistant* (November 1984).

38. Henri Michel at the Yad Vashem colloquium on the Jewish resistance, Jerusalem, April 1968.

39. Pierre Laborie, "Le statut des Juifs de Vichy," in *Actes du colloque du CDJC*, 1 October 1990, 77.

40. *La Propagande sous Vichy*, 11. Sarah Boruchowicz's letter was found in the archives of the Secours national. Extracts, accompanied by the commentary of David Knout, appear in *Le Monde juif* 1 (August 1946).

Chapter Seven. The Inhuman Hunt in the Southern Zone

1. Denis Peschanski, "La France, terre des camps?" in K. Bartosek, R. Galissot, and D. Peschanksi, eds., *De l'exil à la résistance* (Paris: Presses Universitaires de Vincennes et Arcantère, 1989).

2. Léon Daudet in *Action Française* of 28 April 1933, cited in Ralph Schor, *L'Opinion française et les étrangers, 1919–1939* (Paris: Publications de la Sorbonne, 1985), 623.

3. Zosa Szajkowski lists some thirty names, among them Lion Feuchtwanger, Bruno Frei, André Breton, Max Ernst, and Gustav Regler. Many have left memoirs of the period of internment (*Analytical Franco-Jewish Gazetteer*, 18, n. 32). Feuchtwanger's *Devil in France: My Encounter with Him in the Summer of 1940* (New York: Viking, 1941), though it is not without minor errors of fact, deserves special notice.

4. Koestler, *Lie de la terre*, 183. The title, "The Scum of the Earth," was taken from an odious xenophobic article published with the first internments after the beginning of the war. The English-language version of Koestler's book was published in London by Hutchinson in 1941.

5. Anne Grynberg, *Les Camps de la honte. Les internés juifs des camps français, 1939–1945* (Paris: La Découverte, 1991), 270.

6. Ibid., 274.

7. Koestler, *Lie de la terre*; Lion Feuchtwanger reports that some internees used their last resources trying to get cyanide.

8. Some historians argue that this expulsion constitutes evidence the "Final Solution" had not yet been envisaged, and that Berlin was still contemplating the emigration of the Jews under the "Madagascar Plan" that envisioned a "reservation" for Jews on that island.

9. CDJC, CCXV-40.

10. Weill letter to Rabbi Hirschler, 26 May 1941. Departmental archives of Alpes-de-Haute-Provence, 6J12, quoted by Grynberg, *Les Camps*.

11. Vichy, telegram 2765P, 4 August 1942.

12. CDJC, CCXIV-69. Published in the bulletin of the CNI (Commission national pour l'information), *France libre* (London) 10 (1942).

13. Klarsfeld, *Vichy-Auschwitz* 1:318 f.

14. Ibid., 1:356.

15. An interdenominational organization with its seat in Nîmes. It assembled together Catholic, Protestant, and Jewish agencies as well as most of the American and Swiss humanitarian organizations tolerated in unoccupied France (a grand total of twenty-five). YMCA representative Donald Lowrie established the committee in November 1940 with the authorization of Vichy to coordinate aid to detainees in the South of France.

16. See William L. Langer, *Our Vichy Gamble* (New York: Knopf, 1947). The "gamble" ended on 11 November 1942 with the Wehrmacht's invasion of the Southern Zone.

17. Szajkowski, *Analytical Franco-Jewish Gazetteer*, 119.

18. Lion Feuchtwanger escaped disguised as a woman and then boarded a ship in Marseille under a false identity. Other intellectuals and artists who escaped with the help of Fry and his network include Jacques Lipchitz, André Breton, Max Ernst, Heinrich Mann and his wife Golo Mann, and Hannah Arendt. Sick and in poor physical condition, the philosopher and literary critic Walter Benjamin, fearing that the Spanish would refuse him entry, took his own life in the border town of Port Bou rather than face extradition to France.

19. Varian Fry, *Surrender on Demand* (New York: Random House, 1945); and Daniel Benedite, *La Filière marseillaise. Un chemin vers la liberté sous l'Occupation* (Paris: Clancier Guenaud, 1984). Also Grynberg, *Les Camps*, 190 f.

20. Archivio storico del ministero degli Affari esteri, Francia, busta 52, cited in Jan E. Zamojski,"La Résonance de l'insurrection du Ghetto," *Acta Poloniae Historica* 54 (Warsaw, 1986), 121.

21. Henri Manen's text is printed in Jacques Granjonc and Theresia Grundiner, eds., *Zone d'ombres, 1933–1944* (Aix-en-Provence: Alinéa et Erca, 1990), 354–75.

22. Testimony in *Les Camps du silence,* a film by Bernard Mangiante (Paris: Production les Films d'ici-La Sept, 1989).

23. In Szajkowski, *Analytical Franco-Jewish Gazetteer* 120 f.

24. Ibid., 118.

25. CDJC, CCXIII-111.

26. Szajkowski, *Analytical Franco-Jewish Gazetteer* 80, n. 427.

27. Ibid, 80., n. 430.

28. YIVO, HIAS-HICEM Archives, F. 31.

29. Testimony in the film *Les Camps du silence.*

30. Ibid. In April–May 1992 Elsbeth Kasser curated an exhibition in Martigny, Switzerland, of drawings by children at the Gurs camp.

31. Joseph Weill, *Contributions à l'histoire des camps d'internement dans l'anti-France* (Paris: Éditions du Centre, 1946), 177; see also, A. Rayski, "L'UGIF et le CRIF: Les choix de la communauté," *Pardès* 6 (January 1988).

32. Grynberg, *Les Camps.*

33. Archives of the Central Consistory, AIU Library, box 7. In *L'Étoile et la francisque,* 57–59, this text is presented as a resolution of the Central Consistory, a resolution that was never ever acted on, neither in spirit nor letter, unless it was after the creation of the CRIF at the beginning of 1944. Zosa Szajkowski attributes it to the CCOJA (*Analytical Franco-Jewish Gazetteer* 53, n. 22), which seems more correct.

34. Report from the 16th Gendarme Legion (Hérault, Avignon, Lozère, Tarn, Aude, Pyrénées-Orientales), no. 161/4, 27 September 1942.

35. October 1942 (AN 2AG 492).

36. The Rev. Boegner, "Lettre au maréchal," 20 August 1942 (AN, AG II). Rabbi Salzer's remarks are cited in Grynberg, *Les Camps,* 308.

37. Klarsfeld, *Vichy-Auschwitz,* 349.

38. Opening address of Professor Ady Steg at the Meeting between Catholics and Jews, Geneva, 22 July 1986 (*Les Cahiers de l'Alliance israélite universelle,* 220 [February 1990]: 7 f.).

39. Cited by Pierre Truche, public prosecutor in the Paris court of appeals, in "La notion de crime contre l'humanité. Bilan et proposition," *Esprit* 181 (Paris, 1992).

40. For example, a letter from Geneva, addressed to Joseph Fischer in Lyon, intercepted by the postal services, which describes the massacre of Jews of Iași, Romania. AN, 2 AG-4965.

41. See below, chapter 9.

42. Kiefe notes: "Letters to be written . . . to Jardin to provide him with details on the massacre of 11,000 Jews in Poland by means of toxic gas." Did he ever write this letter? We cannot give an answer until access is provided to all the archives of the Central Consistory.

43. See Milton Dank, *The French against the French* (New York, 1974), 234. See also R. de Felice, *Storia degli Ebrei italiani sotto il fascismo* (Milano: Einaudi, 1961); and Michael R. Marrus and Robert Paxton, *Vichy et les Juifs* (Paris: Calmann-Levy, 1981), 291.

44. Meeting on 2 September 1942 between Laval and Oberg, the SS and Police Leader.

45. *Fraternité* 3 (February 1943).

46. "Lettre de S. E. l'archevêque de Toulouse sur la personne humaine," reprinted in *Presse antiraciste,* 271.

47. Ibid., 273.

48. Charles de Gaulle, *Lettres, notes et carnets* (Paris: Plon, 1980), 2:277 f. Also in Charles-Louis Foulon, "La France combattante devant la persécution des Juifs," paper presented at the CDJC colloquium and published in *La France et la question juive* (Paris: Sylvie Messinger, 1981), 331–43.

49. The letter was disseminated by the Toulouse section of the MNCR. See the contribution by Denis Peschanski, "Que savaient les Français," in Stéphane Courtois and Adam Rayski, eds., *Qui savait quoi?* 85 f.

50. CDJC, CIX-127.

51. Interview with Renée Bédarida, May 1990.

52. François and Renée Bédarida, "L'Église catholique sous Vichy: Une mémoire troublée," *Esprit* 181 (May 1992).

53. Free French Information Service.

54. CDJC, CCXXI-73.

55. Claude Vigée, *La Lune d'hiver* (Paris: Flammarion, 1970), 65.

56. Charles Lederman, director of the Lyon center of the OSE, was linked politically to the Lyon organization of Solidarité (MOI), and in September of 1942 assumed responsibility for the MNCR in the Southern Zone.

57. Klarsfeld, *Vichy-Auschwitz*, 399.

58. 1 September 1942, quoted in ibid., 400.

59. Reports of the 14th Legion of the National Police of 29 September and 4 October 1942 (nos. 161/4 and 175/4). The tract is signed "MNCR": "These children are under the protection of the Church. They enjoy the sacred law of right to asylum. And here we have the Vichy regime calling for their extradition. French mothers and fathers! Will you allow this odious crime to happen?" (*Presse antiraciste*, 211).

60. AN-AGII-82.

61. AN-AGII-82. What Lavagne thought of the militiaman Touvier was expressed in a few words: "A Frenchman over whom the cloak of oblivion should fall." (Cf. Rémond et al., *Paul Touvier et l'Église*, 171 f.). Cf. chapter 4, n. 5.

62. *Témoignage chrétien* 1 (16 November 1941). It was written by Father Gaston Fessard.

63. Cf. Léon Poliakov, *Bréviaire de la haine* (Paris: Calmann-Levy, 1951).

64. "Mémoire de la résistance catholique," undated. AN, AGII-83.

Chapter Eight. Drancy: The Last Circle before Hell

1. *Di Yiddishe shtime* ("The Jewish Voice"), an illegal newspaper published jointly by Solidarité and the Amelot Committee, beginning in the summer of 1941. Publication was interrupted for security reasons when members of the Amelot Committee refused to "go underground" because that move would risk a cut-off of the subsidies from the American Jewish Joint Distribution Committee.

2. Some people saw here the hand of the co-opted staff seeking to delay their own departure.

3. Recounted by Szymon Fuchs to the author.

4. Reproduced in *La Presse antiraciste*, 39 f.

5. Testimony, December 1990.

6. Yves Jouffa would become the tenth president of the League for the Rights of Man, serving from 1981 to 1991. The group from Compiègne was part of the sweep of seven hundred and fifty intellectuals and prominent figures arrested by the German police on 14 December 1941.

344 | Notes to Pages 128–138

7. Cf. Maurice Rajsfus, *Drancy, un camp de concentration très ordinaire, 1941–1944* (Paris: Manya, 1991), 205. (The missing document would have had file number DXXXIV-79.)

8. Thomas Wajcman (prisoner No. 9299, stair 20, block V, cell 11) Drancy, 28 January 1942, Wajcman family archives.

9. She was suspected of communist activity, and she was arrested by the same special brigade that was hunting down the Jewish Section of the MOI.

10. Nadia Kaluski-Jacobson, ed., *Les lettres de Louise Jacobson et de ses proches: Fresnes, Drancy 1942–1943* (Paris: Robert Laffont, 1997); Klarsfeld, *Lettres de Louise Jacobson*. Louise was deported on 13 February 1943 in convoy no. 48, her mother on 20 November 1943 in convoy no. 69. Neither was to return. The "Letters" were dramatized and staged by Alain Gintzburger, and read with a great deal of talent by Juliette Battle in 1991 at the Marie-Stuart Theater in Paris and at the Avignon Theater Festival in July 1991.

11. Denise Baumann, *Une famille pas comme les autres* (Paris: Albin Michel, 1985).

12. The camp was named for the township near Toul (Meurthe-et-Moselle).

13. Author's emphasis.

14. *La Vie de la MOI* (organ of the central commission), 3 (1942–43), denounced the scheme in these terms: "At present . . . the Gestapo and so-called French police are busy recruiting spies among the weaker elements, whom they then release from the camps and use to snoop among fellow Jews who are in hiding."

15. Chief rabbi of Nancy, Paul Haguenauer, and his wife, Noémie.

16. Fride, *Une mauvaise historie juive*, 138–40.

17. It is not impossible that Brunner was motivated by a desire to take revenge on them for their attachment to France.

18. Testimony, December 1990.

19. Étienne Rosenfeld, *De Drancy à ces camps dont on ne parle pas* (Paris: L'Harmattan, 1991).

20. Written testimony, February 1992.

21. To be found in S. Courtois, D. Peschanski, and A. Rayski, *Le Sang de l'étranger* (Paris: Fayard, 1989), 356. The last meeting of Hanele Rajman with her two sons took place at a police station. Marcel was felled by the bullets of an execution squad in the Affiche rouge (Red Poster) Incident; the mother and Simon would be deported.

22. Letter communicated by Henri Minczeles, who has the author's thanks.

23. Jean-Marie Lustiger, *Le choix de Dieu: Entretiens avec Jean-Louis Missika et Dominique Wolton* (Paris: Éditions de Fallois, 1987), 76.

24. David Diamant, *Par-delà les barbelés* (Paris, 1986), 47.

25. Georges Wellers, *L'Étoile juive à l'heure de Vichy* (Paris: Fayard, 1973), 228.

26. J. Darville and S. Wichené, *Drancy-la-Juive* (Paris: Bregère Frères, 1945).

27. Courtois, Peschanski, Rayski, *Sang de l'étranger*, 273–301.

28. Diamant, *Par-delà les barbelés*, 163. In addition, Dr. Bacicurinski pointed out in a letter of 6 October 1943 that his comrades from the organization's leadership

would be in truck No. 19 in the event that it were possible to attack it on the road between the camp and the railway station in Bobigny.

29. On the tunnel scheme, see Rajsfus, *Drancy*, 323–32. Rajsfus' work is a well-documented inquiry into a number of details that had remained obscure prior to the publication of his book. See also André Ullmo (a survivor), "Témoignage sur la résistance," *Le Monde juif* 3–4 (September 1964).

30. See chapter 3, above.

31. *Situation à Drancy au 15 juillet 1943* (CDJC, CCXXI-19).

32. R. S. Kapel, *Un rabbin dans la tourmente, 1940–1944* (Paris: CDJC, 1985), 147.

33. "J'ai connu la terreur de Drancy," *Paris Hébdo*, 26 March 1946.

34. Aloïs Brunner took Reich with him when he left Drancy on 17 July 1944. On 8 and 9 February 1949, *Le Monde* published information on the trial and execution of Oskar Reich.

35. Lambert, *Carnet d'un témoin*, 59.

36. Testimony of Jacques London, May 1990.

37. Testimony of Henry Bulawko, August 1990.

38. Testimony of Yvette Bernard-Farnoux as reported by Anne Grynberg, *Les Juifs dans la Résistance*, 106 f.

39. Georges Wellers, 222.

40. CDJC, XXXI-87.

41. Letter from the CGQJ to the Préfecture de police, 12 March 1943 (CDJC, XXXI-87).

42. CDJC, CDXXXIV-44 and A. N AJ 40–548.

43. Diamant, *Par-delà les barbélés*, 114–20.

44. Yad Vashem, P7/1.

Chapter Nine. "Night and Fog": The Battle against Silence

1. Note from the *Judenreferat* Franz Rademacher to the German Ministry of Foreign Affairs on 24 March 1942. Quoted in Hans-Jürgen Döscher, *Das Auswärtige Amt im Dritten Reich. Diplomatie im Schatten der "Endlosung"* (Berlin: Siedler Verlag, 1987), 213.

2. Léon Poliakov, *Chronique du ghetto de Varsovie* (Paris: Robert Laffon, 1959), 309.

3. In *Presse antiraciste*, 45–53.

4. Letter of 21 July 1942, signed by Gaston Kahn (CDJC, CCXIV-6, and the document collection of the Beresniak family).

5. Jean-Claude Favez, *Une mission impossible? Le CICR, les déportations et les camps de concentration nazis* (Lausanne: Payot, 1988), 98 f., with Squire's text in French translation. The original is reproduced in the English version in John and Beryl Fletcher, eds., *The Red Cross and the Holocaust* (New York: Cambridge University Press, 1999), 293–94, and has been incorporated here.

6. Ibid.

7. "This service is carefully organized with a card index and file system." A number of the addressees, affirms the scrupulous bureaucrat R.-R. Lambert, could not be reached. These were requested "to supply the necessary information with all haste in order to make it possible to expedite this correspondence" (CDJC, CCXXI-26).

8. Archives of the Central Consistory in the AIU Library, box 67.

9. Testimony of a deportee (CJDC, CCX VI-91).

10. *J'accuse* 9 (5 February 1943) (*Qui savait quoi?* p. 170).

11. CDJC, XXV-184, and CDJC, CCXIII-15, pp. 1–2.

12. Yad Vashem, 09/10.

13. Archives of the Central Consistory, box 67.

14. *Le Monde juif* 49 (January–March 1968). Wormser's letter was a response to the article in the preceding issue by Adam Rayski, "Contre la nuit et le brouillard."

15. Szajkowski, *Analytical Franco-Jewish Gazetteer,* 36, n. 152.

16. Session of the Permanent Section, 28 December 1942. Archives of the Central Consistory, AIU Library, box 67.

17. Szajkowski, *Analytical Franco-Jewish Gazetteer,* 53.

18. Koestler, *Lie de la terre,* 266. In an overwrought polemic, Simon Schwarzfuchs (*Pardès* 11 [1990]) rhetorically criticizes Courtois and Rayski for having written in *Qui savait quoi?* that the Consistory had not taken care to disseminate news of the extermination of the Jews. It was ignorant of any such measure, and acted in good faith. At that time (1990), the archives of the Consistory were not accessible, except to Schwarzfuchs. We may note that his contribution to the debate would have been much more useful if he had studied the reasons for the astonishing silence of the Consistory, which later never made the slightest reference to the extermination plan that was being implemented, or to the reasons for its overly prolonged attitude of submission to anti-Jewish legislation. The real problem of "knowing" is to be found here.

19. Interview with Gerhart Riegner, Geneva, June, 1989.

20. WJC Archives, formerly in Geneva, now in the Central Zionist Archives, Jerusalem.

21. Riegner interview, June 1989.

22. See chapter 3.

23. *J'accuse,* 2 (20 October 1942).

24. Ringelblum, *Chronique du ghetto de Varsovie,* 308 f. Ringelblum, born in 1900, was a brilliant historian. He began keeping his chronicle in January 1940, three months after the start of the Occupation. He created a kind of brotherhood, the OS (*Oneg Shabbat*), to establish archives of the ghetto, which consisted of information supplied by numerous associates. A large portion of archive was recovered from beneath the ruins of the ghetto, where it was buried at the time of the rising.

25. Excerpt from the "Remerciement" of B. Poirot-Delpech at the Académie Française on 29 January 1987 (*Le Monde* [1–2 February 1987]). Silbermann is the hero of the famous novel by Jacques de Lacretelle, whose chair B. Poirot-Delpech assumed at the Académie (Jacques de Lacretelle, *Silbermann* [Paris: Gallimard, 1922]). We read there on p. 123: "It was a charcoal sketch with a coarse caricature of Silber-

mann. . . . Underneath was written: *Death to the Jews.* No, things like this could not be effaced. The least word of reconciliation seemed to me a disavowal."

26. Youra Riskine was born a French national on 11 April 1928 in the 14th Arrondisement of Paris. He was deported with his mother, a native of Odessa, in convoy no. 55 on 21 June 1943.

27. *La Gazette du Palais,* 24 November 1989.

28. Ringelblum, *Chronique du ghetto de Varsovie,* 21.

29. In E. Tsherikover, *Yidn in Frankraykh: Shtudyes un materialn* (New York: YIVO, 1942), vol. 1.

30. The paper was edited by a group of young "immigrants" (second or third generation), and took an independent stance in relation to the Consistory.

31. Only page one of the first issue has been preserved; it is reproduced in David Knout, *La Résistance juive en France, 1940–1944* (Paris: Éditions du Centre, 1947), 76.

32. *Unzer Kamf* (CDJC, CDLXX-95).

33. Archives du Consistoire central, box 5.

34. Secretary of State for War, Minister's Office, top secret, abstract provided by the civil service for technical control. AN, AG II-461.

35. Synthesis from the *RG,* 19 April 1943.

36. CDJC, CXXVC-246.

Chapter Ten. People of the Shadows

1. Louis Aragon, "Le Médecin de Villeneuve." Written from the underground at Villeneuve-les-Avignon, where the poet was in hiding (cf. Pierre Seghers, *La Résistance et ses poètes* [Paris: Éd. Seghers, 1974], 198).

2. "Marranos" meant "pigs" in Portuguese. Thousands of them were exposed and condemned to the stake during the Inquisition in the fifteenth and sixteenth centuries.

3. Henri Michel, *Paris Résistant,* op. cit., 196.

4. Life experience before deportation and in the camps has been studied by Bruno Bettelheim and more recently in France by Michael Pollak, a researcher at the Institut d'histoire du temps présent, CNRS: *L'Expérience concentrationnaire, Essai sur le maintien de l'identité sociale* (Paris: Éditions Métailié, 1990).

5. Annie Kriegel, "De la résistance juive," *Pardès* 2 (1985). Evoking the diversity of situations, Kriegel tries to win credence for the idea of the impossibility of complete clandestinity for the Jewish organizations. We shall return to this question below. Suffice it to say for the moment that there is nothing in common between the deliberate choice of some leaders to cloak themselves too long in a naïve and dangerous legalism, on the one hand, and the forcibly imposed situations of families and individuals, on the other.

6. Borwine Frenkel (1899–1984), written testimony, Paris, 14 March 1963 (CDJC, DLXXVII-7d).

7. Maurice Lewinbaum, written testimony, Paris, 11 October 1963 (CDJC, DLXXVII-7e).

8. D. Halter, written testimony, Paris, undated (CDJC, DLXXVII-7f).

9. Bernard Morlino, Emmanuel Berl, *Les Tribulations d'un pacifiste* (Lyon: Éd. La Manufacture, 1990), 337 f.

10. At the colloquium organized by the CDJC on the anti-Jewish legislation, Serge Klarsfeld made an important clarification concerning the scale of denunciations of Jews. "The existence of millions of denunciation letters is a legend." He estimates their number to be a few thousand at the very most. *Actes du Colloque*, 134.

11. Interview with Jacqueline Keller, March 1991. She assumed the duties of the directorship of the CRIF in April 1981.

12. See *Le Monde juif* 63–64, (1953).

13. Letter from Isaac Schneerson to his cousin, Chief Rabbi Zalman Schneerson, sent from Mussidan, Dordogne, on 31 August 1944. Kehilat Haredim Collection, Orthodox Community, YIVO Archives, New York.

14. Testimony of Boris Schneerson (Michel's brother), Paris, January 1990.

15. Edgar Morin, *Vidal et les siens* (Paris: Seuil, 1989), 218, 227.

16. Lyon, 25 October 1943. YIVO Archives, New York.

17. "The situation of Jews in France," May 1943. YIVO Archives, New York.

18. Report on the dragnet against Jews by the regional branch of the CGQ J, Toulouse, 28 September 1943. YIVO Archives, New York.

19. Tract signed by the Central Defense Committee, Marseille Region, undated (CDJC, XXII-12).

20. Tract from the Jewish Section of the MOI in the Museum of the Resistance in Champigny. See also Jean-Claude Grunberg, *Zone libre* (Arles: Éd. Actes Sud-Papiers, 1990), an autobiographical dramatic work that had a great success at the Théâtre Nationale de la Colline in Paris in 1990. An optimistic tragedy "caught between laughter and tears" and marked in particular by Jewish humor, which was one of the factors in survival, *Zone libre* is the story of a family that takes refuge in Corrèze. The mother-in-law finds herself day after day being called to order by her son-in-law, Simon. "We're not speaking Yiddish any more!" They tell the farmer who is sheltering them, and who is no fool, that it is an "Alsatian dialect." Simon finished the war as a member of a Jewish underground network run by the MOI.

21. Georges Perec, *W, ou le souvenir de l'enfance* (Paris: Denoel, 1975), 13.

22. Baumann, *Mémoire des oubliés*, 64.

23. Interview with Denise Baumann, December 1985.

24. The testimony of Albert, Lariss, and Charles was gathered by Denise Baumann.

25. For the activities of Dr. Milhaud and his network, see below, chapter 11.

26. Robert Frank, testimony, January 1990.

27. Lacques Lanzmann, "La mort à cache-cache," *L'Arche* 2 (February 1957).

28. R. Gamzon, *Tivliot; harmonie* (Paris: Éclaireurs israélites de France, 1945), 90–92.

29. Ibid., 92 f.

30. Interview, December 1990, in Paris. After the Liberation René was adopted by Sophie Schwartz, who was a UJRE official responsible for saving children. She looked after his education and considered his successful studies as revenge on the past. He is presently [1992] a professor at the University of British Columbia in Vancouver, Canada.

31. Interview, January 1990. Some passages here are drawn from the cardinal's work *Le Choix de Dieu*, 57.

32. J. Bloch-Michel, *Journal des désordres*, quoted in Szajkowski, *Analytical Franco-Jewish Gazetteer*, 52.

33. Léon Poliakov, *L'Auberge des musicians. Mémoirs* (Paris: Mazarine, 1981), 78–158.

Chapter Eleven. Do Not Forget the Children

1. *Je suis partout*, 25 September 1942. Brasillach was a pro-Nazi writer and propagandist; he was executed as a collaborator in February 1945. For this chapter, I have borrowed Eric Conan's title, with his permission: *Sans oublier les enfants. Les camps de Pithiviers et de Beaune-la-Rolande. 19 juillet–16 septembre 1942* (Paris: Grasset, 1991).

2. Tract from the MNCR, November 1942: "Stop these heinous crimes. An appeal to French mothers and fathers, to youth, teachers, and educators" (CDJC, CCIV-9a).

3. Ringelblum, *Chronique*, 306.

4. Georges Garel, who headed the underground network of the OSE, stresses this when he writes: "It does seem to me that the enthusiasm and faith of some, and the experience and clarity of vision of others, allied with the ongoing generosity of America, would still not have been sufficient for the task, were it not for the spontaneous surge of support for us from French people in all parts of a France belabored and exhausted by war"; in *Activités de l'OSE sous l'occupation allemande 1940–1944* (Geneva: OSE, 1947), 17.

5. Harry Roderick Kedward, *Resistance in Vichy France: A Study of Ideas and Motivation in the Southern Zone, 1940–1942* (Oxford: Oxford University Press, 1978); cited from the French translation, *Naissance de la résistance de la France de Vichy: Idées et motivations, 1940–1942* (Seyssel: Champ Vallon, 1989), 186.

6. See above, chapter 7.

7. See chapter 7 for Dr. Joseph Weil's fresh questioning of the narrow, apolitical concept of social aid.

8. R.-R. Lambert, *Carnets*, 234. Author's emphasis. Interned at Drancy, Lambert would witness the arrival of the children from La Verdière and their director at the end of October 1943. See below, chapter 19; and the opening pages of this chapter, too.

9. See above, chapter 7.

10. *L'OSE sous l'occupation,* 47. Henri Wahl directed the Sixth serving in this capacity until the Liberation. His deputy was Ninon Weill-Hait. CIMADE = Comité inter-mouvements auprès des evacués. See Jeanne Merle d'Aubingué et al., eds., *God's Underground: CIMADE, 1939–1945* (St. Louis: Behany Press, 1970).

11. Interview, June 1990. At this writing [1992] Roger Fichtenberg was vice-president of the Union of Jewish Resisters and Deportees of France (URDF).

12. "Le destin des enfants juifs en France, Rapport sur les conditions en 1943" (OSE Files in American Jewish Joint Distribution Committee [AJJDC] Archives, New York).

13. An extremely cultivated Russian Jew, Joseph Millner followed the peregrinations of the OSE from St. Petersburg/Leningrad to Paris by way of Berlin. The invasion of the Soviet Union by the Wehrmacht in June 1941 awakened in him, as in numerous other Russian Jews in France, a certain nostalgia and admiration for the country of their youth. In early 1944 he was introduced to the author, Adam Rayski, by Charles Ledermann. After the Liberation he joined forces with the UJRE and contributed to *Naie Presse,* the Yiddish-language daily of the Jewish Section of the MOI.

14. See n. 8, above.

15. Mme Kogan was at the hospital that day, giving birth to a daughter, Danièlle, who survived after having been hidden by Gaby Cohen, the social worker with the "B Circuit."

16. On the role of the camp commission, see Grynberg, *Camps de la honte,* 181–83.

17. OSE, AJJDC Archives, New York.

18. Yad Vashem, 09/24.

19. Letter of 29 January 1944.

20. Yad Vashem, CZA SG 4565.

21. It would seem that the home in Izieu (Ain) was not taken into account in these statistics. After Mme Sabine Zlatin had left the OSE center in Palavas-les-Flots near Montpellier (Herault) in September–October 1942 with a group of forty-two children whom she took to Izieu, she did not attempt to get in touch with the OSE's "B circuit." The forty-four children and seven staff at Izieu were raided on the order of Klaus Barbie on 6 April 1944. All were gassed or otherwise died at Auschwitz, except one supervisor, Laila Feldblum. See Serge Klarsfeld, ed., *Les enfants d'Izieu, une tragédie juive* (Paris: Édition AZ-Repro, 1984).

22. Zeitoun, *L'Oeuvre de secours aux enfants,* 161. (*Maquis* was the French term for groups of Resistance fighters in the Southern Zone who had gone underground and operated from the *maquis* or scrub terrain characteristic of the countryside in the South of France; trans. note).

23. For the horrible massacre in Place Bellecour on the orders of Klaus Barbie, among whose five victims was Léon Pieller, a member of the FTP-MOI Resistance, see chapter 14 below.

24. Interview, Gerhart Riegner, June 1989.

Toggle

25. Interview, January 1990. Having a premonition that his name would appear on the list of those to be sent to Drancy, he escaped with his friend Neumann by climbing the wall of the Lamarck Center after having torn off his yellow star.

26. Interview, January 1990. (See below, chapter 19).

27. Ida Jidali (née Bialek) in Jean Laloum, "L'UGIF et ses maisons d'enfants," *Le Monde juif* 139 (July–September 1990), 140.

28. Interview, January 1990.

29. The decision was applicable to the centers in Neuilly, La Varenne, Montreuil-sous-Sois, Louveciennes, Saint-Mandé, Montgeron, and those on rue Guy-Patin, rue Lamarck, and avenue Secrétan in Paris.

30. Information from Jean Laloum, 23 June 1992, who has the author's warm thanks. In his opinion, "the decision does not have the value of a historical judgment; its essential objective is to re-establish the rights of these children to reparation on the same terms as other internees."

31. At the colloquium "Le plateau Vivarais-Lignon, accueil et résistance, 1939–1944" organized by la Société d'histoire de la montagne et les Églises réformées du plateau on 12–14 October 1990 at Chambon-sur-Lignon, François Boulet questioned this figure. He thought it due to an "idealization of the phenomenon," and put the number of refugees between eight hundred and one thousand. (Unpublished conference paper.)

32. Cited by Oscar Rosskovsky, "Les Fausses identités," paper given at the colloquium in n. 31. Rossovsky, himself a refugee at Chambon, had created a group to provide false identity papers, for which he received technical assistance from the "Sixth"and the local Resistance.

33. See above, chapter 7.

34. In the film of Pierre Sauvage, *The Weapons of the Spirit,* produced in the United States in 1989.

35. Personal statement in file of Pastor Trocmé, to whom the Medal of the Righteous Among the Nations was awarded, at Yad Vashem.

36. André Chouraqui, *L'Amour fort comme la mort, une autobiographie* (Paris, 1990), 233.

37. Statistics presented by Auguste Rivet at the Plateau Vivarais-Lignon colloquium in 1990.

38. Pierre Vidal-Naquet, *Les Juifs, la mémoire et le présent* (Paris: La Découverte, 1991), 2:194f.

39. AIU, Central Consistory Archives, box 6. Lasting relations between the leaders of the Consistory and l'Amitié chrétienne, for example, had already been established.

40. Charles Guillon had resigned his office in 1940 to play a major role from 1941 as the Geneva-based Ecumenical Council of Churches' representative in France. He successfully transferred the funding for the Council's illegal activity in France and was active in other ways helpful in saving lives and supporting the Resistance. He was posthumously awarded the Medal of the Righteous on 27 April

1992. (The author thanks Herbert Herz, Yad Vashem representative for Switzerland for this information.)

41. Note from 8 April 1943. (YIVO Archives, New York.)

42. Rivet, *Colloquium.*

43. *Lest Innocent Blood Be Shed: The Story of the Village of Chambon, and How Goodness Happened There* (New York: Harper & Row, 1979); translated into French as *Le Sang des innocents* (Paris: Stock, 1980).

44. On 29 June 1943, at the Les Roches residence of the school, twenty-five students (twenty of them Jews) and the director (Daniel Trocmé, the minister's nephew) were arrested. They were subsequently deported, none to return.

45. For example, the testimony given by Eugène Pebellier, mayor of Le Puy, Resistance activist, decorated with the Croix de Guerre.

46. The same sets of factors was decisive for the Protestants who fled persecution after the revocation of the Edict of Nantes (1685).

47. See above, chapter 6, the report of Sophie Schwartz. As of September 1944, the UJRE, whose rescue operations were benefiting from the active participation of the MNCR in both the Northern and Southern Zones, opened homes for rescued children. As of summer 1945, between six hundred and fifty and seven hundred had been sheltered in four homes in Paris and one in Aix-les-Bains.

48. Rayski, *Nos illusions perdues,* 104.

49. Suzanne Spaak, the sister-in-law of the Belgian minister of foreign affairs, whose apartment on rue Beaujolais in Paris served as mailbox for Leib Trepper, the head of the "Red Orchestra," was arrested on 16 September 1943 and executed in the courtyard of the Fresnes prison two weeks before the Liberation of Paris.

50. The Rev. P. Vergara, *Une assistante sociale, Marcelle Guillemot (1907–1960)* (CDJC). The figure of seventy children is doubtless inflated. Teshika Forszteter-Korman, an official with the Union of Jewish Women (MOI), who coordinated the operation, remembers about thirty, of whom some ten did not come from the UGIF but had been brought by a parent (or a member of the Resistance). On rue Grenata, where excitement accompanied the arrival of each new child, there must have been a natural tendency to overestimate numbers.

51. The author thanks Sami Dassa for making available a copy of the registry.

52. Dr. Milhaud had been certified by the military hospital in Val-de-Grâce, despite his origins. See *L'Entreaide temporaire,* a mimeographed booklet published in January 1984 by a group of former "hidden children" of the organization. In addition to the testimony of Dr. Milhaud and Mme Béchard, the booklet includes statements by Robert Frank, Maurice Friedman, Madeleine and Suzanne Fischer, Sami Dassa, Rachel Fleminger, Janine Paul (née Smid), and David and Léon Amzel. (Léon fell in 1948 in Jerusalem during the War of Independence.)

53. On this execution in the town of Brantôme, see Georges Beau and Léopold Gaubusseau, *R 5. Les SS en Limousin, Périgord, Quercy* (Paris: Presses de la Cité), 229–39.

54. Interview, 27 May 1991.

55. Interview, May 1991.

56. The Croix de Guerre was awarded posthumously on 10 December 1945. In 1987–88 an inquiry was mounted by students at the public secondary school in Avon under the direction of their teachers Maryvonne Braunschweig and Bernard Gidel. This resulted in a beautiful and overwhelming book, *Les Déportés d'Avon* (Paris: La Découverte, 1989). Louis Malle experienced these events as a student at the college and based his fine film *Au revoir les enfants* on them.

57. Serge Klarsfeld, *Le Mémorial* (Paris: CDJC, 1978).

58. Cf. Adler, *Jews of Paris*, 3–14.

Chapter Twelve. "Intermezzo," or the Italian Reprieve

1. "We are all beautiful and Jewish." Edgar Morin, *Vidal et les siens* (Paris: Seuil, 1989), 238.

2. See comparative study by Laurence Rosengart in *Communauté nouvelle* 47 (1989). Important extracts in *Le Statut des Juifs de Vichy*, CDJC, 1990, 151–73.

3. Report of Dino Alfieri reproduced in R. de Felice, *Storia degli Ebrei italiani sotto il fascismo* (Milano: Einaudi, 1961).

4. Milton Dank, *The French against the French*, 234; cited in Zamojski, *Résonance de l'insurrection du Ghetto*, 122.

5. Report of the prefect of the Alpes-Maritimes, 14 January 1943 (CDJC, XXXVa-324). Cf. Jean-Louis Panicacci, "Les Juifs et la question juive dans les Alpes-Maritimes de 1939 à 1945," in *Recherches régionales* 4 (1983).

6. Report of 6 April 1943 (CDJC, 1–44).

7. Ibid.

8. Morin, *Vidal et les siens*, 214–38.

9. Some large organizations, such as the Federation of Jewish Societies and the OSE, which were in the course of setting up illegal structures, had delayed such reorganization in the Italian Zone.

10. Prefect's report (CDJC, XXXVa-324).

11. Ibid.

12. Telegram from the Ministry of Foreign Affairs, 22 December 1942, cited in Léon Poliakov, *La condition des Juifs sous l'occupation italienne* (Paris: Éditions CDJC, 1946), 20–22.

13. Prefect's report (CDJC, XXXVa-325).

14. Röthke to Knochen, in Poliakov, *Condition des Juifs*, 74.

15. Lucien Steinberg, *Les Authorités allemandes en France occupée* (Paris: Éditions Polyglottes, 1966), 21.

16. "I was present at a certain number of these telephone discussions." Note by Röthke, May 1943, in Poliakov, *Condition des Juifs*, 101–5.

17. Ibid.

18. Jewish Theological Seminary, New York, B. 12.

19. Philippe Erlanger, *La France sans étoiles* (Paris: Plon, 1974).

20. Among the members were Ignace Fink, Joseph Fischer, Claude Kelman, Dr. Modiano, Michel Topiol, and Wolf Toronczyk. See Renée Poznanski, *Jews in France during World War II* (Hanover, NH: University Press of New England for Brandeis University Press, in association with the United States Holocaust Memorial Museum, 2001), 387.

21. Marshal Badoglio was named head of government by King Victor Emmanuel after the dismissal of Mussolini on 25 July 1943.

22. Donati is not explicit. Poliakov, *Condition des Juifs*, 38–40.

23. AIU, Consistory Archives, box 67.

24. Ibid., box 16.

25. Interview, June 1990.

26. Interview, July 1990.

27. Author's collection.

28. Donati's deposition, June–July 1945 (CDJC CCXVIII-22).

29. Viviane Forrester, *Ce soir après la guerre* (Paris: J.-C. Lattès, 1992), 132. The author's maiden name was Dreyfus, and she was related to the famous captain.

30. Letter from Fischer to Helbronner in the Joseph Fischer Collection at the Yad Vashem Archives.

31. Wolf Toronczyk Collection, YIVO, New York, RG, 116.

32. At Drancy, the internees who had been recruited by Brunner as informers were called by the hunting term *piqueurs,* or literally "lancers."

33. Anonymous, *Cinq mois de persécution antijuive.*

34. Ibid.

35. Written account given to the author in September 1990 by Stanley Hoffmann, professor at the Minda de Guinsburg Center for European Studies at Harvard University. Hoffmann is the author of a remarkable work on Vichy, *Decline or Renewal? France since the 1930s* (New York: Viking, 1960), esp. 58–60, a brief reference to these events.

36. Panicacci, "Juifs et la question juive," 297 (AN, F C III 1 137).

37. Letter of 14 September 1943, cited by David Knout, *La résistance juive en France, 1940–1944* (Paris: Éditions du Centre, 1947), 44.

38. Telex dated 20 October 1943 from the *Militärbefehlshaber* in Paris to headquarters in Berlin (CDJC, XLIX-54).

39. *Presse antiraciste,* 108. *Unzer Wort*'s 15 August 1943 number also asked Jews in the Italian Zone not to delay organization of resistance.

40. Report from *Jeunesse sioniste* (Zionist Youth), 20 December 1943 (CDJC, CC-CXLXVI-64).

41. Léon Poliakov, *L'Auberge des musicians: Mémoires* (Paris: Mazarine, 1981), 127.

42. André Bass was able to establish this liaison thanks to Léon Poliakov, a friend of Spolianski from their university days. In December 1943 he met Rayski in Lyon, and with his group of *maquisards* from Haute-Loire joined the FTP-MOI. After the war he was active in the UJRE-Paris and at the request of the latter founded the publishing house "Pavillons" with Roger Maria, which specialized in "progressive" publications.

43. CDJC, XXXVII-2.

44. This homage was published in January 1944 in Lyon (CDJC, XXII-12).

45. "L'UGIF paravent et piège" ("The UGIF, buffer and snare"), a formula used in the collective work *Les Juifs dans l'histoire de 1933 à nos jours* (Paris: Éditions Pacej, 1984).

46. Letter dated early October 1943 and signed *Zagog* (Glaeser, or 'glazier' in Hebrew). It concludes with wishes for the Jewish New Year.

47. Testimony of Claude Kelman, June 1990.

48. Along with Salomon's testimony appeared that of Jan Karski, the Polish Resistance fighter who succeeded in reaching London after he had been infiltrated into the notorious Belzec camp undercover.

Chapter Thirteen. Jewish Perceptions of the War

1. Rabbi Zalman Schneerson arrived in France from the USSR in 1935. In Paris he created L'Association culturelle des israëlites pratiquants (ACIP—The Cultural Association of Observant Jews), which did not recognize the authority of the Central Consistory. It was part of the celebrated Lubavich "dynasty" which furnished the leaders for this "Hassidic militant and ultraorthodox community with a worldwide influence."

2. Itzhak Kadmi-Cohen was born in Lodz on 20 August 1892 and raised in Palestine. After attending the University of Lausanne he arrived in France in 1914. He enlisted and fought in the Foreign Legion. A graduate of the Faculty of Law, he was admitted to the Paris Bar in 1920. Two years later he graduated at the head of his class from the National School of Oriental Languages.

3. Theodor Herzl (1860–1904) was the founder of modern Zionism. He was a Viennese writer and journalist who witnessed the antisemitic Dreyfus Affair while serving as the Paris correspondent of a major Austrian newspaper. His reflections influenced his book *Judenstaat* (*The Jewish State* [Paris, 1886]). A new French version, *L'État des Juifs* (accompanied by his *Essai sur le zionisme* [Essay on Zionism]) appeared in 1990 (ed. Claude Klein [Paris: La Découverte]).

4. Copy in the private collection of Zosa Szajkowski.

5. The idea that emancipation was a misfortune was current among many East European Jews for it seemed to threaten disappearance through assimilation; nevertheless people who thought this way did not reject the principles of the Declaration of the Rights of Man.

6. Léon Poliakov, *L'Auberge des musicians: Mémoires* (Paris: Grancher, 1999), 116.

7. We learn from an OSE report that eighteen young persons were arrested. After the OSE had disestablished one of the children's homes that was under the supervision of this rabbi, the latter gathered the youngsters and organized a kind of *yeshiva* (rabbinical school). He refused to allow the young people to go underground. "We were able to save only ten of them; the others, picked up by the German police, were all sent to Drancy" (source: Bund archives; see also Szajkowski, *Analytical Franco-Jewish Gazetteer*, 75).

8. *Étude . . . zone occupée* (CDJC, DXXIX-1).

9. The *Renseignments généraux*—was it really so well informed?—notes with regard to him: "In November 1940, the Germans tried to buy him and in September 1941 they punished him with internment at Drancy and Compiègne" (Archives nationales, AG 495).

10. Massada, situated north of Sodom near the Dead Sea, was one of King Herod's fortresses. There the last defenders of Jerusalem took refuge after the city had been captured by the Romans in 70 C.E. They chose suicide over surrender.

11. Cf. Jean-Jacques Bernard, *Le Camp de la mort lente: Compiègne, 1941–42* (Paris, 1944), 130–48.

12. All documents cited below and bearing the reference "2AG"—to which the author had access by special dispensation—are part of the "archival collection of the head of state." The files dealing with Jewish matters have not been explored heretofore. The same is true of numerous documents concerning the attitude of the Roman Catholic Church.

13. Letter of 18 January 1943 (AN, 2AG-495).

14. Cf. Schlomo Lev-Ami, *Be-ma'avek uve-mered* (Tel-Aviv: Ministry of Defense, 1977).

15. Cf. Koestler, *Lie de la terre*, 249. See also, Mitchell Cohen, *Du rêve sioniste à la réalité israelienne* (Paris: La Découverte, 1990), 292–94.

16. AN, 2AG-495.

17. The colored map is drawn very carefully by hand on paper with the letterhead of the civil cabinet of the Marshal, which suggests that Kadmi-Cohen prepared it on the occasion of a visit to Lavagne.

18. AN, 2AG-495.

19. Ibid.

20. Author's emphasis.

21. AN, 2AG-495.

22. Note of 5 March 1943 (AN, 2AG-495).

23. Note to Lavagne, 14 April 1943 (AN, 2AG-495).

24. "Germany does not oppose a Jewish state," Kadmi-Cohen wrote to Lavagne in March of 1943 (AN 2/AG-495).

25. Catry to Lavagne, copy in author's files.

26. The report on the meeting, signed "Dr. Brethauer," was addressed to the chancellery of Alfred Rosenberg in Berlin (CDJC, CXLIV-411). Kadmi-Cohen was deported a month after this meeting in convoy 70, 27 March 1944.

27. This document has not been rediscovered. Quotations are those that were reproduced in "Les Juifs dans la guerre," *Presse antiraciste*, 125–28.

28. Written by A. Rayski. See *La Presse antiraciste sous l'Occupation* (Paris: UJRE Documentation Center, 1950), 125–28 (and in Yiddish as *Dos wort fun Widerstand un zig* [Paris: Édition "Oïfsnai," 1949], 231–35) accessible in the CDJC and the BDIC, University of Nanterre.

29. See above, chapter 3.

30. The quotation, based on reception of a radio broadcast, has been shown to be somewhat inexact; nonetheless, it reflects Ben-Gurion's thought fairly well. As concerns his policy on the military level, see below, chapter 16.

31. Support by the non-Zionist left for a national homeland in Palestine marked a reversal of historical importance for the communist Jews of France. The Consistory followed this course of action during negotiations on the charter of the Conseil représentatif des Juifs de France (CRJF—Representative Council of the Jews of France), founded underground in 1944. See below, chapter 18.

32. See above, chapter 3. This is the first document to reach France that explicitly identified a German project to exterminate the Jewish people.

33. The term "genocide" was not used at the time.

34. YIVO, UJRE collection.

35. After the war, this analysis inspired Adam Rayski to reflect that, "On the clock of history, the hands advance more quickly for the Jews than for other peoples. The time of the others was not our time." See *Nos illusions perdues*, 91. Other historians have adopted it as a key to understanding events; see for example Andre Kaspi, *Les Juifs pendant l'Occupation* (Paris: Seuil, 1991), 285.

Chapter Fourteen. 1943: By the Light of Flames from the Ghetto

1. Survivor from the Warsaw Ghetto Uprising leadership.

2. Cf. Lambert, *Carnet d'un temoin*, 207.

3. Diary of Lucien Vidal-Naquet (private collection of the family); see below, chapter 15.

4. Lambert, *Carnet d'un temoin*, 211.

5. AIU, Central Consistory archives, box 9.

6. Klarsfeld, *Vichy-Auschwitz*, 2:21–22.

7. Robert Kiefe, "Carnet" (AIU, Central Consistory archives, box 9).

8. Serge Klarsfeld, *La rafle de Sainte Catherine*. Klarsfeld also adduces proof of the direct responsibility of Barbie and reproduces the (un-dated) list of persons arrested in rue Sainte-Catherine.

9. Letter of 7 December 1942 (CDJC, CDXXV-29).

10. Victor Sullaper, "Mémoires de Victor," *Le Monde juif* 124 (October–December 1986). Jean-Pierre Lévy confirmed to the author that he remembered having warned Victor of the imminence of a raid.

11. F. Schrager, *Un militant juif* (Paris: Éditions Polyglottes, 1979), 112–14. See also above, chapter 12. On the attitude of the Bund in the matter of scuttling the UGIF, Schrager provides this interesting bit: "We profited by the visit to Grenoble of Raymond-Raoul Lambert, who was an official of the UGIF, in order to explain to him the danger of the situation. Zvi Lewin, Leo Glaeser, and I met him. Unfortunately he did not share our point of view."

12. Ibid., 115.

13. Klarsfeld, *Rafle de Sainte Catherine*.

14. "Le soulèvement du ghetto de Varsovie et son impact en France," *Actes du colloque du CDJC*, Paris, 17 April 1983, 163.

15. Jean Bruller (Vercors), *La Bataille du silence* (Paris: Éditions de Minuit, 1967), 275 ff. Quoted by Dr. Claude Levy at the colloquium "Le soulèvement du ghetto."

16. Neither Robert Gamzon in *Les Eaux claires* nor Jacques Lazarus in *Juifs au combat: Témoignage sur l'activité d'un movement de résistance* (Paris: Éditions du Centre, 1947) mentions the rising of the ghetto. They were simply uninformed.

17. Rachel Chegam (a militant of the Jewish Army), in "Le soulèvement du ghetto de Varsovie et son impact," 166.

18. Ibid., 138.

19. The rebellion of Bar Kokba against the Romans took place from 132 to 135 C.E.

20. Reproduced in *Dos wort fun Widerstand*, 171. This analysis has become dominant in historiography of the uprising.

21. These words belong to Dr. Haïm Slovès (b. Bialystok 1905, d. Paris 1987).

22. Archives of the Bialystok ghetto in Lo'hamei Haghettaot Kibbutz (Ghetto Fighters' House), Israel. Cited by Bronia Klibanksi, *Le Monde juif* 132 (October–December 1988).

23. A. Rayski in *Unzer Wort* 58 (15 June 1943), reproduced in *Dos wort fun Widerstand*, 173.

24. Unsigned document, "*Coup d'oeil sur la situation des Juifs en France*," dated May 1943 (YIVO); see above, chapter 10.

25. Interview with G. Riegner (see above, chapter 9). Note, on the other hand, the bold parachute operation by Palmach (predecessor of the armed underground Haganah) in Yugoslavia undertaken by a commando team including Hana Senesz and Haviva Rajk in order to join Jewish resistance groups in Hungary and Slovakia. We shall return to this in chapter 17.

26. Collection of bulletins of the JTA for 1941–44, American Jewish Archives, Hebrew Union College, Cincinnati, Ohio.

27. It is evident from a report by the Special Brigade of the Prefecture of Police that its agents had shadowed participants to the meeting at 32 rue Guyot (today rue Médéric); these were Édouard Kowalski, Jacques Rawine, Idel Barszczewski, Teshka Tenenbaum-Forszteter, and Adam Rayski. Since they did not have orders from above, the police did not intervene (Archives nationales, Z6 196/2427; reproduced in Courtois et al., *Sang de l'étranger* [Paris: Fayard, 1989], 251).

28. This rupture was aggravated by geographic separation: the noncommunist organizations had regrouped in the "Free Zone," while the communists remained in Paris.

29. F. Schrager broke with the Communist Party in the summer of 1938 and joined the Bund.

30. Schrager, *Un militant juif*, 130–38.

31. The communiqué is published and commented on in the 15 August and September numbers of *Unzer Wort*, as well as in *Notre voix* of 1 September. The CGD would go on to publish its own paper in Yiddish, *Unzer Kamf* ("Our Struggle"), which would be followed by numerous other publications, most of them in French.

32. AN, F. 1A-3754, note 4 054, undated.

33. The UGIF sent subscribers a "dues payment certificate" bearing the name, date of birth, nationality, and address of the person. The fee (in 1943) was 120 francs. The certificate had to be shown in the event of a police check. The bookkeeping was handled by "Aryan" staff, seconded by either the CGQ J or the Ministry of Finance (private archives of Claude Urman).

34. The characterization is Lambert's, who reproached him with "telling everyone that I was a bit of a Quisling for Vallat" (Lambert, *Carnet d'un témoin*, 165). See above, chapter 4, note 17.

35. The signature is without first name. At Yad Vashem the document was attributed to Théo Klein, who was at pains to tell the author that he had never been part of the UGIF and that he had been too young to be entrusted with administrative responsibilities.

36. Yad Vashem Archives.

37. *L'activité des organisations juives en France sous l'Occupation*, 232.

38. Cf. Yerachmiel (Richard) Cohen, "French Jewry's Dilemma on the Orientation of its Leadership," *Yad Vashem Studies* 14 (1981). Cohen analyzes this meeting as revelatory of the power struggle between the Consistory and the UGIF. The thesis is debatable, the more so because the UGIF leaders themselves doubted their raison d'être, while those of the Consistory were more worried in fall 1943 about the unification of the foreign Jewish Resistance groups (CDG).

39. Richard Cohen sees an allusion to Gamzon's involvement with the underground in this remark.

40. Archives nationales, AG II-82 and 84.

41. "Legal or para-legal terrorism was endorsed by Laval as well . . . as Pétain" (Azéma, *De Munich à la Libération*, 305).

42. Georges Mandel, deported to Germany, was brought back to Paris and imprisoned at La Santé and then turned over to the Milice. On 7 July 1944 militiamen took him to the Fontainebleau Forest and murdered him. Some weeks earlier Jean Zay, condemned to life imprisonment by the tribunal in Riom, was similarly "disappeared." Both were targeted particularly for their Jewishness.

43. CDJC, CXXXII-56, signed by Knochen and dated 14 April 1944.

44. This was certainly true.

45. The supervisors were part of Drancy's Jewish Police, established by Brunner. The buses transported the Jews from the train station to Drancy.

46. As a consequence of the agreement reached between René Bousquet and General Karl Oberg on 4 August 1942.

47. Cf. Chertok, *Mémoires d'un hérétique*.

48. Condemned to death by a German military tribunal on 20 September 1943, they were executed at Mont-Valérien on 1 and 2 October. Even though the tribunal considered Engros and Tuchklaper "minors," it made no concessions (AN, AJ40).

49. André Kaspi, who cites the author ("We were obliged to admit that the party's priorities did not coincide with our own" [*Nos illusions perdues*, 146]), generalizes from the continuation in Paris of combat groups to the totality of relations between Jewish communists and the Communist Party, leading to debtable conclusions (*Les Juifs sous l'Occupation*, 318).

50. The phrase belongs to Mao Tse-Tung, who was defining the optimal conditions for guerilla warfare.

51. Identified by the Special Brigade in January–February 1943 during surveillance of a youth group directed by Henri Krasucki, Marcel Rayman was briefly lost but then relocated and placed again under surveillance.

52. Note from de Brinon to the prime minister, 23 November 1943 (AN, AG II).

53. Cited in Klarfeld, *Vichy-Auschwitz*, 2:133. For the circumstances of the assassination plot, see Courtois et al., *Sang de l'étranger*, 320f.

54. Boris Holban resumed his responsibilities as head of the FTP-MOI of Paris after the arrest of Manouchian.

55. Celestino Alfonso, Joseph Boczor, Georges Cloarec, Rino Della Negra, Thomas Elek, Maurice Fingerzwaig, Spartaco Fontano, Jonas Geduldig, Emeric Glasz, Léon Goldberg, Szlama Grzywacz, Stanislas Kubacki, Arpen Levitian, Cesare Luccarini, Missak Manouchian, Marcel Rayman, Roger Rouxel, Antoine Salvadori, Willy Szapiro, Amadeo Usseglio, Wolf Wajsbrot, and Robert Witschitz.

56. David Diamant, *Combattants, héros et martyres de la Résistance* (Paris: Renouveau, 1984), 183. German military law permitted those condemned to death to leave a last letter with the chaplain.

57. Information on Joseph Epstein in Courtois et al., *Sang de l'étranger*, 347–49, 351–54.

58. The next day, in a show of rare spontaneity, throughout the country the posters were covered with graffiti: "No! Patriots!" and "Liberation Army!"; the line "Criminal Army" was struck out.

59. Reprinted in *La Presse antiraciste*, 145–47. Author's emphasis.

60. According to the documentation assembled by Serge Klarsfeld, *Les Fusillés de Mont-Valérien (1941–1944)*, published by the FFDJF (Paris, 1987). The tragic list is very long, from the very first members of the resistance who were executed—Michel Rolnikas, Sameul Tyszelman ("Little Titi," whom Fabien avenged in the Barbès Metro Station), Léon Pakin, Élie Wallach, Mounié Nadler (editor with the underground press), Kaddich Sonowski (seventeen years old), and Simone Schloss (beheaded in Germany)—right up to the executed activists whose faces appeared on the "Red Poster." Trzebrucki, condemned a first time to five years' imprisonment for having distributed underground Jewish newspapers, was arraigned again on 27 August 1942, before a court of the "Special Section," which condemned him to death.

61. The economic or commercial activity of Jews living illegally was inevitably carried on underground and had more to do with simple resourcefulness than the black market.

62. Study by the administration of the Armistice Services, Vichy, 12 November 1943 (Archives nationales, 2AG-530).

63. See below, chapter 16.

64. For the stance of Rabbi Nathan Hosanki on the legal functioning of the Central Consistory, see below, chapter 18.

65. Preface by Serge Ravanel in the booklet "35th Brigade Marcel Langer" (Archives of the Musée de la Déportation et de la Résistance de Besançon).

66. All this information on the Marcel Langer Brigade comes from the archives of Claude Urman; a vital portion has been deposited at the Besançon museum. See Rolande Trempé, "Le rôle des étrangers MOI en guérilleros," in *La Libération dans le Midi de la France*, série A, vol. 35, travaux de l'Université (Toulouse: Éché éditeur et service des publications université de Toulouse-Mirail, n.d.).

67. The boys and girls who fled Paris used to meet at a beach on the Saône, and it was there that ties of friendship and relations with the Jewish Resistance were formed.

68. Acts of reprisal against the judges of the special courts caused dismay among the magistrates according to Jacques Delarue, former Resistance activist and historian of the repression. Death sentences became less frequent.

69. On Pfeiffer's ties with the OSE, see above, chapter 12.

70. We owe to Dr. Joseph Königsberg the assembly of documentation found in the departmental archives of the Rhône on the "Carmagnole Battalion," its actions, and the execution of its fighters. These documents were gathered in a booklet, *Camarades juifs des unités FTP-MOI de Lyon et Grenoble*, published in 1986 by the Fraternal Association of Veterans of Carmagnole-Liberté (Musée de Besançon). The number of those shot, or who fell in action, is thirty-three, one of whom was a woman: Luc Aizenberg, Élie Amselem, Beny Blitz, Albert Brozek, José Elkon, Michel Fred, Charles, Marcel Gaist, Gajewski, Étienne Goldberger, Goldstein, Raymond Grynstein, Maurice Grunstein, Maurice Gurfinkel, Joseph Halaubaumer, Pierre Katz, Jacques Kipman, Alain Klajn, Henry, Guy Landowicz, Marek Majersack, Nathan Nusbaum, Alexandre Ochshorn, Fischel Pfefer, René, Mordka Rosen, Léon Rozenfarb, Chil Rubin, Julien Solanczyk, Léon Szwarcbart, and Tibor Weisz, as well as the two men already cited in this chapter.

71. Rawine was at the head of the combat groups, which one month after their creation had almost one hundred members: Charles Krzentowski, Albert Goldman, Georges Goutchat, Léon Habif, Maurice Benadon, Charles Jacobson, Léon Centner, Gaston Kutas, to cite but a few—men who came from the most diverse backgrounds.

72. Interview with Fernand Kohn, October 1991.

73. The philosopher Mihaïl Sora, "Feuilles d'un carnet de souvenirs," in the collection *Les Roumains dans la Résistance française* (Bucharest: Meridiane, 1971), 250–57.

74. We owe to Annie Kriegel a very fine account of the Jewish communist youth movement in Grenoble, though at points its analysis is debatable because it is inspired by a view more political than historical. We can well believe that this was a very fraught time in her life for it to have left so vivid a memory, engraved with such feeling for both the organization and her comrades, who made her "understand life and the world." (Annie Kriegel, *Ce que j'ai cru comprendre* [Paris: Robert Laffont, 1991], chapter 4, "JC-MOI, 1942–1944," and chapter 5, "Va, laisse couler mes larmes," 186–243.) Kriegel broke with the Communist Party in 1959 primarily over the survival of Stalinism.

Chapter Fifteen. Jews, French and Resistant

1. Léon Blum, *Les Oeuvres. Nouvelles conversations de Goethe avec Eckermann,* vol. 1891–1905 (Paris: Albin Michel, 1954), 197.

2. Diary of Lucien Vidal-Naquet, private archive of his son, the eminent historian Pierre Vidal-Naquet.

3. Session of 20 August 1942. For a counterproposal in the form of a draft bill by Helbronner, see above, chapter 2.

4. Free French Information Service (CDJC CCXIV-85).

5. The remark dates from 28 October 1943, Limagne, *Éphémerides,* op. cit., 1539.

6. Study on the question of arrests in France, Direction des Services de l'Armistice, Vichy, 12 November 1943. Archives nationales, 2AG-530.

7. Meeting of the Permanent Committee of the Central Consistory on 28 February 1943. Cited in Z. Szajkowski, "The French Central Jewish Consistory during the Second World War," *Yad Vashem Studies* 3 (1959).

8. Abundant testimony gathered by André Harris and Alain de Sédouy in *Juifs et français* (Paris: Grasset et Fasquelle, 1979) confirms such a state of mind.

9. Report to WZO, March 1942, Fond 09/24, Yad Vashem.

10. Confidential report of Robert Gamzon, Jules Jefroykin, and Maurice Brener after their trip to Paris from 5 to 15 May 1943 (CDJC CDX-3).

11. *Actes du colloque Églises et chrétiens dans la II Guerre mondiale* (Lyon: Presses Universitaires de Lyon, 1978), 203.

12. Letter from Paul David (Montflanquin, Lot-et-Garonne) to Helbronner, September 1943. AIU, Archives of the Central Consistory, box 5.

13. Julien Samuel to Denise Baumann in *Une famille pas comme les autres,* 222. His reference is to Eastern European Jews, who were very numerous in the OSE administration.

14. Freddy Raphaël and Robert Weyl, eds., *Le Journal du Dr Camille Dreyfus* (Toulouse: author's publication, 1977).

15. *L'Entraide temporaire,* cf. chapter 11, n. 54.

16. Harris and de Sédouy, *Juifs et français,* 46. On retiring Pierre Dreyfus accepted the presidency of the ORT.

17. Azéma, *De Munich à la Libération*, 145.

18. Interview with Claude Bourdet, November 1990.

19. Valentin Feldmann was shot on 27 July 1942, as were Léon Pakin and Élie Wallach of the Second Jewish Detachment of the FTP-MOI. Georges Politzer and Jacques Solomon were shot on 23 May 1942.

20. According to the list of "Companions of the Liberation" reproduced in the booklet published by the Order on 15 March 1951.

21. All citations above are from the diary of Lucien Vidal-Naquet.

22. See above, chapter 4.

23. Stanley Hoffmann, preface to *L'Étrange défaite*, 21.

24. Jean-Pierre Lévy at the Marc Bloch colloquium, 17 June 1986.

25. Drawn up in Clermont-Ferrand, 18 March 1943. In a letter he warns his son that to make his way in this world as a Jew he will have to work harder than others. François Bédarida et Denis Peschanski, eds., "Marc Bloch à Étienne Bloch. Lettres de la 'drôle de guerre,'" *Les Cahiers de l'IHTP* 19 (December 1991). Elsewhere in this correspondence he worries whether his daughter will find a position in the OSE (she did, working with children in the Gurs and Rivesaltes camps).

26. Georges Friedmann, *Fin du peuple juif?* (Paris: Gallimard, 1965), préface, 7–9.

27. Harris and de Sédouy, *Juifs et français*, 44. The Dreyfuses had lived in the same three or four villages of the Republic of Mulhouse for several centuries.

28. Statement from the floor by Dominique Schnapper at the colloquium on the bicentenary of the emancipation of the Jews, organized by the CRIF and the city of Strasbourg, 5–6 October 1991.

29. Baumann, *Une famille*, 35.

30. See above, chapter 11.

31. Baumann, *Une famille*, 211. In reply to the author's question as to what she meant by *juiverie*, with its somewhat perjorative connotation [here translated more neutrally as "Jewishness"], she explained the term as follows: "It is a translation of *yidishkeit*, a notion which to my mind is more comprehensive than *judéité* [approx. 'Jewishness']" (interview, December 1985).

32. Hammel ("Chameau"), *Souviens-toi d'Amalek* (Paris: Éd. CLKH, 1982), 411.

33. André Kaspi (with Ralph Schor et Nicole Piétri), *La Deuxième guerre mondiale. Chronologie commentée* (Paris, 1990), 395.

34. Henri Michel gives this definition of the Resistance: "It is first of all a patriotic struggle for the liberation of the fatherland. . . . It is also a struggle for the liberty and dignity of man against totalitarianism." Cited by François Bédarida in "L'histoire de la Résistance, Lectures d'hier, chantiers de demain," *Vingtième Siècle, revue d'histoire* 11 (July–September 1986), 75.

35. Hoffmann, preface to *L'Étrange défaite*, 26.

36. Declaration of principles of the UJRE published in the summer of 1943. Collection of Joseph Georges Cohen, Archives of the Municipal Library, Toulouse.

37. *Notre parole*, Southern Zone, 3 (8 March 1943).

38. "Appel aux Juifs français," signed MNCR.

39. "Alerte aux Juifs alsaciens! De graves dangers vous menacent!" Tract edited and published by the MNCR, with the collaboration of students and professors from the University of Strasbourg who had withdrawn to Clermont-Ferrand. It may be added that a list of Strasbourg faculty and students who were shot or died during deportation reveals about thirty Jews out of a total of sixty-nine persons. Cf. *Témoignage strasbourgeois. De l'Université aux camps de concentration* (Strasbourg: Presses Universitaires de Strasbourg).

40. A major grain dealer, as the author recalls.

41. *Droit et liberté* (Provence edition) 1 (September 1944, after Liberation).

42. No. 1, May 1944 (CDJC, XXIV-10). In 1940, on the order of Vichy, the Marseille boulevard that bore the name of Gaston Crémieux was renamed boulevard Sidi-Brahmin, a locality in Algeria where the French had defeated the Emir. After the Liberation, the boulevard regained its original name. Information supplied by Pierre Vidal-Naquet.

43. This wartime study, however incomplete, remains the only one on the subject. Text reproduced in *La Presse antiraciste,* 165–77.

44. Testimony of Jacques Zermatti, officer in the Free French parachute corps, at a colloquium organized by the RHICOJ, 7 October 1984, published in *Les Juifs dans la Résistance et la Libération,* 34.

45. Ibid., 38 f. The Americans played the "Admiral Darlan card" before that of General Giraud, consistent with their policy of counterbalancing the position of General de Gaulle. Both Darlan and Giraud made decisions on the use of French forces in North Africa that were contradictory to the Allies, who had conquered French territories there. In the end, Darlan was assassinated on 24 December 1942 and the Americans appointed Giraud as French plenipotentiary in North Africa, a move that enraged de Gaulle.

46. Archives de la Seine.

47. No. 91, December 1943–January 1944. The same issue of *Fraternité* (MNCR, Southern Zone) reproduces an article on the execution of Marcel Langer in Toulouse.

48. *Bulletin* of the Fédération des sociétés juives d'Algérie (no connection with the FSJF), no. 91 (December 1943–January 1944).

49. Declaration published in the *Bulletin* of the FSJA, no. 88 (August–September 1943).

50. *New York Times,* 25 April 1943.

51. Interview, January 1990.

52. At the colloquium organized by the CDJC and the Renouveau juif ("Jewish Renewal"): "Il y a cinquante ans: Le statut de Juifs de Vichy," Paris, 1 October 1990.

Chapter Sixteen. The Jewish Scouts Take Up Arms

1. Founded in 1923 by Robert Gamzon, then aged sixteen, the Jewish Scouts grew rapidly. Although placed under the tutelage of the Consistory and though it fa-

vored religious education, the movement valued pluralism and remained open to immigrants. Under Vichy the scouts came under the Ministry of Youth and were forced to express allegiance to Pétain. Admitted to the Uriage Cadet School, they experienced the ambiguity of a patriotism shackled to the "National Revolution."

2. Contemporary situation report printed in *Activités des organisations juives sous l'Occupation* (Paris: Éditions du Centre, 1947), 68.

3. Oral testimony of Denise Gamzon, Jerusalem, 1989. See also CDJC, CCV-1.

4. Report on the organization of the underground EIF, undated, published after the war (CDJC, CLX-1).

5. Robert Gamzon, *Les Eaux claires. Journal, 1940–1944* (Paris: Éditions EIF, 1981).

6. See Courtois et al., *Sang de l'étranger,* 160–62.

7. Interview with General Redon ("Durenque"), Paris, April 1990.

8. Valérie Ermosilla, "La Résistance juive dans le Tarn. Réalités et représentation" (M.A. thesis under the direction of Jean-Pierre Laborie and Jean Estebe, University of Toulouse-Le Mirail, 1987), 76–78.

9. Written testimony of Denise Gamzon, Jerusalem, 1990.

10. Robert Gamzon, *Les Eaux claires.* The family name of "Jojo" (Josette) is not given by Gamzon. The author has learned that after the war she married Ruven Dassas, with whom she immigrated to Israel, where she died in an accident in 1984.

11. Gamzon, *Les Eaux claires.*

12. A cenotaph erected near Camalières bears the names of these seven Resistance fighters. The body of Gilbert Bloch was buried in the cemetery of Viane. On the tomb is also engraved the name of his mother, who was deported, never to return. See *Les Lieux de mémoire de la Deuxième Guerre Mondiale, Département du Tarn,* published by the Secretary of State for Veterans (Departmental Commission for Historical Information), 61 f.

13. "Mémoire" by General Redon, head of Free French forces of the Tarn department, 96 f., archives of the Museum of the Resistance in Toulouse.

14. Testimony of Lucien Lazare, in Harris and de Sedouy, *Juifs et Français,* 359.

15. *Contribution à l'histoire de la Résistance juive en France, 1940–1944* (Paris: Édition du Centre, 1947).

16. Vladimir Jabotinsky went to America to recruit a Jewish Legion to fight along side the Allies. He died on 4 August 1940 after an intense round of lobbying political figures; his proposal met incomprehension, even among Jewish leaders (cf. Nahoum Summer, *Vladimir Jabotinsky* [New York: Biderman Publishers, 1947]).

17. Lucien Lazare's *Contribution à l'histoire de la Résistance juive* distorts the issue when he writes: "The spirit of . . . Kadmi-Cohen is found in one of the instigators of the AJ [Jewish Army], David Knout." In reality, Kadmi-Cohen worked for a rapprochement with Nazi Germany that would help the Zionists drive Britain out of Palestine and establish a Jewish state (see above, chapter 13).

18. Interview, January 1990.

19. Maquis units generally consisted of between thirty and forty fighters. No counts are available for the other branches of AJ activity.

20. Testimony of Saïa Voldman, in *Les Juifs dans la Résistance*, 141.

21. Ermosilla, *La Résistance juive*, 72.

22. Account of the period 24 July to 18 August 1944, entitled *Journal de marche de Pierre Loeb* (Joseph Georges-Cohen Collection, Municipal Archives of Toulouse).

23. Loeb's written testimony, Brussels, October 1990. Loeb's correction supersedes the version in the document *Comment nos deux maquis ont failli n'en faire qu'un* (Municipal Archives of Toulouse), which is frequently cited in support of the idea of a common organization under the name Organization Juive de Combat.

24. CDXX-48. Cf. also Ariane Bois, "La Résistance juive organisée en France pendant la Seconde Guerre mondiale" (Ph.D. dissertation, Institut d'Études Politiques, Paris, 1984).

25. Ibid.

26. Private archives of Lucien Lublin.

27. Ibid.

28. Testimony of Denise Gamzon.

29. "Rapport sur l'auberge," 25 June 1944 (CDJC, CDLXIX-39).

30. Ibid.

31. Alain Michel, *Les Éclaireurs israélites de France pendant la Seconde guerre mondiale* (Paris: Éd. des EIF, 1984), 188.

32. A detailed account of the first meeting with Porel was published by Henri Pohorylès as *Négotiations avec l'IS* (CDJC, CDLXIX). Lydia Tcherwinska's role remains unclear.

33. Kapel, *Un rabbin dans la tourmente*, 134. He writes: "I found my comrades imprudent. . . . Very worried by what was happening around me, I shared my fears with Jacques Lazarus and asked him to accompany me to the Lyon railway station to find out whether it was still possible to return to Toulouse. We learned that the trains were no longer running because . . . of sabotage organized by the Resistance. There was nothing left for us to do but to bow to the facts, since fate had so decided."

34. Jacques Lazarus, *Juifs au combat* (Paris: Éd. du Centre, 1947), 117.

35. The trial of this group was held at the military tribunal of Paris on 20 November 1952. Those charged: one woman and fourteen men, among them Georges Guicciardini and his two sons, barely twenty years old. Rehbein's case was excluded because he was a German officer performing his military duty, not a traitor to his country. The tribunal gave its verdict on 23 December: eight condemnations to death and seven others in absentia.

36. Interview with Rachel Rubel, Besançon, December 1989.

37. "Note on a Trip to Paris" (CDJC, CDLXIX). The telephone number was doubtless that of Lucien Rubel. It is found in the 1947 Paris telephone book (organized by streets) as registered to 90 boulevard de Coucelles, under the name of a new tenant, "Bony, E." There were no annual phone books between 1942 and 1946

(source: Library of the Ministry of Posts and Telegrams). Rachel Rubel confirms that they used the telephone carelessly.

38. Testimony in Jean Laloum, "L'UGIF et ses maisons d'enfants: L'enlèvement d'un enfant," *Le Monde juif* 124 (October–December, 1986), 175.

39. During an interview, Charles Mandelbaum gave the author various pieces of information allowing a fuller picture of relations between the Jewish Army and the irregular Alerte group of the MLN: "At the beginning of 1944 I joined the irregular Paris group Alerte, which was part of the MLN and was under the direct command of Charcot-Neuville, who in turn reported to Jacques Baumel, today the senator for Hauts-de-Seine. I found there other Jewish fighters who claimed to be part of the Jewish Army, such as Ernest Appenzeller, Isidore Pohorylès [brother of Henri], Lucien Rubel, Marc Lévy, and Max Windmuller. . . . I have no memory of any specifically "Jewish" actions carried out by the Alerte irregulars. On the contrary, my proposal from the UGIF home in Montreuil did not find favor, even though it appeared relatively easy to pull off." Interview, February 1992.

40. Archives nationales, Szekeres Collection, 72 AJ 286.

41. Ibid.

42. Ibid.

43. Ben-Gurion uses the term "anonymous army" with reference to the Jewish unit in the British Army. "Their name was never officially mentioned in any military dispatch. Their Jewish identity was passed over in silence and they were denied the status and rights of all the other military allies of Great Britain in this war. . . . Very recently, after a fresh question in the House of Commons, the minister of war again rejected the bill" (for a Jewish Legion). *Informations de Palestine* (Geneva), 9 July 1942 (CDJC, CCXIV-64 [call no. F 21 in the underground archives of the FSJF]). Negotiations between the Jewish Agency and the War Office concluded in August 1944 with the creation of a "Jewish unit," not composed only of Jews from Palestine, which became known as the Jewish Brigade and fought only in Italy.

44. Michel, *Éclaireurs israélites*, 189. The AJ leadership knew of him: "A captain from de Gaulle's headquarters in London named Castor . . . has had interesting discussions with our Castor [Gamzon]. The English Castor knew with whom he was dealing and addressed him as the commander of a Jewish company."

Chapter Seventeen. The Jewish Resistance in All Its Variety

1. Primo Levi, *If Not Now, When?* (New York: Summit, 1985), 131.

2. Paul Éluard, *Au rendez-vous allemand* (Paris: Minuit, 1945).

3. See above, chapter 3.

4. Adler, *Jews of Paris*, preface, ix.

5. Kriegel, *Ce que j'ai cru comprendre*, 154.

6. Lazarus, *Juifs au combat*, 18–24.

7. Very interesting testimony in *Les Juifs dans la Résistance*, 101 f. Catherine Varlin, who legalized her underground name, would go on to occupy leadership positions in the MOI Resistance in Toulouse and, later, in the east of France.

8. Interview with Henri Krischer, military leader of the "Carmagnole-Liberté" batallion (MOI), December 1989.

9. It is almost impossible, because of the multiple—not to say overlapping—relationships, to draw up a schematic presentation of the whole.

10. This unity was realized with the General Defense Committee, the Representative Council of the Jews of France, and the Youth Action Committee (see above, chapter 15, and below, chapter 18).

11. *L'Arche* 196 (June–July 1973).

12. Wladimir Rabi, "Pour quoi ils ont combattu," *Les Nouveaux Cahiers* 37 (Paris, summer 1974). Arnold Mandel committed a second offense with comments worthy of the collaborationist press that dishonor him: "The Jewish communists of the MOI shot the German troops in the back." (*Informations juives*, May 1985).

13. André Kaspi, *Les Juifs sous l'Occupation*, 317.

14. On this subject, see above, chapter 8 (and also the author's study, "Variations sur le thème de la Résistance," *Cahiers Bernard Lazare* 117 (Paris, 1987).

15. We should recall the homage paid by Robert Gamzon to "Jojo," the young communist who inspired the scouts to armed combat (see above, chapter 16).

16. The former leaders of the Armée juive are critical of the pages that Lucien Lazare devoted to it in his book *La Résistance juive*.

17. Cf. Lucien Steinberg, "Documents allemands sur la Résistance des Juifs en Biélorussie," *Le Monde juif* (October–December 1967).

18. Information supplied by Artur London, Prague, 1948.

19. Cf. Maxime Steinberg, *L'Étoile et le fusil*.

20. "La Résistance juive dans la Résistance européenne" (address given at the colloquium organized by Yad Vashem in Jerusalem in April 1968).

21. Letter from the leadership of the UJRE, "To Jewish members of the FTP," July 1943. Private collection of Henri Krischer.

22. In Yiddish, signed "The Jewish communists," reprinted in *Dos wort fun Widerstand und zig*, 247.

23. See above, chapter 16.

24. Preface to Lucien Lazare, *La Résistance juive*, op. cit., 9 f.

25. Jacques Lazarus, "La Résistance juive en France," *Informations juives* (November–December, 1987).

26. Yehuda Bauer, "Résistance et passivité juive face à l'Holocauste," paper given at the colloquium of the École des hautes études en sciences sociales, *L'Allemagne nazie et le génocide juif*, 403–19.

27. On 19 August 1953 (8 Ellul 5713), the Israeli Knesset passed the "Martyrs and Heroes Commemoration (Yad Vashem) Law . . . to commemorate the six million members of the Jewish people who died martyrs' deaths at the hands of the Nazis and their collaborators, . . . the heroism of Jewish servicemen, and of underground

fighters in towns, villages and forests who staked their lives in the battle against the Nazi oppressor and his collaborators, . . . the heroic stand of the besieged and fighters of the ghettoes who rose and kindled the flame of revolt to save the honour of their people, [and] the high-minded Gentiles who jeopardized their lives to save Jews"; Laws of the State of Israel [in English], vol. 7 (5713 [1952–53]), 119. Yad Vashem is a biblical phrase which literally means "hand" (*yad*) and "name" (*vashem*) but which signifies "monument."

28. In her review of the memoirs of Adam Rayski, *Nos illusions perdues*, "Face au génocide," *Le Figaro*, 16 April 1985.

29. Quote from M. Friedmann in "Les Haredim et la Choa," *Pardès* 9–10 (1989): 161 f. See also chapter 13 above. It is not by chance that Arnold Mandel expresses his preference, in the article earlier cited, for a Jew who taught the Talmud during the Occupation over the Resistance and armed struggle (both attitudes doubtless expressing defiance of adversity).

30. Chouraqui, *L'Amour fort comme la mort*, 229. The rabbinical school in Limoges was created in early 1941 by elements of the Orthodox group *Yeshurun* who had fled Strasbourg.

31. *Le Crépuscule au loin* (Paris: Grasset et Fasquelle, 1987), 120 f.

32. Raul Hilberg, *La Déstruction des Juifs d'Europe* (Paris: Fayard, 1988), 901.

33. Ibid., 13.

34. Claude Vigée, *La Lune d'hiver*, 78 f.

35. Vladimir Jankélévitch, *L'Impréscriptible. Pardonner?* (Paris: Seuil, 1986), 67 f.; a first edition was published in 1971 by Éditions du Pavillon under the direction of Roger Maria.

36. In *Ceux de la Résistance à leur camarade Georges Papillon* (Paris: Imprimerie de presse, 1945), 9.

37. Ibid., 12.

38. *Le Mensonge raciste. Ses origins, sa nature, ses méfaits*, published by the Mouvement national contre le racisme. A copy of the original brochure is preserved in the Municipal Archives of Toulouse.

39. At the time, *inversion* was often used in French to designate homosexuality (trans. note).

40. Jankélévitch, *L'Impréscriptible*, 62 f.

Chapter Eighteen. CRIF: Constructing the Future in the Shadow of Death

1. It emerged in June 1943 in Grenoble from the unification of all the political currents of Eastern European Jewry.

2. Mussolini was removed from power by a vote of the Grand Council of the Fascist Party and arrested by order of the king on 23 July 1943.

3. Kiefe's notebook, AIU Library, Central Consistory Archives, box 9.

4. President of the UGIF-Paris.

5. In fact it concerned Jardin's suggestion to transfer the seat of the Consistory to Challes-les-Eaux in the Italian Zone. Helbronner speaks of it in a letter to Laval. See above, chapter 12.

6. Jean Jardin left Vichy on 1 November to assumed the post of ambassador in Bern. Cf. Pierre Assouline, *Une éminence grise* (Paris: Balland, 1986).

7. André Blumel, *Un grand Juif: Léon Meiss* (Paris: Éditions Guy-Victor, 1967).

8. AIU Library, Central Consistory archives, box 5.

9. CDJC, CDLV-15.

10. Kapel, *Un rabbin dans la tourmente*, 104.

11. See above, chapter 17.

12. In late December 1942 the Consistory Council reconfirmed its intention to observe the anti-Jewish legislation, citing as justification the priority it must assign to religious observance. See above, chapter 9.

13. Letter of 18 September 1942 (CDJC, CCXIV-2). It is to be noted that no trace of a Consistory response is to be found in Jarblum's personal archives deposited at the Yad Vashem or in the files of the FSJF at the CDJC.

14. *Dos wort fun Widerstand*, 211. Subsequent to his arrival in Lyon, Rayski delivered the document to the CGD and to Joseph Fischer in Grenoble (end October 1943).

15. The term *chambre à gaz* appears in the underground press for the first time in August–September 1943.

16. *Unzer Kamf*, organ of the General Defense Committee (CDJC, CDLXX-95).

17. The "White Book," promulgated in 1939 by Great Britain, set the number of "certificates" for Jewish immigration to Palestine without stipulating over how long a period. The result was that from the beginning of the World War II, the immigration of Jews fleeing Europe was made almost impossible.

18. Rayski, *Nos illusions perdues*, 160f.

19. The acronym CRIF (for Conseil réprésentatif des israélites de France) was employed by the Consistory from the first versions of the charter. The UJRE, like the CGD, preferred the acronym CRJF (for Conseil réprésentatif des Juifs de France). But in the course of meetings, it became customary for ease of pronunciation to speak of the CRIF, with the understanding that the Consistory had definitively dropped the use of the French term *israélite*, which had so long served to discriminate between French- and foreign-born Jews.

20. These works include "Une grande date dans la résistance juive: La fondation du Conseil représentatif des Juifs de France," *Le Monde juif* 49 (July–September 1968); "L'UGIF et le CRIF. Les choix de la communauté, 1940–1944," *Pardès* 6 (January 1988), in response to the article of Annie Kriegel, "Pouvoir politique et expression communautaire: le CRIF," *Pardès* 3 (1986).

21. Not catalogued and presently stored under call number 09/11 (information as of 1992 [editor's note]). Thanks to her "Aryan" appearance Bronia Klibanski, a member of Hashomer Hazair in Grodno and Bailystok, was able to ensure liaison between Warsaw and other ghettos.

22. The discussions, begun in October–November 1943 after a general agreement of principle, were prolonged until about 15 August 1944 by differences that emerged during the drafting of the text.

23. "Conference" is the term employed to characterize the series of meetings on the charter.

24. Attention is called to the very interesting study by Jacques Fredj, "Le CRIF, 1943–1966" (M.A. thesis, University of Paris-IV, 1988).

25. Fischer was acting as an ally of the Consistory and was counting on its support in the Palestine question.

26. The Consistory was seeking to assure itself of a majority on the council, probably in order to compensate for some of the basic concessions it was sure to be led to make.

27. My phrasing was inspired by the work of Simon Schwartzfuchs, *Du Juif à l'israélite, Histoire d'une mutation, 1770–1870* (Paris: Fayard, 1989).

28. Robert Badinter, "Les Juifs et la République," closing address at the colloquium on the bicentenary of the emancipation of the Jews, Strasbourg, 6 October 1991.

29. At the bottom of the note the letter G appears. Was this Léo Glaeser? He took an active part in the work. On another sheet his handwritten name is found and the writing has been identified as his.

30. According to the testimony of Tony Grin, agreement had been reached between the Zionist and communist youth groups without further problems. On the other hand, the support of the scouts for the CADJJ was never total. In reality they felt isolated, facing a leftist bloc that included communists, socialist Zionists, and Bundists. The Zionists and communists in Paris established a very successful coordination during the months preceding the Liberation, after Tony Grin, Gaston Griner, and Jacques Tanerman (representing the UJRE combat groups) arrived from Lyon.

31. Note concerning the CDJJ, May 1944, Yad Vashem Archives, Joseph Fischer Collection (temporary call number 09/11).

32. "Aux délégués de la conférence pour la constitution du CRJF," signed "La direction des communistes juifs," 20 June 1944. Adam Rayski is the author of the declaration.

33. This was also (at that time) the point of view of the Marxist-Zionists. The communists subsequently accepted the need for a "national Jewish homeland." Cf. Henry Bulawko, *Le Sionisme* (Paris: Jacques Grancher, 1991).

34. The document, dated 25 April 1944, bears the note "UJRE, IMT archives, alpha 15 (CRIF)."

35. If we do not count the work of the commission considering the liquidation of the UGIF (see below, chapter 19), the CRIF began to operate 5 September 1944, holding its first public meeting in Lyon.

36. This attitude was observed in the Consistory in the 1990s, which for all practical purposes withdrew from the CRIF without explanation.

Chapter Nineteen. A Time for All Fears and All Hopes

1. Letter from Daniel Finkelstein to his wife before his deportation, in David Diamant, *Par-delà les barbelés*, 42.

2. CDJC, CDLXIX-54.

3. Letter from Mme Adamicz to Georges, the son of Léo Glaeser (later professor at the University of Strasbourg).

4. Account of the inquiry into the activity of the ex-militiaman Paul Touvier by Commissioner of Police Jacques Delarue, 10 June 1970; Laurent Greilsamer and Daniel Schneidermann, *Un certain Monsieur Paul: L'affaire Touvier* (Paris: Fayard, 1989), 237–54. In its indictment of 14 April 1992 the prosecutor's office did not deal with the responsibility of Touvier for the Rillieux Massacre but with the question of whether it constituted a "crime against humanity."

5. Report on the tragedy at Guerry drawn up after the Liberation by I. Rozenblat, the FSJF delegate for Cher, 3 January 1945, on the basis of the testimony of M. Krameisen, the only one to escape (CDJ, CCXVII-50a).

6. Report of Jacques Delarue, in Greilsamer and Schneidermann, *Un certain Monsieur Paul*, 237–54.

7. Édith Klein interview, December 1969.

8. Mme Édith Klein urged me to give the date according to the Jewish calendar.

9. See Robert Aron, *Histoire de l'épuration* (Paris: Fayard, 1970), 376f.

10. Excerpt from the Registry of Births, Marriages, and Deaths, town of Saint-Étienne; personal archives of Yves Le Stir of Saint-Étienne, who has the author's warm thanks.

11. The complete text of the testament is preserved at the CDJC but as of 1992 had not been catalogued.

12. Annette Kahn, *Robert et Jeanne. A Lyon sous l'Occupation* (Paris: Payot, 1990), 161 f. I had the sad privilege of being present on 1 or 2 September 1944, at the opening of one of the pits by American GIs who had occupied the airport. It was an indescribable spectacle as the excavation progressed to see emerge now a head, now a woman's leg and foot with a slipper. There were certainly other similar massacres.

13. CDJC, CXI-1.

14. YIVO-UGIF archives, New York (also CDJC, CXI-1).

15. Interview with Mathilde Jaffé, January 1990.

16. More detail on their ages appears in the list for Convoy 77, in Klarsfeld, *Le Mémorial de la déportation*.

17. Darville and Wichené, *Drancy-la-juive*.

18. Almost fifty years later, Aloïs Brunner had still not answered for his crimes, benefiting from protection in Syria against the stubborn effort of Serge and Beate Klarsfeld to have him extradited.

19. Deposition of Dr. Kurt Schendel before Jacques Rabinowitch (brother-in-law of the historian Léon Poliakov), 31 August 1944 (CDJC, CXXI-26, 27). The latter had ties to the MOI and was involved in intelligence along with Raymond Sar-

raute and Igor Krivocheine (Russian group of the MOI). See Knout, *La Résistance juive en France*, 110–12.

20. See above, chapter 11.

21. Testimony in Maurice Rajsfus, *Des juifs dans la collaboration* (Paris: EDI, 1980), 258.

22. Interview with Albert Akerberg, October 1989.

23. "L'UGIF et ses maisons d'enfants," Jean Laloum, *Le Monde juif* 116 (October–December 1984). Dr. Schenkel, consulted by the director of the Montreuil home, is said to have given his consent.

24. *Activité des organisations juives*, 235.

25. Lambert wrote, "You would be acting more boldly if you followed the directions of Dr. Sabord [fictional personal name based on *sabord* ("porthole") and *saborder* ("to scuttle a ship")]. These concessions to the illness will not postpone your entry into the clinic [Drancy]." In Lambert, *Carnet d'un témoin*, 59.

26. André Baur, his wife, and their three children; Lambert, his wife, and their four children; Israelowicz, his wife, and her mother—the remainder of the list is, unfortunately, all too long.

27. Lazarus, *Juifs au combat*, 144 f.

28. Janine Auscher, "Les derniers jours de Drancy," *La Revue de la pensée juive* 3 (April 1950): 118–23.

29. Darville and Wichené, *Drancy-la-juive*. [Editor's note: The Swedish consul-general, Raoul Nordling, negotiated with the German city commandant to arrange a swift end to hostilities once the insurrection in Paris began and Allied troops began to enter the city's suburbs. This did not prevent bloody fighting in some quarters of the city, but it did allow representatives of the Swedish Red Cross to assist in the movement of the prisoners from Drancy to other locations.]

Conclusion. The Weight of the Present and of the Future

1. See above, chapter 14.

2. See Rayski, *Nos illusions perdues*, 183.

3. See S. W. Baron, *Histoire d'Israël*, 1:396.

4. See above, chapter 14. With respect to the colloquium *Penser Auschwitz*, of which he was an initiator, Schmuel Trigano defined the central idea as follows: "Leave historiography, the proof to be shown [and] open instead a theological horizon"; statement made in the course of the TV broadcast "La Source de vie," presented by Rabbi Josy Eisenberg, Second Channel, Paris, 7 May 1989.

5. The phrasing is Baron's, *Histoire d'Israël*, 2:31 (1:396 in the French edition).

6. See above, chapters 5 and 17.

7. R. Hilberg cites the figure of 1,300,000 dead as a result of open-air executions, that is, essentially through the actions of the Einsatzgruppen, (*La Destruction de Juifs d'Europe*, 1033–46). See too François Bédarida, "Le crime et l'histoire: Évaluation

du nombre de victimes d'Auschwitz," *Le Monde,* 22–23 July 1990. This revision was made possible on the basis of research conducted simultaneously by the Auschwitz Museum and Yad Vashem.

8. The Fondation du judaïsme français has created the "George Wellers Collection for the Preservation of Testimony on the Shoah" specifically to make available to researchers testimony not otherwise published.

9. *Le Génocide et le nazisme* (Paris: Presses Pocket, 1992), 9. This is also the view of the Institut d'histoire du temps présent (Institute for Contemporary History).

Afterword. The Twenty-First Century

1. Michael Berenbaum and Abraham J. Peck, eds., *The Holocaust and History: The Known, the Unknown, the Disputed, and the Reexamined* (Bloomington: Indiana University Press in association with the United States Holocaust Memorial Museum, 1998), 616–28.

INDEX

Abetz, Otto, 13, 48–49, 79
Aboulker, Henri, 256
Aboulker, José, 255
Aboulker, Raphaël, 255
Action Française, 66, 333n19
Adamicz (Henri Braun), 230, 293,
    297–98, 309
Ader, Henri, 157
Adler, Jacques, 50, 227, 272–73, 292
Ajdenbaum, Alter, 126
Akerberg, Albert, 308
Alerte (Paris resistance group), 308,
    367n39
Alfieri, Dino, 194
Alibert, Mme, 165
Alibert, Raphaël, 32, 245
Aliens Bureau, 51
Alliance israélite (Jewish Alliance),
    293–94
Alliance israélite universelle (AIU—
    Universal Israelite Alliance), 19,
    64–66
Ältestenrat, 23
Altman, Georges, 248
Amelot Committee, 43–44, 49, 58, 75,
    84–85, 95, 275, 332n5, 343n1
American Jewish Congress, 40
American Jewish Joint Distribution
    Committee (AJJDC), 49, 69, 180,
    204, 343n1

Amitié chrétienne, 122
Amman (fifth century B.C.E.), 328n12
Angeli, Alexandre, 122
Apeloig, Rabbi Georges, 289
Appel, Roger, 183
Arago, Emmanuel, 165
Aragon, Louis, 162
Arbaiter Zeitung (Yiddish underground
    newspaper), 159
Arbeiter Orden (Order of Workers), 43
Arbellot, Simon, 77
Argèles (concentration camp), 20, 103
Armée juive (AJ—Jewish Army), xiii,
    238, 263–69, 274, 277, 279, 311,
    319, 367n39
Armée secrète (AS—Secret Army),
    238, 250, 264–65, 277
Aron, Raymond, 38, 250
Aronson, Robert, 235
Association culturelle israélite du
    rite achkénaze (Jewish Cultural
    Association of the Ashkanazi
    Rite), 201
Association du rabbinate (Association
    of the Rabbinate), 26
Atlas, Joseph, 185
Aubrac, Lucie, 91, 99
Aubrac, Raymond, 251
Auschwitz, 3, 136–38, 141, 150, 157,
    206, 224, 306

375

Defense Committee, 26–27, 293–94
Defferre, Gaston, 38
Der ewige Jude (film), 15
Deutsch, André, 138
Di Yiddishe shtime (The Jewish Voice),
  343n1
Dillard, Father, 75
Direction générale des renseignements
  et les jeux (General Administration
  for Intelligence and Gaming), 19
Direction générale d'étude et de
  renseignement (DGER—General
  Administration for Research and
  Intelligence), 191
Donati, Angelo, 194, 196–201, 205
Doriot, Jacques, 20, 88, 202
Drancy (transit camp), 49, 52–53,
  62, 86–87, 90, 94, 107, 111, 115,
  121–22, 125–43, 149–50, 174,
  179–81, 201, 223, 231, 234, 278,
  289, 305–7, 310–12, 373n29
Dreyfus, Alfred, 245
Dreyfus, Camille, 245
Dreyfus, M., 303
Dreyfus, Pierre, 245, 249
Dreyfus Affair, 6, 12, 27, 252, 298
Dreyfus Trial, 161
Droit et liberté (underground
  newspaper), 250
Dru, Gilbert, 240
Drumont, Édouard, 39
Dubouchage Committee, 197–201,
  204, 206
Dubray, Maurice, 253
Dumas, Georges, 190–91
Dumas, Roland, 190
Dumez, André. See Jankélévitch,
  Vladimir

Éboué, Félix, 38
Éclaireurs israélites de France (EIF—
  Jewish Scouts of France), xiii, 59,
  64, 172, 178–79, 205, 224, 238,

250, 257–64, 266, 271, 273, 277,
  303, 308, 319, 364n1
Edelman, Mark, 221
Edelmann-Kupermann, Hélène, 93
Eden, Anthony, 39
Edinger, Georges, 305, 307–9
Ehrenburg, Ilya, 54, 217–18
Eichmann, Adolf, 22, 78, 161
Einsatzgruppen, 22, 53–54, 220
Eisenhower, Dwight D., 200
Eisenstein, Sergei, 54
Elbogen, Touly, 303
Éluard, Paul, 272
Emergency Rescue Committee, 107
Engros, Roger, 235
Epstein, Joseph ("Colonel Gilles"), 236
Escarra, Jean, 39

Farnoux, Yvette, 141
Faucher, D., 284
Faure-Pinguely, 239
Febvre, Lucien, 249
Fédération des anciens engages
  volontaires étrangers (Federation
  of Former Foreign Enlistees), 21
Fédération des sociétés juives de France
  (FSJF—Federation of Jewish
  Associations of France), 5–6,
  57–58, 60, 67–68, 75, 84,
  159–60, 197, 199, 201, 206,
  223–24, 229, 275, 290–91, 332n5
Federation of Jewish Associations of
  Algeria (FSJA), 256
Feinstein-Wilner, 136
Feldmann, Valentin, 245
Fenkel, Boris, 239
Feuchtwanger, Lion, 15, 340n3, 341n18
FFI. See Forces françaises intérieures
Fichtenberg, Roger, 179
"Final Solution," 42, 53, 72–73, 116,
  118, 150, 152–53, 161, 194, 205,
  211, 220, 222, 233, 275, 310, 340n8
Fink, Ignace, 199, 206

ADAM RAYSKI

left Poland in 1932 for Paris, where he became a full-time journalist working for the *Neie Presse,* a leftist Yiddish-language daily newspaper. From July 1941 until the end of World War II he served as national secretary of the Jewish Section of the French Communist Party and was the head of the most important French Jewish organization, the Union des Juifs pour la Résistance et l'entraide, in which he played a major part in Jewish survival in France.